LEGACIES OF BRITISH RULE

Princeton Studies in Global and Comparative Sociology
Andreas Wimmer, *Series Editor*

Legacies
of British Rule

Colonialism, Statehood, and Nationalist Civil War

Matthew Lange

PRINCETON UNIVERSITY PRESS

PRINCETON AND OXFORD

Published by Princeton University Press
41 William Street, Princeton, New Jersey 08540
99 Banbury Road, Oxford OX2 6JX

press.princeton.edu

GPSR Authorized Representative: Easy Access System Europe - Mustamäe tee 50, 10621 Tallinn, Estonia, gpsr.requests@easproject.com

All Rights Reserved

ISBN 9780691274492
ISBN (pbk.) 9780691274508
ISBN (e-book) 9780691274515

Library of Congress Control Number: 2025938065

British Library Cataloging-in-Publication Data is available

Editorial: Rachael Levay, Erik Beranek, and Tara Dugan
Production Editorial: Nathan Carr
Jacket/Cover Design: Haley O'Neill
Production: Lauren Reese
Publicity: William Pagdatoon
Copyeditor: Natalie Jones

Jacket/Cover Credit: (Top): The History Collection / Alamy Stock Photo; (bottom): Sipa USA / Alamy Stock Photo

This book has been composed in Adobe Text and Gotham

10 9 8 7 6 5 4 3 2 1

To John A. Hall,
A towering academic, generous colleague, and dear friend.

CONTENTS

ILLUSTRATIONS

TABLES

ACKNOWLEDGMENTS

This book has had an unusually long gestation period. It grew out of my dissertation, which was completed in 2004 and explored the developmental legacies of direct and indirect rule in the British Empire. While arguing that the form of British rule commonly shaped postcolonial institutions, I noted cases in which violence transformed these institutional legacies and began questioning whether the form of colonial rule also contributed to postcolonial warfare. This issue was much too large and complicated to add to my dissertation, so I decided to make it a post-dissertation project. My research into this issue raised new questions, leading to new projects, and I put the original project on hold to explore some of these tangential issues. Consequently, I have been working on and thinking about this book for over two decades.

Over this prolonged period, I received invaluable assistance and would like to thank the many people and institutions that helped me along the way. Financially, I received four different grants from the Social Science and Humanities Research Council of Canada, and their generous funding made this research possible. While completing my research, I spent time at the Public Records Office in the UK, the British Library, Cornell University Library, the Archives Nationales d'Outre-Mer in France, the International Centre for Ethnic Studies in Sri Lanka, and the OKD Institute of Social Change and Development in India. This book is based on material from all these institutions, and many people working at them generously assisted my research. My colleagues Peter McMahan and Thomas Soehl gave valuable statistical advice for the project, and my former supervisor Jim Mahoney and old friend Matthias vom Hau gave me encouragement and assistance along the way. Emre Amasyali and Andrew Dawson helped gather data and run earlier statistical analyses published elsewhere. Charlotte Gaudreau and Tay Jeong did the same for the statistical analyses included in this book, and I therefore include them as coauthors of the two chapters in this book that present statistical analyses. Special recognition must be given to Tay, as he gave important advice on statistical methods and models, managed the dataset, and completed most of the programming. Other research assistants—Kalyani Thurairajah and Emma Hebert—helped with literature reviews for different cases. At home, my wife and children kept me going with their constant love and support. The entire production team at Princeton University Press was a pleasure to work with, and three helpful reviewers gave me pages of valuable comments that improved the book in many ways. Last but not least, John A. Hall read multiple drafts of this book, gave detailed comments, and was enormously supportive along the way. This is not the first time he has done this, so I owe him a very big thanks.

ABBREVIATIONS

All Ramanya Mon Association (ARMA)

Bharatiya Janata Party (BJP)

Burma Independence Army (BIA)

Chittagong Hill Tracts (CHT)

East India Company (EIC)

Ethnic Power Relations (EPR)

Front Unifié de Lutte des Races Opprimée (FURLO)

Kachin Independence Army (KIA)

Kachin Independence Organisation (KIO)

Karen National Association (KNA)

Mizo National Front (MNF)

Mizo National Famine Front (MNFF)

Mouvement des Forces Démocratiques de Casamance (MFDC)

Naga National Council (NNC)

Tigray People's Liberation Front (TPLF)

Uppsala Conflict Data Program (UCDP)

Young Lushai Association (YLA)

Introduction

LINEAGES OF WAR AND PEACE

On January 1, 1877, a spectacular imperial pageant occurred in India. The Delhi Durbar, as it was called, revived and repurposed a Mughal ceremony bolstering allegiance between the Mughal Emperor and regional authorities. In its new form, the ceremony enthroned Queen Victoria as Empress of India by having hundreds of maharajas, nawabs, and other Indian authorities proceed one by one in an extravagant ritual to pledge allegiance to the Queen's representative, Viceroy Lytton. Figure I.1 provides one artist's depiction of the extravagant event.

As Cohn (1983) notes, the Delhi Durbar was carefully choreographed to embody and thereby strengthen British colonialism in India. It focused on two elements of British rule, which together promoted a particular form of imperial control: colonial pluralism. One aspect of colonial pluralism is the recognition of communal hierarchies within the polity, and the Delhi Durbar exemplified the hierarchical character of colonial authority, especially the seemingly impenetrable division between colonizer and colonized. At the same time, the ceremony recognized the authority of Indian rulers over their subjects and highlighted a hierarchy among Indian rulers, with the number of guns used to salute each ruler varying according to their colonially designated status. The second component of colonial pluralism—and the one that distinguished it most from other forms of colonialism—was the communalization of populations, and the Delhi Durbar showcased the multicultural character of British rule by bringing together hundreds of Indian rulers to represent and speak for their communities. Striking home this point, Viceroy Lytton asked the audience to look around and observe an India "multitudinous in its traditions, as well as in its inhabitants, almost infinite in the variety of races which populate it, and of the creeds which have shaped their character" (Cohn

1

FIGURE I.1. The Delhi Durbar of 1877. *Source:* Wheeler (1877). Album / British Library / Alamy Stock Photo.

1983: 194). The ceremonial representation of India as infinitely varied acknowledged and valorized several colonial policies that recognized, accommodated, and empowered communities. Notable examples include community-based military units, vernacular education, community-specific family law, and communalized indirect rule.

Ideas moved quickly along well-worn colonial networks, and this repurposed Mughal ceremony traveled beyond British India. Frederick Lugard, who began his first colonial commission in India the year after the first Delhi Durbar, subsequently organized a "Durbar" in northern Nigeria to celebrate customary authorities and cement their support for British rule. In British Malaya, Frank Swettenham began Malay "Durbars" as a means of strengthening both the Malay Federation and Great Britain's power over Malay sultans. In addition to transplanting Durbars, Lugard and Swettenham spread and popularized the form of rule that the Durbars exemplified (Lugard 1922; Swettenham 1907). Many other colonial officials transplanted colonial pluralism to additional colonies, and it quickly became the dominant model of the British Empire (Crowder 1968; Lange 2009b; Mamdani 2012; Mantena 2010).

While colonial pluralism was spreading throughout the British Empire, polities elsewhere were moving in a different direction. The British developed colonial pluralism to limit anticolonial resistance by resurrecting and revamping elements of a defunct land-based empire. During the nineteenth century, however, land-based empires were in decline, and the nation-state was strengthening (Anderson 1983; Gellner 1983; Greenfeld 2019). Instead of dividing populations into distinct communities and bundling them in an imperial state, political leaders increasingly focused on matching Weberian states with Herderian nations to make possible national self-rule. The anachronistic character of colonial pluralism was glaringly apparent as independence approached because global institutions recognized the nation-state as the only legitimate type of polity (Meyer et al. 1997). Many British colonies therefore experienced a double imperial transition: Externally, colonies freed themselves of British control, and, internally, former colonies transformed communalized imperial states into nation-states.

As Wimmer (2013) notes, transitions from empire to nation-state were often violent affairs. Diverse populations did not fit the nation-state model, but postcolonial states forced people into this mold. Nation-state building, in turn, commonly removed the cultural and political autonomy of communities, thereby pitting communities against the new nation-state. One common outcome of contentious transitions to the nation-state was nationalist civil warfare, or wars in which actors fight to increase communal self-rule through either secession or decentralizing reforms. Well-known examples include the nationalist civil wars in Myanmar, Sri Lanka, and Sudan. Importantly, nationalist civil wars were relatively common in places transitioning from empire to nation-state but far from universal, with one in five former colonies experiencing at least one nationalist civil war.

Given the mismatch between colonial pluralism and the nation-state, nationalist civil wars might have been especially concentrated in the former British Empire. By institutionalizing clear communal divisions and providing communities with power and self-rule, colonial pluralism potentially created strong opposition to nation-state-building efforts that removed communal autonomy and promoted conflict over the communal character of the nation. Yet colonial pluralism might have limited nationalist strife in other ways. A large literature argues that pluralist policies can deter nationalist violence by adjusting nation-states to better fit diverse populations, and colonial pluralism might have eased transitions from colony to nation-state by making postcolonial nation-states more Swiss and less German (Aslan 2015; Kymlicka 1995; Lijphart 1977; McEvoy and O'Leary 2013; Stepan et al. 2011). How, then, did colonial pluralism affect postcolonial patterns of nationalist civil war in the former British Empire? Did it promote nationalist civil war or prevent it?

Through a multimethod and comparative analysis of the British Empire, *Legacies of British Rule* explores this question and offers evidence that British colonial pluralism did both, thereby promoting multiple and competing legacies. On average, however, the positive effects were much more powerful than the negative, and nationalist strife is therefore the main legacy of British colonial pluralism. This helps explain why former British colonies have experienced three times as many nationalist civil wars per country as all other former overseas colonies.

The book's analysis pinpoints the extent of precolonial statehood as determining the effects of colonial pluralism, with high and low levels of historical statehood having opposing effects and colonial pluralism magnifying these effects. High levels of historical statehood increase the risk of nationalist civil war by promoting national chauvinism and, thereby, aggressive and discriminatory nation-state-building efforts that remove the cultural and political autonomy of communities. By itself, however, grievances over national chauvinism and lost autonomy are rarely sufficient for nationalist civil war, and I find that colonial pluralism strengthens these effects in three ways: It makes national chauvinism more abrasive, increases sensitivity to the national chauvinism of others, and provides communities with mobilizational resources. In contrast, low levels of historical statehood reduce the risk of nationalist civil war by limiting national chauvinism, and colonial pluralism further reduces this risk by promoting inclusive postcolonial politics in places with weak national chauvinism.

Through these findings, the book makes important empirical and theoretical contributions, the most direct of which speak to a growing literature on colonial legacies. Whereas most previous works describe British colonialism as an omnipotent force that promoted ethnic violence, I recognize that its effects depended greatly on precolonial states, show that it could either promote or deter conflict, and focus on one particular type of ethnic violence: nationalist civil war. Most past analyses, in turn, do not clearly specify the aspects of British rule that promote conflict and the mechanisms through which they do. In contrast, I develop the concept "colonial pluralism," note the different types of policies that were part of this system of rule, and consider the mechanisms through which these policies affected war and peace.

The book also makes contributions by providing more general insight into the causes of nationalist civil war and plurinational peace. At its heart, the analysis highlights a core process that is a common outcome of transitions from empire to nation-state and that lies at the heart of many nationalist civil wars—communities react to aggressive and chauvinistic efforts to remove their autonomy with nationalist movements. Yet lost autonomy at the hands of a chauvinistic state only rarely promotes nationalist civil war, and the book identifies conditions that determine whether communities accept their forced integration into another community's nation-state or organize a nationalist movement to struggle against it. Because British colonial pluralism greatly shaped these conditions, an analysis of the British Empire clearly highlights causes of variation in nationalist civil war. And because the level of historical statehood varies greatly among former British colonies, an analysis of the British Empire highlights how the impact of pluralism depends on historical statehood.

Another contribution that makes the previous contributions possible is the book's rigorous multimethod analysis. The quantitative analysis uses new data on the extent of colonial pluralism and offers a general test of the theoretical framework. The comparative-historical analysis analyzes dozens of nationalist civil wars in 20 countries and uses process tracing and qualitative comparison to highlight mechanisms and processes that promote either nationalist war or plurinational peace. And in combining these analyses to exploit their respective strengths, the book provides an in-depth understanding of both broad patterns and the mechanisms and processes that underly them.

Argument

Nationalism is a principle holding that the nation and state should overlap, and nationalist movements try to improve this match (Gellner 1983; Hechter 2000). National chauvinism commonly inspires nationalist movements that adjust the contours of the nation in ways that—in the eyes of movement supporters—improve the congruence between state and nation. At its core, national chauvinism is a belief that one's community is the true national community. It therefore dichotomizes populations into ingroups or outgroups, and national chauvinists either ignore outgroups or attempt to assimilate, marginalize, or eliminate them.

I provide evidence that large and long-standing precolonial states promote national chauvinism in places transitioning from overseas empire to nation-state. Members of communities that controlled precolonial states, which Paine (2019) refers to as *state communities*, commonly supported national chauvinism and tried to assimilate and establish direct control over communities without large and long-standing precolonial states, or *non-state communities*. One factor promoting national chauvinism is that state communities usually made up the majority of the population at independence, and their members accepted the democratic principle that numbers matter. In addition, members of state communities recognized the precolonial period as a glorious past during which they controlled their own state and ruled over other peoples, and they expected the new nation-state to reflect the precolonial state and reestablish their community's dominance after a destructive colonial interlude. In Myanmar, Sri Lanka, and Sudan, for example, the Bamar, Sinhalese, and Arab state communities asserted their dominance over postcolonial nation-states by assimilating, marginalizing, and eliminating others.

National chauvinism, in turn, can promote strong grievances that motivate nationalist movements. Because national chauvinists desire their own nation-state, they take control of the state and recognize themselves as the true nation. In so doing, they declare their community superior while disparaging and sometimes attacking other communities. Communities, in turn, are angry about and fear losing political and cultural autonomy at the hands of a discriminatory chauvinistic state and seek to protect or retake both through nationalist movements. In this way, different non-state communities reacted to Bamar, Arab, and Sinhalese national chauvinism in ways that promoted nationalist civil war in Myanmar, Sudan, and Sri Lanka.

Such reactions, however, are more exceptional than normal. When faced with national chauvinism and lost autonomy, many actors assimilate more fully into the state community, and others accept a subordinate national status and reduced power by simply keeping their heads low. Nearly all non-state communities in Thailand, Vietnam, and Botswana, for example, have either accepted the dominance of the state community or assimilated. This book finds that colonial pluralism strengthened the reactions of non-state communities to the national chauvinism of state communities in several ways and that this is the most influential way through which colonial pluralism promoted nationalist civil war. One way in which colonial pluralism intensified reactions was by making the national chauvinism of state communities more assertive and discriminatory. In recognizing, accommodating, and empowering communities, colonial pluralism almost always reduced the power and status of state communities relative to non-state communities, and this readjustment caused national chauvinists to target non-state communities as "stooges" who illegitimately benefited from colonialism at their expense. The national chauvinism of state communities was therefore unusually aggressive and vindictive, and this character strengthened the reactions of non-state communities to it.

One reason for the unequal effects of colonial pluralism on the power and status of communities is that state communities posed a much greater anticolonial threat, and colonial officials tried to weaken this threat through divide-and-rule-style policies that benefited non-state communities. In this way, the British actively favored non-Bamar over Bamar, this made Bamar national chauvinism belligerent toward non-state communities, and such belligerence hardened opposition to the national chauvinism of state communities. Even when not explicitly pursuing divide and rule, pluralist colonial policies almost always increased the relative power and status of non-state communities because precolonial states usually ignored and marginalized non-state communities whereas colonial pluralism recognized, accommodated, and empowered them. One sees this in Sri Lanka, where colonial pluralism did not privilege Tamils to squash Sinhalese anticolonialism but increased the relative power and status of Tamils in ways that made Sinhalese national chauvinism aggressive and discriminatory toward Tamils.

Besides making the national chauvinism of state communities more caustic, colonial pluralism increased the sensitivity of non-state communities to reductions in communal autonomy. In recognizing, accommodating, and empowering communities, colonial pluralism politicized communities in ways that caused people to perceive politics in terms of community and focused greater attention on communal power and self-rule. Due to these nationalist frames, non-state communities rarely assimilated into state communities and were more irked by the national chauvinism of others. And by institutionalizing and celebrating communal power and autonomy, colonial pluralism created popular expectations for both after independence, thereby fueling nationalist reactions to lost communal autonomy.

A final way in which colonial pluralism strengthened reactions to national chauvinism was by providing resources that could put grievances into action. To fight nationalist civil wars, anti-state actors require organizational, communication, human, material, and military resources. Colonial pluralism, in turn, provided communities with many mobilizational resources, including their own local governments, parties, associations, schools, and security forces.

Although the colonial state was the main agent of colonial pluralism, other actors also shaped its form and strength. This book highlights the important influence of missionaries—especially Protestants—and offers evidence that they commonly amplified the effects of pluralist colonial states. One way was by strengthening nationalist frames. Missionary standardization of vernaculars, support for vernacular education, and organization of communities all made communal boundaries more rigid and pushed leaders to pursue communal interests in the political arena. Missionaries also contributed to intercommunal grievances by providing some communities with education and lobbying colonial officials in favor of the communities that worked closely with them. Compounding this contention, many communities viewed missionaries as a threat and were angered by, resented, and feared communities working closely with them. And like colonial officials, missionaries affected non-state communities much more than state communities because state communities resisted missionary influence more vehemently, thereby exacerbating conflict between state and non-state communities in places with precolonial states. Missionaries in Myanmar, for example, worked much more closely with non-state communities than with the Bamar, played a central role constructing communal frames among several non-state communities, contributed to transformations in communal hierarchies, and were a cause of fear and resentment among the Bamar.

While colonial pluralism shaped nationalist civil warfare in these ways, its effects were commonly so dependent on precolonial statehood that it is difficult to separate their impacts. Precolonial statehood promoted national chauvinism, and divisive colonial pluralism made national chauvinism more aggressive and vindictive. Colonial pluralism also greatly intensified nationalist reactions to national chauvinism by strengthening nationalist frames and expectations and providing communities with valuable mobilizational resources. At the same time, precolonial statehood affected the character of colonial pluralism in ways that promoted nationalist conflict: Because state communities posed a severe anticolonial threat, colonial officials employed divide-and-rule policies more frequently in places with precolonial states, and this form of colonial pluralism made the national chauvinism of state communities especially aggressive and exclusionary at the same time that it made non-state communities extremely sensitive to any form of national chauvinism.

When not combined, however, colonial pluralism and precolonial statehood had very different effects: Colonial pluralism either had negative or neutral effects in places with limited historical statehood, and the influence of historical statehood was weaker and less consistent in the absence of colonial pluralism. One reason for the contrasting effects of colonial pluralism is that the British usually used colonial pluralism more universally and nondiscriminatorily in places with limited precolonial statehood, and colonial pluralism therefore had similar effects on all communities. Moreover, national chauvinism is usually weak or absent in places with limited precolonial statehood because no community is numerically dominant or can claim a special place in the nation based on their control of a precolonial state. So when limited historical statehood was combined with British colonial pluralism, all communities had similar interests in colonial pluralism, and postcolonial pluralism deterred nationalist civil war by promoting relatively inclusive nation-states in places like Tanzania and Ghana.

Although precolonial states still increase the risk of nationalist civil war in places without a history of colonial pluralism, the analysis provides evidence that their independent effects are weaker and less consistent than their combined effects. This is because colonial pluralism commonly made the national chauvinism of state communities more aggressive, strengthened the nationalist frames and expectations of non-state communities, and provided non-state communities with important mobilizational resources, all of which greatly intensified reactions to the national chauvinism of state communities and their efforts to reduce the autonomy of other communities. Yet colonial pluralism was not the only factor strengthening reactions to the national chauvinism of others, and the book finds that—in the absence of colonial pluralism— communities were most likely to react to national chauvinism and lost autonomy when they themselves were state communities that had been forcibly integrated into a nation-state controlled by another state community. Like colonial pluralism, historical statehood promoted powerful nationalist frames and expectations for self-rule, and both strengthened reactions to the national chauvinism of others. In this way, historical statehood is most likely to promote nationalist civil war on its own when a country has multiple state communities.

Literature Review: States, Pluralism, Colonialism, Missionaries, and Nationalist Conflict

In analyzing the causes of nationalist civil war, this book speaks directly to and builds on distinct literatures on ethnic civil war, states, nationalism and the nation-state, colonialism, and missionaries. This section briefly reviews these literatures to situate the book within them.

ETHNIC CIVIL WAR

Ethnic civil wars are conflicts between states and domestic actors that are motivated in some way and to some extent by ethnic difference. As defined in this book, nationalist civil wars are a subtype of ethnic civil warfare in which the anti-state combatants view their community as a distinct nation and fight for communal autonomy and self-rule. Over the past few decades, the number of analyses of ethnic civil wars has grown exponentially (Cederman et al. 2010; Fearon and Laitin 2003; Sambanis 2002; Wimmer et al. 2009). This literature is dominated by statistical analyses focused on proximate correlates of conflict, and relatively few works consider how macro-historical processes shape nationalist civil war. Wimmer's (2002, 2013, 2018) work, which explores how historical transitions from empire to nation-state contributed to ethnic civil warfare, provides important and influential exceptions, and I build on his insights. That being said, this book differs in terms of scope and analytic perspective.

Concerning scope, *Legacies of British Rule* focuses exclusively on nationalist civil warfare, whereas Wimmer analyzes all types of ethnic civil war. In addition to nationalist civil war, the other major subtype is center-seeking ethnic civil war over a community's control of the state (Cederman et al. 2009; Hunziker and Cederman 2017; Lange and Jeong 2024). The Lebanese civil wars provide examples of center-seeking conflicts, as they pitted communities against one another over their share of state power, not communal self-rule. This book's more limited scope is potentially important because nationalist wars have different correlates than center-seeking ethnic civil wars (Cederman et al. 2009; Hunziker and Cederman 2017; Lange and Jeong 2024; Wimmer et al. 2009). As such, the broad concept "ethnic civil war" might include subtypes with different causal dynamics, and I focus exclusively on nationalist civil war to limit the risk of causal heterogeneity.

This different focus, in turn, promotes a particular analytic perspective that differs from major works on ethnic civil war. I argue that the main causal dynamic underlying nationalist civil war involves communal opposition to aggressive and discriminatory reductions in communal autonomy, whereas the dominant explanation of ethnic civil warfare is political exclusion (Cederman et al. 2013, 2017; Wimmer et al. 2009). This does not mean that analyses of nationalist civil war can ignore political exclusion, however. Indeed, the processes that remove the cultural and political autonomy of communities usually go hand in hand with the exclusion of these communities from political power. And while lost autonomy strengthens nationalist grievances, people might only act on these grievances after political exclusion highlights the costs of lost autonomy.

My emphasis on lost autonomy is similar to earlier analyses of secessionist conflict that consider how a community's past political autonomy affects nationalist warfare (Bunce 1999; Gurr 1993; Jenne et al. 2007; Suny 1994). These works focus on Eastern Europe and find that the communities that fought wars of secession after the demise of the Soviet Bloc had a history of political autonomy. To explain this pattern, the authors argue that past autonomy motivated nationalist movements by shaping identities. Along these lines, I argue that colonial pluralism commonly contributed to nationalist civil warfare by providing a history of political autonomy. My analysis differs, however, in noting how national chauvinism both promotes efforts to curtail the autonomy of communities and makes lost autonomy more unpalatable. And instead of simply being driven by identity, I find that nationalist reactions to lost autonomy depend greatly on expectations and mobilizational resources.

Although focusing more on lost autonomy than exclusion, this book is similar to the literature on political exclusion in recognizing that states are a very important cause of civil war, and I draw on the political sociology literature on states, social movements, and revolutions (Amenta and Young 1999; Clemens and Cook 1999; Goodwin 2001; Johnston 2011; Kitschelt 1986; McAdam 1982; Skocpol 1979; Tilly 1978, 2004). This literature considers the institutional and structural effects of states, with states shaping social environments in ways that affect the form and likelihood of collective action. These works explore how frames, mobilizational resources, opportunity structures, and motives shape social movements and note that states influence all four. In a similar way, I draw on political sociology and analyze how states affect nationalist civil war through their effects on frames, mobilizational resources, and motives.

In addition to focusing on nationalist civil warfare, my approach differs from state-centered literature on social movements in terms of temporality. The social movement literature generally takes an ahistorical perspective in which state characteristics and actions have rapid—although not necessarily immediate—effects on social movements. While acknowledging that rapid effects are influential, I take a historical institutional approach and consider how colonial and precolonial states promote enduring conditions that shape postcolonial nationalist civil warfare (Mahoney 2000a; Steinmo et al. 1992). Different types of long-term effects exist. Structural effects occur when social structures and institutions persist over long periods and shape social processes. Along this line, I argue that large and long-standing precolonial states affect the number and size of communities and that this communal demography persists over long periods and affects nationalist civil war. I also propose that pluralist colonial states promote political institutions, associations, educational networks, and military units that provide communities with mobilizational resources that commonly remain influential after independence.

Historical states can also have long-term effects by shaping cultural views and understandings. For example, states influence the schema that people use to make sense of themselves and the world around them. I argue that historical states—especially precolonial states—shape core elements of what Smith (1986) refers to as myth-symbol complexes, a political schema depicting the nation in particular ways based on select myths, symbols, and understandings. In postcolonial societies, these myth-symbol complexes focus on the precolonial period as the time in which there was a real and unadulterated nation. In a similar way, pluralist colonial states promoted nationalist frames among non-state communities that remained powerful after independence.

Although a historical institutional approach is novel for the literature on social movements, a few historically oriented analyses of ethnic violence and civil war focus on the influence of historical states. Some argue that historical states limit ethnic conflict by increasing the legitimacy of postcolonial states and promoting more homogeneous populations, the latter of which creates a better match between nation and state (Englebert 2000; Wimmer 2018). In contrast, others claim that historical statehood promotes divisions and conflict between state and non-state communities (Paine 2019; Ray 2019). One potential reason for this disagreement is that the type of ethnic conflict matters. For reasons described by Englebert (2000) and Wimmer (2018), historical states deter ethnic civil wars over the control of states, and center-seeking civil wars are therefore very rare in places with historical states. Yet Paine (2019) and Ray (2019) correctly note that places with historical states commonly experience conflict between state and non-state communities. Although they too focus on ethnic civil war or ethnic violence more generally, I argue that conflict between state and non-state communities is most likely to promote nationalist civil war, as non-state communities focus on increasing communal autonomy because of their limited ability to take over the state. In addition to the type of conflict, my work contrasts with that of Paine (2019) and Ray (2019) in that it focuses on different mechanisms through which precolonial states promote conflict, with national chauvinism and lost autonomy playing central roles. Finally, I pay greater attention to colonial pluralism and the ways this form of rule amplifies the impact of historical states.

THE LITERATURES ON NATIONALISM AND COLONIALISM

In exploring the impact of colonial pluralism on nationalist civil warfare, this book also engages with distinct literatures on nationalism and colonialism. Both literatures focus on transitions from empire to nation-state and the influence of pluralism on conflict. Their views of pluralism differ, however, with the nationalist literature focusing on pluralism as a means of deterring nationalist conflict whereas the colonial literature considers how colonial pluralism contributed to postcolonial ethnic violence. In analyzing how colonial pluralism affected the risk of nationalist civil war, I draw on, expand, and integrate both literatures.

Independence initiated transitions from empire to nation-state, and both the colonial and nationalist literatures pay close attention to colonial transitions (Hall 2024; Kumar 2017; Mazrui 1983; Wimmer 2013). Key works within both literatures note that such transitions were neither smooth nor complete, with war being common during transitions and empires often continuing in modified form or having lingering effects (Hall 2024; Kumar 2017; Laitin 1986; Malešević 2019; Mazrui 1983; Wimmer 2013). The literatures also recognize that transitions to nation-states resulted in a varied collection of nation-states that diverge from the nation-state ideal type of a Weberian state ruling over a Herderian nation (Kymlicka 1995; Laitin 1986; Malešević 2019; Stepan et al.

2011; Wimmer 2013, 2018). In this book, I engage with these works by exploring how colonialism shaped postcolonial nation-states. Similar to the colonial literature, I focus on the lingering effects of empire. Like the literature on nationalism, I explore how transitions led to nation-states with different characteristics.

Within the literature on nationalism, several works consider the influence of nationalism on war, focusing on how nationalism contributes to geopolitical competition (Mann 1988, 1993; Posen 1993; Tilly 1992). Within this body of work, some note that the relationship goes both ways, as war also promotes nationalism (Hall and Malešević 2013; Hutchinson 2005). While these works focus on international conflict, others note that nationalism commonly contributes to civil war by promoting opposing understandings of the national community, thereby sparking nationalist conflicts (Aslan 2015; Kymlicka 1995; Lijphart 1977; McEvoy and O'Leary 2013; Stepan et al. 2011). Instead of focusing on the link between nationalism and civil war, however, these works analyze how pluralism can limit nationalist warfare by transforming understandings of nations in ways that make nation-states more inclusive. This position is based in liberal political philosophy and suggests that the exclusion of communities from the nation-state—either formally or symbolically—causes resentment and anger, which, in turn, fuels nationalist movements and warfare. These works therefore argue that the risk of nationalist warfare is much lower when political institutions reflect the communal diversity of national population. This literature highlights three ways in which political institutions deal with communal diversity: ethnic federalism, which provides communities with autonomy; consociationalism, which reserves positions for communities; and multiculturalism, which accommodates community.

While making general claims about the impact of pluralism on nationalist civil war, past works recognize that pluralist reforms are not cookie-cutter policies and that their success depends on a variety of conditions. All types of pluralist reforms, for example, require committed politicians, effective institutions, a long-term effort, and support from all communities. The ethnic federalist subtype, in turn, requires communal geographies and the presence of a relatively effective central state controlled by leaders who are willing to decentralize power (Lange 2017). Lijphart (1977) argues that consociationalism requires even more conditions, including clear communal divisions, a balance of communal power, the presence of an external threat faced by all communities, common loyalty to the state, relative socioeconomic equality among communities, a small population, and a multiparty system with community-based parties.

Despite widespread agreement that pluralism deters violence, some disagree. Social identity theory claims that pluralist policies do more harm than good (Lieberman and Singh 2017; Tajfel 1970, 1974). From this perspective, the categorization of people into different communities—even when random—strengthens or creates social identities and, in so doing, promotes intercommunal discrimination, competition, and antipathy. Social identity theory therefore suggests that pluralist policies are counterproductive and exacerbate contestation.

Although dominated by the pro-pluralism camp, the literature on nationalism and the nation-state is therefore bifurcated. Despite being a popular academic topic, this disagreement shows little sign of being resolved. One reason for the stalemate is that the scholars writing on this topic consider different aspects of conflict and therefore do not engage with one another: The pro-pluralist position focuses on using pluralism to deal with *preexisting* conflict, whereas the anti-pluralist view explores how pluralism contributes to *new* conflicts. Neither, in turn, recognizes that the relationship between pluralism and nationalist violence might be like that between radiation and cancer—able to either treat or cause it. The use of pluralism as a treatment, in turn, creates a severe problem for the empirical analysis of pluralism's effects: Officials implement pluralist policies to limit preexisting conflict, and these conflicts create a heightened risk of warfare regardless of pluralist reforms. As a result, it can be difficult to disentangle the effects of pluralism from the conflict that promoted the pluralist policies in the first place.

Analyses of pluralism focus on noncolonial contexts, but early scholars of pluralism analyzed colonies. Similar to social identity theory, these works argue that colonial pluralism institutionalized communal divisions, competition, and antipathy in ways that contributed to postcolonial contestation. Furnivall (1948) provides an early work and describes colonial Myanmar and Indonesia as plural societies in which diverse communities have a high degree of political and cultural autonomy. Instead of celebrating diversity, he was concerned about how the institutionalization of communal difference affected nation building. In subsequent years, a large literature provided evidence that pluralist colonial policies left a legacy of ethnic violence. While some support social identity theory and claim that the simple act of colonial division contributed to these outcomes (Horowitz 1985; Lieberman and Singh 2017; Mamdani 2012), most argue that colonial officials recognized communal difference as part of divide-and-rule-style policies and focus on the latter as the cause of conflict (de Silva 1986; Idris 2005, 2013; Lange 2012; Mamdani 2001; Newbury 1983; Pollis 1973). These divisive policies physically separated communities to limit contact and collaboration and advantaged communities that posed little threat to colonial rule while disfavoring the communities that posed the greatest risk to colonial control. In so doing, officials sought to weaken anticolonial threats, gain the support of others, and pit colonized communities against one another.

Case studies offer the strongest evidence that divisive colonial pluralism contributed to postcolonial violence (de Silva 1986; Idris 2005, 2013; Mamdani

2001; Newbury 1983; Pollis 1973). For years, however, scholars have questioned these claims, suggesting that past works exaggerate both the extent to which colonizers employed divisive policies and the effect of these policies (Horowitz 1985; Ray 2018). In fact, Wucherpfennig et al. (2016) argue that colonial policies that recognized and institutionalized communal difference deterred postcolonial violence by promoting inclusive postcolonial politics.

Scholars exploring these claims more generally provide limited and inconsistent evidence about the impact of divisive colonial policies on conflict. Most commonly, researchers claim that the British employed divisive and discriminatory policies more than the French and use the identity of the colonizer as a proxy for these policies. Yet this strategy does not offer evidence that the British were more pluralist and discriminatory and overlooks the presence of intra-imperial variation. It is therefore uncertain what the colonial proxies measure. And even if one accepts that the identity of the colonizer is an appropriate proxy for colonial policies, the results of these analyses are inconsistent, with some finding that communal violence was greater in former British colonies (Blanton et al. 2001; Brunnschweiler and Bulte 2009; Collier et al. 2009; Henderson 2000; Lange and Dawson 2009), others that it was more common in former French colonies (Wucherpfennig et al. 2016), and still others that there was no difference in former British and French colonies (Cederman et al. 2015; Collier and Hoeffler 2002; Fearon and Laitin 2003; Paine 2019). Recognizing the potential problems of using the identity of the colonizer as a proxy for divisive colonial policies, a few works have collected data on particular policies for different sets of British colonies and explored their relationships with the risk of postcolonial ethnic conflict, yet these works offer weak and inconsistent findings (Lange and Balian 2008; Ray 2018; Verghese 2016).

Although the literatures on pluralism and colonialism overlap, they do not engage with one another. This is unfortunate, as each has the potential to highlight and correct problems with the other. For example, the colonial literature provides a potential corrective to the nationalist literature by noting that pluralist policies can be discriminatory and that pluralism can be a source of conflict. This omission is not surprising, as the nationalist literature focuses on pluralism as a means of reducing intercommunal tensions in regions with preexisting conflict and such policy solutions would necessarily focus on equitable pluralist solutions. "Equitable" is a very subjective term, however, and the biggest difficulty devising pluralist reforms is coming up with policies that all parties view as fair, suggesting that conflict over pluralism is common.

The study of colonial pluralism also offers a partial solution to the main empirical problem facing studies of pluralism and nationalist violence. Because politicians usually implement pluralist policies in environments with either ongoing nationalist civil wars or a very high risk of nationalist violence, nationalist conflict is a common cause of pluralist policies, and this makes it very difficult to assess how pluralism affects nationalist warfare. In colonies, however, favored models and concerns over control were the main determinants of colonial pluralism. As a result, intercommunal conflict had relatively little effect on the degree of colonial pluralism, and an analysis of colonial pluralism limits problems of endogeneity.

While the colonial literature contributes to the nationalist literature on pluralism in these ways, the nationalist literature also provides two important correctives to the colonial literature. First, key works on pluralism consider how the social environment mediates the impact of pluralism, with pluralist solutions only working when matched with key conditions. The literature on divisive colonial policies, on the other hand, focuses on colonialism as an all-powerful, transformative force and therefore pays little attention to social context (Lange 2015). As a result, colonial scholars potentially overstate the impact of colonialism, overlook the possibility of mixed effects, and miss the influence of other factors.

Second, the nationalist literature can help reorient the colonial literature to consider the type of conflict. Overwhelmingly, the colonial literature analyzes how pluralist colonial policies promote ethnic conflict, including both ethnic violence between civilians and ethnic civil wars between a state and ethnic opponents. The nationalist literature, on the other hand, focuses on nationalist conflict and notes that pluralism has particularly important effects on this type of conflict because it deals with communal character of the nation. As such, colonial pluralism might affect nationalist civil warfare more than other types of ethnic conflict, something that potentially explains the mixed findings of previous analyses of colonialism and ethnic violence.

In the pages that follow, I recognize the strengths and weaknesses of both literatures and explore how colonial pluralism affected the risk of violence. Like past works on nationalism, I focus on nationalist civil war instead of ethnic violence more broadly. I also consider how context shapes the character and effects of pluralism, paying particular attention to how the degree of precolonial statehood interacted with colonial pluralism to affect the risk of nationalist civil war. From the colonial literature, I recognize the common finding that pluralism has polarizing effects and therefore explore how pluralism can cause war. And by focusing on colonial pluralism instead of pluralism in noncolonial environments, I limit problems of endogeneity.

THE LITERATURE ON MISSIONARY LEGACIES

This book also engages with a literature that is inherently linked to colonial studies but remains distinct from it: missionary studies. A growing number of works recognize that Christian missionaries shaped social processes in influential and enduring ways, and these works generally focus on the positive effects of missionaries (Cogneau and Moradi 2014; Gallego and Woodberry 2010; Lankina and Getachew 2012, 2013; Nunn 2014; Okoye and Pongou 2014; Woodberry 2004, 2012). The most common focus is education, and several works find that missionaries expanded it throughout the world. Not all missionaries had the same effect, however, and past works find that Protestants commonly provided more education, especially to females, and were much more likely to provide vernacular education (Cogneau and Moradi 2014; Nunn 2014; Woodberry 2002). Because missionary influence was usually greatest among marginalized communities, missionary education commonly contributed to a reversal of fortunes, whereby the formerly marginalized became the most educated and thereby gained greater access to resources and power (Abernethy 1969; Okoye and Pongou 2014). Others also note that education was one of multiple mechanisms through which missionaries contributed to postcolonial democratization (Lankina and Getachew 2012; Woodberry 2012).

Like the literature on missionary legacies, I analyze the long-term effects of missionaries and pay particular attention to Protestants. My analysis differs from the main currents of the missionary literature in three ways, however. The first concerns the dependent variable: Instead of desirable outcomes like education and democracy, this book analyzes how missionaries affected nationalist violence, a destructive outcome that negatively affects the livelihoods of entire populations. Second, whereas previous works analyze missionaries as an autonomous force, I accept Abernethy's (2000) claim that missionaries were part of colonial systems and analyze the combined effects of colonial states and missionaries. Finally, past works pay little attention to how the social context shapes missionary effects, but I consider how one contextual factor—the degree of precolonial statehood—mediated their influence.

Methodological Design

In addition to integrating distinct literatures, this book combines different methodological traditions to expand insight into causes of nationalist civil war. I use comparative-historical methods to analyze processes and mechanisms promoting nationalist civil warfare or its absence and statistical methods for insight into general patterns of nationalist warfare among a larger set of cases. And given their contrasting strengths and weaknesses, I combine both methods in a division of labor that seeks to exploit their strengths and limit their weaknesses (Lange 2013).

I use comparative-historical methods to explore causal processes leading to nationalist civil war in individual cases, something commonly referred to as process tracing (George and Bennett 2005; Mahoney 2000b). This qualitative method generally involves a detective-style analysis that traces processes back from the outcome to explore its causes. In this book, I employ process tracing in a more structured and focused manner, thereby overlooking all causal determinants and focusing on the place of colonial pluralism and precolonial states in the processes leading to nationalist civil war. When structured and focused in this way, process tracing is as forward-looking as it is backward-looking. I therefore trace processes backward from nationalist civil war, trace processes forward from colonial pluralism and precolonial statehood, and explore how both sets of processes connect. As part of this analysis, I use counterfactuals— either implicitly or explicitly—to consider whether nationalist civil wars would have occurred in the absence of colonial pluralism and precolonial states, thereby assessing how central precolonial states and colonial pluralism were to the processes leading to nationalist warfare. Although one cannot turn back history to see if removing colonial pluralism or precolonial states would have prevented nationalist civil warfare, I consider the centrality of each in the processes for evidence into counterfactuals, and these counterfactuals guide my causal assessments.

To strengthen the within-case analysis, I make several qualitative comparisons. These comparisons are qualitative in that they occur in narrative form and focus on complex characteristics—such as processes and mechanisms— that are not easily operationalized (Lange 2013). Similar to Mill's (1843/2012) Methods of Agreement and Difference, the comparisons pair cases based on key similarities and differences to maximize insight into the causes of nationalist civil war. Different from Mill's methods, however, my comparisons are neither independent nor deterministic, and their strength depends on the evidence from the case studies. The main way I use these comparisons is to isolate the influence of precolonial states and colonial pluralism, and such comparisons inform counterfactuals by offering insight into what might have happened if precolonial states were absent or colonialism either did not occur or took a different form.

Instead of using them independently, I combine process tracing and qualitative comparison, and both strengthen and are difficult to separate from one another. The qualitative comparisons bolster the within-case analysis by raising issues for the within-case analyses to explore and highlighting key factors within processes that shape the outcome. In contrast, the within-case analysis highlights the factors and processes that the qualitative comparisons subsequently compare, and an understanding of the processes that occurred in the cases is needed to gain insight from the comparisons.

While the comparative-historical analysis offers insight into causal processes and patterns within particular cases, statistical methods highlight general patterns among a larger set while formally controlling for other factors that might influence the outcome. Using this method, I explore how colonial pluralism, the extent of precolonial statehood, and their combinations are related to the odds of nationalist civil war onset. The goal of these analyses is to highlight general patterns, and I use statistics to test whether these broad patterns support my hypotheses.

In recent years, there has been growing concern that within-case and statistical methods are distinct methodologies with opposing epistemologies, ontologies, and cultures (Goertz and Mahoney 2013). A major conclusion of this literature is that their differences shape empirical analysis in important ways, and quantitative and qualitative methods can therefore produce incompatible results. One way to mitigate this problem is to better integrate within-case and statistical methods by using within-case methods to supplement and test the statistical analyses (Rohlfing 2008; Seawright 2016). Examples include using the within-case analysis to test variable measurements, the possibility of omitted variable bias, and the direction of causation.

I agree that a better integration of comparative-historical and statistical methods can help prevent incompatible findings. I take issue, however, with simply using comparative-historical methods to supplement statistics, a strategy that places all emphasis on the statistical analysis and overlooks the extremely important insight into causal processes that within-case methods and qualitative comparisons provide. Instead of using one method to supplement the other, I attempt to integrate them by completing both comparative-historical and statistical analyses simultaneously, something that allows a continuous back-and-forth between the two. When doing this, within-case analysis can supplement the statistical analysis by exploring possible measurement error, omitted variable bias, and the like. At the same time, a simultaneous analysis enables researchers to exploit the main benefits of comparative-historical methods—insight into causal processes—while supplementing the comparative-historical analysis with insight from the statistical analysis. For example, if the statistical analysis highlights a particular relationship, the within-case analysis can explore processes and mechanisms that might explain the relationship. And, if the within-case and statistical findings contrast, researchers can explore potential reasons for the discrepancy. In completing this book, I therefore continually compared the findings of the comparative-historical and statistical analyses.

To complete such a back-and-forth analysis, an understanding of each methodological tradition is necessary. Just as people can navigate between different cultures by gaining an understanding of each, an understanding of both comparative-historical and statistical methods is needed to integrate them. If not, one dominates, and the main benefits of the other are discarded. A very important part of this understanding is recognizing the strengths and weaknesses of both methodological traditions and attempting to combine them in ways that minimize the disadvantages while maximizing the advantages. I recognize that comparative-historical methods provide powerful insight into processes and mechanisms that explain social outcomes whereas statistical analysis provides important insight into patterns that are needed to make general causal claims. I combine both methodologies to exploit their contrasting advantages, thereby promoting a more rigorous analysis than either methodology could provide on its own.

Given this back-and-forth between statistical and comparative-historical findings, a realistic representation of the research process would be excruciatingly complex. For ease of presentation, I only present the outcome of this process. Because it is easier for readers to follow, I generally present the statistical and comparative-historical analyses separately. As a result, the order of presentation does not represent the order in which the analysis occurred.

Another way in which I limit potentially conflicting results from multi-method analysis is by using comparative-historical methods to analyze a relatively large number of cases—dozens of nationalist civil wars in 20 countries. Any single case is unique in a variety of ways, and the risk that the qualitative and quantitative findings conflict are high when including only one or two case studies. By increasing the number of cases, the comparative-historical analysis offers insight into broader patterns, and the match between statistical and comparative-historical findings should improve. And if the findings do not converge, the researcher must explore why they do not.

To analyze how colonial pluralism and precolonial states affect the risk of nationalist civil war, I could analyze any number of former overseas colonies. I focus on the former British Empire because it offers superior insight into interactions between colonial pluralism and historical states: British rule was exceptionally pluralist, and the extent of precolonial statehood varied greatly within the British Empire. More generally, different aspects of the British Empire help highlight common causal dynamics of nationalist civil war. For one, former British colonies have experienced three times as many nationalist civil wars as the former colonies of other European powers, but only one in four former British colonies have suffered nationalist civil wars. As a result, the factors promoting nationalist civil war should be unusually concentrated in some former British colonies but weaker or absent in others. In addition, there are three dozen former British colonies, and this relatively large number makes possible a systematic analysis of the causes of nationalist civil war. And because of the number of British colonies and the concentration of nationalist civil war in them, over one-third of all nationalist civil wars since 1946 have occurred in former British colonies, a share that allows analyses to highlight broader patterns and provide more general insight.

My case-selection strategy for the comparative-historical analysis is to include all nine former British colonies that experienced nationalist civil war (Bangladesh, India, Iraq, Israel/Palestine, Myanmar, Nigeria, Pakistan, Sri Lanka, and Sudan). For comparative purposes, I also select seven former British colonies that have not experienced nationalist civil war (Botswana,

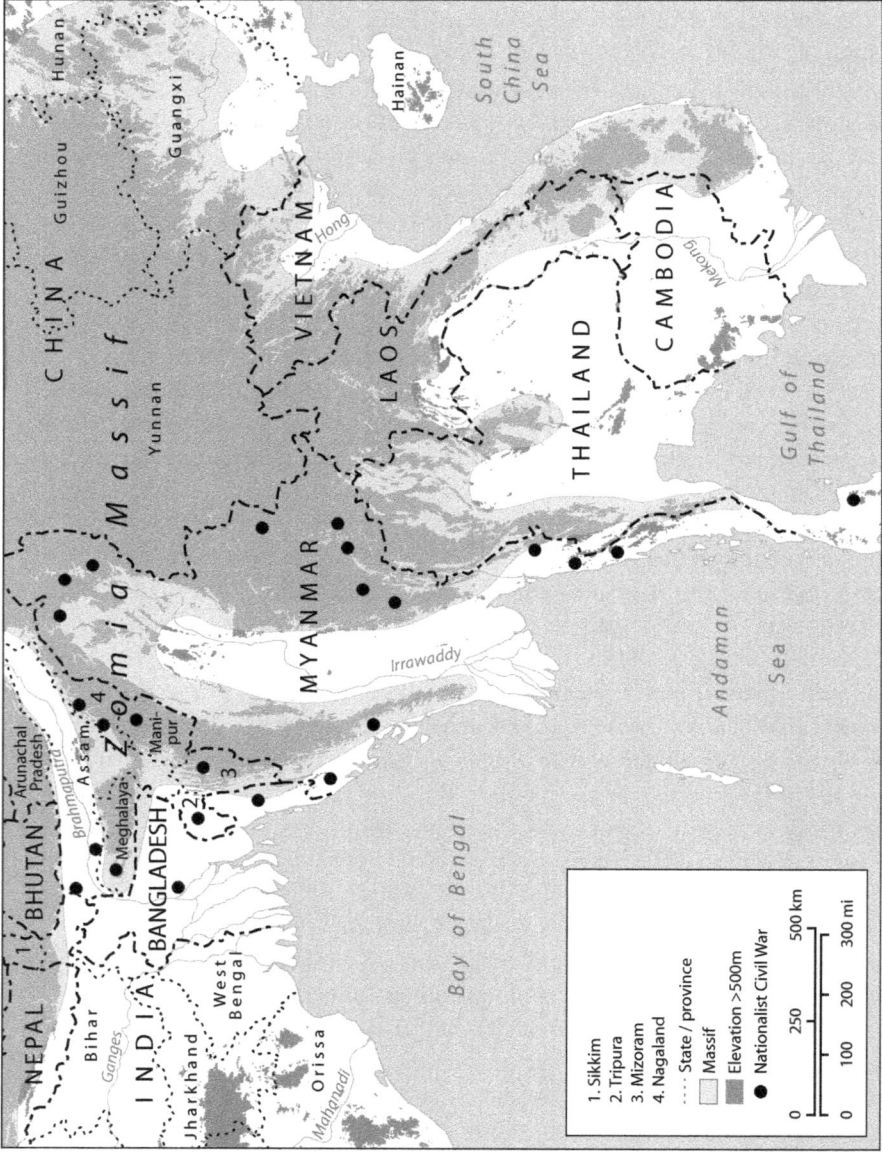

FIGURE I.2. Nationalist Civil Warfare in Southeast Asia, 1946–2020. Adapted from "The Southeast Asian Massif" by Jean Michaud, *Journal of Global History*, 2010.

Ghana, Egypt, Malaysia, Sierra Leone, Singapore, and Tanzania), two former French colonies that either did not experience nationalist civil war (Cambodia) or experienced a relatively minor conflict (Vietnam), and two countries that (mostly) avoided European colonialism and experienced either one (Thailand) or seven nationalist civil wars (Ethiopia). I selected these cases based on variation in the focal independent variables, theoretical considerations, their pairing with other cases, and their fit with the statistical analysis.

While analyzing cases in different regions of the world, I pay particular attention to Southeast Asia for different reasons. Most importantly, 22 of the 35 nationalist civil wars in the former British Empire occurred in Southeast Asia, so any analysis of how British colonial pluralism affected nationalist civil war must pay close attention to this region. Similarly, nationalist civil wars are much more concentrated in Southeast Asia than any other region of the world, making the region important for more general understandings of the causes of nationalist civil war. The region is also ideal for testing my main hypotheses because all countries in the region have very high levels of historical statehood and communal demographies characterized by one large state community and several smaller non-state communities. Scott (2009), in turn, notes that conflict in the region is common between lowland states and upland non-state communities, with upland communities fighting to maintain their autonomy from lowland states. Finally, the British colonized three of the eight countries in the region, thereby allowing me to explore how historical statehood affects nationalist conflict with and without histories of colonial pluralism. As highlighted in figure I.2, 22 of the 23 nationalist civil wars in the region occurred in former British colonies, and I explore whether the combination of colonial pluralism and historical statehood explains this pattern.

Book Outline

The remainder of this book includes nine chapters. Chapter 1 presents the book's theoretical framework, which takes a mid-level, mechanism-centered approach that draws on social movement and statist theories. The majority of the chapter describes mechanisms through which colonial pluralism and precolonial statehood potentially affect nationalist civil war, and it ends by considering how these effects can endure after colonialism to shape postcolonial patterns of nationalist conflict. Chapter 2 analyzes the pluralist character of British colonial rule. For this, it provides a brief history of British colonialism, describes the main characteristics and policies of colonial pluralism, explores the prevalence of colonial pluralism in the British Empire, and analyzes the origins of colonial pluralism. For insight into the extent to which British colonialism was uniquely pluralist, the chapter also compares the form of rule in the British Empire with other European overseas empires, focusing primarily on the French. Chapter 3 uses statistics to test whether general patterns support chapter 1's theoretical framework. For this, I measure the extent of colonial pluralism and precolonial statehood and test their relationships with the onset of nationalist civil war between 1946 and 2020. Chapters 4 through 8 complete the book's comparative-historical analysis. Chapters 4 and 5 analyze Myanmar and India, respectively. Both regions are extreme cases that had highly pluralist forms of colonialism and subsequently experienced many nationalist civil wars. If colonial pluralism affects nationalist civil warfare, these cases are therefore ideal for highlighting the mechanisms and processes linking colonial pluralism and nationalist conflict (Goertz 2016). Chapter 6 provides more abbreviated analyses of all remaining former British colonies that experienced nationalist civil warfare to see if the findings parallel those of Myanmar and India. For insight into why colonial pluralism did not promote nationalist civil warfare in all cases, the chapter also includes a comparative analysis of Malaysia, Singapore, Sierra Leone, Ghana, and Tanzania. Chapters 7 and 8 turn the attention to the impact of historical statehood on nationalist civil warfare. Chapter 7 returns to cases reviewed in chapters 4, 5, and 6 and analyzes ways in which precolonial statehood interacted with colonial pluralism to affect nationalist civil warfare. By including cases with different levels of precolonial statehood, the chapter explores the different ways in which precolonial statehood combined with colonial pluralism to shape nationalist civil warfare. Chapter 8 explores the independent effects of historical statehood. For this, it analyzes six cases with high levels of historical statehood but limited or no colonial pluralism—Vietnam, Cambodia, Thailand, Botswana, Egypt, and Ethiopia. The concluding chapter summarizes the findings and considers their generalizability. For the latter, it investigates whether the book's findings can be applied to noncolonial settings and whether they offer insight into patterns of postcolonial conflict in the former French and Spanish Empires.

1

Theoretical Framework

PRECOLONIAL STATES, COLONIAL PLURALISM, AND NATIONALIST CIVIL WARFARE

In this chapter, I present a mid-level theoretical framework that focuses on causal mechanisms and that is most influenced by the sociological literature on states and social movements. The social movement literature considers how states create institutional settings that affect the character and success of social movements through motivational, framing, and mobilizational mechanisms (Amenta and Young 1999; Clemens and Cook 1999; Goodwin 2001; Johnston 2011; Kitschelt 1986; McAdam 1982; Skocpol 1979; Tilly 1978, 2004). While recognizing that social movements and nationalist civil wars are distinct phenomena, nationalist civil wars and social movements are both clear examples of contentious politics in which civilians mobilize to make demands on states, and most nationalist civil wars begin after nationalist movements turn to violent repertoires in reaction to state repression. Given these similarities, social movements and nationalist civil wars likely have similar causal dynamics, and I focus on how states shape nationalist civil wars through motivational, framing, and mobilizational mechanisms.

The theoretical framework suggests that nationalist civil wars are usually fought after chauvinistic states remove the cultural and political autonomy of communities. The motive of lost autonomy is usually not sufficient to mobilize a nationalist civil war, however. Different factors must therefore be present to make the loss of autonomy especially hurtful, heighten sensitivity to lost autonomy, and empower communities to mobilize in opposition to it.

I apply the framework to former British colonies. Chauvinistic reductions in communal autonomy were common during transitions from empire to nation-state. In particular, state communities regularly reduced or eliminated the cultural and political autonomy of non-state communities in their efforts to build their own nation-states after independence, thereby increasing the risk of nationalist civil war in former colonies with large and long-standing precolonial states. British colonialism, in turn, was usually highly pluralist, and this form of rule magnified the effects of lost autonomy. For one, colonial pluralism made the national chauvinism of state communities unusually aggressive and vindictive, which increased fear and anger over lost communal autonomy. It also increased the sensitivity of non-state communities to lost autonomy by strengthening their nationalist frames and expectations. Finally, colonial pluralism provided communities with important resources that allowed communities to mobilize opposition to lost autonomy. The risk of nationalist civil war was therefore extremely high in places with both historical statehood and a history of British colonial pluralism.

While the combination of historical statehood and colonial pluralism created a very elevated risk of nationalist civil war, I argue that colonial pluralism had the opposite effect when combined with low levels of historical statehood. Limited historical statehood weakens national chauvinism, so no community claims the postcolonial nation-state as its own. And without national chauvinism, communities experience less fear and anger when they lose autonomy to postcolonial nation-states. Colonial pluralism, in turn, has similar effects on all communities when historical statehood is limited, and this promotes popular support for pluralism and the continuation of pluralist policies after independence in places with weak national chauvinism.

Precolonial Statehood and Nationalist Civil Warfare

While all countries have states, some states have existed for much longer than others. The first large-scale independent polity in Papua New Guinea, for example, was formed less than a century ago, thereby promoting very low levels of historical statehood. In contrast, the first large state controlling most of contemporary Myanmar has been present over most of the past millennium, giving the country unusually high levels of historical statehood. I argue that the level of historical statehood has important implications on the risk of nationalist civil war because large and long-standing states commonly initiate a causal sequence leading to nationalist conflict: Historical statehood shapes communal demographies and myth-symbol complexes in ways that strengthen national chauvinism, national chauvinism promotes assertive and discriminatory efforts to remove the political and cultural autonomy of communities, and these changes spark nationalist movements.

HISTORICAL STATEHOOD AND NATIONAL CHAUVINISM

Communal demography deals with the number and relative size of communities within a polity. For example, Japan has one overwhelmingly dominant community, Myanmar has one majority community and several smaller communities, and Papua New Guinea has thousands of small communities. Demographic dominance is an important cause of national chauvinism, as communities that are the largest and make up most of the population accept the democratic principle that numbers matter. Indeed, if your community is very large and all others are very small, it seems only natural that your community should be *the* national community. Places like Japan and Myanmar therefore have unusually strong national chauvinism. In contrast, national chauvinism is weak or absent in places like Papua New Guinea because all communities are very small and make up a small fraction of the population, causing people to view their community as one of several national communities.

Unipolar communal demographies like those in Japan and Myanmar are not distributed randomly throughout the world: They are heavily concentrated in places with large and long-standing states. The first states that controlled most of Japan and Myanmar, for example, were founded in the first millennium AD, providing more than 1,000 years of rule. As Wimmer (2018) notes, historical statehood promotes homogeneous populations by assimilating non-state communities. Both overt efforts to spread the language and religion of the state community and informal incentives—such as access to education or positions of authority—promote assimilation. Such assimilation usually occurs over generations, so a long period of historical statehood is key.

Even with very long periods of statehood, however, assimilation into state communities is rarely complete, and most regions with high levels of historical statehood have one demographically dominant community and several smaller communities, making the communal demography of Myanmar more typical of places with historical states than Japan. The most important reason for continued diversity is that most large and long-standing historical states were imperial states controlling core and peripheral regions, and these states granted considerable cultural and political autonomy to communities in peripheral regions (Elliot 1992; Hall 2015; Lattimore 1962; Mann 1986; Tilly 1992). Indirect rule was widespread in imperial states out of necessity: They lacked the communication, transportation, and organizational technologies needed to establish direct control over large and distant lands, so outlying communities were allowed to rule themselves if they paid allegiance to the imperial state.

In addition to demographic size, cultural ideas of community inform national chauvinism and affect its strength. These ideas are commonly organized into what Smith (1986) calls myth-symbol complexes, which combine myths, symbols, historical memory, and core values of a community in ways that promote popular understandings of communities and strong communal frames and schema that shape how people perceive themselves and the world. Myth-symbol complexes focus largely on the origins of communities, the historical triumphs and struggles that define them, and their "natural" homelands.

All communities have myth-symbol complexes, but historical statehood promotes myth-symbol complexes that strengthen national chauvinism. Historical statehood provides a plethora of material for building myth-symbol complexes, as it highlights the distant origins of communities, suggests the continuity of a national community over time, and provides a great variety of mythic events that highlight the grandeur and character of national communities. Given the centrality of a long history of statehood in the myth-symbol complexes, members of state communities recognize themselves as the rightful heirs of past states, and historical statehood promotes popular beliefs that the state community has always lived there and that the state has been passed down from one generation to the next. This creates genealogical understandings of the national community that make national membership exclusive and based on heritage. Anyone not from the state community is therefore not a natural member of the nation-state, making them outsiders or, at best, lesser nationals. And when these myth-symbol complexes are combined with demographic dominance, national chauvinism is very strong.

In contrast, the myth-symbol complexes of non-state communities are not compatible with national chauvinism because they are more localized and do not match the history of contemporary states. Indeed, these myth-symbol complexes focus on local history and pay little attention to the history of the nation-state. Members of communities with limited or no historical statehood might view themselves as the truest members of a particular region, but this rarely translates into national chauvinism because the nation-state was never theirs, is much larger than their homeland, and is comprised overwhelmingly of people from other communities.

NATIONAL CHAUVINISM AND NATIONALIST CIVIL WAR

Through its effects on national chauvinism, I hypothesize that historical statehood contributes to nationalist civil war. National chauvinism pushes state communities not only to remove the political and cultural autonomy of non-state communities but to declare their community the sole national community, and non-state communities commonly oppose both. And because of their chauvinism, state communities commonly deal with this opposition inflexibly, thereby escalating conflict into nationalist civil war.

The construction of a nation-state requires both nation building and state building, and national chauvinism pushes actors to purify the nation and take exclusive control of the state. In their efforts to assert national supremacy and build a unified nation, national chauvinists try to either assimilate, marginalize, or eliminate other communities (Mann 2005; Weber 1976). National chauvinism therefore severely threatens the cultural autonomy of other communities, with language, religion, dress, and other aspects of culture seemingly under attack. At the same time, the ideal-typical nation-state is based on a Weberian state that is infrastructurally powerful, monopolizes the legitimate use of violence within the state's territory, and rules all regions directly (Mann 1986; Tilly 1992; Weber 2019). Because national chauvinists believe their communities must run the state, they remove local authorities, replace them with members of their community, and create bureaucratic structures making possible more centralized control. In this way, communities confronted by the national chauvinism of others face double jeopardy during transitions to the nation-state: They lose their cultural autonomy through efforts to build a cohesive nation around the state community, and they lose their political autonomy through the creation of more infrastructurally powerful and direct states run by the "true" community for the well-being of the "true" community.

When people value their community, the loss of political and cultural autonomy creates strong grievances because such policies threaten the very existence of their community, and these grievances can therefore motivate opposition to lost autonomy. This opposition is strongest when the state is run by national chauvinists who arrogantly claim that their community is the only true national community, denigrate others as lesser communities, and demand that other communities assimilate or leave. Yet because of their national chauvinism, members of the state community see resistance to their nation-state-building efforts as illegitimate and target those who oppose it with anger and resentment. This, in turn, only increases the fear and anger of communities facing lost autonomy and therefore strengthens opposition to it. At some point, this vicious circle of escalating conflict pushes communities to mobilize nationalist movements to maintain or regain their autonomy, and national chauvinists try to suppress this movement through any means, resulting in a nationalist civil war.

In contrast, the risk of nationalist civil war is much lower in places with limited historical statehood. In this situation, there are many small communities, and none has populations or myth-symbol complexes that support ideas of national supremacy. National chauvinism is therefore limited or absent, and reductions in communal power and autonomy—while still common during transitions to the nation-state—are much less galling when the state is not run by arrogant national chauvinists from another community.

Although an influential cause of nationalist civil war, the impact of national chauvinism is not universal. For one, nationalist civil war depends on the presence of multiple communities. Although national chauvinism is present in Japan, its extremely homogeneous population creates a very low risk of nationalist civil war because no community is large enough to mobilize opposition. In contrast, the state community in Myanmar—the Bamar—makes up approximately two-thirds of the population, and dozens of non-state communities make up the rest. Non-state communities are therefore large enough to mobilize against Bamar national chauvinism and the loss of communal autonomy to a chauvinistic state.

Yet even when national chauvinism is present in places like Myanmar, non-state communities rarely react violently. One reason is that the strength of national chauvinism varies, and milder national chauvinism is less likely to spark strong fear and opposition. Moreover, some communities are less sensitive to the national chauvinism of others because they have weaker nationalist frames and expectations. And even if some communities are aggrieved by the national chauvinism of others and their loss of autonomy to a chauvinistic state, they commonly lack the mobilizational resources to do anything about it.

Colonial Pluralism and Nationalist Civil War

Certain conditions make national chauvinism more aggressive, increase sensitivity to lost autonomy at the hands of chauvinistic states, and strengthen the mobilizational resources of communities. In this section, I argue that colonial pluralism promoted all three, thereby creating a very high risk of nationalist civil war in places with historical statehood. When colonial pluralism was combined with limited historical statehood, however, the risk of nationalist civil war was low. In this setting, national chauvinism was weak, colonial pluralism recognized and empowered all communities, and both combined to promote pluralist postcolonial states that allowed communities to maintain power and autonomy. And even when postcolonial states reduced autonomy, pluralist policies and an inclusive nation-state weakened grievances over it.

COLONIAL PLURALISM AND MOTIVATIONAL MECHANISMS

As noted previously, pluralist policies recognize, accommodate, and empower communities. Of these three, I argue that pluralist policies are most likely to motivate nationalist civil war when they empower communities in regions with large and long-standing precolonial states. In this context, empowering pluralist policies strengthen non-state communities at the expense of state communities, and this readjustment promotes grievances, competition, and conflict over pluralism and the communal character of the postcolonial nation-state.

In the British Empire, the most common empowering pluralist policies were the provisioning of communal autonomy through indirect rule, the reservation of legislative seats for communities, and the creation of community-based military regiments. Communities that had great autonomy through indirect colonial rule and that received special legislative or military representation had strong interests in retaining their privileged positions after independence. Similarly, past practice created expectations for the retention of pluralist policies and a belief that their communities needed and deserved them. Alternatively, communities that did not benefit from pluralism had an interest in removing pluralist policies. Thus, when the leaders of postcolonial states refused to retain pluralist policies, those communities benefiting from colonial pluralism experienced strong grievances, thereby creating a high risk of nationalist conflict.

While common in places with a history of colonial pluralism, I argue that this conflict depends greatly on the combination of colonial pluralism and precolonial states. As noted previously, state communities commonly support national chauvinism given their size and myth-symbol complexes, and colonial pluralism gave this chauvinism sharp teeth. Although pluralist colonial policies that recognize and accommodate non-state communities likely strengthen the national chauvinism of state communities, pluralist policies that empower non-state communities have much more powerful effects because they fly in the face of the national chauvinism of state communities by increasing the power and status of non-state communities. Even more, the state communities see indirect rule, communal legislative representation, and communalized security forces as nefarious means of divide and rule that underpinned colonialism, thereby seeking to remove these colonial practices as part of the decolonization process and regain the power that is "rightfully" theirs. As a result, state communities target non-state communities as a danger and seek to reinstate their dominance by removing their powers. And when faced with the arrogant, aggressive, and vindictive national chauvinism of state communities and their vehement opposition to postcolonial pluralism, non-state communities react by demanding the retention of pluralist policies, thereby creating a political deadlock that promotes nationalist civil warfare.

A central component of this process is the readjustment of the relative power and status of state and non-state communities through pluralist policies. In general, state communities mounted the greatest resistance to colonialism, whereas non-state communities put up less resistance and were a much weaker threat. As a result, regions with large and long-standing precolonial states were ideal for divide-and-rule-style policies that limited the anticolonial threat of state communities by granting special power and privileges to non-state communities. Yet even when colonial pluralism did not overtly discriminate against state communities, pluralist policies promoted grievances among state communities by readjusting the relative power and status of communities. State communities had high levels of power and status prior to colonialism, whereas non-state communities usually had very low levels of both. By recognizing, accommodating, and empowering non-state communities, colonial pluralism increased their power and status relative to state communities, and state communities no longer dominated non-state communities. In this situation, leaders of state communities popularized and pursued aggressive and revisionist forms of national chauvinism that targeted non-state communities as colonial "stooges" and "cronies" who unfairly benefited from colonialism and thereby endangered the heritage and future of state communities.

Different works within the sociology of emotions offer insight into how this situation motivates violence. Following Kemper's (1978) theory, state communities assessed their power and status as inadequate due to colonial pluralism, and this created anger, fear, and resentment that was directed at the colonized communities that had gained power and status at their expense. The national chauvinism of state communities therefore strengthened and targeted non-state communities as a danger and made the national chauvinism of state communities aggressive, exclusionary, and vindictive. At the same time, state communities viewed their diminished power and status at the hands of colonial "collaborators" as immoral given myth-symbol complexes that declared themselves the true national community, and this promoted moral rage (Turner and Stets 2006).

In contrast, non-state communities saw their power and status as adequate under colonial pluralism and viewed pluralist policies that safeguarded their power and autonomy as necessary and moral. In this situation, the efforts of state communities to repeal colonial pluralism increased their anger, fear, and resentment and focused these emotions on state communities. Non-state communities therefore opposed the national chauvinism of state communities and demanded the retention of or return to pluralism. This opposition, in turn, began a vicious circle of escalating conflict, as state communities perceived non-state resistance to their national chauvinism as illegitimate, immoral, and dangerous and thereby further intensified the anger and resentment of state communities, which, in turn, strengthened the opposition of non-state communities.

These motivational effects result from pluralist policies empowering non-state communities more than state communities and a belief among state communities that they are the true national community, and both effects depend on the presence of precolonial states. Due to this dependence, colonial pluralism had very different effects in the absence of precolonial statehood. Without large and long-standing precolonial states, populations were usually more diverse, demographically dominant communities were rare, and communities seldom viewed themselves as the only true national community. And with limited national chauvinism, the risk of nationalist civil war is low. At the same time, colonial officials usually applied pluralism more universally in places with limited precolonial statehood because all communities posed similar threats, and pluralist colonial policies therefore had similar effects on the relative power and status of all communities. Because of limited national chauvinism, communal elites from all communities had similar interests in retaining or reforming colonial pluralism, and popular postcolonial pluralism further reduced the risk of nationalist civil war. One way it did so was by formally recognizing all communities as equal members of the nation-state. In addition, postcolonial pluralism helped maintain a certain degree of communal power, thereby reducing opposition to nation-state-building policies that curbed communal autonomy.

COLONIAL PLURALISM AND FRAMING EFFECTS

Although shaping nationalist civil war in important ways, the motivational effects of precolonial statehood and colonial pluralism depend greatly on communal frames. These frames focus attention on communities, affect interests and expectations, and push actors to interpret situations from the perspective of their community. Without communal frames, actors are much less likely to assess the relative power and status of their communities and have expectations for both. While many factors contribute to communal frames, I argue that colonial pluralism strengthened and nationalized them, especially among non-state communities.

Cognitive frameworks influence how people see themselves and the world around them, and communal frames promote communal perceptions whereby people perceive themselves and the world in terms of community (Brubaker 2004; Jenkins 2008). A central claim of social identity theory is that communal frameworks contribute to intercommunal conflict (Tajfel 1970, 1974). While seemingly innocuous, these frames make possible discriminatory behavior, as one cannot discriminate against communities without perceiving communal categories. Communal frames also allow people to perceive communal interests and feel aggrieved by communal inequalities, thereby promoting motives for communal conflict. Building on this literature, I argue that colonial pluralism is most likely to promote nationalist civil warfare when it promotes politicized communal frames focused on communal power and self-rule, a subtype of communal frame that I refer to as a nationalist frame. And with nationalist frames, people are more likely to expect communal power and status, perceive nationalist grievances when these expectations are not met, and address them through nationalist movements.

Several works note that colonial pluralism clearly shaped community-based categorical frameworks in ways that contributed to communal conflict (Horowitz 1985; Mamdani 2012; Lieberman and Singh 2017). Along these lines, Mazrui (1983) claims, "British approaches to colonial rule, by being culturally relative and ethnically specific, helped to perpetuate and in some cases create the kind of ethnic consciousness which could seriously militate against nation building" (29). According to this view, pluralist policies that recognized, accommodated, and empowered communities promoted communal frameworks that shaped how people perceived the world and themselves. Empowering pluralist policies, in turn, were most likely to promote nationalist frames, especially through indirect rule and communal legislative representation. As Kasfir (1972) notes, indirect rule "sanctioned the notion that an ethnic group was a valid basis for an administrative unit . . . and provided an institutional expression for cultural unity" (72). As a result, indirect rule promoted nationalist frames that depicted the community as the natural political community and suggested that communities should rule themselves. In a similar way, communal legislative representation promoted the idea that community is the main unit of politics and that communities need to focus on protecting communal interests in the political arena. Communities in places with communal legislative representation were therefore more aware of their relative power and status and had expectations for formal communal powers.

Although nationalist frames can have independent effects on nationalist civil war by promoting discriminatory behavior, I hypothesize that they are most likely to promote nationalist civil warfare when combined with motivational mechanisms. In seeing the world in terms of community, actors look out for the well-being of their community and feel aggrieved when their community faces hardships. As such, communities with nationalist frames are much more likely to feel strong grievances when experiencing lost cultural and political autonomy at the hands of a national chauvinist state. Even more, nationalist frames create expectations for communal power and self-rule, and impediments to both promote powerful grievances that can motivate nationalist civil warfare. Discriminatory and empowering pluralist policies were particularly influential in this regard, as they strengthened nationalist frames, created expectations for continued communal power and self-rule, and motivated conflict between communities that were either helped or hurt by pluralist policies.

In contrast to social identity theory, I argue that the presence of several communal—or even nationalist—frames need not promote conflict. In places with pluralist policies but limited communal competition and conflict, the recognition, accommodation, and empowerment of communities promotes more pluralist understandings of the nation-state. As a result, community and nation-state are compatible and complementary instead of competing and antagonistic, thereby promoting a type of plurinationalism in which people perceive the nation as inherently diverse. This outcome is most likely in places with many non-state communities and pluralist policies that treat all communities similarly, thereby lowering risk of nationalist civil war in places with limited historical statehood but high levels of colonial pluralism.

COLONIAL PLURALISM AND MOBILIZATIONAL EFFECTS

Nationalist civil warfare depends on collective action. And even with motives and frames, collective action commonly requires resources that make possible the mobilization of large numbers of people. In addition to shaping motives and frames, colonial pluralism increased the risk of nationalist warfare in places with precolonial states by providing communities with organizational and military resources that allowed them to recruit fighters and mobilize and sustain nationalist civil wars.

Colonial pluralism provided a variety of organizational resources that leaders could employ to mobilize nationalist movements. Communalized indirect rule, for example, provided communities with their own semiautonomous polities equipped with administrations, courts, and security forces, all of which created a very strong organizational base to launch a nationalist movement. Communal legislative representation, in turn, spurred the creation of community-based parties, which were also powerful organizations that mobilized communities. Communal representation was not necessary for the founding of communal parties, however, as colonial pluralism promoted communal organizations by simply recognizing and politicizing communities. The provisioning of vernacular education, for example, provided communities with their own schools and communalized education in ways that facilitated and encouraged the organization of community-based educational associations, which commonly popularized nationalist causes while endowing nationalist movements with important human, communication, and organizational resources.

Besides organizational resources, nationalist civil wars require a variety of military resources, and colonial pluralism often provided non-state communities with these resources. Most importantly, the creation of community-based military units was a common pluralist policy, and this provided communities with ready-made fighting forces. Moreover, indirect rule commonly gave communal authorities control of local security forces. And through both, colonial pluralism provided some non-state communities with military leadership, fighting experience, trained soldiers, and weapons.

Importantly, the use of these mobilizational resources to organize nationalist movements and nationalist civil wars depends on motive. When confronted with national chauvinism and lost autonomy and possessing nationalist frames, communities use their mobilizational resources to fight nationalist civil wars. In the absence of nationalist motivations, actors do not.

PROTESTANT MISSIONARIES AND COLONIAL PLURALISM

Studies of colonial legacies focus on colonial states, and this focus is especially appropriate for analyses of colonial pluralism because the colonial state was the main actor implementing pluralist policies. As Abernethy (2000) correctly notes, however, economic and religious actors were commonly either formal or informal colonial agents. In this book, I pay particular attention to the ways in which missionaries—especially Protestants—strengthened colonial pluralism in ways shaping framing, motivational, and mobilizational mechanisms. Although they affected colonial pluralism in multiple ways, I focus largely on their educational effects and, in so doing, draw on literature linking communalized education to ethnic violence and civil war (Bush and Saltarelli 2000; Davies 2004; King 2014; Lange 2012).

The growing historical and social scientific literature on missionaries notes that Protestant missionaries differed from their Catholic counterparts in important ways (Cogneau and Moradi 2014; Gallego and Woodberry 2010; Lankina and Getachew 2012, 2013; Nunn 2014; Okoye and Pongou 2014; Woodberry 2004, 2012). Of greatest relevance to this work, Protestant missionaries recognized and accommodated communities much more than Catholics. Because Protestantism believed all Christians must read the Bible, Protestant missionaries placed great emphasis on literacy and education. The ability of people to read the Bible and live according to its word also required the translation of the Bible into local vernaculars, and Protestant missionaries therefore actively translated it into many languages. Thus, when Protestant missionaries began their activities, among the first things they did was to standardize a system of writing in places that lacked one, translate the Bible into local vernaculars, found printing presses, and establish schools teaching in these languages. In this way, Protestant missionaries promoted pluralist education accommodating the languages of diverse communities.

Through vernacular education and the printing of material presenting communities as real, Protestant missionaries strengthened—and sometimes created—nationalist frames. One reason for this is that the missionaries possessed nationalist frames, saw the communities they worked with as nations, and helped spread nationalist understandings. As a result, people were more likely to perceive and be concerned about communal power and autonomy.

Missionaries also created infrastructures that supported nationalist frames and provided communities with mobilizational resources. According to Woodberry (2004, 2012), Protestant missionaries promoted a vibrant associational life in a variety of ways. One way was established printing presses that produced large amounts of printed material. Because newspapers were widespread in the missionary homelands (primarily the United States and Great Britain) and because printing newspapers was seen as a means of attracting followers, Protestant missionaries founded many of the first newspapers in Africa and Asia. Newspaper readership is, in turn, a strong predictor of associationalism. Woodberry (2004, 2012) also notes that Protestantism introduced organizational reforms that strengthened associationalism, and a selection effect also increased associationalism: Missionaries were generally very active in civil societal associations prior to joining a mission, and they brought their active associationalism to the missions.

The literature on civil societal associationalism generally focuses on cross-cutting, or bridging, ties that bring people from diverse backgrounds together in ways that increase trust, compromise, and mutual respect and understandings (Putnam 2000). The associations founded by Protestant missionaries, however, rarely had such breadth. Missionaries usually catered to Christians from their denomination. And because the missionaries invested in learning local languages, missionaries usually worked exclusively with one linguistic community. Even more, missionaries were very concerned about protecting "their flock," and they often helped the communities they worked with organize themselves politically. For these reasons, Protestant associations promoted bonding ties within communities much more than bridging ties between communities. In so doing, they not only politicized communities but helped build associations focused on communal power and interests.

Protestant missionaries, in turn, commonly strengthened motives that put these mobilizational resources into action by readjusting communal hierarchies and threatening the religions of state communities. Because missionaries provided most of the education in the British Empire, educational access depended on missionary influence (Cogneau and Moradi 2014; Woodberry 2004). In general, missionaries worked much more closely with non-state communities because the state communities resisted missionary influence much more strongly. In addition, the attraction of missionary education was usually greater for non-state communities because they commonly lacked their own formal system of education, did not have their own systems of writing, and saw missionaries as a potential means of freeing themselves from dependent relationships with state communities. And because education was the main means of mobility in colonies, missionaries contributed to a reversal of fortune benefiting non-state communities at the expense of state communities (Abernethy 1969; Okoye and Pongou 2014).

Missionary influence also contributed to the overrepresentation of non-state communities in key colonial institutions, and this was another important source of grievances. In some cases, missionaries encouraged their followers to join the colonial military forces for a variety of reasons—to protect the mission, to gain the favor of colonial officials, to increase the standing of communities within the colonial hierarchy, and to modernize and strengthen the community. Of equal or greater importance, colonial officials sought indigenous soldiers who they could trust, and many believed that the most loyal colonial subjects were Christian. Missionary education, in turn, provided the credentials that allowed some soldiers to work their way up the military hierarchy. In a similar way, colonial officials were more likely to reserve legislative seats for communities working with missionaries because of missionary lobbying, because missionaries organized communities in ways that strengthened their demands for special representation, and—especially—because colonial officials wanted "friends" in the colonial legislature and believed that Christian communities would side with the colonizers in heated legislative debates.

A final way in which Protestant missionaries motivated conflict between state and non-state communities was by threatening the religions of the state communities. Although state communities usually did not convert to Christianity, many members of state communities feared that Christianity could destroy their religion. One reason for this is that some members of state communities eventually converted, and many went to missionary schools because they were their best or only educational option. In fearing Christianity, state communities targeted those communities that worked closely with missionaries as both dangerous and degenerate.

While education, overrepresentation in the colonial military and legislature, and religious conversion strengthened state community resentment and outrage against non-state communities, missionaries also created expectations among non-state communities for continued power and status. Communities benefiting from missionary influence believed they deserved desirable jobs because they were better educated, and special communal representation created expectations for its continuation. State communities therefore targeted non-state communities and sought to reassert their dominance over them, whereas non-state communities opposed these efforts and sought to protect the advantages they had gained through missionary influence.

As this discussion suggests, the influence of Protestant missionaries depends greatly on the presence of a large and long-standing precolonial state. In this context, missionaries worked most closely with non-state communities, thereby strengthening the communal frames of non-state communities, providing them with community-based mobilizational resources, and benefiting non-state communities in ways that motivated conflict between state and non-state communities. In the absence of precolonial states, however, Protestant missionaries did not promote nationalist civil war through these mechanisms for three reasons. First, the religions of all communities were usually more localized and less institutionalized, causing similar levels of missionary influence among all communities and weakening missionary efforts to isolate and protect "their" communities from the neighbors. Second, yet in combination with the first, most regions without precolonial statehood had limited communal hierarchies, and missionaries had little effect on reversals in communal status and power in this situation. Finally, postcolonial states were less likely to target communities influenced by missionaries as degenerate and dangerous when missionaries were active among all communities.

———

In summary, I propose a series of factors that interact to increase the risk of nationalist civil warfare. First, precolonial states commonly promote communal demographies and myth-symbol complexes that strengthen national chauvinism, and national chauvinism creates a moderate risk of nationalist conflict during and after transitions to the nation-state by promoting fear and anger of lost cultural and political autonomy. When combined with a history of colonial pluralism, however, this risk increases greatly. For one, colonial pluralism intensifies the aggressive and vindictive character of this national chauvinism, making it more likely that non-state communities react to it with nationalist movements. Moreover, colonial pluralism commonly promotes nationalist frames that cause people to pay great attention to, be concerned about, and expect communal power and autonomy, all of which make non-state communities very sensitive to the national chauvinism of state communities and promote strong grievances when state communities threaten to remove pluralist policies. Finally, colonial pluralism provides communities with organizational, human, and military resources that allow actors to put their motives into action. Protestant missionaries, in turn, were part of colonial pluralism and commonly strengthened these motivational, framing, and mobilizational mechanisms.

The combination of precolonial statehood and colonial pluralism is crucial: Precolonial states have weaker and less consistent effects without colonial pluralism, and colonial pluralism either has no effect on nationalist civil war or has suppressive effects when combined with limited historical statehood. Instead of canceling each other out, the positive effects of colonial pluralism likely outweigh the negative effects. This is because colonial pluralism greatly increases the risk of nationalist civil war when levels of historical statehood are high, thereby promoting many nationalist civil wars in places with historical statehood that would not have occurred without it. In contrast, the risk of nationalist civil war was already low in places with limited historical statehood, and most cases with limited historical statehood therefore would *not* have experienced a nationalist civil war even without a history of colonial pluralism.

Theorizing the Legacies of Colonial and Precolonial States

A large literature notes that colonialism has lingering effects on postcolonial ethnic violence, and a separate literature describes how precolonial states affect postcolonial conflict (Englebert 2000; Lange and Dawson 2009; Ray 2012,

2018, 2019; Wimmer 2018; Wucherpfennig et al. 2016). To date, these works pay little attention to the ways in which the effects of historical states can endure, and I consider such a possibility in this section. For many cases, I note that colonial effects did not have to last very long, as the conflicts began during the independence process and transformed into violent civil wars shortly thereafter. For the cases in which a lag separated the civil wars from independence, however, I argue that nationalist divisions and goals as well as disagreements over the communal character of the nation-state—while fluctuating over time in terms of strength—rarely disappeared. As a result, the framing and motivational mechanisms described in the previous sections commonly persisted. In contrast, the mobilization mechanism likely weakened to some extent, as communal organizations generally persisted after independence but military equipment and soldiers commonly disappeared. And while the different mechanisms of colonial pluralism had the potential to persist, so did the framing and motivational effects of precolonial states, and the combination of precolonial statehood and colonial pluralism therefore created a heightened risk of nationalist civil warfare that persisted after independence.

Popular assessments of the causes of nationalist civil war usually focus on proximate causes that spark conflict, and this type of causal assessment suggests that colonialism has only limited effects on postcolonial nationalist civil warfare. Several nationalist conflicts, however, began during the independence process and transformed into a civil war within a few years of independence, suggesting that colonialism could be a proximate cause of postcolonial conflict. Over a quarter of all nationalist civil wars in former British colonies, for example, occurred within a decade of independence. As Wimmer (2013) notes, conflict over the control of the nation-state was great at colonial independence, and the risk of ethnic civil wars was therefore very high during the independence period. Although Wimmer focuses on ethnic civil warfare more generally, the risk of nationalist civil warfare seems particularly high during the independence period because independence requires negotiations over the communal character of the nation-state and the maintenance of colonial pluralism. When both sides of these negotiations dug in, these disagreements became heated and started conflicts leading to nationalist civil warfare.

In contrast to analyses focusing on proximate causes, a common finding of statistical analyses is that previous conflict is a strong predictor of future conflict. One interpretation of this finding is that violence intensifies intercommunal divisions and antipathy in long-lasting ways. In a similar way, I argue that colonial pluralism has long-term effects on the risk of nationalist civil warfare by institutionalizing intercommunal competition, polarization, and antipathy, which perpetuates communal frames and motives and maintain important organizational resources.

My main argument is that empowering and discriminatory colonial pluralism politicizes community and communalizes politics in ways that contribute
to conflict between state and non-state communities over the communal character of the postcolonial nation-state. Undoubtedly, political reforms, population changes, events, and individuals can reduce the extent to which communities are politicized, politics is communalized, and communities disagree
over the character of the nation-state. Yet power, interest, and socialization
mechanisms commonly reproduce communal divisions at the macro level in
a path-dependent fashion (Lange 2020; Mahoney 2000a; Ruane and Todd
2004; Wimmer 2008). It is therefore likely that the communal divisions that
were present at independence persisted after colonialism.

In a similar way, mechanisms of reproduction likely affect communal
politicization and conflict over the communal character of the nation-state.
A communalized political environment empowers communal leaders, and
these leaders have an interest in the maintenance of communal politics. Communalized politics, in turn, affects the views and understandings of people
in ways that shape their political participation and that, thereby, perpetuate
the status quo.

Similarly, ideas of the character and composition of nations and nation-
states commonly spread from generation to generation, thereby perpetuating
conflict over the communal character of the nation-state. Because the position
of communal elites depends on the power and autonomy of communities, they
have an interest in continuing to pursue greater communal autonomy. Parents
and communal organizations, in turn, socialize children and members to have
similar views about the place of their community in the nation-state. In particular, communities that receive power and autonomy during colonialism likely
socialize members to romanticize the colonial past and maintain expectations
for communal power and self-rule. In this way, colonial pluralism can shape
the myth-symbol complexes of communities.

So far, this discussion has focused on elements related to framing and motivational mechanisms, but it is also possible that mobilizational mechanisms
persist to different extents. At one extreme, many of the military resources
provided by colonialism likely disappeared over time, as non-state communities lost their overrepresentation in militaries and former soldiers aged and lost
access to weapons. Organizational resources, however, likely remained and
enabled communities to mobilize nationalist civil warfare. As noted previously,
this is especially the case when communal frames, political competition, and
disagreement over the communal character of the state persist.

In similar ways, the influence of precolonial statehood likely persists over
long periods. For one, communal demography usually changes very slowly,
thereby suggesting the persistence of national chauvinism. Moreover, the
myth-symbol complexes of state communities likely adapt to include colonial

experiences, focusing on the devastating effects of colonialism and the ways non-state communities supported and benefited from colonialism.

Thus, although one cannot assume that colonial and precolonial effects persist after independence, such persistence is not only possible but likely. If colonial pluralism and precolonial states promote nationalist civil warfare through motivational, framing, and mobilizational mechanisms, these effects have the potential to shape patterns of nationalist civil warfare long after independence.

2

The British Pluralist Model in Comparative Perspective

with Tay Jeong and Charlotte Gaudreau

English landscape gardening and French formal gardening highlight two starkly contrasting relationships between humans and nature. The French model was a by-product of the Enlightenment and represents humankind's domination over nature through reason. This overtly modernist style combines an almost obsessive ordering with complex geometric designs while destroying nature and replacing it with domesticated organic artwork. The Versailles gardens is one notable example (see figure 2.1). English landscape gardening turned its back on the Enlightenment in favor of Romanticism, thereby focusing on emotions, nature, the exotic, and mysticism. This model works with and celebrates nature by accentuating key elements of the environment. To do so, it tames parts of the surroundings so humans can stroll around and admire natural monuments. This style therefore purposefully disentangles nature's diverse components, and the result is a garden divided into distinct sections that display nature in humanized settings. The park in figure 2.2 exemplifies this style.

Although very different phenomena, gardening and colonialism have surprising similarities. Both involve humans taking over and transforming territories for their personal benefit. Both colonial officials and landscape architects must also consider their own physical and symbolic positions within the territory while struggling against and deciding what to do with the preexisting inhabitants, whether trees, rabbits, or people. Leading colonial officials recognized these parallels and argued that the dominant colonial models of

FIGURE 2.1. Engraving of the Versailles Gardens. *Source:* Pérelle (1680).

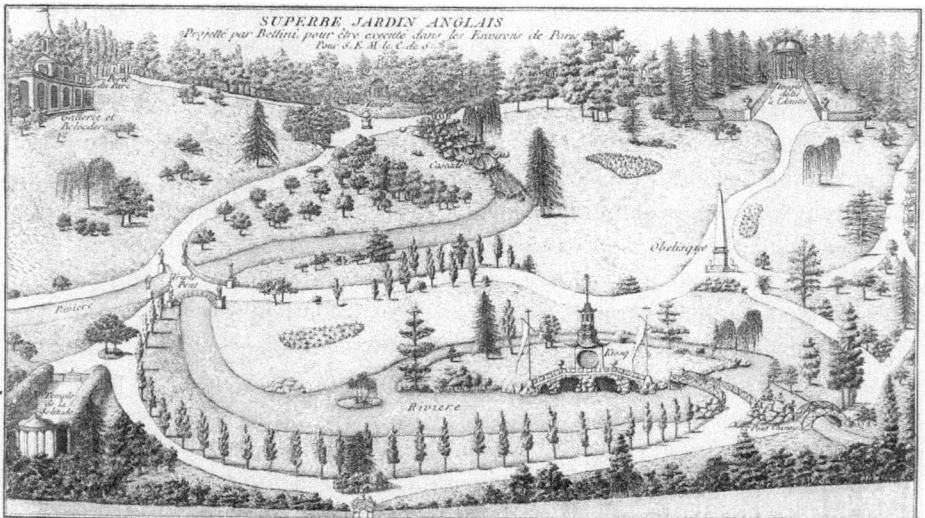

FIGURE 2.2. Engraving of English Landscape Gardening. *Source:* Bettini (1788), gallica.nf.fr/Bibliothèque nationale de France.

Great Britain and France conformed to their national gardening styles (Judicial Advisers' Conference 1957).

Similar to French formal gardening, the dominant French colonial ideology was powerfully modernist and transformative and emphasized *la mission civilisatrice*. Thus, just as French formal gardening destroys nature and replaces it with supposedly superior human designs, the French colonial model sought to uproot indigenous cultures and institutions and replace them with their more "enlightened" French counterparts. Two core elements of this colonial model were a Republican state and a focus on the assimilation of subjects into French civilization. Yet the French colonial model was commonly much more ideological than practical, and actual colonial policies were usually limited in scope and scale. In effect, French colonial gardens proved unruly and difficult to tame, and the colonial gardeners were usually either unwilling or unable to implement grand modernist designs.

In contrast to the French model, the British colonial model began as practice and subsequently developed into a powerful colonial ideology that reinforced and expanded practice. As such, English landscape gardening is a more appropriate analogy of the form of rule in the British Empire. This model was a form of pragmatic pluralism that sought to dominate foreign lands and peoples by recognizing, accommodating, and empowering colonized communities while clearly separating them from the colonizers. For this, colonial actors and institutions celebrated the supposedly natural and exotic and downplayed the need to modernize the colonized. Similar to how English landscape gardening compartmentalized and accentuated select natural features, British rule implemented a variety of policies that strengthened communal boundaries in ways promoting plural societies instead of a single cultivated nation. The British, for example commonly completed censuses to recognize and count communities and used this information to guide and—thereby communalize—other colonial policies. They also used vernacular education and customary law to accommodate communities by allowing them to attend school in their native tongue and access legal systems based on their traditions. Finally, the British empowered communities by reserving legislative seats for them, providing them with their own military units, and giving them their own legal-administrative institutions.

Whereas subsequent chapters analyze the effects of British colonial pluralism (and precolonial statehood), this chapter provides a base for this analysis by presenting a brief history of the British Empire and investigating the form and origins of British colonial pluralism. The chapter also situates the British Empire within the larger set of European empires through a comparative analysis exploring the extent to which British colonialism was uniquely pluralist.

The British Empire: A Historical Overview

Over a relatively short period, England (and, subsequently, Great Britain and the United Kingdom)[1] went from being a small country on Europe's periphery to possessing the largest empire in the world. To accomplish this feat, the British relied on colonial officials as well as explorers, pirates, mercenaries, merchants, entrepreneurs, religious minorities, and missionaries. In this way, the British Empire clearly highlights Abernethy's (2000) claim that European overseas expansion occurred through the combined and (usually) collaborative efforts of political, economic, and religious actors.

Because Britain and Ireland are separated by the Irish Sea, Ireland was Great Britain's first "overseas" possession. Yet given the short distance between the two and—especially—the integration of Ireland into the English polity, most colonial scholars consider Ireland an internal colony and recognize colonies in the Americas as the first official members of the British Overseas Empire. Early attempts to found colonies in Roanoke (North Carolina), Guyana, St. Lucia, and Grenada failed, and the first successful British settlement was in Jamestown, Virginia, in 1607. Thereafter, several additional settlements were founded in what became the 13 American colonies. British colonialism in Canada began with the declaration of a colony in Newfoundland in 1610 and the founding of the Hudson's Bay Company in 1670. At this time, the British also established colonies in the Caribbean, including St. Kitts (1624), Barbados (1627), Nevis (1628), and Jamaica (1655). Because the economies of Britain's colonies in the Caribbean and the Southern United States were plantation-based and depended on slave labor, British traders established posts along the West African coast to buy and sell slaves, including in Gambia, Ghana, and Sierra Leone.

As the British were establishing their first colonies in the Americas, they began to lay the foundations of their Asian imperial branch, although these colonies took longer to materialize. In 1599, the British government formed the East India Company, and shortly thereafter it established several factories and trading posts in present-day India and Bangladesh. Over the next century and a half, Company rule expanded to establish a strong foothold in South Asia. By the mid-eighteenth century, the Company was increasingly meddling in Indian politics, and it won the Battle of Plassey in 1757, thereby taking control of Bengal and establishing the Company as a real colonial power. Over the next century, the power of the East India Company continued to grow. After the Great Indian Revolt of 1857, however, Company rule was replaced by formal

---

1. In this book, I analyze the country over time and therefore look at England, Great Britain, and the UK. When considering the country during multiple periods, I refer to it simply as Great Britain instead of as England/Great Britain, Great Britain/UK, or England/Great Britain/UK.

British colonialism, and British India continued to expand, eventually including contemporary Bangladesh, India, and Pakistan.

At the same time that British rule was developing in the Americas and India, it also spread to other regions of the world. Two notable additions were the settler colonies of Australia and New Zealand, both of which resulted from British naval exploration in the South Pacific. Instead of exploration and conquest, European warfare was the most common cause of British colonial expansion during the late eighteenth and early nineteenth centuries. With the rise of empires, European warfare spread to the colonies, and the British were usually on the winning side during this period, allowing them to take many colonial possessions from their opponents. In addition to a number of tiny colonies, such as Malta, St. Lucia, St. Kitts, and the Seychelles, the British took possession of all of Canada and added Sri Lanka, South Africa, Trinidad and Tobago, Guyana, and Mauritius to their empire. Similar to India, South Africa began with the British controlling colonial outposts along the coast, but their rule gradually expanded inland. Along the same lines, the Dutch had only controlled a thin coastal belt in Sri Lanka prior to British rule, but the British gained control of the entire island in 1817.

Prior to India, South Africa, and Sri Lanka, British possessions were either settler colonies, forced settlement colonies based on plantation agriculture with imported laborers, trade-based colonies that were little more than forts along the coast, or some combination of the three. With these three colonies, however, we see the transformation of colonial outposts into vast colonies ruling over very large indigenous populations, thereby founding the first British colonies of occupation (although the large number of settlers in South Africa made it a mixed colony). A similar process occurred in colonial Malaysia, with the British gaining footholds over coastal regions and subsequently expanding to form the Colony of Malaya in 1867. In 1824, the British organized a military expedition against Myanmar to stop the Konbaung dynasty's expansion into colonial India and thereby established a new colony along the Myanmar coast, and the British gained control over all of Myanmar through subsequent wars in 1852 and 1885. Great Britain colonized Hong Kong in 1841, although unlike Malaysia and Myanmar, it did not succeed at expanding beyond the small coastal enclave.

As the British were finalizing their colonial possessions in Asia, the scramble for Africa began, and the British founded many more colonies of occupation in this region. Former British slaving (and subsequently anti-slaving) posts provided footholds for British colonial expansion in Ghana, Sierra Leone, and the Gambia. In the late nineteenth and early twentieth centuries, British colonialism expanded to include Nigeria in West Africa, took control of several new colonies in southern Africa (Lesotho, Botswana, Eswatini, Zambia, and Zimbabwe), and established Kenya, Sudan, and Uganda as new colonies in eastern Africa.

British influence in the South Pacific and Oceania also expanded around this time. British officials established a colony in Fiji in 1874, added the Solomon Islands in 1893, and took control of British New Guinea in 1888. British rule was short-lived in New Guinea, as they handed control of the territory over to Australia—a newly established dominion—in 1902. In 1878, the British also strengthened their position in the Mediterranean by negotiating a deal with the Ottoman Empire to take control of Cyprus.

Great Britain's final colonies were acquired after the First World War. The British established de facto control of Egypt in 1882 but continued to recognize the region as part of the Ottoman Empire. With the outbreak of the First World War, however, the British disregarded Ottoman authority and made Egypt a formal colony. After the war, the League of Nations awarded the British three other Ottoman territories—Iraq, Jordan, and Palestine—as Mandate Territories. The League also gave German Tanzania and parts of German Togoland and Cameroon to the British.

Although the British Empire became the world's largest overseas empire by continually expanding, there were periods of contraction. The major settler colonies were the first possessions freeing themselves from British overrule. This began with the loss of the 13 American colonies in the late eighteenth century. Almost 100 years later, the British government made Canada a dominion, thereby providing Canada full control over domestic affairs. In 1901, they also made Australia a dominion, followed shortly by New Zealand in 1907 and—after the Boer War—South Africa in 1910. Among colonies of occupation, the last colonial conquests became the first to gain their independences, with Egypt receiving formal independence in 1922, Iraq in 1932, and Jordan in 1946. The next year, India gained its independence, followed a year later by neighboring Myanmar and Sri Lanka. Another wave of independence began a decade later, with Sudan (1956), Ghana (1957), and Malaysia (1957). Due to South African claims over Botswana, Lesotho, and Eswatini, independence was postponed for these three colonies until the late 1960s, and the settlers living in Zimbabwe unilaterally declared their independence in 1965 in their effort to exclude black Zimbabweans from power. By the early 1970s, the only colonies left were small territories that the British were unsure could rule themselves, although most of these eventually left the Empire as well, with the independence of Hong Kong in 1997 being the last major departure. Today, the British Empire is little more than a handful of tiny overseas territories with permanent populations ranging from zero (the British Arctic and Indian Ocean Territories) to 68,000 subjects (Cayman Islands).

As noted previously, religious and economic actors commonly helped colonial officials build the British Empire. This is clearly evident in the British colonies that started off as companies before changing to formal colonies, such as the East India and Hudson's Bay Companies. The influence of missionaries was less evident but more influential in most colonies. Although

Catholic missionaries played an earlier role in Spanish, Portuguese, and French colonialism, Protestant missionaries only became an influential force in the British Empire in the late eighteenth century. Most notably, the Baptist Missionary Society was founded in 1792, the London Missionary Society in 1795, the Church Mission Society in 1799, and the Colonial Missionary Society in 1836. Unlike most other colonial powers, the British usually welcomed missionaries of any denomination and from any country. American Protestant missionaries gained influence in the early nineteenth century, and Catholic missionaries from a variety of countries and orders usually followed them to compete for the souls of British colonial subjects.

With rare exceptions, missionaries were not formal members of the colonial apparatus in the British Empire. That being said, they commonly worked hand in hand with the colonizers due to broadly complementary goals: Many colonial officials supported missionary endeavors because they were Christians and approved of missionary work; other officials viewed Christianity as a means of pacification through the conquest of "souls" instead of bodies, and missionaries commonly offered services that British officials valued. Colonial officials were especially supportive of missionary education, and missionaries were the main providers of education in nearly all British colonies. Colonial governments commonly supported missionary schools financially, influenced their curricula, and provided missionaries with other types of assistance.

Although common, missionary influence varied within the British Empire. The receptiveness of colonized peoples explains much of this variation, as some peoples proved easier to convert than others. In addition, the British formally limited missionary activities when missionary influence was a disruptive impediment to colonial control. This was usually the case in colonies of occupation with large precolonial states and organized world religions, as missionaries commonly caused political and religious backlashes in this context.

British Colonial Models of Political Community

At its most basic, politics involves the rules and institutions central to collective decision-making, and a political community for whom decisions are made is therefore a core element of politics. Because these communities are not natural, polities must delineate and define political community, and the way they do determines the model of political community. Officials of all types of polity must consider models of political community, but the characteristics of these models commonly vary by the type of polity. In overseas colonies, models of political community are similar to what Steinmetz (2003) refers to as "native policy," which involve "state interventions organized around a specific stabilizing representation of the character of the colonized" (45). Such characterizations have two key elements—the internal and external dimensions of models of political community. The external side is vitally important for imperial polities and considers the relationship between the colonizers and the colonized. Should the colonial powers recognize the colonized as distinct from the colonizers, enforce strong communal boundaries, and create different sets of institutions for the colonized and the colonizers? Should the colonizer force the colonized to assimilate into their culture and institutions? Or should the colonizers assimilate into the culture of the colonized? The internal dimension, on the other hand, is central to all types of polity and deals exclusively with the relationships between peoples living within the polity. In colonies, this dimension asks whether political institutions should consider all colonized peoples the same or recognize communal differences, treat communities differently, and rule communities separately.

British colonizers did not use the same model of political community throughout their overseas possessions. Instead, they used different models in different places, and the models used in some colonies transformed over time. One important reason for variation is that there is no perfect model of political community that suits all environments, and views of the appropriateness of different models varied from official to official, from place to place, and over time. Moreover, all models of political community have advantages and disadvantages, and officials reformed models to deal with disadvantages. While recognizing this variation, several factors contributed to clear family resemblances within the British Empire, and most British colonies had pluralist models of political community. As Abernethy (2000) describes, the British recognized the presence of many national communities by acknowledging "differences of religion, language, continental origin, culture, and political tradition among its non-European subjects" (161). The colonial community was therefore conceptualized as inherently diverse. At the same time, Mazrui (1983) notes that this internal dimension was paired with an external dimension that created powerful racialized barriers between the colonizer and the colonized, and colonial pluralism therefore promoted very strong boundaries both among the colonized and between the colonized and the colonizers.

One potential cause of British colonial pluralism was the transfer of the metropolitan model to overseas possessions. Over the past few centuries, the dominant model of political community in the British metropole has become increasingly pluralist, something epitomized by the recognition of four national communities within the aptly named United Kingdom of Great Britain and Northern Ireland. Within this plural national community, however, there was a clear hierarchy, with the English being the core nation and the others having varying degrees of Englishness (Kumar 2003). Given this model, many colonial officials were undoubtedly open to seeing colonized populations as plural and creating a hierarchy among communities. Yet there was never an organized effort to transfer the British model to the colonies.

Instead of dissemination from metropole to colony, events in the "Crown Jewel" of the British Empire played a much more important role popularizing and proliferating pluralist colonial models. During the early period of British rule in India, many officials of the East India Company had considerable respect for Indian culture and assimilated into it by taking Indian concubines, learning local languages, and adopting local dress and cuisine (Ballhatchet 1980; Dalrymple 2002). In this way, the line between colonizer and colonized was sometimes blurred. The East India Company became concerned about their employees going "native" and subsequently forbid practices that weakened boundaries between British and Indian. At the same time, the Company began to privilege British culture and institutions and weakened traditional Indian authorities by removing them and attempting to create a more direct form of rule based on British institutions. These officials were influenced by liberal utilitarianism and believed in the perfectibility of all humans. But believing in the cultural superiority of Great Britain, they attempted to spread the "superior" elements of British "civilization" to India (Mamdani 2012; Mantena 2010; Metcalf 1960, 2016). Early British rule in India was therefore nonpluralist.

The Indian Rebellion of 1857 radically transformed the model of political community in India. Subjects who were supposedly benefiting from British rule turned against their colonizers. As Metcalf (1960, 2016) describes, the rebellion changed the views of leading British officials, who increasingly saw Indians as incapable of becoming "civilized," and these officials blamed the violence on past colonial policies that erroneously sought to impose British institutions and culture on Indians. In the years following the war, the British established a highly pluralist model in India (Belmekki 2008; Dirks 2001; Mamdani 2012; Metcalf 1960, 2016).

As Mamdani (2012) notes, the pluralist reforms in colonial India involved a transition "from civilization to conservation and from progress to order" (8). By this, he notes that ideas of British cultural superiority and the desire to "enlighten" colonial subjects now took a back seat to the need to maintain colonial control, and the retention of "customary" institutions was seen as the most effective means of colonial control. The key figure behind this change was Sir Henry Maine, an extremely influential legal scholar who spent a decade in India codifying Indian law and subsequently educated many colonial officials at Oxford, Cambridge, and the Inns of Court (Mamdani 2012; Mantena 2010). Maine rejected Enlightenment claims of human perfectibility in favor of racial claims of British superiority and therefore demanded that British colonialism maintain strict divisions between the British and the Indians. He saw efforts to "civilize" the Indians as a failure and key cause of the Indian Rebellion and therefore concluded that British colonialism should maintain indigenous institutions as much as possible. Influenced by these views, one of the first post-rebellion reforms was to replace policies that tried to weaken and eliminate

Indian princely states with new policies that sought to promote greater stability by celebrating "tradition" and granting Indian authorities considerable autonomy (Fisher 1991; Metcalf 1960, 2016; Metcalf and Metcalf 2006). In this way, the dominant British model of indirect rule was formalized. Yet this form of rule required an understanding of India's complex social landscape, and the British therefore began constructing an "ethnographic" state that documented India's great social diversity to make its population more legible (Dirks 2001; Mamdani 2012; Mantena 2010: 57). Censuses and other forms of documentation were therefore used to gain "knowledge" of all communities (Cohn 1987). The British also began using community-specific personal law, communal electorates, and recognized indigenous languages.

As an early and important colony, India subsequently influenced the form of rule in other British possessions, thereby helping to make colonial pluralism the dominant model of political community in the Colonial Office (Fisher 1991; Kirk-Greene 1980). Maine himself instructed many colonial officials in training, including key colonial administrators like Cromer, Gordon, Ibbertson, Lyall, MacMichael, Swettenham, and Tupper (Mamdani 2012: 7; Mantena 2010). Lord Lugard—who was born in India and served in the Indian military—was greatly influenced by Maine's ideas and played a particularly important role transplanting colonial pluralism in African soil and turning it into a powerful colonial ideology. And with the ascendancy of the pluralist model, indirect rule, legal pluralism, vernacular language policies, communal legislative representation, and communalizing censuses became common practice in the British Empire.

Variation in British Colonial Pluralism

While pluralism was clearly the dominant form of rule in the British Empire, the extent of colonial pluralism varied from colony to colony. This section explores the causes of variation in colonial pluralism in the British Empire. It begins with a historical assessment and ends with a statistical analysis.

HISTORICAL PATTERNS

One clear pattern in the British Empire is that early colonies were less pluralist than later colonies. Timing helps explain this pattern: Pluralism only became dominant in the British Empire during the second half of the nineteenth century and therefore had little influence in early British colonies. Just as the model of political community changed in India, however, colonial officials in early colonies could have modified the form of colonialism to make it more pluralist, but there was usually little effort to do this. While institutional stasis helps explain limited pluralist reforms in early colonies, the main reason for staying the course is that most early colonies were settler or forced settlement colonies, not colonies of occupation, and settler and forced settlement colonies had demographic conditions and power configurations that opposed colonial pluralism. Pluralist policies are usually used to recognize diversity among indigenous communities, but colonialism decimated indigenous populations in settler and forced settlement colonies, thereby creating a mismatch between populations and the pluralist model. On top of this, white settlers and plantation owners were the dominant colonial actors in these colonies, and both believed British culture was superior and felt no need to recognize, accommodate, and empower either indigenous peoples or imported laborers.

In addition to the type of colony, Protestant missionaries also affected the extent of colonial pluralism in British colonies. Most notably, vernacular missionary education accommodated communal language practices and therefore promoted pluralism (Woodberry 2012). Many missionaries, in turn, encouraged colonial officials to recognize and protect the communities with whom they worked, something that commonly reinforced or even expanded other pluralist policies. In colonial Myanmar, for instance, Protestant missionaries lobbied the colonial government to provide Karens with special legislative representation. Moreover, missionaries often mobilized to protect "their" communities when colonial officials sought to reverse or weaken policies recognizing, empowering, or accommodating the communities working with the missionaries. For example, missionaries successfully fought reforms proposed by Resident Commissioner Rey to reduce the power and autonomy of Tswana chiefs in colonial Botswana. Rey never forgave missionaries for this, referring to them as his "mortal foes," "intriguer[s]," and "useless, lying idle, hypocritical, canting swine" (Rey 1988: 19, 132, 174) and wishing he could "blow the whole damned lot to the heaven they're always bleating about" (51).

Historical statehood also affected colonial pluralism. Instead of promoting more pluralist policies in general, historical statehood increased the use of certain types of pluralist policies: discriminatory policies that empowered non-state communities at the expense of state communities. State communities usually mobilized the strongest resistance to colonialism, whereas non-state communities were much less threatening. Some British colonial officials therefore devised discriminatory pluralist policies that strengthened non-state communities at the expense of state communities as a means of divide and rule. In Myanmar, for example, the British provided minority communities with special communal representation in the Burmese colonial legislature, stacked the military with "loyal" communities to counter the influence of Bamar nationalists, and only provided non-state communities with political autonomy through indirect rule. To justify such unequal treatment, the British drew on liberal philosophy and claimed minorities required special recognition, accommodation, and empowerment to protect them from larger communities.

STATISTICAL PATTERNS

For more systematic evidence into variation in the extent of British colonial pluralism, this section completes an OLS analysis of the correlates of colonial pluralism. To complete the analysis, it creates an index measuring the extent of colonial pluralism and regresses this indicator on different factors that might have shaped it. The set of cases includes all formal overseas possessions that were ruled by the British and had more than 400,000 inhabitants at independence.[2] When a colony was simultaneously controlled by multiple powers, the foreign power that ruled over the largest population at colonial independence is recognized as the colonizer. When a colony was ruled by multiple colonizers in succession, the last power that formally colonized the region for at least 10 years is considered the colonizer. Finally, internal colonies, informal overseas colonies, and overseas territories in which the colonizers only controlled foreign policy are all excluded from the set. Based on these criteria, the set includes 36 British overseas colonies.

For the analysis, the dependent variable measures the extent of colonial pluralism. This "pluralist index" is based on four variables measuring different aspects of colonial pluralism. Three indicators focus on the internal side of colonial pluralism that differentiate between colonized communities: One focuses on a policy recognizing communities, one on a policy accommodating communities, and one on a policy empowering communities. The final indicator focuses on the external side of political community and measures a policy formally separating the colonizer and the colonized. All four variables are equally weighted to create an index ranging from 0 (low colonial pluralism) to 1 (high colonial pluralism).[3] Table 2.1 presents the scores of the pluralist index and its components for the set of British colonies.

The first indicator measures the extent to which colonial censuses recognized the presence of diverse types of communities, as such recognition is a core element of the pluralist model. This variable is based on data from Lieberman and Singh (2017) measuring whether censuses gathered information on caste, linguistic, racial, religious, and tribal categories and calculates the largest number of types of categories ever collected in a colonial census. The scores range from 0 (no types of communal categories collected) to 5 (caste, ethnic, racial, religious, and tribal categories all collected). Colonies that never had a census are scored as 0, as the colonizers in these cases never used censuses to document communal difference.

The second indicator measures communal representation in colony-level legislatures, something that empowers communities by providing them with

---

2. See Lange et al. (2022) for more information on rules for delineating the set.
3. See Lange et al. (2021) for more information on the scoring of the variable.

TABLE 2.1. Pluralist Index of British Colonies

Country	Census Categories	Legislative Representation	Vernacular Education	No Legislative Representation in Metropole	Pluralist Index
Australia	2	0	0	1	0.35
Bangladesh	5	1	1	1	1.00
Botswana	3	0	0	1	0.40
Canada	2	0	0	1	0.35
Cyprus	3	1	1	1	0.90
Egypt	3	0	0	1	0.40
Eswatini	3	0	0	1	0.40
Fiji	3	1	1	1	0.90
Gambia	3	0	0	1	0.40
Ghana	3	1	0	1	0.65
Guyana	3	0	0	1	0.40
India	5	1	1	1	1.00
Iraq	2	1	1	1	0.85
Israel/Palestine	1	1	1	1	0.80
Jamaica	2	0	0	1	0.35
Jordan	0	1	0	1	0.50
Kenya	2	0	0	1	0.35
Lesotho	3	0	1	1	0.65
Malawi	3	0	1	1	0.65
Malaysia	5	0	1	1	0.75
Mauritius	3	0	0	1	0.40
Myanmar	5	1	1	1	1.00
New Zealand	2	0	0	1	0.35
Nigeria	4	1	1	1	0.95
Pakistan	5	1	1	1	1.00
Sierra Leone	3	1	1	1	0.90
Singapore	4	0	1	1	0.70
South Africa	3	0	1	1	0.65
Sri Lanka	5	1	1	1	1.00
Sudan	2	1	0	1	0.60
Tanzania	4	0	0	1	0.45
Trinidad & Tobago	2	0	0	1	0.35
Uganda	3	1	1	1	0.90
United States	0	0	0	1	0.25
Zambia	2	0	1	1	0.60
Zimbabwe	2	0	1	1	0.60
AVERAGE	2.92	0.42	0.53	1	0.63

political representation. This indicator is based on whether colony-level legislative institutions ever reserved seats for one or more indigenous colonized communities. The variable is dichotomous, with 1 measuring the presence of communal legislative representation and 0 denoting its absence. Cases that only gave special representation to non-indigenous peoples—such as white settlers—are scored as 0.

The third variable measures linguistic accommodation in colonial schools. It measures whether primary education was taught in multiple vernaculars at independence, which was a clear pluralist policy accommodating communal interests. Cases with multiple educational vernaculars are scored as 1, and all others are scored as 0. The variable score is based on the languages used in colonial primary schools at or just prior to independence.

The final variable operationalizes the external side of colonial pluralism by measuring whether a colony's population ever received representation in the metropole's parliament, a policy that removes barriers between colonized and colonizer. Because pluralism separates the colonized from the colonizer, the variable is inverted, with 1 measuring colonies that never received legislative representation in the metropole and 0 measuring colonies that did.

To explore the correlates of colonial pluralism, the analysis includes a variety of control variables measuring precolonial and colonial conditions that might have shaped the extent of colonial pluralism. Six variables measure historical and structural conditions that potentially shaped the form of colonialism: latitude, territorial size, mountainous terrain, precolonial statehood, population size, and proportion of arable land. As noted by Alesina et al. (2003), a country's latitude measures ecological conditions that have shaped long-term trajectories of development and communal diversity, both of which might have influenced the form of colonialism. And because the size of territories also provides a proxy for precolonial communal diversity, the analysis controls for the natural log of a colony's total land size. The third historical control measures the natural log of the extent of a country's territory that is mountainous. Mountains facilitate resistance to colonialism and affect precolonial communal diversity, and both potentially shape the colonial model of political community. The fourth historical control measures the presence of a large and long-standing precolonial state, as the presence of states might shape colonial models of political community. The variable is based on data from Borcan et al. (2018) measuring the extent to which there was a long-standing and autonomous precolonial state that controlled the same territory as a contemporary state. The score ranges from 0 to 50 and measures 50-year periods, and the variable averages the scores for all periods between 1001 and 1700 AD. The next independent variable measures the log of the total population in 1900, as colonial powers might have considered the size of the population when implementing polices related to the model of political community. For colonies that received their independence prior to 1900, the population is measured at independence. Finally, because the presence of fertile land might affect the form of colonialism, the analysis includes a measure of the proportion of arable land in 1961 from the World Bank database.

In addition to precolonial conditions, the analysis includes variables measuring conditions shaped by the interaction between precolonial and colonial conditions. Because the timing of colonialism might have influenced the extent of colonial pluralism, the models include a variable measuring the time of onset of British colonialism. This variable measures the year in which British colonialism began, so higher values suggest later onset.

The second colonial variable measures the type of colony, something that potentially shaped the extent of colonial pluralism. This variable measures the percentage of the colonial population that was either European or the descendants of African slaves and Indian laborers. Lower scores therefore measure colonies of occupation, whereas higher scores measure settler and forced settlement colonies.

Finally, the analysis includes a variable measuring Protestant missionaries per capita in 1923 as an indicator of Protestant missionary influence (Woodberry 2012). All settler colonies lack data for this variable, so the models with this variable exclude these cases.

Table 2.2 presents of the OLS analysis using these variables. With the exception of logged variables, all variables are standardized, meaning that the variable coefficients estimate the change in the dependent variable associated with an increase in the independent variable by one standard deviation. The first model includes the controls of historical and structural factors as well as the time of colonial onset, Model 2 adds the variable measuring settler and forced settlement populations, and Model 3 adds the measure of Protestant missionaries per capita to Model 1.

The results of Model 1 show that the extent of historical statehood and the percentage of arable land are both positively and significantly related to colonial pluralism. Although the coefficient of the variable measuring colonial onset suggests that late colonies were more pluralist on average, the variable is not significantly related to the extent of colonial pluralism. Subsequent analysis suggests that state history captures much of the effect of time of colonial onset, as colonial onset was almost always late in places with historical states. With the addition of the variable measuring settler and forced settler populations in Model 2, the variable measuring settler and forced settler populations is negatively and significantly related to the extent of colonial pluralism, but no other variable has significant relationships. One interpretation of this finding is that state history and arable land influenced the type of colony, which, in turn, shaped the extent of colonial pluralism. Places with old states and arable lands, for example, commonly had dense, large, and organized populations with immunity to many diseases, thereby promoting colonies of occupation instead of settler or forced settlement colonies. Model 3 adds the variable measuring Protestant missionary

TABLE 2.2. OLS Analysis of Colonial Pluralism in British Empire

	(1)	(2)	(3)
Extent of Historical Statehood	0.480**	0.175	0.546**
	(0.173)	(0.214)	(0.185)
Latitude	−0.256	−0.078	−0.317+
	(0.156)	(0.168)	(0.185)
Log Proportion Mountainous	0.116	0.017	0.196
	(0.156)	(0.153)	(0.165)
Log Population 1900	−0.063	0.149	0.199
	(0.270)	(0.272)	(0.330)
Log Land Area	−0.006	−0.102	−0.116
	(0.215)	(0.206)	(0.263)
Percent Arable Land	0.324+	0.140	0.381+
	(0.188)	(0.195)	(0.198)
Lateness of Colonial Onset	0.166	−0.162	0.247
	(0.155)	(0.209)	(0.245)
Log Settler & Forced Settler Population		−0.593*	
		(0.271)	
Protestant Onset			0.442+
			(0.223)
Constant	−0.000	−0.000	−0.019
	(0.131)	(0.123)	(0.163)
Observations	36	36	32
R^2	0.504	0.579	0.491
Adjusted R^2	0.380	0.454	0.315

Note: +$p < 0.1$; * $p < 0.05$; ** $p < 0.01$; *** $p < 0.001$

influence to Model 1, and the variable is positively and significantly related to colonial pluralism, suggesting that Protestant missionaries promoted pluralist policies. All in all, these findings offer evidence that the type of colonialism— which was influenced by precolonial statehood and arable land—was the most important factor shaping the extent of colonial pluralism in the British Empire and that early Protestant missionary influence also promoted it.

British Pluralism in Comparative Perspective: The Case of the French Empire

For insight into the uniqueness of British colonial pluralism, this section compares the British Empire with the French, Spanish, and Portuguese Empires. These empires were the largest: 93 percent of all former European overseas colonies with more than 400,000 people at independence were in the British, French, Spanish, and Portuguese Empires. Of the French, Spanish, and Portuguese, the French Empire is most appropriate for comparison with the British Empire, and I therefore focus on it and provide much briefer analyses of the Spanish and Portuguese Empires. One reason for my focus on French colonialism is that the British and French had more colonies than any other empire, and systematic comparison depends on the number of cases. In addition, the analysis in the previous section finds that colonial pluralism was concentrated in colonies of occupation, and most French colonies were colonies of occupation. In contrast, the presence of only four Portuguese colonies limits systematic comparison, and colonial pluralism was less likely in the Spanish Empire because nearly all Spanish colonies were mixed settler colonies.

FRENCH COLONIAL MODELS: A REPUBLICAN BIAS

The dominant colonial model in the French Empire was Republican. In contrast to the dominant British model, the French Republican model was present in France, and colonial officials subsequently exported it to the colonies. This transfer was both intermittent—due to the fall of French Republics—and halfhearted—due to limited resources, on-the-ground complexities, and opposition from colonial officials. As a result, French colonial Republicanism was more ideological than practical, and it had only limited influence on colonial policies. That being said, weak French Republicanism limited the extent of colonial pluralism.

In France, the leaders of the French Revolution were greatly inspired by the Enlightenment and sought to create an advanced system of government by creating a rational and scientific system of law and administration and a legal and territorial conceptualization of citizenship. Regardless of language, culture, and religion, legal residents of France were considered French and allowed to participate in government. The French Revolution also inspired a powerful Republican ideology and took a central place in the French national myth-symbol complex, both of which allowed the Revolution to have long-term effects on the French model of political community.

At the same time that it was being implemented in France, postrevolutionary officials exported the French Republican model to the first generation of French colonies (Betts 1961; Cooper 2014; Crowder 1964, 1968; Kumar 2017; Lawrence 2013; Owolabi 2023; Wilder 2005). French colonial Republicanism pursued assimilation, institutional isomorphism, and integration into the metropole and turned colonial subjects into French citizens. These imperial policies were influenced by Republican ideology, but political considerations also promoted their transfer to the colonies, as the extension of citizenship to the colonies and colonial representation in the French National Assembly strengthened the hands of Republicans against their Royalist opponents. After Napoleon cemented his control of the postrevolutionary state, he severely weakened Republicanism in the overseas empire. In subsequent years, the model strengthened during the Second French Republic, weakened with the Second French Empire, and reemerged once again with the founding of the Third French Republic.

During the Third French Republic, the French Republican model spread to the next generation of French colonies in Africa, Asia, and the Pacific. At this time, a new motive strengthened the model: Officials concerned about France's geopolitical strength after the Franco-Prussian War viewed the integration of the empire into the metropole as a means of making France a nation 100 million people strong (Lewis 1962). This motive also influenced a brief effort to integrate the empire into the metropole after the Second World War (Julien 1950). Although most colonies subsequently gained their independence, many early colonies—such as Reunion, Martinique, and Guadeloupe—remain integral parts of France (Lawrence 2013).

Even if Republicans were in power from 1870 until the end of the French Empire and supported colonial Republicanism, the Republican model was much more watered down in the second generation of French colonies relative to the first, with some officials trying to create a greater partnership between colonial and indigenous actors through associationalism while others employed policies recognized communal differences among the colonized, such as Gallieni's and Lyautey's famous *"politique des races"* (Betts 1961; Conklin 1997; Wyrtzen 2015). In this way, colonial Republicanism might have been the official colonial ideology, but it had only limited effect on actual colonial practice in the second generation of French colonies. A number of factors limited the strength of French colonial Republicanism, including the perceived failure of assimilationist policies in early colonies and fear that the colonized would take over the metropole. In addition, the implementation of Republican policies that favored French culture and institutions were costly and could be very disruptive, causing some leading French colonial officials to question their value and explore alternatives. Finally, official colonial Republicanism—which was based on ideas of cultural superiority—competed with unofficial French racism, and some colonial officials opposed Republican policies because they did not believe the colonized could or should become French. As a result of these factors, French colonial policies in Asia and Africa commonly did little more than pay lip service to Republicanism (Fatih 2013).

Although usually very watered down, French colonial Republicanism still affected the form of colonial rule in various ways. For example, the French paid much more attention to integrating the colonies into the metropole than the British. Of greater concern to this book, it also focused more attention on national unity than communal diversity, and French colonialism was therefore less pluralist than British rule on average. Indeed, French officials commonly believed in their *mission civilisatrice*, had little interest in communal divisions, gave little respect for communal authorities, and rarely provided communal autonomy (Betts 1961; Conklin 1997; Crowder 1968; Kumar 2017; Lewis 1962; Mazrui 1983). This relatively nonpluralist character is apparent when considering five policies: indirect rule, communal legislative representation, vernacular education, communal census categories, and representation in metropolitan legislatures.

Indirect Rule

Indirect rule commonly recognizes communal difference by providing communities with some degree of self-rule (Kasfir 1972; Lange 2009b). It is therefore a core pluralist policy, and the classic literature on comparative colonialism claims that the British employed indirect rule whereas the French ruled directly. Over the past several decades, these claims have been increasingly questioned and even disregarded. Some provide evidence that the British used both direct and indirect rule and combined them in different ways and to different extents, thereby creating considerable variation in the extent of indirect rule (Lange 2009b). And within the French Empire, the minuscule number of French officials meant that colonial rule depended greatly on indigenous actors to control vast territories and populations, and this contributed to indirect forms of rule (Mamdani 1996).

Despite these important corrections, there were common differences between British and French indirect rule, and the British form was, on average, much more pluralist than the French. The British form commonly focused on ruling through communities in a way that celebrated tradition and promoted high levels of communal autonomy (Collier 1982: 83–87; Firmin-Sellers 2000; Iliffe 1995; Lange 2009b; Miles 1994; Müller-Crepon 2020). The British usually used indirect rule to incorporate indigenous institutions into the system of colonial control, with colonial officials collaborating with the authorities of these institutions to control the colonies (Lange 2009b). In working with and institutionalizing indigenous political institutions, British indirect rule generally placed greater emphasis on "customary" authority and gave indigenous authorities control over their land and laws. As a result, British rule created a bifurcated form of rule that depended on indigenous customary authorities for local control and a bureaucratic "European" administration that ruled cities and managed the customary authorities. This form of rule commonly provided communities with considerable autonomy, thereby institutionalizing communal self-rule. In some instances, however, British indirect rule was not communalized. Most princely states in colonial India, for example, ruled over diverse communities and did not rule in the name of any one community.

In French colonies, on the other hand, indirect rule was used as a technique to gradually integrate peoples into the colonial state and—with rare exceptions—did not promote communal self-rule. The use of indigenous intermediaries in the French Empire rarely conformed to British indirect rule because it neither recognized indigenous institutions, maintained customary authorities, nor endowed intermediary authorities with control over customary law and land. Instead, the use of indigenous intermediaries at the local level served as a low-cost means of extending the reach of the colonial state while limiting resistance to colonial interference. The French *commandants de circle* were almost always French nationals, dominated colonial rule outside of the colonial capital, and directed local indigenous agents whose authority rested on their positions within the colonial state, not customary authority. A very important aspect of this is that the commandants de circle were in charge of implementing the *indigénat*, or the native legal code, whereas chiefs and other customary authorities controlled "customary" courts in British colonies. In addition, the French usually chose indigenous intermediaries based on their assimilation into French culture, their willingness to follow colonial orders, and their service within the colonial military, not customary authority. In fact, Albaugh (2014) notes that the French variety of indirect rule sought "to erase feudal aristocracies, undermine hereditary chiefs, and promote instead francophile elites" (31). Similarly, Kirk-Greene (1995) compares British and French colonial West Africa and concludes that the French consistently and successfully destabilized traditional rulers to such an extent that they were fewer and weaker by independence (28). Highlighting this general difference, Müller-Crepon (2020) finds that precolonial polities in British Africa were two and a half times more likely to survive colonialism than in French Africa.

The French used another variety of indirect rule outside sub-Saharan Africa, although this too was very different from the normal British model of indirect rule and did not conform to pluralist models. In an effort to avoid the stiff anticolonial resistance that they faced in Algeria, French officials in Cambodia and Tunisia developed a form of indirect rule that retained the paramount precolonial authority—the Cambodian King and the Bey of Tunis—in order to transfer legitimacy from the precolonial states to the colonial states, thereby making Cambodia and Tunisia "protectorates" instead of "colonies" (Aldrich 2021; Meyer et al. 1991: 628). Due to the apparent success of this policy, officials created similar systems of rule in Vietnam and Morocco. Yet these indigenous authorities were figureheads at the colony level with little actual power, and they simply facilitated the construction of relatively centralized colonial states that did not provide communities with self-rule.

As these descriptions show, the extent to which indirect rule promoted pluralism varied by the identity of the colonizer. British indirect rule commonly recognized and empowered communities in ways that institutionalized communal self-rule. In contrast, the French variety was rarely pluralist because it usually did not recognize communities or rule through designated "customary" authorities, instead using indirect rule as a pragmatic and noncommunalized means of either stretching the reach of the colonial state or limiting opposition to it.

Communal Legislative Representation

Communal legislative representation is another pluralist policy that affected the power of communities. As Wight (1950) notes, the British used communal legislative representation in many colonies (85–90). In so doing, they institutionalized the principle that communities require representation to protect their interests, thereby emphasizing communal difference instead of national integration. Alternatively, historians overlook any effort by the French to recognize communities through special legislative representation because the French rarely used it.

In 14 British colonies, at least one indigenous community received special representation on colony-level legislative assemblies. The British never used communal legislative representation in settler and forced settlement colonies without large indigenous populations, so communal legislative representation was therefore completely concentrated in British colonies of occupation. In total, 52 percent of British colonies of occupation had communal legislative representation giving special representation to at least one indigenous community at some time. Overwhelmingly, these cases include colonies with large state communities and smaller non-state communities, and the British justified communal legislative representation as a means of allowing smaller communities to receive representation. Alternatively, most colonies of occupation without communal representation were in sub-Saharan Africa and had communal demographies characterized by many small communities.

The French, on the other hand, usually restricted political participation to French citizens and paid more attention to representing colonial peoples in Paris than providing colonized communities with special representation in colony-level legislatures. In fact, no *conseil coloniaux* or *conseil généraux*—the colony-level legislatures in formal French colonies—ever reserved seats for an indigenous community. In the French protectorates and Mandate Territories of Lebanon, Syria, Tunisia, and Morocco, however, at least one indigenous community received special representation. In Tunisia and Morocco, this representation was for Jewish communities and was both informal and a brief one-time measure in preparation for independence. All in all, no formal French colony had communal legislative representation, only 17 percent of all French colonial possessions (including protectorates and Mandate territories) had communal legislative representation for indigenous communities, and this figure decreases to 9 percent if focusing on formal communal legislative representation. Communal legislative representation was therefore much more common in British colonies.

Language and Colonial Education

In addition to empowering communities by providing them with self-rule or political representation, pluralist policies sometimes accommodate communities by providing public goods catered to their cultural needs. The language of education offers one important example, as the pluralist model favors vernacular education. A comparison of British and French colonies offers clear evidence that the British colonial model of political community was much more pluralist (Albaugh 2014; Cogneau and Moradi 2014; Gifford and Weiskel 1971).

Although hardly universal, the British commonly encouraged the use of major indigenous languages. A British colonial report on education policies in Africa, for example, proclaimed that "every people have an inherent right to their Native tongue" and declared that lower elementary education must be taught in vernaculars (Jones 1925: 26). While British officials made grandiose statements about the need for vernacular education, their French counterparts made equally powerful claims about French being the exclusive language of colonial education (Albaugh 2014; Michelman 1995). As the governor-general of French West Africa proclaimed in 1912, "The goal of elementary teaching is the diffusion among the indigenous people of spoken French. The French language is the only one to be used in schools. It is forbidden for teachers to use local speech with their students" (Albaugh 2014: 34).

Evidence from former British and French colonies highlights these differences. Among all former British colonies, 53 percent had primary education that was taught in multiple indigenous languages at independence. And when excluding British settler and forced settlement colonies, this percentage increases to 67 percent. Alternatively, only two former French colonies—Morocco and Vietnam—had colonial primary education in multiple indigenous languages at independence, representing 8 percent of French colonies of occupation.

This data on the language of education is based on schools run by the colonial state and therefore overlooks missionary education, which was commonly the most important source of education in colonies. Data on the language of education in missionary schools are not available, but missionary influence provides a crude proxy of missionary education. Moreover, the denomination of missionaries offers insight into vernacular missionary education because Protestants favored vernacular education whereas Catholics were more supportive of education in the language of the colonizer (Cogneau and Moradi 2014; Woodberry 2012). And when Catholic missionaries taught in vernaculars, they usually did so because they were competing with Protestant missionaries (Gallego and Woodberry 2010).

Table 2.3 provides data from Woodberry (2012) on the average number of Protestant and Catholic missionaries per 10,000 inhabitants in the British and French Empires in 1923. Like the statistical analysis in the previous section, the analysis includes all formal overseas colonies that had more than 400,000 people at independence. Within the British Empire, however, data

TABLE 2.3. Missionary Influence in the British and French Empires

	Protestant Missionaries per 10,000	Catholic Missionaries per 10,000
Great Britain	1.05	0.45
France	0.29	0.46

on missionaries is not available for the settler colonies (Australia, Canada, New Zealand, and the United States). Based on these figures, there were 3.6 times as many Protestant missionaries in British colonies relative to French colonies. At the same time, the average per capita presence of Catholic missionaries was nearly identical for the British and French Empires. In recognition of qualitative findings on missionary vernacular education, these statistics suggest that missionaries were providing much more vernacular education in the British Empire relative to the French both because the Protestants provided vernacular education and because the Catholics copied Protestant educational techniques when competing with them.

Colonial Censuses

Of all ways to recognize communities, the most widespread is to do so through censuses. There is variation in the extent to which this is done, however, with some censuses ignoring communal difference completely whereas others gather data on a great variety of communal categories. Colonial censuses therefore offer insight into the extent to which colonial powers recognized communal diversity and, thereby, whether they employed pluralist models.

Lieberman and Singh (2017) provide data on the presence of colonial censuses and whether they collected data on language, caste, race, religion, and tribe. Based on this data, the average score of the highest number of types of communal categories ever collected on a colonial census is 2.9 among British colonies, and the average increases to 3.2 when excluding British settler and forced settlement colonies. In contrast, the average number of communal census categories in French colonies was only 1.25. Thus, a simple comparison suggests that the British used colonial censuses to document two and a half times as many types of communal categories in their colonies of occupation relative to the French.

Metropolitan Legislative Representation

One rallying cry behind the American Revolutionary War was no taxation without representation, but the British refused to give the American colonies seats at Westminster. In subsequent years, no overseas colony ever had formal political representation in the British Parliament. For the British, colonial subjects—even those of British descent—were separated from the metropole and could not be a part of it.

TABLE 2.4. Pluralist Index of French Colonies

Country	Census Categories	Legislative Representation	Vernacular Education	No Legislative Representation in Metropole	Pluralist Index
Algeria	3	0	0	0	0.15
Benin	0	0	0	0	0.00
Burkina Faso	0	0	0	0	0.00
Cambodia	1	0	0	1	0.30
Cameroon	2	0	0	0	0.10
Central African Republic	3	0	0	0	0.15
Chad	0	0	0	0	0.00
Congo, Republic	1	0	0	0	0.05
Cote d'Ivoire	1	0	0	0	0.05
Gabon	0	0	0	0	0.00
Guinea	2	0	0	0	0.10
Haiti	0	0	0	0	0.00
Laos	0	0	0	1	0.25
Lebanon	2	1	0	1	0.60
Madagascar	2	0	0	0	0.10
Mali	2	0	0	0	0.10
Mauritania	0	0	0	0	0.00
Morocco	4	1	1	1	0.95
Niger	0	0	0	0	0.00
Senegal	3	0	0	0	0.15
Syria	2	1	0	1	0.60
Togo	2	0	0	0	0.10
Tunisia	0	1	0	1	0.50
Vietnam	0	0	0	1	0.25
AVERAGE	1.25	0.17	0.04	0.29	0.19

Although varying over time and by region, things were very different in the French Empire. All French colonies were given political representation in the French National Assembly shortly after the French Revolution, although Napoleon abruptly ended this practice. With the founding of the Second French Republic in 1848, colonial representation in the French National Assembly returned, with Algeria, French India, French Guyana, Guadeloupe, Martinique, Reunion, and Senegal all receiving representation in Paris. Although colonial legislative representation continued after the end of the Second Republic, the French government now appointed colonial representatives, and the French did not provide new colonies with any representation in Paris. During the Third Republic, representatives were once again elected, but new colonies did not receive representation due to beliefs that the newly colonized were not sufficiently assimilated and fears that the rapidly growing colonial population would have undue influence in the National Assembly. In 1946, however, nearly all French colonies—with the exceptions of Cambodia, Laos, Morocco, Tunisia, and Vietnam[4]—were given representation in Paris (Weber 2010: 25). At this time, the colonies received 63 colonial representatives, making up 15 percent of seats in the French National Assembly.

STATISTICAL ANALYSIS OF BRITISH AND FRENCH COLONIALISM

Having considered inter-imperial differences more qualitatively, this section uses quantitative methods to explore variation in the extent of colonial pluralism between empires. Table 2.4 presents the pluralist index scores of former French colonies, and a comparison of tables 2.1 and 2.4 shows that former British colonies were, on average, considerably more pluralist than former French colonies: Whereas the average pluralist index among former British colonies was 0.63, the average of former French colonies was only 0.19. The difference is even greater if excluding the British settler and forced settlement colonies, with the British average increasing to 0.71.

Despite these large differences, it remains possible that factors other than the identity of the colonizer promoted general differences between British and French models. For insight into this possibility, table 2.5 presents the findings of an OLS analysis exploring the relationship between the identity of the colonizer and the pluralist index while controlling for other factors. The main focal independent variable is a dichotomous measure of whether a territory was a British colony, and the models include the independent variables from Table 2.2 as controls. The findings show that the identity of the colonizer is very strongly and significantly related to the extent of colonial pluralism in all models, and the coefficients suggest that a history of British colonialism increases the pluralist index by over one standard deviation. The coefficients of the remaining variables are similar to those in table 2.2, although late colonial onset is now significantly related to the extent of colonial pluralism in Models 1 and 3 due to French pluralism being most common in regions with very late colonial onset. As in table 2.2, all other control variables lose significance when the variable measuring settler and forced settler population is added,

---

4. Although French citizens in Morocco, Tunisia, and South Vietnam had representatives.

TABLE 2.5. OLS Analysis of Colonial Pluralism in British and French Empires

	(1)	(2)	(3)
British Colony	1.233***	1.149***	1.048***
	(0.196)	(0.197)	(0.218)
Extent of Historical Statehood	0.321**	0.203	0.333**
	(0.118)	(0.132)	(0.124)
Latitude	−0.089	0.028	−0.111
	(0.107)	(0.122)	(0.126)
Log Proportion	0.124	0.098	0.135
Mountainous	(0.106)	(0.105)	(0.108)
Log Population 1900	0.063	0.144	0.196
	(0.168)	(0.170)	(0.186)
Log Land Area	−0.115	−0.184	−0.106
	(0.135)	(0.137)	(0.150)
Percent Arable Land	0.257*	0.153	0.295*
	(0.124)	(0.134)	(0.129)
Lateness of Colonial Onset	0.230*	0.020	0.246+
	(0.106)	(0.154)	(0.139)
Log Settler & Forced		−0.316+	
Settler Population		(0.170)	
Protestant Onset			0.283*
			(0.137)
Constant	−0.740***	−0.689***	−0.619***
	(0.148)	(0.147)	(0.156)
Observations	60	60	56
R^2	0.586	0.612	0.617
Adjusted R^2	0.521	0.543	0.542

Note: + $p<0.1$; * $p<0.05$; ** $p<0.01$; *** $p<0.001$

suggesting that factors like state history and the time of colonial onset shape the extent of colonial pluralism through the type of colony.

THE FORM OF COLONIALISM IN THE SPANISH AND PORTUGUESE EMPIRES

The evidence therefore suggests that British colonialism was usually much more pluralist than French colonialism and that the identity of the colonizer promoted this difference. Former French colonies, however, make up only 46 percent of all non-British overseas colonies, so it is uncertain whether nonpluralism was the norm outside the British Empire. After the British and the French, the Spanish and the Portuguese were the third and fourth largest European overseas empires, respectively. And together, the French, Spanish, and Portuguese Empires had 86 percent of non-British European overseas colonies.

Spanish colonialism was unique among the European overseas empires in that nearly all colonies were mixed settler colonies with either sizable indigenous populations or African slaves. As in the British settler, mixed settler, and forced settlement colonies, colonial pluralism was very rare, if not completely absent, in the Spanish Empire. This was because the Spanish settlers and their descendants dominated colonial institutions and viewed their cultures as superior to those of the indigenous and slave populations. As a result, they did not recognize communal diversity among the non-European population or try to accommodate their cultures. Importantly, because many more European men migrated to Spanish America than European women, the men found non-European partners, and a large segment of the colonial population was mestizo. Given the dominance of Europeans and assimilationist pressure, people therefore focused on the extent to which they were white instead of on communal differences among the non-white population, thereby promoting assimilation and the "whitening" of the population. In Mexico, for example, 54 percent of the Mexican population was categorized as Indigenous in 1825, but this figure decreased to only 8 percent in 1970 (Wimmer 2002: 144).

Portugal's mixed settler colony—Brazil—and its forced settlement colonies—Cape Verde and São Tomé and Principe—were similar to the Spanish Empire in that European settlers dominated all colonial institutions and opposed pluralism. Even more than French colonial Republicanism, colonial ideology and policies focused on assimilation and national integration (Owolabi 2023). Similar to Spanish America, pressure to whiten the population was present in Portuguese colonies, with larger segments of the population self-identifying as "white" over time even though population growth was lower among the European population (Marx 1998: 163).

In addition to these colonies, the Portuguese also had three large colonies of occupation: Angola, Guinea Bissau, and Mozambique. These cases parallel French colonies of occupation in that colonial Republicanism was present but weak (Keese 2007). Most importantly, the Portuguese paid considerable attention to assimilation and integration into the metropole, even if racism, resources, and complications limited both (Keese 2007; Mazrui 1983: 40; Owolabi 2023). Those assimilating into Portuguese culture—the *assimilados*—gained rights and citizenship and had access to Portuguese law instead of colonial law (Owolabi 2023). And in focusing on assimilation and political integration, Portuguese colonialism in Angola, Guinea Bissau, and Mozambique did not employ pluralist policies that recognized, accommodated, and empowered colonized communities anywhere to the same extent as the British.

Finally, whereas Protestant missionaries commonly strengthened colonial pluralism, colonial authorities restricted their influence in the Spanish and Portuguese Empires even more than authorities in the French Empire. Throughout the colonial period, Catholicism was the official religion of Spain and Portugal, and Spanish and Portuguese colonial officials forbid Protestant missions. Thus, whereas British colonies averaged 1.05 Protestant missionaries per 10,000 people in 1922, this figure was only 0.19 and 0.46 for Portuguese and Spanish colonies, respectively (Woodberry 2012). And while the Spanish figure is moderate, Equatorial Guinea is the only Spanish colony in which Protestants founded a mission before independence (Woodberry 2012). In this way, the average score of Protestant missionaries per capita is driven almost completely by postcolonial missionary influence.

Conclusion

This chapter focuses on the forms, origins, and uniqueness of British colonial pluralism. It considers the characteristics of British colonial pluralism and explores the factors that promoted its use in the British Empire, noting how its adoption in India led to its transfer to most other colonies of occupation. The analyses of the British Empire also offer evidence that the type of colonialism (settler, forced settlement, or occupation) and Protestant missionaries shaped the extent of colonial pluralism in the British Empire. Precolonial statehood and arable lands are also positively related to colonial pluralism, although these relationships disappear when including settler and forced settlement populations in the same model, offering evidence that these factors shaped the extent of colonial pluralism by promoting colonies of occupation.

The chapter also compares British colonialism to other empires to explore whether non-British colonizers employed pluralist policies. In addition to brief analyses of the Spanish and Portuguese Empires, the chapter provides a multimethod analysis of the French Empire. All in all, the comparative analysis offers evidence that colonial pluralism was much more prevalent in the British Empire than other European overseas empires.

3

A Statistical Analysis of Colonial Pluralism, Precolonial Statehood, and Nationalist Civil War

with Tay Jeong and Charlotte Gaudreau

Over the past decade, a number of scholars have used "natural experiments" to explore the causal effect of a random historical "treatment," and this type of analysis is potentially applicable to analyses of colonial legacies (Diamond and Robinson 2010). To the extent that different colonial powers preferred opposing models of political community, the identity of the colonizer determined the extent of colonial pluralism, and researchers can explore how the colonial treatment affected postcolonial outcomes (Wucherpfennig et al. 2016). So, since the British implemented highly pluralist policies whereas the French did not, researchers can compare the incidence of nationalist warfare in former British and French colonies for powerful insight into how pluralist colonial policies affected the risk of nationalist civil warfare.

As Kocher and Monteiro (2016) note, natural experiments require a random treatment, something that is very difficult to prove. When the treatment is not generated randomly, some factor or set of factors can cause variation in both the treatment and the outcome. Although finding that the identity of the colonizer greatly influenced the extent of colonial pluralism, chapter 2's analysis shows that British colonialism only accounts for part of the variation in colonial pluralism. Evidence therefore suggests the presence of influential nonrandom determinants, making colonialism a poor treatment.

While not solving these problems, multivariate statistics allow researchers to address some of them. When researchers are unable to use an experimental design that manipulates one factor while holding all other variables constant, multivariate statistical methods allow them to use observational data to calculate relationships between variables while controlling for other factors. Multivariate statistics are unable to establish causation but highlight general relationships, something that provides vital insight into the *possibility* of systematic causal relationships among a large set of cases. This chapter completes an initial test of chapter 1's theoretical framework by using multivariate statistics to explore relationships between the extent of colonial pluralism, historical statehood, and nationalist civil warfare. Before completing the analysis, however, the next section presents hypotheses based on chapter 1's framework, and the subsequent statistical analysis tests these hypotheses.

Hypotheses

Chapter 1's theoretical framework makes several hypotheses, but not all are of equal value. Some are central to the theoretical framework, and others are more tangential. Although no statistical test can prove this book's theory, those that test core hypotheses approach "hoop tests," meaning that they cannot prove the theory but can provide powerful evidence against it (Collier 2011). The tests of other hypotheses are closer to "straw-in-the-wind" tests that are inconclusive but still offer some insight into the theory (Collier 2011).

This book's core claims deal with colonial pluralism, precolonial states, and nationalist civil warfare. When formulated for statistical tests, these claims generate five hypotheses:

H_1: The level of colonial pluralism is positively related to nationalist civil warfare.

H_2: Pluralist colonial policies that are discriminatory and empowering are more strongly related to nationalist civil warfare than other pluralist policies.

H_3: The level of precolonial statehood is positively related to nationalist civil war.

H_4: High levels of colonial pluralism are strongly and positively related to nationalist civil war when the level of precolonial statehood is high.

H_5: High levels of colonial pluralism are either unrelated or negatively related to nationalist civil war when the level of precolonial statehood is low.

These hypotheses provide important insight into the theory and therefore approach hoop tests. Tests of H_1, however, are more uncertain than tests of the other hypotheses, and the interpretation of tests of H_1 depends on tests of H_2, H_4, and H_5. This uncertainty and dependence result from the complexity of

H_1: The theory suggests that colonial pluralism has mixed effects that depend on the type of pluralist policy and the presence of historical states but that—overall—the positive effects outweigh the negative. As a result, a negative relationship between colonial pluralism and nationalist civil war provides strong evidence against H_1, a positive and significant relationship provides evidence supporting H_1, but a positive relationship without significance provides uncertain results that suggest either mixed effects or no effect. In the case of uncertain results, tests of H_2, H_4, and H_5—which focus on the type of pluralist policy and the effects of historical statehood—provide important insight into how to interpret tests of H_1.

The next hypothesis deals with communal demography:

> H_6: Unipolar communal demographies with one dominant community and sizable minority communities are positively related to nationalist civil warfare.

This hypothesis focuses on one potential mechanism through which historical states affect national chauvinism and, thereby, nationalist civil war. As argued in chapter 1, historical statehood commonly promotes communal demographies characterized by one demographically dominant community and one or more smaller non-state communities, and this communal demography increases the risk of nationalist civil war by strengthening the national chauvinism of the dominant community. If historical statehood promotes nationalist civil war through its effects on communal demography, places with one large community and several smaller communities should have a high risk of nationalist civil war.

The final two hypotheses deal with Protestant missionaries:

> H_7: Protestant missionary influence is positively related to nationalist civil warfare.
> H_8: The relationship between Protestant missionary influence and nationalist civil war is especially strong in places with high levels of precolonial statehood.

These hypotheses are both "straw-in-the-wind" tests because—as described in the next section—the measure of missionary influence is imprecise. Like H_1, H_7 can also provide uncertain results because the theory suggests that missionaries have mixed effects but that the positive effects outweigh the negative. Tests of H_8 therefore inform interpretations of tests of H_7.

Variables and Methods

Statistical tests of these hypotheses require the operationalization of colonial pluralism, historical statehood, communal demography, Protestant missionary influence, and nationalist civil warfare. Because all focal independent variables vary by degree, this chapter employs continuous measures of them. To control for other factors that might mediate relations between the focal independent and dependent variables, the models include several control variables.

To measure the level of colonial pluralism, this analysis employs the pluralist index presented in chapter 2. Because this variable is limited to the British and French Empires, the findings of models including this variable might not apply to a larger set of cases. For insight into this possibility, some models use the set of all former European overseas colonies and include British colony of occupation as a proxy for colonial pluralism.

To test the hypothesis that empowering and discriminatory pluralist policies are especially likely to promote nationalist civil war, the analysis also disaggregates the pluralist index and tests the relationships between the individual components and the odds of nationalist civil war onset.[1] As described in chapter 1, communal legislative representation was more empowering and discriminatory than either census categories or vernacular education. As a result, communal legislative representation should be more strongly related to the odds of nationalist civil warfare onset than either communal census categories or vernacular education.

To test H_3 and H_4, the analysis uses data from Borcan et al. (2018) on the level of precolonial statehood. As described in chapter 2 in greater detail, this variable measures the extent to which an independent state controlled the territory of a contemporary state between 1001 and 1700 AD.

The analysis uses data by Fearon (2003) on ethnic fractionalization to operationalize communal demography for tests of H_6. This variable measures the likelihood that two randomly selected co-nationals are from different ethnic communities, with 0 therefore designating a situation of complete communal homogeneity and 1 designating a country with complete communal heterogeneity. H_6 suggests that communal demographies characterized by one dominant community that makes up more than half the population and several smaller communities have a high risk of nationalist civil war because they promote national chauvinism and reactions to it. Countries with this communal demography generally have ethnic fractionalization scores around 0.5. With its ethnic fractionalization score of 0.52, for example, Myanmar has one majority community making up two-thirds of the population and dozens of smaller communities that make up the rest.

---

1. Because H_2 concerns pluralist policies that recognize, accommodate, and empower colonized communities and because metropolitan representation does none of these, metropolitan representation is not included as an independent variable. When including metropolitan representation as an independent variable, the coefficients of the other components of the pluralist index are substantively identical to models without it.

One problem with using ethnic fractionalization to measure communal demography is that moderate levels of ethnic fractionalization can also measure the presence of two equally sized communities that make up nearly all the population. Belgium, which is almost equally divided between Flemish and Walloon, for example, has a score of 0.56. A review of former British and French colonies shows that most countries with moderate levels of ethnic fractionalization have unipolar communal demographies similar to Myanmar, but a few cases have populations that are closer to a bipolar ethnic configuration. To test H_6, models therefore exclude countries with bifurcated communal demographies.[2]

Finally, the analysis uses data by Woodberry (2012) to measure Protestant missionary influence. The variable subtracts the year of Protestant missionary onset from 1960, so higher numbers signify earlier onset and thereby greater influence. Woodberry also provides a variable measuring Protestant missionaries per capita in 1923, but the onset variable is more appropriate for testing H_7 and H_8. According to this book's theory, missionaries are most likely to contribute to nationalist civil warfare when they work with non-state communities, but per capita measures of missionary influence are particularly low in places with historical states because missionaries rarely worked closely with state communities and because state communities make up the majority of the population. In regions with high levels of state history, however, earlier onset increases the chances that missionaries worked closely with non-state communities, suggesting that the year of missionary onset provides a better proxy of missionary influence among non-state communities.

The dependent variable measures the year of onset of nationalist civil wars involving a community that fights the state for greater autonomy and self-rule and is based on information from the Uppsala Conflict Data Program (UCDP) and Ethnic Power Relations (EPR). UCDP data identify all civil wars between 1946 and 2020 causing at least 25 yearly battle deaths on each side of the conflict. It also includes a variable measuring whether the conflict was over "territorial incompatibility," a category including wars in which anti-state combatants seek greater control of territory to increase their autonomy through either state decentralization or secession (Pettersson and Öberg 2020). While suggesting that civil wars over territorial incompatibility are nationalist civil wars, some conflicts over territorial incompatibility—such as the American Civil War—were not over communal self-rule and therefore do not fit this book's definition of nationalist civil war. The analysis therefore supplements UCDP data with data from EPR to identify which civil wars over territorial incompatibility pursued *communal* autonomy and self-rule (Vogt et al. 2015). For all civil wars in the UCDP dataset, EPR provides information on whether the anti-state actors (1) make ethnic claims, (2) recruit based on ethnicity, or

2. Models including these cases produce substantively identical results.

(3) receive support from particular ethnic communities. This analysis codes civil wars over territorial incompatibility as nationalist if EPR scores anti-state combatants as ethnic for at least two of the three indicators.

Using this measure, the year in which a nationalist civil war begins is scored 1 whereas all other years are scored 0. Yet many nationalist civil wars in the UCDP dataset have temporal breaks during which fighting either ceases or is so minor that it is no longer considered a civil war. For this analysis, civil wars are categorized as having a new onset if the break between the end of fighting and the beginning of new fighting is greater than a decade (i.e., eleven years or more). In addition to this variable, models also employed a dependent variable measuring whether a nationalist civil war was ongoing in a country in any given year, with all years in which a nationalist civil war is ongoing scored as 1. Because the results are similar to the models using nationalist civil war onset as the dependent variable and because the theory focuses on the occurrence of civil war instead of its duration, the analysis only presents the results of nationalist civil war onset.

The models include two sets of control variables, the first of which includes measures of geographic conditions, previous conflict, and time since independence. One geographic control variable measures a region's latitude. As noted by Alesina et al. (2003), a country's latitude measures ecological conditions that have shaped long-term trajectories of development and communal diversity, both of which might have influenced precolonial states, colonial pluralism, and historical patterns of warfare. A second geographic control measures the natural log of the extent of a country's territory that is mountainous (Fearon and Laitin 2003). Mountains facilitate resistance and affect communal diversity, and both potentially shaped the form of colonialism, precolonial statehood, and postcolonial warfare. The third geographic control variable measures the natural log of territorial size in square kilometers, as the physical size of colonies might have shaped the form of colonial rule and nationalist warfare. Most notably, the size of a territory is related to communal diversity, which potentially promotes both colonial pluralism and nationalist civil warfare. Finally, all models include variables measuring geographic region to account for unobserved background factors that may vary by region, with sub-Saharan Africa as the reference category.

All models also include a dichotomous measure of the number of previous nationalist civil wars because analyses find that past war increases the odds of future war. Because the data on nationalist civil war begin in 1946, this variable only measures wars that occurred on or after 1946. All models also use a cubic polynomial to control for years since independence because independence is a particularly contentious period during which communities compete for control of the postcolonial state (Carter and Signorino 2010; Wimmer 2013).

The second set of control variables measure factors that past analyses find are commonly related to ethnic warfare: the natural log of a country's per

TABLE 3.1. Nationalist Civil War by European Overseas Empire

Empire	Average Nationalist Civil Wars per Colony	Average Years of Nationalist Civil Wars per Colony
British	0.97	14.1
French	0.38	2.3
Other	0.32	2.3

capital GDP (Feenstra et al. 2015), the natural log of total population (Feenstra et al. 2015), the natural log of oil production (Our World in Data 2024), and level of democracy (Marshall and Gurr 2020). Notably, the polity2 variable measuring level of democracy has several missing values, and the value of a previous or subsequent year is used to impute missing values when possible.

Because colonial pluralism and precolonial statehood potentially influenced the second set of control variables, their inclusion might cause the analysis to underestimate the association between the focal independent variables and nationalist civil war onset. That being said, the second set of controls potentially has independent effects on nationalist civil war onset. To deal with the possibility of endogenous selection bias, some models exclude these control variables. To deal with the possibility of omitted variable bias, other models include them.

Using these variables, the analysis employs panel regressions to estimate how independent variables are related to the odds of nationalist civil war onset between 1946 and 2020. The analysis uses a pooled logistic regression with regional fixed effects. To account for within-country clustering, it uses "Sandwich" standard errors (Zeileis et al. 2021).

The analysis uses country year as the unit of analysis. Community year, however, is an alternative unit that might offer superior insight if a community's risk of nationalist civil war depends on how the pluralist policies were applied to that community. Jeong (2023) uses community-level data on communal legislative representation to replicate previous analyses of ethnic civil warfare based on country-level data and finds that the unit of analysis does not change the results. Moreover, he finds that communal legislative representation has institution-level effects on communities that did not receive reserved seats, suggesting the appropriateness of country-level measures.

Statistical Analysis

As shown in table 3.1, the average number of nationalist civil wars of former British colonies is approximately three times greater than those of the former French Empire and all other former European overseas empires. The average number of years of nationalist civil wars in former British colonies, in turn, is

TABLE 3.2. Logistic Regression Analysis of British Colonialism, Historical Statehood, and Nationalist Civil War Onset, 1946–2020

	(1)	(2)	(3)	(4)	(5)	(6)
British Colony of Occupation	1.241	1.304				0.085
	(0.68, 2.26)	(0.61, 2.79)				(0.00, 1.71)
Extent of Historical Statehood			2.179**	2.875**	1.678+	2.035*
			(1.25, 3.79)	(1.45, 5.71)	(0.99, 2.84)	(1.09, 3.81)
British × Historical Statehood					9.218*	7.692+
					(1.39, 61.24)	(0.94, 62.87)
Ethnic Fractionalization	1.221*	1.221*	1.355**	1.428*	1.532**	1.510**
	(1.04, 1.44)	(1.05, 1.42)	(1.10, 1.67)	(1.09, 1.88)	(1.17, 2.01)	(1.13, 2.03)
Latitude	2.108**	2.137**	1.682*	1.559+	1.598+	1.450
	(1.27, 3.49)	(1.31, 3.50)	(1.08, 2.62)	(0.99, 2.47)	(0.98, 2.61)	(0.87, 2.41)
Log Proportion Mountainous	0.993	1.007	0.972	1.068	0.772	0.869
	(0.67, 1.47)	(0.69, 1.46)	(0.66, 1.43)	(0.72, 1.59)	(0.52, 1.14)	(0.59, 1.27)
Log Land Area	2.283***	2.570**	1.988**	2.368**	1.802*	1.786*
	(1.52, 3.43)	(1.39, 4.74)	(1.28, 3.09)	(1.37, 4.10)	(1.07, 3.03)	(1.02, 3.12)
Number of Previous Wars	1.157*	1.143*	1.117+	1.097	1.011	1.021
	(1.03, 1.30)	(1.00, 1.31)	(0.10, 1.26)	(0.96, 1.25)	(0.90, 1.14)	(0.89, 1.17)
Asia & Oceania	3.818**	4.191**	2.557*	2.142	3.609***	2.517*
	(1.66, 8.76)	(1.49, 11.79)	(1.07, 6.12)	(0.83, 5.52)	(1.71, 7.62)	(1.01, 6.25)

	(1)	(2)	(3)	(4)	(5)	(6)
North Africa & Middle East	1.338	1.431	1.173	1.080	1.741	1.655
	(0.49, 3.69)	(0.49, 4.18)	(0.48, 2.86)	(0.49, 2.37)	(0.78, 3.87)	(0.77, 3.57)
Americas	0.000***	0.000***	0.000***	0.000***	0.000***	0.000***
	(0.00, 0.00)	(0.00, 0.00)	(0.00, 0.00)	(0.00, 0.00)	(0.00, 0.00)	(0.00, 0.00)
Extent of Democracy		1.188		1.310		1.315
		(0.77, 1.83)		(0.87, 1.98)		(0.85, 2.03)
Log GDP pc		0.717+		0.792		0.811
		(0.49, 1.04)		(0.54, 1.17)		(0.55, 1.19)
Log Population		0.760		0.703		0.898
		(0.40, 1.46)		(0.39, 1.26)		(0.48, 1.67)
Log Oil Production		1.042		1.011		1.011
		(0.91, 1.19)		(0.89, 1.15)		(0.86, 1.19)
Years since Independence	0.937	0.942	0.941	0.964	0.939	0.954
	(0.84, 1.05)	(0.84, 1.05)	(0.84, 1.05)	(0.86, 1.08)	(0.84, 1.05)	(0.85, 1.07)
Years since Independence^2	1.002	1.001	1.001	1.001	1.002	1.001
	(1.00, 1.01)	(1.00, 1.00)	(1.00, 1.00)	(1.00, 1.00)	(1.00, 1.01)	(1.00, 1.00)
Years since Independence^3	0.987	0.988	0.989	0.993	0.986	0.990
	(0.96, 1.01)	(0.97, 1.01)	(0.97, 1.01)	(0.97, 1.02)	(0.97, 1.01)	(0.97, 1.011)
Constant	0.003***	0.002***	0.001***	0.001***	0.000***	0.000***
	(0.00, 0.01)	(0.00, 0.01)	(0.00, 0.01)	(0.00, 0.01)	(0.00, 0.01)	(0.00, 0.01)
N country-years	5848	5684	5848	5684	5848	5684

Note: + p<0.1; * p<0.05; ** p<0.01; *** p<0.001

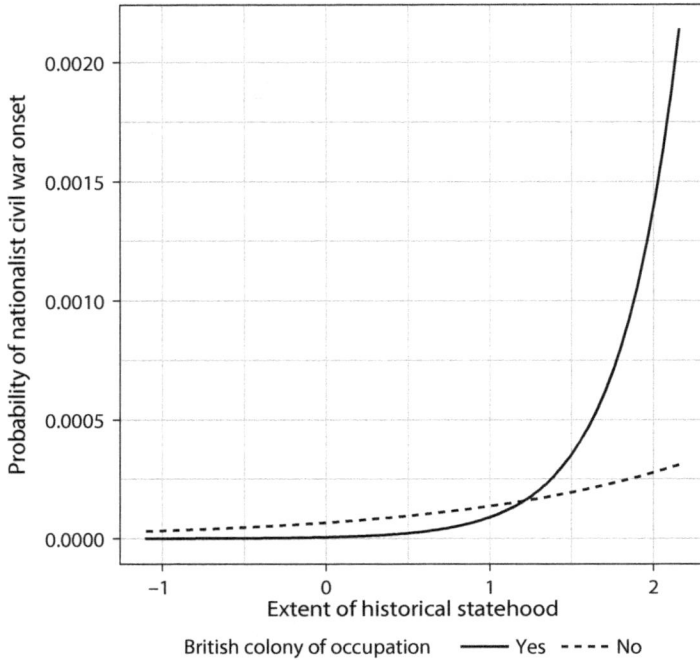

FIGURE 3.1. Probability of Nationalist Civil War Onset by State History and Colonizer.

six times greater than former French colonies and three and a half times greater than former colonies of other European overseas empires. Nationalist civil war is therefore unusually concentrated in the former British Empire.

Table 3.2 analyzes the relationship between British colonialism and nationalist civil war more rigorously by completing logistic regression analysis of nationalist civil war onset between 1946 and 2020 using the set of all former European overseas colonies with at least 400,000 people at independence. Because the goal is to isolate the impact of colonial pluralism and because chapter 2 provides evidence that colonial pluralism was unusually concentrated in British colonies of occupation, the focal independent variable is dichotomous and measures whether a country is a former British colony of occupation.[3] This and all subsequent tables present the 0.05-level confidence intervals in parentheses. For ease of interpretation, all variables in this and subsequent tables are standardized except for dichotomous variables and time since independence, so the coefficients estimate how an increase in a

---

3. The findings are substantively identical when the variable includes the British settler and forced settlement colonies.

variable by one standard deviation is associated with the odds of nationalist civil war onset.

In table 3.2, Models 1 and 2 use British colony of occupation as the focal independent variable, Models 3 and 4 use state history as the focal independent variable, and Models 5 and 6 include an interaction term multiplying British colony of occupation by state history. Although well above one, the coefficients of the variable measuring British colony of occupation are not significant in Models 1 and 2. Given variation in the extent of colonial pluralism among British colonies of occupation and the hypothesis that the colonial pluralism has mixed effects that depend on precolonial statehood and the type of pluralist policy, this finding is uncertain and neither supports nor opposes H_1. In Models 3 and 4, the coefficients of historical statehood are well above one and significant, showing that an increase in historical statehood by one standard deviation is associated with an increased odds of nationalist civil warfare by between 220 and 290 percent. Finally, the coefficients of the interaction term in Models 5 and 6 are both very large and significant, suggesting that former British colonies of occupation with high levels of historical statehood have extremely high odds of nationalist civil war onset. With the addition of this interaction term, the coefficients of British colony of occupation are now well below one and significant at the 0.1 level in Model 5. In this way, British colonies of occupation with high levels of state history have very high odds of nationalist civil warfare relative to all other overseas colonies, whereas British colonies of occupation with average levels of state history have odds of nationalist civil war onset that are similar to or even below those of other colonies.

Figure 3.1 is based on Model 6 of table 3.2 and presents the predicted probability of nationalist civil war onset by level of historical statehood for former British colonies of occupation and all other former European overseas colonies separately. Among cases that are not former British colonies of occupation, the predicted probability of nationalist civil war increases slowly over the entire range of state history, suggesting a moderately strong and linear relationship between historical statehood and nationalist civil war onset in places with limited colonial pluralism. In contrast, the predicted probability of nationalist civil war for former British colonies of occupation is below the predicted probability of other colonies and flat until the z-score of state history passes 0.5, at which time it increases exponentially and quickly surpasses the predicted probability of non-British colonies of occupation with like levels of historical statehood. All in all, the results using the entire set of European overseas colonies offer evidence that nationalist civil warfare is heavily concentrated among former British colonies of occupation with high levels of historical statehood but that nationalist civil war is relatively rare in former British colonies of occupation with limited precolonial statehood. Given high levels of colonial pluralism among British colonies of occupation, this finding

TABLE 3.3. Logistic Regression Analysis of Colonial Pluralism and the Nationalist Civil War Onset, 1946–2020

	(1)	(2)	(3)	(4)
Pluralist Index	1.901**	2.153**		
	(1.23, 2.93)	(1.27, 3.66)		
Legislative Representation			4.570***	6.598***
			(1.88, 11.09)	(2.75, 15.81)
Vernacular Education			0.920	0.911
			(0.37, 2.31)	(0.34, 2.47)
Census Categories			1.175	1.284
			(0.80, 1.74)	(0.84, 1.97)
Latitude	1.179	1.113	1.282	1.153
	(0.84, 1.66)	(0.70, 1.78)	(0.87, 1.88)	(0.71, 1.88)
Log Proportion Mountainous	1.058	1.002	1.046	0.926
	(0.71, 1.57)	(0.68, 1.48)	(0.67, 1.63)	(0.61, 1.41)
Log Land Area	2.709***	3.126***	2.577***	3.654***
	(1.95, 3.76)	(1.61, 6.07)	(1.82, 3.65)	(1.87, 7.14)
Number of Previous Wars	1.184***	1.127+	1.150**	1.078
	(1.08, 1.30)	(1.00, 1.28)	(1.04, 1.27)	(0.95, 1.22)
Americas	0.000***	0.000***	0.000***	0.000***
	(0.00, 0.00)	(0.00, 0.00)	(0.00, 0.00)	(0.00, 0.00)
North Africa & Middle East	1.008	1.453	0.644	1.198
	(0.32, 3.16)	(0.38, 5.62)	(0.21, 2.00)	(0.30, 4.73)
Asia & Oceania	1.283	1.488	1.159	1.563
	(0.68, 2.42)	(0.65, 3.38)	(0.63, 2.13)	(0.68, 3.61)
Extent of Democracy		1.189		1.206
		(0.73, 1.94)		(0.74, 1.96)
Log GDP pc		0.493*		0.449*
		(0.27, 0.90)		(0.24, 0.84)
Log Population		0.749		0.639+
		(0.46, 1.21)		(0.40, 1.03)
Log Oil Production		1.014		0.991
		(0.88, 1.17)		(0.84, 1.17)
Years since Independence	0.944	0.953	0.946	0.963
	(0.84, 1.06)	(0.84, 1.08)	(0.85, 1.06)	(0.85, 1.09)
Years since Independence^2	1.002	1.002	1.002	1.002
	(1.00, 1.00)	(1.00, 1.01)	(1.00, 1.00)	(1.00, 1.01)
Years since Independence^3	0.985	0.986	0.985	0.986
	(0.97, 1.00)	(0.97, 1.01)	(0.97, 1.00)	(0.97, 1.01)
Constant	0.012***	0.005***	0.005***	0.001***
	(0.00, 0.04)	(0.00, 0.02)	(0.00, 0.02)	(0.00, 0.01)
N country-years	3763	3763	3763	3763

Note: + p<0.1; * p<0.05; ** p<0.01; *** p<0.001

TABLE 3.4. Logistic Regression Analysis of Historical Statehood, Colonial Pluralism, and Nationalist Civil War Onset, 1946–2020

	(1)	(2)	(3)	(4)
Extent of Historical Statehood	3.379*** (2.04, 5.60)	3.695*** (2.16, 6.33)	3.199*** (1.66, 6.17)	3.115*** (1.71, 5.69)
Pluralist Index			0.990 (0.49, 1.98)	1.310 (0.68, 2.54)
Historical Statehood × Pluralist Index			1.811* (1.04, 3.16)	1.683* (1.06, 2.66)
Latitude	1.298 (0.74, 2.28)	1.315 (0.66, 2.61)	1.153 (0.70, 1.89)	1.013 (0.58, 1.78)
Log Proportion Mountainous	1.066 (0.70, 1.62)	1.165 (0.77, 1.76)	0.769 (0.52, 1.15)	0.817 (0.53, 1.26)
Log Land Area	2.744*** (1.55, 4.86)	1.880* (1.02, 3.45)	3.104*** (1.76, 5.47)	3.804*** (1.73, 8.35)
Number of Previous Wars	1.144* (1.03, 1.27)	1.147* (1.02, 1.29)	1.048 (0.93, 1.18)	1.032 (0.92, 1.15)
Extent of Democracy		1.554[+] (0.98, 2.47)		1.424 (0.87, 2.33)
Log GDP pc		0.672 (0.38, 1.20)		0.630[+] (0.39, 1.01)
Log Population		1.048 (0.66, 1.67)		0.753 (0.51, 1.11)
Log Oil Production		1.043 (0.90, 1.22)		0.935 (0.78, 1.12)
Americas	0.000*** (0.00, 0.00)	0.000*** (0.00, 0.00)	0.000*** (0.00, 0.00)	0.000*** (0.00, 0.00)
North Africa & Middle East	0.415 (0.09, 1.87)	0.421 (0.09, 2.00)	0.639 (0.14, 2.93)	1.051 (0.19, 5.97)
Asia & Oceania	0.976 (0.44, 2.16)	0.572 (0.23, 1.45)	0.821 (0.39, 1.72)	0.700 (0.32, 1.52)
Years since Independence	0.950 (0.85, 1.06)	0.974 (0.87, 1.10)	0.947 (0.85, 1.06)	0.980 (0.87, 1.11)
Years since Independence^2	1.001 (1.00, 1.00)	1.001 (1.00, 1.00)	1.002 (1.00, 1.00)	1.001 (1.00, 1.00)
Years since Independence^3	0.987 (0.97, 1.01)	0.994 (0.97, 1.01)	0.985[+] (0.97, 1.00)	0.989 (0.97, 1.01)
Constant	0.007*** (0.00, 0.03)	0.006*** (0.00, 0.03)	0.005*** (0.00, 0.02)	0.002*** (0.00, 0.02)
N country-years	3763	3763	3763	3763

Note: + p<0.1; * p<0.05; ** p<0.01; *** p<0.001

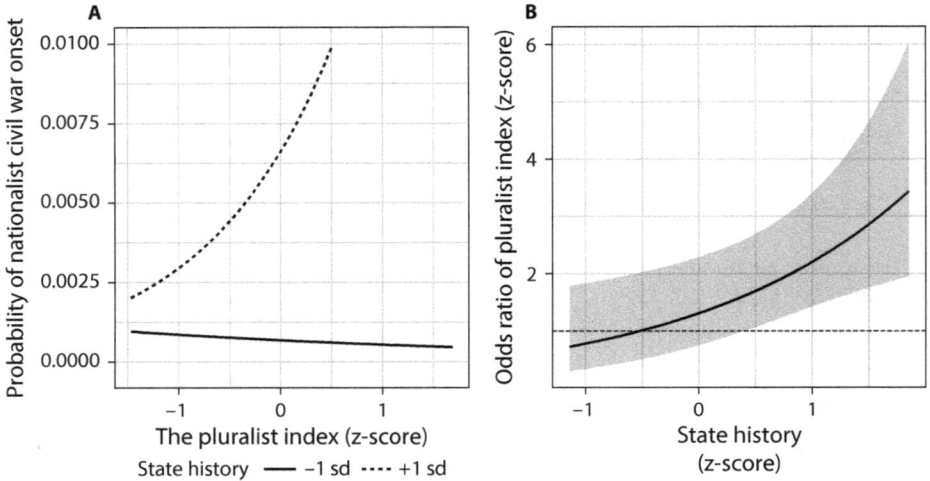

FIGURE 3.2. State History, British Colonial Pluralism, and Nationalist Civil War Onset.

supports H_4 and H_5 and thereby suggests that the insignificant relationships between British colony of occupation and nationalist civil war onset in Models 1 and 2 highlight mixed effects.

While the large set used for table 3.2 makes possible more generalizable insight, the results are potentially biased due to an imprecise proxy of colonial pluralism. To test the hypotheses on colonial pluralism with a better measure, table 3.3 presents the results of the panel regressions using the pluralist index as the focal independent variables. The first two models include the pluralist index, and the next two models include the individual components of the pluralist index. Because the pluralist index is only available for former British and French colonies, the set is limited to these cases.

In the first two models, the coefficients of the pluralist index are well above one and significant and estimate that an increase in colonial pluralism by one standard deviation is associated with an increase in the odds of nationalist civil warfare by between 190 and 215 percent. These findings therefore support H_1. Models 3 and 4 of table 3.3 test the hypothesis (H_2) that empowering and discriminatory pluralist policies have the greatest impact on the odds of nationalist civil war onset by disaggregating the pluralist index. The coefficients of communal legislative representation—which is the most empowering and discriminatory pluralist policy of the three—are large and significant, estimating that the odds of nationalist civil war onset are 4.6 to 6.6 times greater in places with a history of communal legislative representation. Alternatively, communal census categories and multiple educational vernaculars

TABLE 3.5. Logistic Regression Analysis of Ethnic Fractionalization, Colonial Pluralism, and Nationalist Civil War, 1946–2020

	(1)	(2)	(3)	(4)
Ethnic Fractionalization	1.742[+]	0.905	1.957**	2.340**
	(0.93, 3.27)	(0.41, 2.00)	(1.22, 3.15)	(1.270, 4.32)
Ethnic Fractionalization^2	0.231***	0.157***		
	(0.10, 0.52)	(0.06, 0.39)		
Pluralist Index			2.332**	3.039***
			(1.34, 4.05)	(1.57, 5.88)
Ethnic Fractionalization × Pluralist Index			0.490**	0.495**
			(0.31, 0.77)	(0.30, 0.80)
Latitude	1.155	0.814	1.146	1.113
	(0.74, 1.79)	(0.47, 1.40)	(0.72, 1.82)	(0.66, 1.88)
Log Proportion Mountainous	0.690	0.699	0.895	0.731
	(0.34, 1.41)	(0.33, 1.50)	(0.55, 1.47)	(0.46, 1.16)
Log Land Area	3.354***	2.323*	4.368***	5.766**
	(1.95, 5.78)	(1.05, 5.15)	(2.09, 9.13)	(1.95, 17.02)
Number of Previous Wars	1.145**	1.113	1.152**	1.085
	(1.04, 1.26)	(0.98, 1.27)	(1.05, 1.27)	(0.95, 1.24)
Extent of Democracy		1.235		1.272
		(0.75, 2.02)		(0.74, 2.20)
Log GDP pc		0.494**		0.468*
		(0.30, 0.83)		(0.26, 0.85)
Log Population		1.778[+]		0.567*
		(0.93, 3.41)		(0.35, 0.96)
Log Oil Production		1.012		1.023
		(0.87, 1.18)		(0.86, 1.22)
Americas	0.000***	0.000***	0.000***	0.000***
	(0.00, 0.00)	(0.00, 0.00)	(0.00, 0.00)	(0.00, 0.00)
North Africa & Middle East	2.314	3.140	2.668	3.376
	(0.76, 7.08)	(0.50, 19.93)	(0.72, 9.91)	(0.50, 22.71)
Asia & Oceania	6.849***	2.384	2.029	3.513[+]
	(2.34, 20.09)	(0.55, 10.28)	(0.79, 5.20)	(0.85, 14.51)
Years since Independence	0.938	0.951	0.930	0.944
	(0.84, 1.05)	(0.84, 1.08)	(0.83, 1.04)	(0.83, 1.07)
Years since Independence^2	1.002	1.001	1.002	1.002
	(1.00, 1.00)	(1.00, 1.00)	(1.00, 1.01)	(1.00, 1.01)
Years since Independence^3	0.984	0.991	0.981[+]	0.981[+]
	(0.96, 1.00)	(0.97, 1.01)	(0.96, 1.00)	(0.96, 1.00)
Constant	0.015***	0.020***	0.006***	0.002***
	(0.00, 0.06)	(0.00, 0.16)	(0.00, 0.02)	(0.00, 0.01)
N country-years	3411	3411	3411	3411

Note: + p<0.1; * p<0.05; ** p<0.01; *** p<0.001

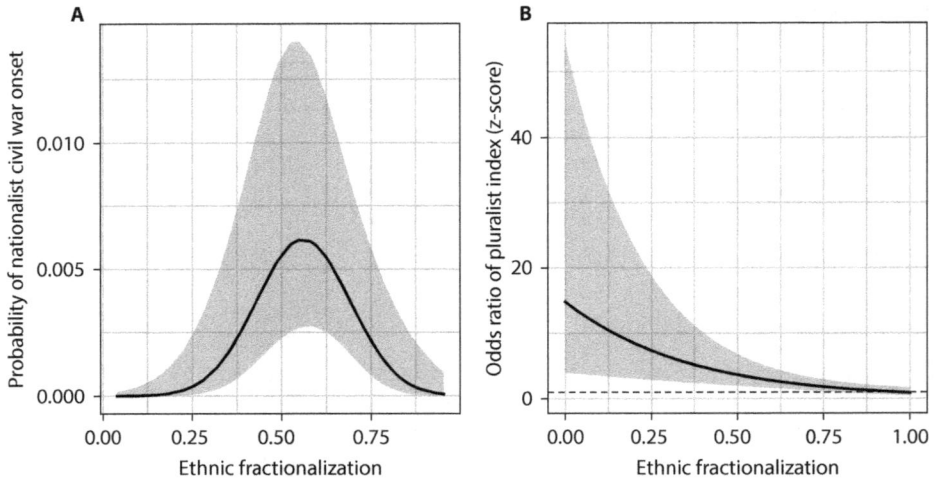

FIGURE 3.3. Ethnic Fractionalization, British Colonial Pluralism, and Nationalist Civil War Onset.

have coefficients near one, suggesting that the relationship between colonial pluralism and nationalist civil war is driven by empowering and discriminatory pluralist policies.

Table 3.4 analyzes interactions between the pluralist index and state history, with Models 1 and 2 using state history as the focal independent variable and Models 3 and 4 including the interaction term multiplying state history by the pluralist index. Similar to the analysis of the larger set in table 3.2, state history is positively and significantly related to the onset of nationalist civil war. In Models 3 and 4, the coefficients of the interaction term are significantly above one in both models and show that the relationship between colonial pluralism and nationalist civil war onset is strongest when combined with high levels of historical statehood.

Figures 3.2a and 3.2b are based on Model 4 of table 3.4 and offer more insight into this nonlinear relationship. Figure 3.2a shows the predicted probability of nationalist civil war onset by level of pluralism when the z-score of state history is either one standard deviation above or below the mean. With high levels of state history, the estimated probability of nationalist civil war onset is low when colonial pluralism is low but increases rapidly as the pluralist index increases. With low levels of historical statehood, however, the estimated probability of nationalist civil war is low when the level of colonial pluralism is low and declines gradually throughout the range of the pluralist index. Similarly, figure 3.2b graphs the odds ratio of the pluralist index by level of state history and estimates that the odds ratio is small when state history is low, increases rapidly with higher level of state history, and becomes significantly greater than 1 when the z-score of state history surpasses 0.5. Both figures therefore strongly support H_5 and H_6.

Table 3.5 analyzes the relationship between communal demography and nationalist civil war onset, thereby testing the hypothesis (H_6) that state history shapes nationalist civil warfare, in part, through its effects on communal demography. Because some models include the pluralist index, the set is limited to former British and French colonies. To test the hypothesized quadratic relationship between ethnic fractionalization and nationalist civil war onset, the first two models include ethnic fractionalization and its squared term as the focal independent variables. The coefficients of ethnic fractionalization and its squared term in Models 1 and 2 provide evidence of a nonlinear relationship between ethnic fractionalization and nationalist civil war. Figure 3.3a visualizes these findings by plotting the predicted probably of nationalist civil war by ethnic fractionalization using Models 2. The figure clearly shows an inverted-u-shaped relationship, with the probability of nationalist civil war onset greatest when ethnic fractionalization is moderate. The analysis therefore strongly supports H_6.

Models 3 and 4 of table 3.5 remove the squared value of ethnic fractionalization and add an interaction term multiplying colonial pluralism by ethnic fractionalization. In both models, the coefficients of the interaction term are significantly below one, suggesting that colonial pluralism is associated with reduced odds of nationalist civil warfare when combined with high levels of ethnic fractionalization. This finding therefore supports the hypothesis that colonial pluralism either has a weak relationship with or is negatively related to nationalist civil warfare in regions with highly diverse populations (and limited precolonial statehood). Figure 3.3b visualizes these findings by presenting that the odds ratio of the pluralist index by ethnic fractionalization based on Model 4, and it shows that the odds of onset are high when ethnic fractionalization is low and decline as ethnic fractionalization increases.

A comparison of figures 3.3a and 3.3b suggests that colonial pluralism transforms the effects of ethnic fractionalization, as low ethnic fractionalization is associated with limited nationalist civil war in general but is strongly related to nationalist civil warfare when combined with high levels of colonial pluralism. This pattern conforms with the general ideas presented in chapter 1: Very large communities are more likely to impose aggressive national chauvinism on very small communities; small communities usually do not react to this national chauvinism because they lack powerful nationalist frames, expectations, and mobilizational resources; but colonial pluralism strengthens the frames, expectations, and resources of small communities in ways promoting nationalist reactions. Even with high levels of colonial pluralism, however, ethnic fractionalization should not be associated with nationalist civil war

TABLE 3.6. Logistic Regression Analysis of Protestant Missionaries, State History, and Nationalist Civil War Onset, 1946–2020

	(1)	(2)	(3)	(4)
Protestant Onset	0.999	1.118	0.473*	0.507*
	(0.85, 1.17)	(0.83, 1.50)	(0.23, 0.98)	(0.27, 0.97)
Extent of Historical Statehood			2.805**	3.437***
			(1.34, 5.89)	(1.65, 7.15)
Protestant Onset × Historical Statehood			1.762*	1.745*
			(1.00, 3.10)	(1.04, 2.93)
Ethnic Fractionalization	1.218*	1.179+	1.467**	1.433*
	(1.04, 1.42)	(0.99, 1.40)	(1.15, 1.87)	(1.09, 1.89)
Latitude	2.142**	2.259**	1.665+	1.428
	(1.35, 3.39)	(1.30, 3.92)	(0.95, 2.92)	(0.74, 2.75)
Log Proportion Mountainous	0.996	1.054	0.968	1.117
	(0.68, 1.47)	(0.72, 1.54)	(0.65, 1.43)	(0.73, 1.70)
Log Land Area	2.336***	2.818**	1.795*	1.922*
	(1.51, 3.61)	(1.40, 5.66)	(1.08, 2.98)	(1.12, 3.31)
Number of Previous War Onset	1.163*	1.148*	1.073	1.066
	(1.02, 1.33)	(1.00, 1.31)	(0.97, 1.18)	(0.95, 1.20)
Asia & Oceania	4.074***	3.611*	3.431*	1.933
	(1.83, 9.07)	(1.35, 9.70)	(1.34, 8.79)	(0.62, 5.99)
North Africa & Middle East	1.357	1.345	1.512	1.345
	(0.51, 3.61)	(0.42, 4.30)	(0.69, 3.33)	(0.64, 2.82)
Americas	0.000***	0.000***	0.000***	0.000***
	(0.00, 0.00)	(0.00, 0.00)	(0.00, 0.00)	(0.00, 0.01)
Extent of Democracy		1.236		1.392
		(0.81, 1.88)		(0.91, 2.14)
Log GDP pc		0.731		0.802
		(0.50, 1.07)		(0.54, 1.20)
Log Population		0.723		0.822
		(0.35, 1.51)		(0.46, 1.48)
Log Oil Production		1.002		0.996
		(0.86, 1.17)		(0.86, 1.16)
Years since Independence	0.939	0.954	0.945	0.969
	(0.84, 1.05)	(0.85, 1.07)	(0.85, 1.06)	(0.86, 1.09)
Years since Independence^2	1.001	1.001	1.001	1.001
	(1.00, 1.00)	(1.00, 1.00)	(1.00, 1.00)	(1.00, 1.00)
Years since Independence^3	0.988	0.991	0.990	0.995
	(0.96, 1.01)	(0.97, 1.01)	(0.97, 1.02)	(0.97, 1.02)
Constant	0.003***	0.002***	0.000***	0.000***
	(0.00, 0.01)	(0.00, 0.01)	(0.00, 0.01)	(0.00, 0.01)
N country-years	5552	5388	5552	5388

Note: + $p<0.1$; * $p<0.05$; ** $p<0.01$; *** $p<0.001$

when it is zero or very close to zero because nationalist civil war requires some diversity. One likely explanation for this discrepancy is that the set lacks cases to test the interaction when ethnic fractionalization is low: No case in the set pairs an ethnic fractionalization score lower than 0.20 with a pluralist index score above 0.7.

Table 3.6 completes the statistical analysis by testing the hypotheses about Protestant missionaries (H_7 and H_8). Because data on Protestant missionary onset are available for all former overseas colonies (excluding the settler colonies), this analysis includes all former overseas colonies with more than 400,000 people at independence. Models 1 and 2 of table 3.6 use Protestant missionary onset as the focal independent variable, and the results fail to support H_7, as the coefficients of Protestant missionary onset are near one. One potential reason for this finding is measurement error, as year of missionary onset might be a poor indicator of Protestant missionary influence among non-state communities. Another possible explanation is that Protestant missionaries have mixed effects that depend on historical statehood. To test the second possibility (and H_8), Models 3 and 4 include an interaction term multiplying Protestant missionary onset by state history, and the coefficients of the interaction term are well above one and significant. While showing that Protestant missionary influence is associated with greater odds of nationalist civil war onset when combined with high levels of historical statehood, the coefficients of Protestant missionary onset are now below one and significant, showing that Protestant missionary onset is associated with lower odds of nationalist civil war onset when combined with moderate levels of precolonial statehood. The results therefore suggest that the context in which missionaries worked mediated their impact.

Conclusion

This chapter presents eight hypotheses based on chapter 1's theoretical framework and tests them using statistical methods. The results strongly support the hypotheses: Colonial pluralism, state history, and moderate ethnic fractionalization are all positively related to nationalist civil war onset; the relationship between colonial pluralism and nationalist civil war onset is strongest for pluralist policies that are both empowering and discriminatory; colonial pluralism is most strongly related to nationalist civil war onset in places with high levels of historical statehood; and colonial pluralism is either unrelated to or negatively related to nationalist civil war onset in places with limited historical statehood and great communal diversity. Although Protestant missionary influence is not positively related to nationalist civil war onset on its own, it is strongly and positively related to nationalist civil war onset when combined with high levels of historical statehood. The chapter's analysis therefore offers evidence that colonial pluralism and precolonial statehood combined to create a high risk of nationalist civil warfare. At the same time, the analysis provides evidence that colonial pluralism and state history have different relationships with the odds of nationalist civil war onset when not combined. This is especially the case for colonial pluralism, as it either has no relationship with or is negatively related to nationalist civil war onset when combined with low levels of historical statehood.

Although supporting the hypotheses, correlation based on observational data cannot prove causation because it does not offer insight into causal mechanisms and processes. Thankfully, comparative-historical methods specialize in analyzing actual processes and mechanisms. The next five chapters employ comparative-historical methods to explore potential mechanisms and processes through which colonial pluralism and precolonial statehood affected nationalist civil war, with chapters 4 through 6 focusing on colonial pluralism, chapter 7 analyzing the combined effects of colonial pluralism and historical statehood, and chapter 8 considering the independent effects of historical states.

4

Myanmar

COLONIAL PLURALISM AND
NATIONALIST CIVIL WAR

In reaction to the country's military coup in 2021, a number of nationalist civil wars quickly erupted in Myanmar. Nationalist civil warfare is nothing new to Myanmar, however, and most of these wars simply reignited previous conflicts that had weakened or ended in previous years. Indeed, based on the data on nationalist warfare used in chapter 3, Myanmar experienced more nationalist civil wars than any other former British colony between 1946 and 2020.

In addition to being an extreme case of nationalist civil warfare, British colonialism was unusually pluralist in Myanmar and included several discriminatory and empowering pluralist policies, and chapter 3 offers evidence that discriminatory and empowering pluralist policies are very strongly related to nationalist civil war onset. Because extreme cases that conform to general relationships are ideal for highlighting common causal mechanisms that explain broad patterns, an analysis of Myanmar is especially likely to highlight general mechanisms linking colonial pluralism to nationalist civil war if the statistical relationship between the two is causal (Goertz 2016). I therefore begin the comparative-historical analysis with this case.

Myanmar: History, Society, and Warfare

Previously known as Burma, Myanmar is located east of India and Bangladesh and was ruled as a nonintegral part of India for most of its colonial history. Ironically, Myanmar's strength was the main reason why the British conquered it. The Konbaung dynasty ruled precolonial Myanmar and began expanding to the west with the conquest of Arakan (1785), Manipur (1814), and Assam (1817–1819). In so doing, Konbaung rulers threatened British India, and British officials decided to protect their "Crown Jewel" by attacking the Konbaung dynasty during the First Anglo-Burmese War (1824–1826). After defeating the Konbaung dynasty, the British took control of Arakan, Manipur, Assam, and Tenasserim. Two decades later (1852), the British began the Second Anglo-Burmese War, in which they successfully gained control of the Pegu region linking Arakan to Tenasserim, thereby separating the Konbaung dynasty from the ocean. And due to growing concerns over French colonialism in Indochina, the British began the Third Anglo-Burmese War in 1885, thereby conquering all Myanmar.

The British incorporated the late Konbaung conquests of Assam and Manipur into India, and both remain part of India to this day. Although the remaining territories of the Konbaung dynasty were formally controlled by the Indian colonial administration, the British made Myanmar a separate, autonomous district. As a result, there were administrative links with India and Myanmar, Indians were free to migrate to Myanmar during British rule, but Myanmar remained a distinct region with its own colonial government, administration, and legislative assembly. In 1937, the British formalized this division by creating the Colony of Burma. Five years later, the British lost control of Myanmar to the Japanese, but they retook it by the end of the Second World War. In 1948, the country regained its independence.

Close to 70 percent of Myanmar's population self-identify as Bamar. In addition to speaking the Bamar language, Bamar are overwhelmingly Buddhist. Although dispersed more broadly, the Bamar population is concentrated in the Irrawaddy Valley, which runs down the center of the country and was the heartland of different precolonial Bamar kingdoms. Non-Bamar communities, in contrast, are concentrated in the country's more mountainous borderlands. Prior to British rule, Bamar states claimed authority over non-Bamar communities, and the extent of Bamar control depended largely on how far the communities were from the Irrawaddy Valley. Presently, over 100 recognized communities live in Myanmar.

Once in control of Myanmar, the British institutionalized different forms of rule that varied by region and community. Along the Myanmar coast, the British created a direct form of rule, and these regions became the most economically valuable regions of the colony and had the greatest colonial presence. Most notably, the coastal region became the "rice basket" of the British Empire and the colony's main center of trade. Given its peripheral location within precolonial kingdoms, the region's population was mostly non-Bamar. Because of the region's economic dynamism during the colonial period, however, many Bamar and Indians migrated to the region, resulting in the very mixed population that Furnivall (1948) famously described as a plural society. The British also ruled the former heartlands of the Konbaung dynasty directly, thereby exiling the Konbaung royal family and employing colonial officials to control the region's administration, legal system, and security forces. All remnants of the former Konbaung dynasty were effectively removed.

In contrast to the coastal regions and the Bamar heartland, the British employed indirect rule in the mountainous regions of northern and northeastern Myanmar and referred to them as the "Frontier Areas" (Bowerman 1946). In these regions, the British recognized "traditional" authorities and allowed them to maintain considerable administrative and legal autonomy within the colony. Without exception, the traditional authorities were non-Bamar and ruled in the name of their communities. In addition to the different form of rule, British officials forbid nonresidents from visiting the Frontier Areas without permission.

Different factors contributed to these contrasting forms of rule. Most notably, economic interests and the influx of large numbers of Indians promoted direct rule in the coastal regions. In the Bamar heartland, security and control were the dominant motives for establishing costly direct rule. Indeed, the British faced considerable resistance in this region, and officials concluded that indirect rule through Bamar authorities would further endanger British control and therefore created a particularly militarized form of direct rule (Callahan 2003: 23–25). In the Frontier Areas, two factors pushed the British to copy the form of rule in Northeast India's excluded areas. First, the British saw little economic value, and—after initial resistance—local authorities agreed to work with the British if allowed to maintain considerable autonomy. On top of this, officials were worried that Bamar anti-colonialism would spread to upland communities, something that influenced their decision to isolate the Frontier Areas.

Based on the pluralist index, Myanmar has the maximum score: Colonial censuses collected information on all five types of communal categories, some communities had reserved legislative seats, colonial primary schools provided education in multiple indigenous vernaculars, and Myanmar was not represented in Westminster. The colony's model of political community was pluralist in other ways as well. As noted previously, some regions had communalized indirect rule, a form of rule that gave communities political autonomy. In addition, the British recognized communities and institutionalized divisions through communal recruitment in the colonial security forces. Because the Bamar-led anticolonial movements threatened colonial control, the British stacked these forces with non-state communities (Callahan 2003: 35). Within the colonial police, for example, Bamar were underrepresented by 70 percent (Ray 2012). In the colonial military, the British formally excluded Bamar for most of the colonial period, and Indians and non-state communities made up the majority of soldiers. Among the non-state communities, Karens, Chins, and Kachins had their own units and provided the bulk of the colony's indigenous forces. Finally, Protestant missionaries were very active among some communities but had very limited influence among others, especially the Bamar, who strongly opposed missionary influence. And through vernacular education and colonial lobbying, the missionaries further strengthened communal divisions.

As several of these examples highlight, colonial pluralism in Myanmar was discriminatory in that it privileged non-state communities more than—and commonly at the expense of—Bamar. Recognizing this character, Gravers (1999) claims that the "British colonial model [in Myanmar]—'plural society'—was based on the principle of 'divide and rule'" (7), and Taylor (2009) notes that the British sought to legitimize colonial rule by protecting the rights of non-state communities against the Bamar (288). And in protecting and advantaging non-state communities, discriminatory pluralism promoted antagonistic and competitive relations between Bamar and other communities.

The threat of anticolonial resistance greatly influenced the discriminatory form of colonial pluralism, as many Bamar strongly opposed colonialism and the British viewed them as a severe threat because of their numerical strength, mobilizational capacity, and military prowess. This threat was very real and present throughout the colonial period: Bamar fought against the British militarily during the wars of colonial conquest, the British needed several years to gain control over Myanmar after formal conquest, a violent and widespread uprising against British rule occurred in the 1930s, and dacoity was a common form of personal resistance to British rule throughout the colonial period. In addition, Bamar began a nationalist movement by the early twentieth century and, shortly thereafter, organized their own paramilitary forces. This nationalist paramilitary eventually sent representatives to Japan for special training and helped the Japanese conquer Myanmar.

In contrast, non-Bamar communities posed little threat to British rule given their small size and greater readiness to accept British overrule, and the British systematically advantaged them through a variety of policies. Some communities, especially the Karens, actively sided with the British during the wars of colonial conquest, as missionary influence pushed them to help the British fight the Konbaung dynasty. Others, such as the Shan, fiercely resisted British rule and fought as members of the Konbaung dynasty against the British during the first war of conquest, but they refused to support the Konbaung during the subsequent wars of conquest and were willing to work with the British in exchange for regional autonomy. Colonial Myanmar therefore provided an ideal situation for so-called divide and rule, whereby the British received support from non-state communities to limit the anticolonial resistance of the state community. As postcolonial history shows, this situation provided considerable fodder for nationalist civil war.

Based on UCDP and EPR data, eight different communities have fought seventeen nationalist civil wars against the Bamar-dominated state between 1948 and 2020. As nationalist civil wars, all were over either secession or

TABLE 4.1. Nationalist Civil Wars in Myanmar

Community of Anti-State Combatants	Approximate Years of Active Warfare	Percent of Population	Number of Civil Wars
Mon	1949–1963, 1990–1996	2.0	2
Kachin	1949–1950, 1961–1992, 2011–2019	1.5	3
Karen	1949–2013	7.0	1
Karenni	1957, 1987–2005	1.8	2
Arakanese	1948–1957, 1964–1973, 1977, 2018–2020 1.7	1.7	2
Rohingya	1948–1961, 1973–1978, 1991–1994, 2016–2017	2.6	4
Shan	1959–1973, 1985–2015	9.0	2
Wa	1997	0.2	1

greater recognition and self-rule within Myanmar. Table 4.1 lists the communities involved in these wars, the years in which major fighting occurred, the demographic size of the non-state community, and the number of nationalist civil wars. In the remainder of this chapter, I explore whether British colonial pluralism contributed to these conflicts. Before analyzing particular conflicts, however, I consider how colonial pluralism affected Bamar national chauvinism, something that potentially contributed to all nationalist civil wars in postcolonial Myanmar.

Colonial Pluralism and Bamar National Chauvinism

All evidence suggests that discriminatory colonial pluralism played an important role promoting aggressive and exclusionary Bamar national chauvinism, which Gravers (1999) refers to as "nationalistic paranoia" and "fundamentalistic nationalism" (2, 22). By exiling the Konbaung royal family, removing Bamar from positions of power, and advantaging communities that had previously been ruled and sometimes enslaved by Bamar, British colonialism created widespread rage and resentment among Bamar and focused these popular emotions on taking back what was "rightfully" theirs while putting colonial "agents" in their place. Bamar nationalist understandings, in turn, were historical, viewing the Konbaung dynasty as an ideal and heroic polity. The nationalist movement focused on the race, language, and religion of Bamar as defining elements of the nation, thereby giving it an exclusive character. At an extreme, the Bamar nationalist movement explicitly recognized minorities who "collaborated" with the British as dangerous and degenerate "others" who were not true members of the nation.

Bamar nationalism gained considerable strength after the First World War and became an aggressive anticolonial force by the early 1930s with the founding of the Dobama movement. "Dobama" translates into "our Burma," and the nationalist movement asserted the place of Bamar as the rightful rulers of Myanmar and demanded the return of a Bamar-dominated state. Members of the movement accepted the title *thakin*, which means "master" in Bamar, to reassert their status, as they believed that British colonialism had removed them from their deserved places of power and made them impoverished and weak subjects of an illegitimate intruder.

Dobama leaders recognized the need to modernize Myanmar and decided to use Japan as an example to emulate. At the same time, they clearly drew on history and religion to popularize a myth-symbol complex describing Myanmar as a great and glorious Bamar civilization that was destroyed by the British and needed rejuvenation. They praised the Konbaung dynasty, held ceremonies on sacred Konbaung grounds, and pushed for policies—such as the repatriation of the bodies of the exiled king and queen—that emphasized the importance of their Konbaung heritage. The Konbaung kings, in turn, were Buddhist leaders, and their rule was perceived as making possible a society based on Buddhist principles. The Dobama movement therefore clearly incorporated Buddhism into Bamar nationalism. Finally, the Dobama leaders recognized a long Bamar literary tradition while noting that Bamar was a second- or third-class language in colonial Myanmar, and they sought to reinstate Bamar as the exclusive language of education, literature, and the public sector.

As Nemoto (2000) notes, the Dobama movement had a clear "other" that was used to define the Bamar nation, thereby juxtaposing "our Burma" (*dobama*) with an illegitimate and dangerous "their-Burma" (*thudo-bama*). Their-Burma consisted of the British and all communities that supported colonial rule. The latter included Indian shopkeepers and laborers, who Bamar associated with the British and perceived as taking away "their" jobs and money, and Bamar nationalism was vehemently anti-Indian. The Bamar nationalist movement also vilified indigenous non-state communities that held privileged positions within colonial institutions, especially the military and Burmese Legislative Council. Even worse, many of these minorities had converted to Christianity, making them both political collaborators and religious traitors. The educational advantages provided by Christian missionaries and the favorable treatment that colonial officials gave Christian subjects, in turn, made Bamar nationalists even more enraged and resentful over the privileged position of Christian minorities. In this way, colonial pluralism was a major source of Bamar resentment and rage against minorities and influenced the character of Bamar national chauvinism.

The importance of the "other" is clearly evident in the processes leading to the founding of the Dobama Association. In 1930, Bamar laborers took the jobs of Indian dockworkers after the latter went on strike, and the Indian workers insulted the Bamar when they returned to their jobs after reaching an agreement. The Bamar reacted to the insults by attacking and killing approximately 250 Indians (Yi 2018). In the midst of the violence, students and intellectuals founded the Dobama movement and mobilized support by noting how Bamar—with their glorious past—were now subordinate to and subject to the insults of lowly Indian "coolies." They therefore demanded the expulsion of the British and their "cronies" and the reconstruction of an independent Bamar state based on Buddhist principles.

In contrast to India's nationalist movement, the Dobama movement was aggressive and rejected pacifism, arguing that pacifism breeds subjugation and that force is the only route to freedom (Yi 2018: 5). Dobama leaders organized volunteer militias, or tats, to create a military force that could prepare Bamar to retake their country (Callahan 2003). These militias were an important source of military training, as Bamar were excluded from the military throughout most of the colonial period due to their perceived untrustworthiness. Even after the British opened the colonial military to Bamar, however, very few joined because Bamar nationalists viewed members of the colonial military as traitors.

Shortly before the Second World War, Dobama leaders and Japanese officials recognized their mutual interests, and 30 Dobama leaders traveled to Japan to complete guerrilla training. During the war, the Bamar forces formed the Burma Independence Army (BIA) and fought with the Japanese against the British and their non-Bamar supporters, and many Bamar soldiers took revenge on the thudo-bama by attacking villages and killing thousands. Eventually, the Dobama leaders realized that the Japanese were unwilling to grant Myanmar autonomy and were losing the war, and they therefore switched sides and helped the British reconquer Myanmar during the final months of the conflict. After retaking Myanmar, the British did not trust the Dobama leaders and excluded them from power in the initial postwar government. British officials soon realized that Myanmar must gain its independence quickly and that Bamar nationalists needed to play a leading role in the independence process. Through their interactions with the leader of the Dobama movement, Aung San, British officials gained greater trust in him. Colonial officials therefore began working with Bamar nationalists and prepared Aung San to take power. Minorities felt betrayed by this reversal, but Aung San worked diligently to assuage minority fears. Aung San's reconciliatory position, however, sparked opposition among Bamar nationalists, and a Bamar chauvinist assassinated him shortly before independence. Thakin Nu, a prominent leader of the Dobama movement and a devout Buddhist, subsequently became prime minister and led the country to independence, thereby completing the Dobama movement's path to power.

Nu subsequently rescinded agreements Aung San had made with most non-state communities, thereby confirming the fears of many non-state communities that he was a die-hard national chauvinist. In reaction, many demanded greater autonomy or secession. Using "Burman" to refer to "Bamar," Silverstein (1980) remarks, "What moved [non-state communities] were their common fears of Burmanization, loss of cultural identity, interference in their affairs by the national government and a belief that the Burmans were creating an internal colonial system in which they would not share the wealth of the country, the growth of the economy and their right of self-determination" (239). Similarly, Win (1994) notes that "the crux of all these [ethnic] problems is Myanmar chauvinism. The Burman tribe . . . are in the majority, and want perpetual domination" (41).

Bamar national chauvinism is therefore a key cause of nationalist civil war in Myanmar, and British colonial pluralism strengthened Bamar national chauvinism and made it more aggressive and vindictive. The case studies analyzed in the remainder of this chapter provide more specific evidence linking British colonial pluralism to Bamar national chauvinism. On top of this, the case studies highlight how British colonial pluralism contributed to nationalist civil warfare in two additional and influential ways: by making non-state communities more sensitive to Bamar national chauvinism and by empowering them to mobilize resistance.

The Karen Civil War

The first case study analyzes the Karen nationalist civil war. Relative to subsequent cases, I complete a more detailed analysis that describes pluralist policies and the ways they influenced this war. Subsequent case studies are less detailed and more comparative, thereby highlighting similarities with and differences between cases. I did not choose the Karen conflict because it is the most typical case; it is not. Instead, I begin with it because multiple pluralist policies clearly affected the conflict, thereby highlighting different ways in which colonial pluralism can affect nationalist civil war.

The Karen civil war began during the independence period and continued nearly nonstop until 2012. By 2012, between 15,000 and 70,000 soldiers and combatants had died, an unknown number of noncombatants had lost their lives, and government violence and security measures had displaced nearly all Karen civilians. After the 2021 coup, Karen nationalists resumed fighting, and the war continues at the time of writing.

The most proximate cause of the Karen nationalist civil war was disagreement over communal power and autonomy during the lead-up to independence. Karens benefited from reserved seats in the colonial legislature and had their own military units, and missionaries had great influence on the community and helped many Karens climb to the top of the communal hierarchy by the late colonial period. As independence approached, Bamar national chauvinists demanded the replacement of all pluralist policies with more assimilationist policies and insisted that they gain complete control over the postcolonial nation-state (Callahan 2003: 120). And because of their privileged position in the colonial hierarchy, Bamar national chauvinists targeted Karens as a severe threat to the nation. Karens strongly opposed Bamar national chauvinism. Seeing how other communities in colonial Myanmar received great autonomy through indirect rule, Karen leaders requested that the British create an autonomous Karen homeland to protect Karens from Bamar national chauvinists. In the end, the British did not support Karen demands.

In reaction to this decision and continued Bamar aggression, Karen leaders transformed their main communal association—the Karen National Association (KNA)—into a nationalist organization—the Karen National Union—and mobilized in pursuit of an independent Karen homeland. Shortly thereafter, ethnic violence erupted between Bamar and Karens, with Bamar civilians and members of Union Military Police attacking Karen villages during Christmas celebrations and killing nearly 100 people. Given suspected government complicity and deep communal division in the Myanmar military, Karen soldiers deserted and formed the military wing of the Karen National Union, the Karen National Defence Organisation, and open conflict between Karen and government forces began in January 1949.

As this description shows, the most proximate cause of the war was conflict over pluralist policies. To more fully understand how colonial pluralism led to this conflict, however, it is necessary to analyze three key aspects of colonial pluralism: missionary influence, communal legislative representation, and Karen military units. These policies helped create a powerful Karen nationalist frame, pitted Karens against Bamar over the communal character of the postcolonial nation-state, and provided Karens with vital resources that they ultimately used to fight a long nationalist civil war.

PROTESTANT MISSIONARY INFLUENCE AMONG KARENS

American Baptists began their mission in Myanmar in 1813, more than a decade before Great Britain began to colonize the region. Early missionary efforts to gain followers failed, but their luck changed after a missionary bought a Karen slave to free him. This former slave accepted Christianity and subsequently helped the American Baptists establish a mission among Karens. Because of their success, other missionaries followed, and missionaries greatly shaped Karen social relations. These missionaries contributed to the nationalist civil war in four main ways: They were instrumental in the construction of a Karen national consciousness, increased conflict between Karens and Bamar, helped organize Karens politically, and provided Karens with key mobilizational resources. Along these lines, Keyes (1977) notes that "the activities of the Christian missionaries among the Karen must be recognized as perhaps the most important factor in the development of a Karen national movement" (56).

The fact that a Karen nationalist movement fought for an independent homeland over several decades suggests that many Karens have a strong sense of nationhood, yet in the early 1800s Karens lacked almost all characteristics that are commonly associated with nations: They spoke several languages, practiced multiple religions, lacked a history of statehood, and had very localized political identities (Jørgensen 1997: vi). It therefore comes as little surprise that there is no evidence of an overriding "Karen" collective identity when the Baptists founded their mission. Indeed, there was no term to refer to Karen peoples, and American Baptist missionaries coined "Karen" to refer to a diverse group of non-Bamar peoples. The missionaries wore communal lenses and believed that Karens were a distinct "race" and "nation," something that was influenced by growing attention to nation and race in the United States and Europe as well as missionary interests in separating Karens from Bamar to facilitate their conversion. At the same time, the missionaries saw the Karen "nation" as primitive and needing assistance to gain the attributes of an "advanced" and "modern" nation. As one prominent missionary remarked, "From a loose aggregation of clans we shall weld them into a nation yet" (Smeaton 1920: 19). Another missionary noted the success of their nation-building endeavors: "These scattered tribes were becoming a united people. Instead of each clan acting for itself, they proposed to unite; and this was undoubtedly the legitimate result of the new life from the Deliverer. Satan divides and destroys. Jesus unites and saves" (Bunker 1902: 237).

Several missionaries worked hard to unify Karens. Only a few years after arriving, American Baptists made the first Karen flag (Mason 1862: 267). They also spearheaded the organization of the KNA, which had the stated goals of promoting Karen unity and looking out for the well-being of the community (Gravers 1999: 24, 148). Over the next century, this association proved very influential and eventually transformed into the leading nationalist organization. Missionaries also standardized three Karen languages and thereby helped create a common linguistic base on which to build an imagined community. As one British official remarked, "No people can long survive the extinction of their language. . . . The missionaries, headed by the great Judson, have rescued the Karen language from oblivion and given it a certain permanency by reducing it to writing in the Burmese character" (Smeaton 1920: 219–20).

Although missionaries were delighted that their linguistic work helped build a Karen community that could resist Bamarization, the main reason for their standardization of Karen languages was something very different: It made the gospel more accessible to Karens. To allow Karens to read the scripture, in turn, American Baptist missionaries made an enormous effort to educate Karens through the establishment of schools, and many flocked to them. This education was in one of the three Karen languages used by missionaries, meaning that Karens learned standard dialects shared by many others and made investments in these languages. Because of the success of the American

Baptists, other Christian missionaries set up missions among Karens and copied the techniques of the American Baptists, thereby expanding missionary influence even further. French Catholic missionaries in the area, for example, differed from their missions elsewhere by focusing on providing education and offering vernacular education (Societé des Missions Étrangères 1890: 202).

Through missionary education, Karens went from being illiterate to among the most educated community in colonial Myanmar. Mass literacy, in turn, gave Karens access to literary depictions of the Karen community as real and important and therefore helped strengthen a sense of Karenness. Lewis (1924) notes this in his early analysis of processes affecting the assimilation of Karens into Bamar society, concluding that "the new literature is indefinitely postponing the assimilation of the Karen" (84–85). The Baptist missionaries established their first press shortly after founding their mission among Karens, and the press was prolific, printing tens of millions of pages of material in Karen languages. Most notably, the missionaries established the *Morning Star* newspaper in 1842, which was written in Sgaw Karen and stayed in circulation until the Second World War. Articles from the newspaper presented issues from a Karen national perspective, provided a history of the Karen people, and emphasized the importance of community. One article from 1855, for example, claimed that the Karen were once a great nation, declined after becoming illiterate, but would reunify once again to take the place that they deserve (Mason 1860: 75–76). Another from 1916, entitled "The Karen Language and Karen Loyalty," described how language is the basis of the Karen identity and demanded respect for it as well as for all Karens (American Baptist Historical Society 2015).

As the previous examples highlight, missionaries and the missionary press played an important role popularizing myths supporting a Karen consciousness. American missionaries were extremely interested in Karen customs and culture, as a knowledge of both proved vital to evangelical success. Dr. Francis Mason (1870), who helped translate the Bible into Karen, also collected and published Karen myths and traditions. On this, he writes: "The Karens had no books, but I found they had an abundance of traditions, and I went to work collecting all I could find of every description. I pretty well exhausted the Tavoy Karens from one end of the province to the other, for whenever I found a man who knew something that others did not, I had it written down on the spot" (276–77). Although gathering many myths of the origins of Karens, Mason popularized one version describing how Karens migrated from the Gobi Desert thousands of years ago, and this myth became part of the Karen myth-symbol complex. By giving this myth a scientific character and describing the origins of the Karens in concrete terms, Mason and other missionaries strengthened a Karen national consciousness (Rajah 2002).

In addition to the ideal bases of community, missionaries shaped the more physical foundations on which a Karen consciousness could flourish by promoting interactions among Karens from all over colonial Burma. One way this occurred was through schools, especially secondary schools that brought Karens together from different regions. In addition, churches emerged as a central social institution and allowed Karens to interact with one another. As one colonial official described, "The local church takes the place of the clan-unit, or village. These churches are federally united into associations or missions, which look up to the missionary as their leader. These associations take the place of the confederacies of clans" (Smeaton 1920: 196). Missionaries and their converts organized regular meetings bringing pastors and other Christians together to talk about local and regional affairs, and annual meetings for all Karen Christians assembled the leaders of the Karen community to discuss church governance for the entire community. Such meetings played an important role making the imagined Karen community seem real, especially since the little contact between Karen clans that existed prior to the arrival of the missionaries was often conflictual. One British official noted and clearly described the unifying effects of the meetings, writing: "Opportunities are thus given for the Karen to have friendly and social gatherings, which serve to cement a better understanding among the different tribes, who for many years were jealous and suspicious of each other" (McMahon 1876: 255). Finally, Baptist missionaries worked closely with Karens to found the KNA in 1881 with the goal of increasing Karen national unity (Gravers 1999: 24, 148). The KNA was the main Karen political organization over the next 70 years and served as a de facto political party after Karens gained reserved legislative seats.

Importantly, missionary influence varied greatly among Karens, and only a minority of Karens possesses a strong Karen national consciousness (Buadaeng 2007; Jørgensen 1997). If missionaries were the main cause of ethnic consciousness, we would therefore expect that the strongest Karen nationalists were most influenced by the missions, and the evidence supports this expectation. Missionaries had much greater influence on the Sgaw Karen, and nearly all leaders of the Karen nationalist movement have been Sgaw even through only 15 percent of Karens are Sgaw (Harriden 2002; Stern 1968; Thawnghmung 2012). In contrast, non-Christian and non-Sgaw-speaking Karens commonly oppose the nationalist movement (Thawnghmung 2012).

In addition to contributing to a Karen national consciousness, missionaries affected Karen relations with Bamar by increasing Bamar anger and resentment against Karens. One reason for this is that many Bamar resented that Karens sought to isolate themselves from Bamar, rejected Buddhism, and converted to Christianity. As noted previously, Buddhism is a core element on which Bamar-ness is based, and many Bamar therefore saw Christianity as a severe threat. Given this situation, many Bamar viewed Christian Karens as traitorous stooges who rejected and opposed Bamar nationalism and embraced the colonizers. Christianity therefore played an important role in making Karens despised thudo-bama.

The targeting of Karens as a threat to the Bamar nation was also influenced by the impact of missionaries on the status of Karens. Whereas Karens had been marginalized and even enslaved prior to British colonialism, missionary influence allowed Karens to climb the social ladder and receive many of the best white-collar jobs available to non-Europeans. The main reason for this mobility was missionary education, which transformed an illiterate community into one of the most educated in the colony. Given its focus on disciplines taught in British schools and its teaching of English, colonial officials recognized missionary education as vastly superior to the Buddhist education that most Bamar received, and Karens therefore had much better access to jobs. As one missionary remarked with notable pride in 1931: "Risen from a place of servitude and fear without a written language or any chance of growth, they now occupy positions and honour throughout the country, in high Government positions and in places of responsibility and trust in business enterprises of all kinds. A large percentage of teachers of the province, in Government as well as mission schools, are Karens. The positions of trust of various kinds occupied by Karens, are out of all proportion to their numbers as compared with the other races of the country" (American Baptist Foreign Mission Society 1931: 5).

Missionaries also improved Karen mobility in additional ways: They actively lobbied colonial officials to protect Karen interests and influenced colonial views of the Karens. Missionaries repeatedly presented Karens as "loyal" subjects who strongly supported British colonial rule. For this, they reminded the British that missionaries had led their Karen communities to fight with the British during their wars of colonial conquest. Given the loyalty and support of Karens as well as the special access missionary leaders had to colonial officials, many colonial officials gave special treatment to Karens. And just like Karen acceptance of Christianity, the mobility of Karens and the special treatment they received made them thudo-bama in the eyes of the Bamar.

COMMUNAL LEGISLATIVE REPRESENTATION

Through their influence, missionaries affected British colonial policies in ways that recognized, accommodated, and empowered Karens. That being said, the British were predisposed to pluralist policies by the time they had conquered all Myanmar, and Bamar-led anticolonial resistance created incentives to recognize and empower Karens. Formal colonial policies, in turn, had similar effects as Protestant missionary influence. Most notably, they strengthened a Karen national consciousness, promoted conflict with Bamar, and provided Karens with important mobilizational resources that helped organize the nationalist movement.

Although in different ways than the missionaries, British colonialism contributed to a widely held Karen national identity. Colonial censuses made

"Karen" a legitimate category of community and even sparked contentious debates that hardened boundaries between the Bamar and Karens. With growing Bamar nationalism in the late 1920s, for example, Karen and Bamar politicians debated who should be categorized as Karen in the colonial census (Indian Statutory Committee 1929: 37–38). The boundaries of this communal category were quite blurry given great social diversity among Karens and that fact that many "Karens" had assimilated to different extents into Bamar culture. The censuses, in turn, counted the number of Karens in Myanmar, and Bamar politicians argued that many non-Karens were "miscategorized" as Karen in the census. The main reason why Bamar politicians were paying attention to census numbers, however, was because it had implications on the representation of Karens in the colonial legislature. And communal legislative representation both strengthened a Karen national identity and proved a major source of conflict between Karens and Bamar.

During the colonial period, officials estimated that Karens made up 10 percent of the total population, making them the second largest ethnic community behind the Bamar majority. Due in large part to their size and location in directly ruled regions of colonial Myanmar, Karens were the only "indigenous" community that received reserved seats in the Burmese Legislative Council.[1] Karen communal representation began informally with the appointment of one representative in 1916 and was formalized and expanded to include 5 seats in 1923 and 12 seats in 1935. Legislative representation organized Karens to look out for the well-being of their community and continued the work that missionaries had begun in nationalizing Karens. Tellingly, Dr. San C. Po, the first Karen representative on the Legislative Council, is recognized as the father of the Karen nation and wrote what is commonly referred to as the "bible" on Karen nationalism after over a decade of fighting against Bamar politicians in pursuit of Karen interests in the Legislative Council (Fink 2001). Indeed, Karen leaders point to the reservation of legislative seats as awakening Karens as a nation (Burma Reforms Committee 1921: 232, 238). And in his early analysis of Karen-Bamar relations, Lewis (1924) notes that Karens had continued to assimilate into Bamar culture after the onset of colonial rule but that—in combination with Karen missionary literature—the reservation of legislative seats played a decisive role halting this process (96).

In addition to creating a stronger Karen national consciousness, the reservation of legislative seats for Karens politicized community and pitted Karens and Bamar against one another in ways that contributed to nationalist

---

1. The line between indigenous and non-indigenous was blurry. Mixed Burmans also received reserved seats and were arguably much more indigenous than foreign. And although Indians were considered non-indigenous and received reserved seats, indigenous Muslims were categorized as Indian.

conflict. Even before its formalization, communal legislative representation caused conflict between Bamar and Karens. During public meetings in 1921 that considered whether a formal system of communal representation should be created, Karen leaders supported reserving seats, but Bamar nationalists decried this policy as a divisive ploy to weaken the anticolonial movement (Burma Reforms Committee 1921: 21–24). In the heated debate that followed, Bamar organized a public protest against the policy and physically prevented Karens from testifying at the meetings (Keenan 2017).

Once formalized, communal legislative representation became an even more divisive force. The policy strengthened communal boundaries by recognizing the Karens as a distinct national community and empowering them to look out for the well-being of their community in the legislature. A review of the minutes of the Legislative Council proceedings highlights this communalization of politics by showing that Karen representatives refrained from general discussions but spoke up to pursue Karen interests. Karen representatives, for example, inquired about the representation of Karens in the Military Police (Burma Legislative Council 1932: 583), the Judicial Services (Burma Legislative Council 1936: 146, 262), the Legislative Council (Burma Reforms Committee 1921: 22, 78), the Imports Advisory Committee (Burma Legislative Council 1946: 277), and education and teacher training (Burma Legislative Council 1938: 3). They also demanded greater funding of Karen schools (Burma Legislative Council 1938: 5–7), the use of Karen languages in schools and the government (Burma Legislative Council 1929: 197), and the suppression of crimes against Karens (Burma Legislative Council 1929). The political demands of Karen representatives, in turn, increased the concerns of Bamar politicians over the privileged position of Karens and pushed them to protect Bamar interests, commonly at the expense of Karens (Burma Legislative Council 1928: 95; 1929: 43, 60, 413; 1930: 130, 368; 1932: 298; 1935: 169; 1936: 269–70).

The communalization of the Legislative Council, in turn, greatly intensified intercommunal antagonisms. In addition to resenting minorities as illegitimate thudo-bama who were only concerned about their own community, many Bamar nationalists were enraged at them for opposing Bamar interests. In an electoral system that prevented Bamar from ever having a majority, minority representatives consistently voted with colonial officials to oppose Bamar demands, and this practice strengthened popular Bamar anger by solidifying stereotypes of Karens as colonial stooges (Cady 1958: 256–57; Maung 1990: 8). For example, many Bamar were furious when a Karen representative argued in a debate that Myanmar was not prepared for independence and required many more years of British tutelage (Smith 1991: 50–51).

At the same time that Bamar were angry and resentful, many Karens feared what they saw as growing Bamar national chauvinism and attempts to weaken the Karen community. Karen representatives therefore assertively demanded not only the maintenance of Karen legislative representation but the expansion of Karen power and autonomy. Most importantly, Karen politicians observed the indirect form of rule present among Karennis, who many Karens viewed as their brethren, and began lobbying for an indirect form of rule that would make possible self-rule for the entire Karen community. This demand only intensified Bamar anger and resentment, especially since Bamar formed the majority of the population in the regions that Karen leaders claimed as their homeland. Karen self-rule was therefore seen as another ploy to make Bamar strangers in their own land. Most Bamar politicians were therefore unwilling to make any concessions to Karens and, in fact, desired the removal of all special recognition, accommodation, and empowerment that the Karen community had received under British rule. The resulting conflict over Karen power and autonomy was a central cause of the civil war.

KAREN MILITARY RECRUITMENT

Throughout most of the colonial period, Bamar were excluded from the colonial military, which was the major source of power in colonial Myanmar given the very militarized form of direct rule used throughout much of the colony. Along with Indians and two other indigenous minority communities (Chin and Kachin), Karens had their own military units and were greatly overrepresented in the colonial military. Evidence suggests that discriminatory military recruitment contributed to the Karen nationalist civil war in three influential ways.

First, inequalities in the military promoted strong grievances and competition over its control, and this further strengthened conflict between Karens and Bamar. Given their exclusion form the colonial military and their resentment of the colonial military after they were allowed to join it, many Bamar organized and joined militias, and the militias were a major force behind the rise of a more assertive, exclusive, and combative Bamar national chauvinism in the 1930s that clearly demarcated between "collaborators" and "nationalists" (Callahan 2003: 37). The Bamar nationalist militias, in turn, formed the bulk of the BIA, which fought with the Japanese to expel the British from Myanmar. And after the Second World War, the composition of the military proved a difficult and contentious issue. Although Bamar forces eventually switched support to the British, the British did not trust them and disbanded Bamar militias, stacked the postwar military with minority troops who had supported the British throughout the war, and placed the army under the control of two Karens. After long and difficult negotiations, the British agreed to incorporate Bamar militias into the military, although they kept them separate from non-Bamar units (Callahan 2003: 95–96). At independence, two distinct militaries were therefore present, and Bamar nationalists greatly resented the powerful minority forces and sought to disband them. The resulting conflict between

Bamar and Karen forces played an important role sparking the nationalist civil war by leading to the mass desertion of Karen soldiers.

The second way in which discriminatory military recruitment contributed to nationalist civil warfare was by promoting open military conflict between Bamar and Karens, which further intensified the Bamar views of Karens as thudo-bama and strengthened animosity between Karen and Bamar communities. The British used minority military units to combat Bamar anticolonial forces, with Karens assisting the British militarily during the wars of colonial conquest, helping to contain the Saya San Rebellion of 1932, and fighting Bamar and their Japanese supporters during the Second World War. The resulting violence enflamed relations between Bamar and Karens and cemented Bamar views of Karens as dangerous collaborators who had no place in the great Bamar nation. Notably, tension over minority military support during the wars of colonial conquest had weakened by the turn of the twentieth century, but communal legislative representation rekindled these antagonisms (Lewis 1924). Alternatively, minority military assistance against Bamar anticolonial movements in the 1930s and 1940s occurred after the colonial legislature had institutionalized intercommunal contention, and this assistance further intensified conflictual relations. After minority troops played an important role putting down the Saya San Rebellion, for example, the Bamar nationalist movement focused on the minorities that collaborated with the British as a dangerous and degenerate threat and increasingly characterized them as "thudo-bama" (Callahan 2003: 36). The conflict during the Second World War was even more polarizing. Karens and other minority communities supported the British and joined the guerrilla intelligence unit "V Force," which included 16,000 soldiers by the end of the war (Callahan 2003: 71). The Japanese trained militia leaders, and members of Bamar nationalist militias formed the BIA in their effort to expel the British, thereby pitting Bamar and Karen soldiers against one another in bloody combat (Callahan 2003: 75).

The third and most direct way through which the overrepresentation of Karens in the colonial military contributed to nationalist civil warfare was by providing Karens with valuable resources needed to wage and maintain a war against the postcolonial state. In addition to having their own military units, Karens were greatly overrepresented in the upper levels of the colonial military at independence, this despite efforts by Bamar nationalists to Bamarize the military. Given the communal split in the military at independence and efforts by Bamar officials to take control of it, Karen soldiers were targets and suffered hostilities and threats, and conflict between Bamar and Karen soldiers erupted. As a result of this and the continued attacks on Karen civilians, Karen soldiers—including many officers—deserted and formed the Karen National Defence Organisation in 1947, thereby creating the military wing of the Karen National Association. Weapons, soldiers, and skilled military leaders, in turn, allowed Karen nationalists to mount and sustain a bloody civil war.

———

All in all, the Karen nationalist civil war highlights five complementary processes through which colonial pluralism promoted nationalist civil war: (1) colonial pluralism contributed to an aggressive Bamar national chauvinism that targeted Karens, (2) pluralist policies and missionary influence politicized and nationalized the Karen community in ways that made them sensitive to Bamar national chauvinism, (3) British colonial pluralism promoted conflict between Bamar and Karens, (4) discriminatory colonial pluralism created expectations for Karen power and self-rule, and (5) colonial pluralism provided Karens with diverse resources that allowed them to quickly organize a nationalist movement and fight a civil war. In this regard, colonial pluralism was the core component of the process leading to nationalist civil warfare; if you remove it, the Karen nationalist civil warfare likely would not have occurred.

A more detailed counterfactual analysis supports this conclusion. The Karen civil war is a classic example of a conflict over the form of the postcolonial nation-state, with Karen nationalists demanding greater political and cultural autonomy and Bamar nationalists pursuing a centralized state controlled by Bamar in the name of the Bamar. If precolonial conditions promoted the Karen civil war, one would expect that some combination of assertive Karen nationalism, Bamar resentment and fear of Karens, and intercommunal antipathy and competition would have occurred without the British colonial interlude. Available evidence does not support this view. Prior to British rule, Karens held a marginalized position within the sociopolitical system. While their position could have motivated collective mobilization to counter Bamar dominance, there is no evidence of this ever occurring prior to British rule, largely because Karens were not in a position to counter or threaten Bamar dominance in any way. Karens, for example, lived in the same region as Bamar and were dependent on them, and the Bamar had an extremely powerful military force that could easily overwhelm Karens. Of even greater importance, Karens were not organized into a coherent political community prior to British rule and did not share an overriding Karen communal identity that could frame and inspire such a movement (Jørgensen 1997: vi).

Although a Karen political community might have strengthened and organized a military to counter Bamar might without a history of British rule, this scenario seems extremely unlikely given the influence of colonial pluralism on the formation of a Karen nationalist frame and the organization and militarization of the Karen community. While colonial censuses made "Karen" a legitimate category of community, legislative representation helped organize Karens to look out for the well-being of all Karens, and Karen military units strengthened the divide and animosity between Karens and Bamar and empowered Karens to resist Bamar dominance. Missionaries also played an important role molding Karens into a powerful political community. And although missionaries were not formal colonial agents, their influence depended on British rule: Whereas the British allowed missionaries to work in Myanmar and provided them assistance, precolonial leaders forbid missionaries from proselytizing and threatened to execute converts.

The Shan, Karenni, and Kachin Nationalist Civil Wars

The Karen conflict highlights important mechanisms through which colonial pluralism promoted nationalist civil war, but the case lacks the pluralist policy that was the most influential cause of nationalist conflict in Myanmar: communalized indirect rule. The British did not rule Karens indirectly, and indirect rule only contributed to the Karen conflict—indirectly—by providing an example of communal self-rule that inspired Karen leaders. Several other communities in colonial Myanmar were ruled indirectly in a way making possible communal self-rule, and this form of rule promoted a common sequence leading to nationalist civil war: Non-state communities demanded the retention of communal self-rule after independence, the Bamar state refused and forcibly integrated regions into the Bamar nation-state, and the removal of communal power and autonomy triggered nationalist civil war.

THE SHAN NATIONALIST CIVIL WAR

The Shan are one of several Tai-speaking groups in Southeast Asia, with others located in Thailand, China, India, Laos, Malaysia, and Vietnam. The Shan migrated to Myanmar hundreds of years ago and established dozens of relatively small "princely states" in the hills and mountains north and east of the Bamar heartland. These lands were sparsely populated by non-Bamar, and the Shan established feudalistic states controlling these peoples. Shan polities were rarely autonomous, however, and generally paid allegiance to one or more regional powers. At the onset of British rule, there were over 40 Shan states.

From early on, the southern Shan states had close contact with Bamar, and many assimilated into Bamar culture. In fact, assimilated Shan founded the Ava Kingdom in the late fourteenth century, which controlled much of contemporary Myanmar. Both the Toungoo Empire and the Konbaung dynasty had limited control over the Shan states, with Shan princes supporting the kingdoms in exchange for autonomy. During the early Konbaung period, Shan rulers worked closely with the Konbaung imperial state and actively helped the Konbaung dynasty fight the British during the first war of conquest. After the war, however, the king reduced Shan autonomy in an effort to strengthen the state, and these reforms greatly weakened Shan support for the Konbaung king.

The British were interested in controlling the Shan states to prevent French influence and to open a trade route to Yunnan. After the third war of conquest,

British officials therefore sent an expeditionary force to the region (Mangrai 1965: 52–54). Although some Shan fought British incursions, the British military was powerful, and most Shan princes were open to British influence, especially because the British promised that the princes would retain autonomy if they allowed free trade and respected British interests (Mangrai 1965: 90). The British therefore quickly and easily established an indirect form of rule whereby the princes retained power over local police, law, services, and administration. Copying the Scheduled Areas Act of 1874, which established the excluded areas in Northeast India, the British proclaimed the Shan states as part of the Frontier Areas that were administered separately from "Burma Proper" with minimal colonial interference and in which people from other regions were not allowed to travel without colonial permission (Ferguson 2021: 30; Sadan 2013: 168). The main motives for this form of rule were the low cost of indirect rule and fear of Bamar anticolonialism spreading to the Shan.

Prior to British rule, the Shan were politically and culturally divided, and few Shan shared a communal or national consciousness. Indeed, "Shan" is a Bamar term used to refer to the diverse population in what is presently northwestern Myanmar (Ferguson 2021). According to Ferguson (2021), British colonial pluralism played a very important role creating a Shan national consciousness (40–45). Charles Crosthwaite, the Chief Commissioner of Burma between 1887 and 1890, noted the lack of unity among the Shan and "saw the British administration as a step toward creating a unified Shan country" (Ferguson 2021: 42). To create this unity, the British recognized the Shan as a community, counted them on censuses, created a special school for the sons of Shan princes that used a very nationalistic Shan curriculum, and—especially—institutionalized Shan self-rule in the Frontier Areas. A very important reason why the British strengthened Shan communal frames and provided Shan with power and autonomy, in turn, was to drive a wedge between Shan and Bamar and thereby weaken the anticolonial threat.

After the Second World War, Shan princes—and the British administrators who had worked with them—actively lobbied for the retention of Shan autonomy, much to the chagrin of Bamar national chauvinists. Due to these efforts, the British allowed the Shan princes to retain considerable political autonomy at independence and gave them (as well as Karennis, another community in the Frontier Areas) the option to secede from Myanmar after ten years of independence. Before independence, however, Shan princes and Bamar leaders had reconciled many of their differences, with Bamar leaders pledging to maintain Shan autonomy in exchange for support (Brown 1988: 69). As part of the entente, a Shan prince was named the first president of independent Myanmar. Although the president's power was primarily symbolic, he was able to use his influence to placate Shan fears. In addition, the Shan princes were conservative leaders of feudalistic polities, students and peasants demanded reforms, and the Myanmar government helped protect

Shan elites during the unstable independence process (Brown 1988: 70; Callahan 2003: 157; Ferguson 2021: 66–67).

The actual Shan nationalist civil war began a decade after independence and was led by a handful of different organizations that all demanded an independent Shan state. Two proximate factors led to the rise of these organizations and, thereby, the nationalist civil war. First, Myanmar leaders were increasingly worried that the Shan would exercise their right to secede after ten years of independence and began undermining the position of the Shan princes, beginning with smear campaigns and subsequently removing their powers completely (Brown 1988: 69–70; Ferguson 2021; Yawnghwe 2010: 107–9). These policies were not popular and pushed many Shan to demand the use of the independence clause. As Ferguson (2021) notes, many Shan saw the removal of local autonomy "as yet another critical step toward military and cultural Burmanization of the area," and this resentment motivated the nationalist movement (72). Second, thousands of Bamar troops had entered the region after independence to combat hostile forces (Burmese communists and KMT troops after their expulsion from China) and subsequently ruled the region in a violent and heavy-handed manner (Callahan 2003: 155–57; Yawnghwe 2010: 106). In addition to the hardships that they imposed on the local population, the presence of Bamar soldiers was a sign that Shan autonomy—which was the rule throughout the colonial period and was expected by many Shan—had been removed by the hands of violent and disrespectful Bamar. Thus, with their autonomy removed and living under Bamar military rule, the autonomy and protection provided by the British caused many Shan to view the period of British rule as a "Golden Age" (Ferguson 2021: 50; Yawnghwe 2010: 75). And to regain autonomy, students organized nationalist associations, and police defectors and ex-soldiers joined them to begin armed nationalist conflict in 1959.

As this short history shows, colonial pluralism affected the Shan civil war in very different ways than the Karen civil war. In contrast with the Karens, the Shan did not have any reserved seats in the Burmese Legislative Council. In fact, being in the Frontier Areas, the Shan were not eligible to participate in the council in any way. Moreover, Buddhism was popular among the Shan prior to British rule, and Christian missionary influence among the Shan was limited. In combination with their isolation, limited missionary influence hindered educational and economic development among the Shan, and the Bamar therefore did not resent them as colonial whippersnappers. That being said, Bamar nationalists did resent Shan as collaborators who had unfairly gained autonomy under British rule (Ferguson 2021: 51).

As this last point suggests, another important difference played a central role in the Shan nationalist civil war: The British ruled the Shan through an extreme form of indirect rule that nationalized the Shan and focused their attention on self-rule. Prior to British rule, Shan polities were vassal states with limited autonomy, and the Shan lacked political and cultural unity and commonly fought one another (Ferguson 2021). The extreme form of British indirect rule, however, strengthened an idea of "Shanland" as an ancient and powerful state on par with the Konbaung dynasty, thereby causing many Shan to view Shanland as "a bona fide sovereign nation-state that deserves a place in the international order" (Ferguson 2021: 64). Even more, the British created the Frontier Areas to isolate non-Bamar from Bamar anticolonialism and stop the process of Bamarization, and this form of protective isolationism nourished a fear of Bamar rule. In contrast, Bamar leaders—who noted that Shan regions had historically been part of Bamar kingdoms—viewed themselves as the rightful rulers of the Shan and sought to integrate them more fully into the postcolonial nation-state (Ferguson 2021: 51). Indeed, Bamar nationalists commonly viewed Shan autonomy as illegitimate and resulting from colonial divide-and-rule policies. They therefore demanded the removal of Shan autonomy, which sparked a civil war.

In addition to creating powerful expectations for autonomy and fear of Bamar rule, indirect rule also provided important mobilizational resources. This form of rule created a decentralized administrative structure that Shan leaders could use to mobilize the nationalist movement. It also provided military resources that proved vital to the nationalist conflict. Although the Shan did not have their own military regiments like Karens, they were greatly overrepresented in the colonial military during the Second World War, when 10,000 Shan soldiers fought with the British against Japanese and BIA forces (Callahan 2003: 27). After the war, Shan princes—as the customary authorities of the system of indirect rule—recruited these soldiers into their own security forces (Callahan 2003: 156). And when the Myanmar government removed the powers of Shan princes in 1959, members of the princes' security forces joined the nationalist movement (Ferguson 2021: 72).

Communalized indirect rule is therefore at the heart of the process leading to nationalist civil war. It helped forge a strong Shan national consciousness, promoted expectations for self-rule, strengthened resentment against Bamar rule, and provided Shan with the ability to fight for autonomy. At the same time, Shan indirect rule increased Bamar resentment against the Shan, with Bamar nationalists targeting them as thudo-bama who had sold out the Bamar to gain favors from the British. Communalized indirect rule, in turn, is one important aspect of colonial pluralism. Given the centrality of colonial pluralism in the processes leading to nationalist civil war, it is unlikely the nationalist civil war would have occurred without it.

THE KACHIN AND KARENNI NATIONALIST CIVIL WARS

Although the Shan are the largest community in the Frontier Areas, Chin, Kachin, Karennis, and Wa also live in the region and have fought wars against the Bamar state. Of these, Kachin, Karennis, and Wa have fought nationalist civil wars over secession, and the Chin have fought to create a plural and federal state that provides non-state communities with a high degree of self-rule within Myanmar. In this section, I focus on the Kachin and Karennis and explore how communalized indirect rule contributed to these nationalist conflicts.

The Kachin live in the Kachin Hills in the extreme North of Myanmar wedged between India and China. Kachin speak several different languages, although one—Jinghpaw—is the dominant written language. "Kachin" is therefore a regionally based and inclusive umbrella category that unites diverse communities but that is most closely associated with Jinghpaw speakers (Sadan 2013: 176). The Kachin make up 1.5 percent of the total Myanmar population.

A nationalist civil war between Kachin nationalists and the Myanmar state began in 1949 and ended the following year. In 1961, a second and much more violent conflict began, and it lasted until 1992. Although limited violence continued after this date, a third nationalist civil war began in 2011 and continues at the time of writing.

British colonial pluralism influenced the Kachin nationalist civil wars in three main ways. Like the Shan, the Kachin were located in the Frontier Areas, received great autonomy during the colonial period, and were effectively isolated from the rest of colonial Myanmar. And when the postcolonial government ended indirect rule, the Kachin rebelled. The loss of autonomy at the hands of Bamar national chauvinists is therefore at the heart of processes leading to the wars.

Communal military recruitment also increased conflict between Kachin and Bamar and provided Kachin with important military and organizational resources. The British considered the Kachin a "martial" race and created a Kachin battalion, something that helped instill a sense of Kachinness among soldiers (Sadan 2013: 234–37). Similar to Karens, these forces fought Bamar during both the Saya Rebellion and the Second World War, with the BIA committing atrocities against Kachin communities. As Sadan (2013) notes, the Second World War "became a battle for local [Kachin] autonomy from both Burmese and Japanese nationalist incorporation" (258). And with weapons and military training, the Kachin were able to effectively fight a nationalist civil war despite their relatively small size.

Kachin are also similar to Karens in that Baptist missionaries contributed to the conflict. In fact, missionary influence was greater among Kachin, with approximately 90 percent of Kachin presently being Christian. Paralleling processes linking missionary influence to Karen nationalism, vernacular education, the printing of material depicting the Kachin as a real nation, and the founding of a Kachin nationalist association all contributed to the strengthening of a Kachin national consciousness (Pelletier 2021; Sadan 2013: 50, 53, 234–35, 242–43). As Pelletier (2021) notes, "Christian churches, with their capacity to organize, proselytize, and make use of modern print technologies, shaped the emergence of a nascent Kachin public sphere. The development of educational institutions . . . helped to create an educated Kachin elite that began to aspire and promote a 'multigroup Kachin nationalist identity.' Christian elites and Christian educational institutions also contributed to the representation of a uniform Kachin identity and history centered on Christianity and the success of religious conversions in the Kachin Hills" (78).

The combination of indirect rule, military recruitment, and missionary influence made Kachin very sensitive to Bamar national chauvinism. Laoutides and Ware (2016) interviewed Kachin civilians about the causes of the conflict, and a nearly universal response was that the "deep-seated paternalistic and chauvinistic attitudes" of Bamar governments motivated the nationalist movement (56). As independence approached, Kachin leaders did not trust Bamar leaders and feared they would lose their autonomy and suffer under Bamar rule (Sadan 2013: 276). These fears diminished after meeting with Bamar leader Aung San in a last-minute negotiation before independence and agreeing that the Kachin State would retain considerable autonomy within a unified Myanmar. Shortly thereafter, Aung San was assassinated, and subsequent leaders refused to acknowledge Aung San's agreement with the Kachin, thereby reinvigorating Kachin fears of Bamar domination (Jaquet 2018; Laoutides and Ware 2016). With the desertion of Karen military units shortly after independence, the leader of Kachin forces—Naw Seng—also deserted with his soldiers and began the first Kachin nationalist civil war. After Naw Seng fled to China in 1950, the first Kachin war ended.

The combination of lost autonomy, missionaries, and Bamar national chauvinism also contributed to the second Kachin nationalist civil war. Postcolonial governments made Buddhism the sole national religion, confiscated church property, and closed Christian schools in 1960. As a consequence, Kachin were no longer able to attend schools teaching in Jinghpaw, with Bamar being the sole language of instruction (Jaquet 2018). Because Christianity was a core component of the Kachin identity, these school closures was seen as an attack on the Kachin. In reaction, a number of Kachin—including former military officials—formed the Kachin Independence Organisation (KIO) and, shortly thereafter, the Kachin Independence Army (KIA), and the latter began a war of secession (Jaquet 2018). Notably, the KIO worked very closely with the Kachin Baptist Convention, which was formed by Baptist missionaries in 1890. This organization was the main Kachin nationalist association and played a vital role mobilizing and supporting the population during the second nationalist civil war (Pelletier 2021: 79). Showing the link between religion and the nationalist conflict, a popular Kachin saying is "If you want to hear about God, join the KIA. If you want to hear about the war, go to church" (Pelletier 2021: 79).

The nationalist civil war among Karennis has close parallels with the Shan and Kachin nationalist civil wars and therefore does not require thorough analysis. Like the Shan, Karennis received great autonomy within the Frontier Areas and were given the right to secede from Myanmar ten years after independence. And fearing that the Bamar-led state would remove this autonomy, Karenni leaders began a nationalist civil war at independence.

In terms of timing, the Karenni nationalist civil war is more similar to the Kachin civil war than the Shan, as the conflicts began during the independence process. Two factors promoted the early onset. First, Karennis—like the Kachin—were much less assimilated into Bamar culture than the Shan. Indeed, many Shan spoke Bamar, and most were Buddhist. In contrast, Bamar had little influence on Karenni culture, especially in terms of language and religion. Moreover, missionaries were very influential among Karennis, with most converting to Christianity. Missionary schools, in turn, taught in local vernaculars and provided histories of the Karenni people. Bamar nationalist rhetoric about the Bamarization of minorities therefore posed a greater threat to Karennis, and they quickly mobilized to fight for independence.

A second important factor causing Karennis to start a civil war during the independence process is the close relationship between Karennis and Karens. Like Karens, the Karenni community includes many distinct subgroups, and—as the terms "Karen" and "Karenni" suggest—both communities are related. In fact, each view one another as brethren communities, and colonial officials commonly referred to Karennis as the "Red Karens" in recognition of their distinctive red clothing. [2] Moreover, Karen and Karenni leaders were Christians, and many Karens lived near the Karenni State and interacted with Karennis regularly. Due to all of these factors, Karenni and Karen nationalists had close ties with one another, and Karen nationalist mobilization influenced Karennis. Thus, when Karens began their nationalist civil war, many Karennis joined them.

Additional Cases: Mon, Arakanese, and Rohingya Nationalist Civil Wars

The Karen, Shan, Kachin, and Karenni cases highlight how British colonial pluralism contributed to nationalist civil war though different combinations of communal legislative representation, communalized indirect rule, missionary influence, and overrepresentation in the security forces. Yet Mons, Arakanese, and Rohingyas have also fought nationalist civil wars against the Myanmar state even if few—if any—of these pluralist policies directly affected them. Although colonial pluralism appears to have had less influence on these

---

2. The Myanmar government changed the official name of Karennis to Kayahs in an effort to separate Karenni and Karen communities.

conflicts, it still affected them in important ways. Most notably, colonial plural-ism strengthened Bamar national chauvinism, which increased support for all three of these nationalist movements. Furthermore, colonial pluralism com-munalized politics and created expectations for recognition, accommodation, representation, and autonomy among all communities, not simply those that were directly affected by pluralist policies. Finally, other nationalist civil wars provided inspiration, encouragement, and assistance.

THE MON NATIONALIST CIVIL WAR

Similar to Karens, Mons were concentrated in the directly ruled region of southern Myanmar. In fact, Karens and Mons commonly lived close to one another and interacted regularly. Different from Karens, however, colonial plu-ralism had more limited effects on Mon communal consciousness and conflicts between Mons and Bamar. Although recognizing Mons as a distinct people in censuses, briefly attempting to create a Mon military regiment, and contem-plating bringing the descendants of Mon royalty to Myanmar from Thailand to create an indirect form of rule, the British ultimately did very little to separate Mons from Bamar. And, given a long history of Buddhism, missionaries had limited influence among Mons. With the formal incorporation of Mons into colonial Myanmar and great influx of Bamar into southern Myanmar during the colonial period, Mon cultural autonomy diminished, and the Mon community decreased in size due to assimilation and intermarriage (South 2003: 22, 32).

Despite these differences, British colonial pluralism contributed to the Mon nationalist civil war both directly and indirectly. For one, politics in colo-nial Myanmar was highly communalized and competitive, and this environ-ment created expectations for pluralism even among communities that were not directly affected by pluralist colonial policies. In the 1930s, Mon leaders founded the All Ramanya Mon Association (ARMA), a political organization looking out for Mon interests. Due to Mon cultural erosion during the colo-nial period, this association focused on the protection and promotion of Mon language and identity (South 2003: 87). While this movement could have occurred without colonial pluralism, British rule provided an environment facilitating and encouraging such behavior, and Mon leaders modeled ARMA after the communal associations of other communities, especially the KNA.

At the same time, missionary influence strengthened concerns over the demise of Mon culture by kickstarting a Mon literary tradition and growing interest in Mon affairs. Baptist missionaries working with Karens attempted to convert the neighboring Mons and began printing a large quantity of material in Mon, thereby helping to revitalize a Mon literary tradition (South 2003: 91–92). In fact, a Baptist missionary—Robert Halliday—is considered the father of Mon studies. Through their influence, a printing press and newspaper in the Mon language were founded, and considerable research on the long history of the "great" Mon civilization began. As noted earlier, however, the missionaries had very little success converting Mons.

Bamar national chauvinism—which was strengthened by British colonial pluralism—also contributed to a nationalist movement. During the independence process, Mon leaders worked with Bamar politicians to end British rule and secure a position for Mons in the postcolonial nation-state. Thus, instead of fighting against the BIA, many Mons supported it (South 2003: 95). Over time, however, it became apparent that Bamar politicians were unwilling to recognize or protect the Mon community (South 2003). Bamar politicians justified their lack of recognition by claiming that Mons were Bamar, and Mon leaders reacted to the denial of their very existence by mobilizing a nationalist movement (South 2003: 110).

To mobilize their community against Bamar national chauvinism, Mon leaders employed a nationalist frame and narrative based on Mon history that targeted the Bamar as an enemy. In particular, large Mon empires had been present in the region long ago, but Bamar kingdoms conquered them and persecuted Mons, with many fleeing to present-day Thailand. In addition, Mons had brought both Buddhism and the first system of writing to the region, and the Bamar adopted both. In the face of Bamar national chauvinism, Mon nationalists therefore emphasized the presence of a long-standing and proud Mon civilization that declined at the hands of ungrateful Bamar kingdoms. A poem by a Mon monk clearly highlights these elements of the Mon nationalist myth-symbol complex:

> Our history is rich
> Our future is bright
> We gave Southeast Asia Buddhism
> Here we were the first peoples to write
> The Thais and the Burmans were our pupils
> How do they treat their teacher now? (South 2003: 34)

The implied answer to this question was badly, and this view helped politicize Mons in ways that promoted the nationalist movement.

In addition to politicizing Mons and strengthening Bamar national chauvinism, British colonial pluralism had indirect effects on the Mon nationalist movement through the Karen nationalist movement and civil war (South 2003: 102–4). Because early efforts to protect Mon interests by supporting Bamar nationalists failed, several Mon leaders looked to the more militant Karen nationalist movement as an example to follow. Karen and Mon communities, in turn, lived near one another and had relatively cordial relations, and Karen and Mon leaders quickly agreed to work together to pursue their interests collectively. For example, the first armed Mon nationalist organization—the

Mon National Defence Organisation—was modeled after the Karen National Defence Organisation, and Karen and Mon leaders entered an agreement to aid one another (South 2003: 106–8). As one Mon nationalist declared about this relationship, "fate had determined the coming together of Mons and Karens as eternal allies" (South 2003: 108). Within this relationship, the Mon leaders were clearly the junior partner due to the much greater military prowess of Karens within the colonial regime, and Karens helped organize and train Mon forces. And over the next several decades, Karen and Mon nationalist movements coordinated their battle against the Myanmar state.

THE ARAKANESE AND ROHINGYA CIVIL WARS

Similar to Mons, colonial pluralism did little to formally privilege the Arakanese or Rohingyas, but both have fought nationalist civil wars against the Myanmar state. The cases are also similar to the Mon conflict in that colonial pluralism contributed to both civil wars indirectly by strengthening Bamar national chauvinism and providing examples and openings for nationalist civil warfare. Of these cases, however, the Arakanese case is most similar to the Mon conflict, as the presence of a historical state that was conquered by the Bamar only a few decades before British colonialism created expectations for self-rule. In contrast, extreme discrimination and exclusion politicized the Rohingya community and sparked the nationalist civil war.

Both the Arakanese and Rohingyas are concentrated in the Rakhine State, a region known as Arakan until Myanmar independence. Although previously living in mixed communities, ethnic cleansing during the Second World War pushed Rohingyas north and Arakanese south, thereby communalizing the territory. Rohingyas and Arakanese speak different languages, with Arakanese related to Burmese and Rohingya similar to Bengali. The Arakanese, in turn, are overwhelmingly Buddhist, whereas most Rohingyas are Muslim.

The Arakanese peoples have historically been active in the maritime trade and had a diverse population by the time of Konbaung conquest. Although Buddhism was—and remains—the dominant religion, large Muslim and Hindu populations were present. Arab traders proselytized in the region, but most Muslims either migrated to Arakan from Bengal as soldiers or were forcibly brought to the region as slaves. After British colonial conquest, many Muslim Indians migrated to Arakan, thereby creating a larger and more vibrant Muslim population. Although it is uncertain how many Muslims moved to Myanmar during the colonial period, experts agree that the size of the Muslim community increased several-fold under British rule (Ibrahim 2016; Ware and Laoutides 2019).

Both the Arakanese and Rohingya civil wars began during the independence transition and simultaneously supported and fought one another. During the

Second World War, the Arakanese actively participated in the BIA, whereas many Rohingyas supported the British. As a result, they fought each other, and ethnic violence between Arakanese and Rohingya civilians was widespread, leading to ethnic cleansing and the formation of communal enclaves. Antipathy between Arakanese and Rohingyas was therefore great during the final years of colonialism. At independence, however, Arakanese and Rohingyas recognized their similar interests and agreed to cooperate in their fight against the Myanmar state. Continued antipathy and violence between civilians, however, severely impeded this cooperation.

Although the Arakanese joined the BIA to fight the British, were Buddhist, and spoke a language similar to Burmese, Arakanese leaders demanded autonomy either within Myanmar or through secession. Like the Mons, Bamar claimed Arakanese were Bamar and refused to make any concessions, and Arakanese soldiers in the BIA deserted and started a war of secession even before colonial independence. Given the lack of pluralist policies that increased competition and antipathy between the Bamar and Arakanese communities and the religious and cultural similarities between the two, the presence of an Arakanese nationalist movement differs from most cases analyzed in this chapter. Like the Mons, however, the general communalization of politics pushed Arakanese nationalists to look out for their community, and Bamar national chauvinism—which denied the existence of an Arakanese community—motivated them to do just this. Importantly, British colonial pluralism contributed to both the communalization of politics and Bamar national chauvinism.

A comparison with the Mons also shows that precolonial histories of statehood combined with the communalization of politics and Bamar national chauvinism to promote a myth-symbol complex focused on the presence of a "glorious" past civilization, and Arakanese leaders employed this frame to mobilize and justify the nationalist movement. Between the mid-seventeenth and late eighteenth centuries, the independent Kingdom of Mrauk-U controlled Arakan and was wedged between the Bengal Sultanate and the Bamar-dominated Toungoo Empire. Prior to that, the region had been a tributary state of either the Bengalis or the Bamar but retained considerable autonomy from both. In 1784, the newly dominant Konbaung dynasty defeated the Kingdom of Mrauk-U and incorporated it into its territory. After conquest, the Konbaung plundered the population before placing the region under Bamar rule. For the Arakanese, this event is commemorated every December 31, known as Black Day (Holt 2019: 15). And with the communalization of politics during the colonial period and the strengthening of Bamar national chauvinism, Arakanese nationalists decried the removal of their autonomy and Bamar efforts to stamp out their existence, thereby pursuing autonomy to protect the Arakanese nation and reestablish Mrauk-U. As Ware and Laoutides (2019) note,

From a Rakhine perspective, centuries of Arakanese independence culminating in the glorious kingdom came to a tumultuous end in 1784, when the Burmese King Bodawphaya invaded. While most Rakhine today are not necessarily familiar with the text of the *Razawin* [a royal chronical of Mrauk-U], they know the stories, and the destruction of Mrauk-U is etched deeply into their collective memory. Indeed, the destruction of Mrauk-U and the plunder of Arakan is usually top of their list of grievances against the Burman-led state today. (109)

While the Arakanese civil war has been almost completely ignored by the international community, the Rohingya nationalist civil war received great public scrutiny after the forced exodus of hundreds of thousands of Rohingyas from Myanmar in 2017. Although exceptional in scale and suffering, this event was only a recent aspect of a civil war that first began during the independence process. Over the years, the civil war has had different phases and involved different anti-state organizations. In 1948, the Mujahid Party began a nationalist civil war seeking to merge northern Arakan with Bangladesh (then East Pakistan), but the Mujahid disbanded by the mid-1950s. In subsequent years, new organizations formed and fought the Myanmar government, although they differed from the Mujahid in pursuing greater Rohingya autonomy within Myanmar. Because the government claimed that all Rohingyas are foreign noncitizens, these organizations also demanded full Myanmar citizenship for Rohingyas. Throughout this period, nationalist violence was usually limited and sporadic. Then, after Rohingya nationalists attacked police stations and killed civilians in 2017, the Myanmar government responded with a "final solution" involving a systematic effort to remove all Rohingyas from Myanmar soil.

A major cause of the Rohingya conflict was consistent efforts to exclude Rohingyas from the Bamar nation-state, something that British colonialism contributed to in important ways. For many centuries before British rule, Muslims had settled in Arakan, although many more arrived during the British colonial period (Ware and Laoutides 2019: 79–90, 131–34). In their censuses of colonial Myanmar, the British categorized all Muslims as Indians, thereby merging indigenous and non-indigenous Muslims into the same category. In so doing, the British effectively declared all Muslims foreigners regardless of whether their ancestors had lived in the region. Due to this situation, Muslim leaders lobbied the colonial government for a new census category—Burman Muslim—that would declare their indigeneity (Upper Burma Muslims 1929). Bamar politicians learned of these demands, however, and asked the government to reject them, and the government sided with the Bamar (Burma Legislative Council 1933a: 29).

This decision had major ramifications on the Muslim population, as it made them one of the biggest targets of Bamar national chauvinism. Most notably, the Dobama movement became a powerful force in colonial Myanmar at this time and demanded that all Indians return to India, and acts of aggression and violence against Indians—while already common—increased during the final decades of colonialism (Yi 2018). A legislative debate over separating Myanmar from colonial India clearly highlights this antipathy, with a Bamar politician asking threateningly, "If we separate [from India] can we drive out the Indians?" (Burma Legislative Council 1933b: 298). Around this time, a publication by a Muslim scholar making anti-Buddhist statements sparked a riot killing hundreds of Muslims (Frydenlund and Jerryson 2020: 86). Given growing Bamar harassment, intimidation, and violence against Muslims, Rohingyas feared what Bamar would do to them after independence and turned to the British for support. In this situation, many joined British forces and fought BIA and Japanese forces during the Second World War. Thus, just like Karens, Rohingya soldiers fought Bamar (and Arakanese) forces, and all sides attacked civilians (Frydenlund and Jerryson 2020: 87).

After the war, it was clear that British rule would end soon, and Rohingya leaders argued that they would face rampant discrimination and violence if they remained part of Myanmar and therefore demanded the merger of northern Arakan with Bangladesh. Given their loyalty and assistance to the British during the war, Rohingya leaders expected that the British would respect their interests, but the British rejected their request. After independence, most "Indians" left Myanmar to avoid violence, but the majority of Rohingyas stayed. It was at this time that Muslim Arakanese started referring to themselves as "Rohingya," meaning "from Arakan."

As many Rohingyas had feared, postcolonial governments refused to grant them citizenship and formally discriminated against and attacked them, and vindictive and exclusionary acts sparked the Rohingya nationalist movement as well as civil war (Frydenlund and Jerryson 2020: 92–93). At one point, the government offered to recognize Rohingyas as non-indigenous citizens, but Rohingya leaders refused because many Rohingyas had ancestors with historical roots in Arakan and feared they would continue to face formal discrimination if categorized as non-indigenous. As a result of this refusal, the government denied Rohingyas citizenship and—faced with Rohingya anti-state violence—declared them personae non gratae, eventually resulting in the expulsion of these "foreigners" from Myanmar soil (Ibrahim 2016).

While influenced by a variety of things, the belief that Rohingyas are dangerous and degenerate "foreigners" is at the heart of the Rohingya nationalist civil war: Because of this, Rohingyas have faced extreme marginalization, persecution, and violence, all of which pushed some to take up arms to either join Bangladesh or gain greater autonomy within Myanmar. Importantly, British colonialism contributed to this situation in a variety of ways. One was through population transfers: After colonial conquest, the British opened Myanmar to Indian migrants, and the sheer number of Indians increased Bamar antipathy toward them. Exacerbating the effects of this population movement, Indians were commonly economic middlemen, causing Bamar to revile them as "parasites" (Bowser 2021: 120–22). And because the British categorized all Muslims as Indians regardless of their origins, Bamar targeted Rohingyas with anti-Indian sentiments. As "Indians," Rohingyas also received communal legislative representation and cooperated with the British to stifle Bamar nationalist demands in the legislature, and this special treatment and "traitorous" opposition only strengthened anti-Muslim sentiments. Finally, the use of Rohingyas as soldiers to combat BIA forces during the Second World War reinforced the belief that Rohingyas were colonial agents out to get Bamar and greatly increased Rohingya-Bamar antipathy right before independence.

While some of these colonial effects were not the direct result of colonial pluralism, pluralist policies influenced the processes leading to nationalist civil war in important ways. Most importantly, colonial policies that benefited non-state communities and discriminated against Bamar contributed to a Bamar national chauvinism that targeted non-state communities as colonial collaborators and, thereby, promoted a schema that amplified and legitimized anger, resentment, and fear against non-Bamar. Given this righteous rage and a powerful desire to resurrect a great Bamar kingdom, Bamar nationalists despised the Indian "colonial agents" and sought to expel them. And for the Bamar, Rohingyas were Indians. In this way, discriminatory colonial policies promoted anger, resentment, and fear among Bamar, who then targeted Rohingyas as collaborators and foreigners in ways promoting a Rohingya nationalist movement.

Conclusion

Myanmar has experienced numerous nationalist civil wars, and it also had a highly pluralist and discriminatory colonial model of political community. If discriminatory colonial pluralism promotes nationalist civil warfare, the case is therefore ideal for highlighting mechanisms and processes that link the two. The analyses of the Karen, Shan, Kachin, Karenni, Mon, Arakanese, and Rohingya nationalist civil wars highlight multiple ways through which discriminatory colonial pluralisms contributed to the conflicts. The mechanisms are interrelated and affected both the Bamar state community and diverse non-state communities.

First, discriminatory colonial pluralism contributed to an aggressive and vindictive national chauvinism among the Bamar that targeted other communities as dangerous and degenerate, thereby provoking nationalist movements among non-state communities. The main way it did this was by downgrading the status of the Bamar while increasing the status of the communities that the Bamar dominated prior to British rule. In this way, the state community resented losing its power and status and targeted non-state communities as collaborating colonial cronies. While it is impossible to know the strength and character of Bamar national chauvinism without a history of British colonial pluralism, British colonialism clearly exacerbated the exclusive and aggressive character of Bamar national chauvinism and thereby contributed to all the nationalist civil wars analyzed in this chapter. This is especially the case for Rohingyas, as Bamar associated this community with Indian "intruders" and therefore focused on their elimination from the national homeland.

A second mechanism through which British colonial pluralism contributed to nationalist civil warfare was the strengthening of communal frames, something that was necessary for communities to perceive and be concerned about communal affairs. While the use of communal census categories helped make communities concrete and legible, indirect rule and communal legislative representation forced communities to observe politics from a communal perspective. Missionaries, in turn, commonly spread communal frames through literacy and by creating communal associations.

Many of the same processes that strengthened communal frames also contributed to the communalization of colonial politics, which is a third mechanism through which colonial pluralism contributed to nationalist civil wars. The communalization of politics effectively nationalized communal frames by focusing them on communal power and self-rule and, in so doing, created powerful expectations for both. And when communities were confronted by a chauvinistic state that sought to remove all pluralist policies and Bamarize the population, these expectations motivated nationalist movements and civil war. The special protection and isolation of the Frontier Areas, for example, created particularly strong expectations for self-rule, whereas Karen communal legislative representation created expectations for communal power. Yet the Mon and Arakanese cases show that these nationalist expectations and orientations were present in the absence of both communalized indirect rule and legislative representation. While the general communalization of politics contributed to this outcome by creating expectations for communal power and self-rule among all communities, histories of precolonial statehood also strengthened nationalist frames and expectations in both cases.

The cases analyzed in this chapter also highlight how British colonial pluralism contributed to nationalist civil war through mobilizational mechanisms whereby communities gain the capacity to mobilize nationalist movements and fight wars. Although present in the other civil wars, the Karen nationalist civil war clearly highlights the influence of a mobilizational mechanism: Discriminatory pluralist policies provided minority communities with resources that empowered them and facilitated the mobilization of powerful nationalist movements. Nationalist organizations are one important resource facilitating the mobilization of nationalist movements, and pluralist policies contributed to the main Karen nationalist organization—the KNA—in two main ways. First, by providing Karens with reserved legislative seats, colonial pluralism politicized and nationalized the Karen community, and the KNA served as a de facto political party pursing Karen interests. In addition, missionaries emphasized and exacerbated intercommunal differences and helped Karens found and run this association. Military personnel and weapons, in turn, are additional resources that made possible the nationalist civil wars. Indeed, the organization of a fighting force to counter state aggressions is usually very difficult. Karens, however, possessed communal military units, and the soldiers and officers from the Myanmar military quit and joined the nationalist movements, thereby creating a ready-made nationalist fighting force. In addition to these resources, colonial pluralism also provided the Shan, Karenni, and Kachin communities with another: Communalized indirect rule in the Frontier Areas provided them with their own polities, which included both administrations and security forces.

Although providing evidence that British colonial pluralism was most likely to promote nationalist civil war among communities that were ruled indirectly, provided with communal legislative representation, given advantaged opportunities in the colonial military, or greatly influenced by missionaries, the cases show that colonial pluralism affected all communities. Bamar national chauvinism targeted some communities more than others, but all were negatively affected by it. Similarly, some pluralist policies politicized certain communities more than others, but all communities were politicized because colonial pluralism communalized politics at the colony level. Finally, while communal military units provided Karens with particularly important military resources to fight their wars, Karens helped train and organize Mon and Karenni forces, suggesting that this resource was partially transferable.

All in all, the analysis offers evidence that colonial pluralism contributed to widespread nationalist civil warfare in postcolonial Myanmar. Although it is impossible to know exactly what would have happened in the absence of British colonial pluralism, the qualitative evidence suggests that far fewer nationalist civil wars would have occurred if the British never colonized the region. Confidence in this conclusion is strongest for cases in which multiple mechanisms combined to promote nationalist civil warfare and weakest in cases in which colonial pluralism influenced the nationalist civil war more indirectly.

5

Colonial Pluralism and Nationalist Civil War in India

A large literature analyzes communal conflict in India, some of which links violence to colonialism (Brass 1997; Lee 2020; Mukherjee 2021; Varshney 1997; Verghese 2016; Wilkinson 2004). Most of this research explores conflict between Hindu and Muslim civilians and therefore does not analyze nationalist civil war. Scholars of nationalist violence in India, in turn, commonly claim that postcolonial India experienced only limited nationalist conflict and argue that linguistic federalism and other pluralist policies helped limit nationalist strife in such a large and diverse country (Stepan et al. 2011; Tudor 2013; Wilkinson 2015). While making an important point, such praise ignores another side of the Indian story. As Deol (2000) notes, identities based on language, caste, and region have been accommodated by the Indian state, but non-Hindu "religious identity assertions, particularly in conjunction with a geographical region, are regarded as posing a grave threat to India's political integrity" (30). The Indian state has therefore sought to stifle the political demands of religious minorities outside the Hindu heartland, thereby attempting to build unity out of diversity by "pursu[ing] unity violently and eradicate[ing] diversity" (Franke 2009: 66). And in so doing, the Indian state has contributed to several nationalist civil wars.

India's independence transition was rife with religious-based nationalist conflict, as the region gained independence through the partition of colonial India into India and Pakistan. Estimates of deaths resulting from partition range from 500,000 to nearly 4 million, and tens of millions were displaced (Singh and Shani 2021: 104–5). Technically speaking, this violence was not a nationalist civil war because it pitted civilian against civilian. After partition,

TABLE 5.1. Nationalist Civil Wars in India

Nationalist Community	Years of Active Warfare	Region	Percent of Population
Naga	1956–1968, 1992–2000	Northeast	0.2
Mizo	1966–1968	Northeast	0.1
Tipuri	1979–2004	Northeast	0.1
Manipuri	1982–2009	Northeast	0.2
Sikh	1983–1993	Northwest	1.7
Bodo	1989–2014	Northeast	0.1
Assamese	1990–2010	Northeast	1.1
Kashmiri Muslims	1990–2020	Northwest	0.2
Garo	2012–2014	Northeast	0.1

nine different communities have fought ten nationalist civil wars in India. As highlighted in table 5.1, 8 of the 10 wars were located in Northeast India, and all communities fighting nationalist wars were relatively small. And with a few exceptions, the members of the communities fighting the wars are non-Hindu. In the analysis that follows, I explore whether colonial pluralism contributed to these conflicts. I analyze all the wars but categorize them into four groupings: nationalist civil wars in Northeast India's excluded areas, nationalist civil wars in in Northeast India's former princely states, the two remaining nationalist civil wars in Northeast India, and nationalist civil wars outside the Northeast. Before these analyses, however, I describe the main aspects of colonial pluralism in India.

Colonial Pluralism in India

British colonialism in India began as "Company rule" with the founding of the British East India Company (EIC) in 1599. A few years later, the Company established its first factories in Gujarat and Madras. For this, the EIC required permission from Indian rulers to trade and build factories, and local authorities made concessions giving the EIC control over small enclaves. Over time, Company lands expanded, making the EIC a political entity controlling extensive territories. With its victory in the Battle of Plassey in 1757, the Company took over the territories of the Nawab of Bengal, and many historians consider this victory the time at which formal British colonialism began in India. Less than a decade later, the EIC won rights over Orissa and Bihar through the Battle of Buxar, and they gained control over much of southern India by the end of the eighteenth century. In the nineteenth century, the Company began to expand into the North and Northwest, thereby ending the Mughal Empire. Around this time, the EIC had a military numbering 300,000 strong, which was double the size of the British army.

Company rule in India took a variety of forms, although there were two main types of control. In many regions, the EIC annexed territory and ruled it directly. In other territories, Company officials left Indian authorities in power and ruled indirectly through them. Indirect rule usually involved princely states in which Indians who had been regional authorities in the Mughal Empire recognized the Company's hegemony and accepted a British adviser in return for considerable autonomy. In between these two forms of rule, the EIC frequently established more hybrid institutions. In large parts of Bengal, for example, the British established quasi-indirect rule in regions that were formally recognized as directly ruled by retaining the Zamindari land system through the Permanent Settlement Act of 1793.

In 1857, Indian soldiers working for the EIC revolted and nearly ended British rule. First termed the "Sepoy Mutiny," most refer to it today as either the Indian Rebellion of 1857 or the First Indian War of Independence. Anti-British violence lasted until mid-1859 and shook the Company to its core, with the Company losing control of most of India. After the anticolonial war, the British government decided to dissolve the EIC and take direct control of India in the hopes of creating a more stable system of rule, and India became a formal British colony at this time. As described in chapter 2, influential officials believed that the Company's liberal reforms sparked the anticolonial war and concluded that retaining or reverting to customary authorities and traditional institutions was the best way to contain anti-British sentiments. They therefore reversed the course set by the Company and established a pluralist system of rule that recognized the diverse communities and tried to limit the disruptive effects of colonialism by maintaining or reestablishing "traditional" institutions.

Colonial pluralism in India subsequently took a variety of forms. One important element was strengthening and expanding indirect forms of rule. Thus, whereas the Company had been weakening and eliminating princely states prior to the war, the British now retained and strengthened them. With subsequent colonial expansion, the British also established indirect forms of rule in Northeast India, including the founding of "excluded areas," which had a form of rule nearly identical to Myanmar's Frontier Areas. Another pluralist policy was using censuses to recognize and count communities. Believing that a better understanding of Indian society would facilitate colonial control of it, the British began the monumental task of completing a census of colonial India shortly after the Rebellion of 1857. A major element of the colonial censuses was to document the different types of communities in India, thereby recording the religions, castes, tribes, languages, and ethnicities of the Indian subjects. Such an undertaking required that the British study and gain an understanding of the different categories of community in colonial India, thereby promoting what some refer to as an "ethnographic" state (Cohn 1987; Dirks 2001). Beyond recognizing communal difference, the British implemented multicultural policies that accommodated diversity by providing public goods and services that catered to cultural needs, such as providing education in a variety of vernaculars and enforcing community-specific personal law.

Some of these pluralist policies were discriminatory. The British used indirect rule selectively, for example, thereby giving only some regions and communities autonomy. Other pluralist policies were more overtly discriminatory. Because both Hindu and Muslim soldiers turned against the British in the Indian Rebellion whereas most Sikh soldiers fought alongside the British, colonial officials stacked the colonial military with Sikhs immediately following the rebellion. By the late nineteenth century, Hindus dominated the independence movement whereas Muslim elites were supportive of British rule. To deal with the Hindu threat, the British began to recruit Punjabi Muslims into the military, and they became the largest group in the Indian military (Wilkinson 2015). The British also empowered Muslims by giving them special legislative representation, something that ultimately allowed British officials and Muslim representatives to outnumber Hindu nationalists in the legislature. Through a policy that was ultimately repealed because of strong opposition, the British also divided Bengal into eastern and western halves, as Hindu anticolonialists dominated politics in the region and the separation of Bengal allowed the Muslims to dominate politics in East Bengal. Although not motivated by pluralism, the British used pluralism to justify these and other discriminatory policies. For example, they argued that splitting Bengal allowed Muslim Bengalis to receive their fair share of political representation and power and that reserved legislative seats were needed for religious minorities to participate in politics. Like Myanmar, the case therefore shows how anticolonial resistance contributed to discriminatory pluralist policies that favored "loyal" subjects over anticolonial opponents.

Colonial India is also similar to Myanmar in that missionary influence was sporadic and concentrated in regions with non-state communities. The British recognized that Hindus and Muslims greatly resented missionaries and therefore commonly limited missionary activities among these communities. When working among other communities, however, missionaries reinforced pluralist communal differentiation by using, standardizing, teaching in, and printing material in vernaculars. They also organized communities politically and lobbied officials to protect "their" communities.

Excluded Areas and Nationalist Civil Warfare

Also called "scheduled" or "backward" areas, excluded areas were concentrated in Northeast India and had a form of colonial rule that was nearly identical to that in Myanmar's Frontier Areas. In fact, the model of rule in the excluded areas was transferred from India to the Frontier Areas. Excluded areas therefore provided communities with self-rule and extreme isolation from other more "advanced" communities. Although less than 1 percent of the Indian population lived in former excluded areas, 40 percent of the nationalist civil wars have occurred in them, making them easily the most prone to nationalist conflict. And like Myanmar's Frontier Areas, colonial pluralism promoted nationalist civil war when postcolonial states removed the cultural and political autonomy of communities.

THE NAGA NATIONALIST CIVIL WARS

Conflict between Naga nationalists and the Indian state began during the independence process and resulted from Nehru's refusal to acknowledge Naga demands for autonomy. In reaction to increasingly heavy-handed and violent repression, Nagas began a nationalist civil war over secession in the mid-1950s. For over a decade, the fighting was intense. It began to wane in the 1970s, and most Naga combatants surrendered in 1975. Some Nagas refused to accept the agreement, however, and an underground movement continued. Fighting intensified in the 1990s, thereby starting the second Naga nationalist civil war, and continued more sporadically until a ceasefire in 2015.

Similar to Karens, Karennis, and Kachin in Myanmar, "Naga" is a recently created umbrella term used to refer to diverse peoples who speak dozens of different languages and, until recently, lived in village-based polities and did not self-identify as a community (Franke 2009). In fact, Naga villages commonly fought one another, and Nagas gained a reputation as vicious warriors (and headhunters). The British had little interest in Nagaland, the region inhabited by the Nagas, but Nagaland separated British Assam and Manipur. The British therefore conquered it to create a corridor linking the two. Given the marginal position of Nagaland in colonial India and the absence of easily exploitable resources, the British employed an indirect form of rule that left Nagas high levels of autonomy. Unlike most systems of indirect rule, the British did not recognize and rule through a prince or chief, as most Naga communities traditionally ruled by council. The British therefore maintained and formalized these councils during the colonial period. Although previously separate, Naga villages became more unified during the colonial period. Most notably, British officials organized a pan-Naga council that included representatives from local councils and made decisions for all Nagaland.

British pluralism therefore maintained but readjusted indigenous institutions while creating a new level of Naga self-rule at the regional level. This regional government included administrations and councils that empowered Naga leaders to rule the Naga nation, and these institutions provided extremely valuable mobilizational resources: They were ready-made organizations with links to all local councils that could engage all people and implement policies throughout the territory. At the same time, communal self-rule helped construct powerful Naga communal frames. As noted, Nagas were not unified politically prior to British rule and had considerable cultural diversity. British rule recognized the Nagas as a coherent community and helped nationalize them by providing them with their own national council. The institutionalization and celebration of Naga self-rule, in turn, created popular and powerful expectations for cultural and political autonomy.

In addition to institutionalizing Naga self-rule, the few British officials working in the area sought to limit outside influence as much as possible, and this also strengthened Naga nationalist frames and expectations. Some refer to these officials as "anthropologist" colonialists who were fascinated with Naga culture and sought to protect it (Das 2022; Thomas 2015: 33). In so doing, they tried to limit the impact of the "plains" peoples living near the Nagas, who the British believed were more "advanced" and would overrun the Nagas if given the opportunity. This isolationism and the colonial justification for it heightened Naga mistrust of the "plains" Indians. Indeed, British officials in Nagaland constantly emphasized that the plains Indians posed a serious threat, and this recognition and fear of the other strengthened reactions to the forced incorporation of Nagaland into the Indian nation-state.

Protestant missionaries were influential informal colonial agents in Nagaland and shaped colonial pluralism. Nearly half of all Nagas converted to Christianity by independence; almost all Nagas are Christian today. Missionary influence further isolated Nagas from the "plains" Indians and strengthened Naga nationalist frames and expectations for self-rule. By standardizing languages, making them written languages, printing a variety of materials about Nagas, and making religion an important marker of community, missionaries strengthened a Naga consciousness and increased "pride in their culture and traditions" (Chadha 2005: 276; Thomas 2015). They also provided a strong organizational base for a more unified national community by creating the Council of Naga Baptist Churches and overseeing the founding of the Naga Club in 1918 (Baruah 2020: 106). This Club developed into a nationalist organization and, among other things, actively lobbied the colonial government to retain Nagaland's "excluded" status during the various constitutional reforms (Franke 2009: 39; Thomas 2015: 78). And because the missionaries saw the religions of the plains communities as competition, they also viewed the plains communities as a danger and favored isolationism.

During the tumultuous lead-up to Indian independence, the Naga Club transformed into the Naga National Council (NNC), a political party that represented Nagas and lobbied the British to retain Naga autonomy (Chadha 2005: 280–82; Maxwell 1973). The NNC argued that Nagaland were not part of India prior to colonialism and therefore insisted that Nagas retain their autonomy (Singh 2013: 798–99). British officials had contradictory views, at once fearful that Nagas would be overwhelmed if given to India but also worried that the "backward" Nagas could not possibly run their own country (Franke 2009: 42–45). In the end, they gave in to Indian pressure and awarded the region to India. In the face of the Indian National Congress's refusal to accept the NNC's demands and the subsequent incorporation of Nagaland into the Indian regional state of Assam, the NNC organized a nationalist movement and unilaterally declared Nagaland independence. On learning of this declaration, Nehru supposedly pounded his fists on the table and shouted, "Whether heavens fall or India goes into pieces and blood runs red in the country, whether I am here or anyone else, Nagas will not be allowed to be Independent" (Anderson 2013: 122). In the end, Naga leaders did not push their demands and grudgingly accepted integration into postcolonial India as part of the Assamese regional state. This was facilitated by the fact that the Indian and Assamese governments did little to disrupt Naga politics during the first years of independence, leaving Naga leaders to take control of the colonial administration.

In time, however, both national and regional governments increasingly interfered in Naga affairs, including making Assamese the official language. In reaction, Naga nationalists borrowed Congress's civil disobedience techniques to mobilize a secessionist movement. They held a plebiscite in 1950, and the overwhelming majority of Nagas voted for the creation of an independent Naga state. In reaction, the national and state governments sent police and soldiers into the region, and these troops used extreme force. Naga nationalists countered with their own violence in 1955, and government forces were soon frustrated by the Naga guerrillas, who were able to avoid them and seemingly attack at will. In an effort to weaken the guerrillas, the Indian military forced civilians to relocate their villages to guarded enclosures; effectively gave soldiers the license to murder at will; and committed numerous atrocities against civilians, including mass murder, systematic rape, the public display of mutilated corpses, and the aerial bombing of villages. Such violence, in turn, only intensified resentment and anger among Naga nationalists.

As this description shows, the processes leading to the Naga conflict were very similar to those of the Shan, Karenni, and Kachin conflicts in Myanmar: Colonial pluralism created an extreme form of communal self-rule and isolationism, which made communities very sensitive to losing their cultural and political autonomy. Colonial officials and missionaries told Nagas that they were distinct people, declared Indians a menace, allowed Nagas to rule themselves, and isolated Nagas from Indians. And with the help of colonial officials, Naga leaders organized their community and lobbied for the maintenance of their autonomy. As Suykens (2015) notes, Nagas—who decades earlier were divided and lacked a collective identity—now viewed themselves as having a "natural" state and requiring national self-rule (142–43).

Protestant missionaries also contributed to the nationalist civil war, as religion became a bone of contention between the opposing sides of the conflict. Most Naga leaders were Christian, and Christianity was a defining element of the Naga community, something that is evident in the popular nationalist slogan "Nagaland for Christ" (Wouters 2019: 17–18). Nehru and other Indian leaders greatly resented Christian missionaries and saw Christianity as a threat to the Indian nation, and they argued that the Naga nationalist movement was the work of Baptist missionaries (Shannon 1953). As a result, Nehru expelled missionaries from Indian soil. In this way, the Indian government saw Nagas as dangerous and degenerate because they were Christian, whereas Nagas saw Indian policies as an attack on their faith and, thereby, their nation, something that they believed justified secession.

The case also shows how colonial pluralism provided important mobilizational resources that allowed nationalists to act on their grievances. For one, British rule provided Nagas with their own administration and council, and both helped organize the nationalist movement and—after going underground—the civil war. Similarly, missionaries were instrumental in organizing the NNC, which became the main nationalist party. This party organized resistance against the Indian military and took over the regional administration after the British left (Suykens 2015: 143). As Suykens (2015) notes, the NNC was able to use these organizational resources to complete a variety of necessary activities to sustain the war effort, including taxation, protection, and the provisioning of justice and basic services.

THE MIZO NATIONALIST CIVIL WAR

The nationalist civil war in Mizoram was postcolonial India's second nationalist civil war and began less than a decade after the Naga conflict. Mizoram is located south of Nagaland in the extreme southeast of Northeast India and borders both Bangladesh and Myanmar. Similar to the Naga nationalist civil war, Mizo nationalists fought for an independent Mizo state. And like Nagas, Mizos lived in an excluded area during the colonial period, and the history of extreme colonial autonomy and isolation contributed to the nationalist civil war.

Prior to colonialism, Mizos lived in small community-based polities, and the British believed they needed protection from the more "advanced" communities in colonial India, thereby declaring the Mizo Hills (also known as the Lushai Hills) an "excluded area." Whereas precolonial Naga politics was based on councils, Mizos had a history of chiefs, and the British ruled Mizos through chiefs. As in other British colonies, indirect rule greatly empowered the chiefs and promoted exploitative and autocratic rule (Lange 2009b; Mamdani 1996). As a result, many opposed the power of Mizo chiefs at independence, especially educated Mizos (Chadha 2005: 328–29; Goswami 2009: 580; Holt 2022).

Mizoram is similar to Nagaland in that Protestant missionaries (Welch Presbyterian and British Baptist) were very influential, and Christianity was the dominant religion by independence (Lalchungnunga 1994: 50–52; Sarbahi 2021). In addition to converting Mizos, missionaries standardized the Mizo language, set it to writing, and created an effective system of education. In so doing, missionaries "bound the fragmented tribes together giving them a common 'Mizo' identity" (Chadha 2005: 327), and Mizos understood "their identity to be inextricably linked to their Christianity" (Pachuau 2014: 137). Missionary and church leaders founded the Young Lushai Association (YLA) in 1935. This association played a very important role organizing the Mizo community and promoting national unity, and it developed into a political organization (Pachuau and van Schendel 2015: 248; Singh 2017).

During the independence process, chiefly power was the key political issue in Mizoram, and Mizo educated elites—usually with links to the YLA—formed the Mizo Union to demand the removal of chiefs (Chadha 2005: 328–29; Maxwell 1973: 18). Although still very concerned about Mizo autonomy, the leaders of the Mizo Union aligned with Congress and agreed to merge Mizoram with India, employing the slogan "Joining India means the overthrow of the chiefs/ Wanting Independence means the [continued] rule of chiefs" (Pachuau and van Schendel 2015: 248). Yet the party was divided, and many opposed union with India in favor of self-rule.

After independence, Mizoram joined the Assamese regional state. Many Mizos believed the regional and national governments neglected them and greatly resented their loss of autonomy (Chadha 2005: 333; Holt 2022). Popular resentment mushroomed in 1959, when the national and state governments did little to deal with a famine that killed 5 percent of the population despite being warned about it in advance (Holt 2022; Maxwell 1973: 18; Pachuau and van Schendel 2015: 300; Panwar 2017: 979). Compounding this lack of responsiveness and empathy toward Mizos, the postcolonial Assamese government made Assamese the official language of the entire state at a time when Mizos were still recovering from the famine (Chadha 2005: 334; Holt 2022; Lalchungnunga 1994: 57). Mizo leaders formed the Mizo National Famine Front (MNFF) to provide food to the population during the famine, and the organization gained great popular support. After the famine, the MNFF was renamed the Mizo National Front (MNF) and—because the governments were more interested in forcing assimilation than providing famine relief—shifted its focus to demanding that the Indian government reinstate the autonomy that Mizos had lost at independence (Goswami 2009: 581). After new elections, the MNF easily defeated the Mizo Union and mobilized a secessionist movement. As in Nagaland, the Indian state used increasingly repressive tactics to combat the movement, and aggressive and unbending government policies promoted an escalation in conflict leading to nationalist civil war in 1966.

Available evidence suggests that support, recruitment, and resources for the MNF came disproportionately from three groups strengthened by colonial pluralism: chiefs, Christians, and soldiers. Because they lost their powers after union with India, chiefs kickstarted the nationalist movement by founding the United Mizo Freedom Organisation in 1947 (Lalchungnunga 1994: 79; Panwar 2017). Christian Mizos also spearheaded the nationalist movement, and churches provided the movement with a strong mobilizational base. The MNF emphasized that Hindu-dominated India sought to thrust Hinduism upon them and declared the need to keep Mizoram a "land of Christians" (Singh 1994: 203). Sarbahi (2021) explores the geographic variation in recruitment into the MNF and finds that—due to this religious dimension of Mizo nationalism—recruitment was greatest in regions with Presbyterian churches and YLA branches. Finally, approximately 5,000 Mizos fought with the British during the Second World War, and ex-Mizo soldiers—who had experience in guerrilla warfare—trained nationalist troops (Ray 1982: 161). On top of this, the government disbanded the Second Battalion of the Assam Regiment in 1964 because the soldiers—who were Mizos—requested more culturally appropriate food, and many of these soldiers joined the movement and helped train combatants (Chatterjee 1994: 186; Lalchungnunga 1994: 83; Panwar 2017: 980–81; Ray 1982: 161). In this way, lost autonomy was the main motive behind the nationalist movement, chiefs and Christians were especially fearful and resentful, and the soldiers from former Mizo regiments provided the Mizo nationalists with military support. Like the Naga conflict, the case therefore shows how extreme autonomy in excluded areas made Mizos sensitive to rule by others by strengthening communal frames and creating expectations for autonomy while simultaneously providing them with resources to fight a war.

THE GARO NATIONALIST CIVIL WAR

The Garo nationalist civil war began in 2014, and most violence ended by 2017. Relative to the Naga and Mizo conflicts, the Garo nationalist civil war was much later, smaller in scale, and shorter. Despite these differences, the Garo conflict follows a similar trajectory: The region was ruled as an autonomous zone, and Garo militants fought a war to restore the autonomy they had lost after union with India.

Even before colonial times, Garo were more influenced by larger "plains" communities than Nagas or Mizos. Because British officials viewed them as "primitive tribals" and were concerned over Garo raids on plains peoples, however, the British sought to isolate them. This began in 1822 and became more formalized in 1869, when the Garo Hills was given an "exclusionary" status and ruled through local headmen (de Maaker 2022: 301–2). Similar to the Naga and Mizo cases, exclusionary status resulted in "isolating the area politically, economically and socially" (Bhattacharjee 1973: 519). Yet similar to Nagaland and Mizoram, this isolationism did not affect missionaries, and Baptist missionaries were the main providers of education and set the local languages to writing (de Maaker 2022: 303). Unlike the Naga and Mizo cases, however, restrictions on population movements were repealed in the Garo Hills when its status was changed to "partially" excluded area in 1935. This change allowed nonresidents to travel in the territory, and Bengalis began to settle in the region during the final decade of colonialism.

After independence, the Garo Hills were fully incorporated into India and the regional state of Assam. The Khasi Hills, which border the Garo Hills, were also a partially excluded area, and both successfully lobbied the Indian government to separate the regions from Assam and create a new regional state—Meghalaya—in 1972. In recent decades, the Garo have found themselves marginalized economically and politically. Khasis are Meghalaya's largest community, making up 45 percent of the state's population versus the Garo's 33 percent (Singha and Nayak 2015: 1–2). The Khasi Hills are also more economically developed than the Garo Hills, and the Garo have lost considerable land due to the settlement of many migrants in the Garo Hills. On top of this, Khasi nationalists have demanded the recognition of Meghalaya as a Khasi state and implemented policies benefiting Khasis at the expense of Garo (Nayak and Singha 2015). In reaction to their political weakness, losing control of lands to immigrants, and Khasi chauvinism, Garo leaders began a movement to regain the autonomy that they had during the colonial period (Singha and Nayak 2015: 5–8). When faced with stiff government opposition at all levels, Garo leaders used violence to force the government's hand, thereby beginning the nationalist civil war.

Because seven decades separate the Garo's loss of autonomy and the beginning of the nationalist civil war, it is difficult to link the Garo nationalist civil war to colonial pluralism. Yet Garo leaders did not forget their history of autonomy and demanded its return when faced with the growing threats of political weakness, cultural loss, and land alienation. Such demands could have happened without indirect colonial rule, but colonialism legitimized these demands by declaring the Garo Hills the homeland of the Garo peoples and providing them with self-rule. Moreover, Garo are like Mizos, Nagas, Karens, and others in that missionaries helped forge a collective "Garo" consciousness by standardizing Garo, putting it to writing, and teaching in the vernacular. The Garo conflict therefore clearly fits the general pattern highlighted in other cases of nationalist civil warfare in Northeast India and Myanmar.

Nationalist Civil Wars in Princely States: Manipur and Tripura

The excluded areas were one important type of indirect rule in colonial India, but the most common form of indirect rule was princely states. Three nationalist civil wars occurred in regions that were princely states, including the Kashmiri, Manipuri, and Tripuri wars. Although much less concentrated than in the excluded areas, nationalist civil wars in the princely states still make up a disproportionate share of nationalist civil wars, as the princely states had one-quarter of the population of colonial India but have 30 percent of nationalist civil wars (Lange 2009b: 177).

The form of indirect rule in the princely states differed from the form of rule in the excluded areas in several ways. For one, princely states were more centralized, with one paramount "customary" authority, whereas excluded areas had more decentralized polities with many local authorities. In addition, and of greater relevance to this book, excluded areas were organized to make possible communal self-rule, whereas the princely states had maharajas, nawabs, or other Indian officials who ruled over diverse communities, thereby retaining the multicultural and imperial character of the Mughal Empire that preceded them. Because of this, indirect rule in princely states made possible a form of self-rule that was less likely to promote nationalist civil wars than in the excluded areas. There were exceptions, however, with the Tripuri and Manipuri princely states having "tribal" rulers who governed in the name of their communities. These were therefore abnormal princely states making possible communal self-rule, and this situation contributed to nationalist civil wars in similar ways as the excluded areas.

THE MANIPURI NATIONALIST CIVIL WAR

Manipur was an independent kingdom for nearly 1,000 years and avoided Mughal rule. The kingdom was controlled by ethnic Meiteis, or Manipuris, who speak their own language, are overwhelmingly Hindu, and presently make up more than half of the region's population. Most of the remaining population are Zo peoples, a broad term referring to a number of "tribal" communities, including Nagas and Mizos. In addition to the nationalist civil war, ethnic conflict between Manipuri and Zo communities has been common since independence.

In 1814, the Konbaung dynasty conquered Manipur, and the EIC— which had signed a treaty of mutual defense with the Manipuri Maharaja in 1762—fought with Manipuri forces to retake the region in 1826, thereafter restoring the Manipur Kingdom while retaining influence over it as a "protected state" (Meetei 2015: 149). In 1891, Manipuri leaders attempted to curb

British influence, causing the British to launch a military campaign and take complete control of the region during the Anglo-Manipuri War. Although subsequently recognizing and ruling through Manipuri Maharajas, the British exerted great influence over Manipuri politics.

The British did not force princely states to merge with India or Pakistan at independence. The Maharaja and other Manipuri nationalists recognized that Manipur had never been part of the Mughal Empire and had a long and proud history prior to British rule, and they sought Manipuri self-rule within India. The Maharaja of Manipur therefore conceded security and foreign affairs to India while establishing an independent Manipuri government with its own constitution, and elections were held in 1948. Shortly thereafter, the Maharaja of Manipur was effectively kidnapped by Indian security forces during a visit to Assam and forced to sign an agreement completely merging Manipur with India, thereby removing all Manipuri political autonomy and dissolving the Manipuri parliament (Baruah 2005: 59–60). In signing, the Maharaja did not consult with the Manipuri Legislative Assembly, and many therefore viewed the merger as both forced and illegitimate. The coerced incorporation of Manipur, in turn, is at the heart of the nationalist narrative in Manipur, with the two main Manipuri organizations fighting the Indian state citing the Merger Agreement as the root cause of the nationalist civil war (Baruah 2005; Sanatomba 2015: 206; Verghese 1996: 116).

After the forced union with postcolonial India, the Indian government ruled Manipur directly, thereby dismantling the preexisting state and removing Manipuris from positions of authority (Brara 2022: 292). Over time, many Manipuris became concerned about their lost autonomy and increasingly resented what they saw as India's illegitimate and forced integration of Manipur, and a nationalist movement strengthened in the 1950s. The Indian state reacted by vigorously repressing the movement and creating a highly militarized form of rule, and state coercion only strengthened grievances (Hanjabam 2008). Thus, in 1964, the United National Liberation Front was formed and began training members to fight for national self-rule (Sharma 2000; Tarapot 2003: 177–79).

With Manipuri nationalism strengthening in the face of state repression, the Indian state made Manipur a separate regional state within India in 1972 (Singh 2002: 219–25). Regional autonomy was a farce, however, as the Indian military controlled a shadow government that held real power (Baruah 2005: 59–70). And military rule and state violence intensified after the Indian state declared a state of emergency in 1975 and enacted the Armed Forces Act in 1980. It was in this context that the nationalist civil war began, and it continued over the next three decades (Singh 2011: 1000).

Similar to the Naga and Mizo conflicts, the root cause of the Manipuri nationalist civil war was therefore the forced incorporation of the region into a postcolonial nation-state that they viewed as alien. Manipuris were sensitive to lost autonomy because a long history of precolonial statehood and a communalized form of indirect rule strengthened both nationalist frames and expectations for self-rule. By the time the nationalist civil war began, postcolonial nation-state-building reforms had weakened or eliminated the political institutions that had supported indirect rule during the colonial period, and regional political institutions therefore offered less mobilizational resources than in Nagaland and Mizoram (Brara 2022: 292). Given strong nationalist frames and expectations, geographic isolation, and rugged terrain, Manipuri nationalists were still able to organize a nationalist movement.

THE TRIPURI NATIONALIST CIVIL WAR

Tripura is also a former princely state located in Northeast India that, like Manipur, has a long precolonial heritage, with a line of nearly 200 precolonial Tripuri rulers (Chadha 2005: 357). It paid tribute to the Mughal Empire at times but remained autonomous from it, and its ruler—the Maharaja—retained his position after the British took control of Tripura. Presently, 19 "tribes" live in Tripura, with ethnic Tripuris making up over two-thirds of the tribal population. The tribal communities, however, make up only one-third of the total population, and most of the remainder are Bengalis. Tripura is surrounded by Bangladesh on three sides, and a long history of Bengali migration promoted both Hinduism and the use of the Bengali language among elites prior to British rule. With the partition of colonial India, Bengali migration exploded, with some 600,000—equal to the size of the total population of Tripura in 1951—fleeing violence in East Pakistan (now Bangladesh) and migrating to the region (Kumar 2016: 159). As a result, the tribal population declined from 56 percent of the total population in 1921 to only 32 percent in 1961 (De 1998: 9).

Relative to Manipur, the nationalist movement in Tripura focuses less on the illegitimate union of Tripura with India because Tripuri elite were more willing to join India (Debbarma 2015). The main reason for this difference is security concerns: Tripura is surrounded by Bangladesh, and Pakistan attempted to gain control of Tripura during the independence transition (Mohanta 2004: 33–34). As in Manipur, however, resentment over union with India quickly grew, as Tripuris found themselves under the rule of outsiders and excluded from power.

Similar to Manipur, the central Indian government ruled Tripura without local participation after union, something that excluded local elites from government and allowed Congress to rule the region without local support (Mohanta 2004: 140). The main reason for this nondemocratic form of rule is that the Communist Party of India was the strongest party in Tripura at the time of union, and Congress wanted to keep communists from gaining control of the region. Congress cooperated with Bengalis to keep Tripuris out of power (Mohanta 2004: 141). Under Congress rule of Tripura, Bengalis had easy access to land, indigenous communities were not allowed to organize their tribal councils, and no effort was made to fill government positions with indigenous peoples (Khan 2023; Mohanta 2004: 63). The Congress-led government also made Bengali the sole official language in 1964 and refused to allow any education in Kokborok, the main language of Tripuris (Khan 2023: 132, 162).

Resentment over these policies quickly arose, and a Tripuri nationalist movement began in 1967 (Mohanta 2004: 59–62). The movement emphasized three problems that resulted in large part from the massive immigration of Bengalis into Tripura: landlessness, indebtedness, and the decline of the Kokborok language (Debbarma 2015; Gan-Chaudhuri 1980: 155; Khan 2023: 131–32). By the time India granted Tripura its own regional government in 1972, Bengalis were numerically dominant and therefore able to control the government (Kumar 2016; Saha 2002). And because Tripuri interests commonly opposed those of Bengalis and because radical Tripuri nationalists with ties to the Communist Party of India called for the expulsion of recent Bengali migrants, Bengali politicians and their supporters in Delhi were unwilling to address these grievances. As a result, some Tripuris "began to think that they were socially cornered, politically outnumbered, and economically deprived. They suffered from an apprehension that their language, culture, and every sphere of their way of life and tribal identity were at stake" (Khan 2023: 133). The resulting fear radicalized many and pushed some to join the nationalist movement. And because they were the targets of radical nationalist, some Bengalis actively opposed Tripuri nationalist demands and declared Tripura their own (Khan 2023: 139). By 1979, the resulting conflict turned violent, and the nationalist civil war lasted until 2004.

The Tripuri nationalist civil war therefore differs from those in Nagaland, Mizoram, and Manipur in that Bengali immigrants caused the most powerful grievances motivating the conflict. That being said, all four cases share three features that were central to the processes leading to nationalist civil war: the institutionalization of formalized communal self-rule, forced incorporation into a postcolonial state that removed cultural and political autonomy, and nationalist reactions. And because colonial pluralism promoted the first and the third, it was a vital—and possibly necessary—cause of the Tripuri nationalist civil war.

Colonial Pluralism and the Assamese and Bodo Nationalist Civil Wars

So far, this chapter has reviewed all nationalist civil wars in Northeast India except two: the Assamese and Bodo conflicts. British colonial pluralism did not promote these civil wars in the same way as the other conflicts in the region, as neither Assam nor Bodoland were ruled indirectly. Despite this difference, British colonial pluralism still contributed to both conflicts.

The Assamese and Bodo nationalist civil wars occurred in Assam, were over autonomy, and began in 1990 and 1989, respectively. Students, in turn, were the driving force behind the mobilization of both nationalist movements and emphasized that Bengali immigrants threatened their cultures and economic well-beings. Both movements also turned violent and demanded autonomy after concluding that governments were unwilling to protect their interests. Importantly, the movements are also related in another way: In their fervor to pursue their own interests, Assamese nationalists disregarded and disparaged Bodos, who are a plains tribe that has historically lived in contact with the Assamese, and the Bodo movement was in large part a reaction to what they saw as aggressive Assamese national chauvinism.

The Assamese recognize themselves as descendants of the Ahom Kingdom. Like the Shan in Myanmar, the Ahom were a Tai community that conquered much of the Bramhaputra Valley in the early thirteenth century and ruled it until Myanmar's Konbaung dynasty conquered the region in the early nineteenth century. With Bamar aggressions approaching British India, the British attacked the Konbaung dynasty in 1826, took control of Assam, and incorporated it into India. Although it had weakened by the time of Bamar conquest, the Ahom Kingdom had been large and powerful, being one of the few regions in South Asia that had successfully fended off Mughal aggressions and expanded greatly in the sixteenth century. Before this expansion, the Ahom had assimilated local peoples into their culture, but their military success reversed this process, as the Ahom adopted the Assamese language and Indic religions.

At independence, Assamese nationalists successfully lobbied to create a large Assamese state in Northeast India, thereby providing the Assamese with some degree of self-rule within India. The Assamese heartland is located in the Brahmaputra Valley, and other communities live in the surrounding hills and plains. These non-Assamese areas were also included in the Assamese state at independence, making the Assamese a minority in a regional state that they dominated. Many minorities, in turn, had not been ruled as part of colonial Assam. Given their minority position in their own regional homeland, postcolonial Assamese governments sought to protect their power by assimilating other communities, something that—as noted previously—contributed to the Naga and Mizo conflicts.

Although Assamese national chauvinism was present at independence and contributed to multiple incidents of ethnic violence against non-Assamese, Assamese national chauvinists did not use violent methods to increase Assamese self-rule until the 1990s. Similar to other regions in India's Northeast, many Bengali migrants entered the region during and after the independence process, which not only affected the economic opportunities of Assamese but threatened their political dominance. And viewing the Indian state as complicit with these problems, a small number of Assamese nationalists took up arms and began a guerrilla-based nationalist civil war.

One way in which British colonial pluralism contributed to this civil war was by providing examples. The Naga, Mizo, Manipur, and Tripuri conflicts all occurred in neighboring lands, and Assamese leaders knew about these conflicts. Thus, when some Assamese felt aggrieved by government nonresponsiveness to their demands and feared losing control of a regional state that they viewed as their homeland, they copied the model provided by these communities.

Protestant missionaries also influenced the nationalist civil war by strengthening and politicizing the Assamese community. Relative to nearly all other communities in Northeast India, missionaries had very little success converting Assamese. Despite this, they influenced Assamese society and politics in important and long-lasting ways. The Assamese are a linguistic-based community, and the dominant Assamese discourse claims that missionaries revitalized the Assamese language and prevented it from disappearing, thereby saving the Assamese community from certain destruction (Dutta 2005: 11; Misra 1987: 3; Price 1997). Prior to the arrival of the American Baptist missionaries in 1813, there was a variety of related dialects instead of a single Assamese language. And although different Assamese dialects had a written script, writing was very undeveloped, hardly used, and in decline. Upon their arrival, missionaries quickly standardized a single Assamese language, thereby creating a more unified linguistic community. Using this language, the missionaries also developed a vibrant vernacular literature. They began by translating the New Testament into Assamese, writing the first Assamese dictionaries and grammar books, and establishing the first Assamese press. They also founded the first Assamese journal, *Orunodoi*, which published a wide variety of nonreligious articles written by local intellectuals and was instrumental in starting a literary movement that popularized written Assamese (Dutta 2005: 15; Misra 1987: 67; Sharma 2002: 113–15). The importance of *Orunodoi* is evident in the fact that the word *orunodoi*—which means "the dawn"—became a generic term to refer to any journal (Sharma 2002: 115).

The standardization of the Assamese language and the growth of Assamese literature played a particularly important role promoting a strong Assamese communal identity because the British ruled the region as part of the Bengal presidency and—viewing Assamese as a close dialect of Bengali—declared Bengali the official language of the region. By standardizing the language and creating a vibrant literature in Assamese, the missionaries helped galvanize an Assamese identity and prevent the Assamese from becoming Bengalis. Missionaries also prevented this assimilation more directly: They actively lobbied the colonial government to make Assamese the official language of Assam and to separate Assam from Bengal, efforts that eventually proved successful and that provided an institutional environment that cultivated an Assamese national consciousness (Lange 2017: 183–84). As part of these efforts, the missionaries worked with several Assamese intellectuals, thereby mobilizing the Assamese politically.

Like the Assamese case, missionaries also influenced the Bodo nationalist civil war, but communal legislative representation was also important. The Bodo community includes a variety of tribes living primarily in the Brahmaputra Valley in western Assam. The British considered them "plains tribes," and Bodos lived in proximity to the Assamese during the colonial period and were more integrated into the Assamese economy and society than "hills tribes" like Nagas. Although the British did not create an excluded area for Bodos, they believed Bodos were at risk of "disappearing" and therefore created a "line system" to prevent nonlocals from settling in Bodo lands. Although the system never functioned effectively, it strengthened ideas that particular regions were Bodo and that non-Bodos were outsiders who did not belong.

Given their growing integration into Assamese society, colonial officials in the late nineteenth century feared that Bodos would assimilate into Assamese society. A major reason for this is that Bodos lived in proximity with the Assamese, and many accepted Assamese as their mother tongue and converted to Hinduism. Supporting colonial fears, the Bodo-speaking population decreased by 25 percent between 1881 and 1891 (Sarmah 2018: 9).

By the early twentieth century, Bodo numbers stabilized, and Bodo leaders worked hard to organize their community. Several Bodo cultural associations were founded at this time, and they lobbied the colonial government to protect and pursue Bodo interests. One early and important activity was participating in a government commission about electoral reform in 1929, during which Bodo leaders lobbied the government for reserved legislative seats (Chadha 2005: 259). As Pathak (2010) notes, Bodo leaders "used the colonial imagery of the tribe as backward, semi-savage, ignorant to put forward their political claims and for seeking colonial protection" (62). Shortly thereafter, the British reserved five seats for Bodos in the Assam Legislative Council. In 1933, Bodo leaders founded the Tribal League, a political party that actively pursued the interests of Bodos and other neighboring plains tribes. Given that Bodo votes were commonly needed to break deadlocks, the Tribal League was very influential and effectively protected Bodo interests. After independence, the renamed Plain Tribal Council continued to pursue Bodo interests, and in 1966 demanded the creation of a new state for Bodos. Like Karens in Myanmar, pluralist policies dealing with political representation therefore pushed Bodos to organize their community, enter colonial politics, and seek greater self-rule.

Baptist missionaries played an equally important role in the organization of the Bodo community. Although the missionaries had relatively little success converting Bodos (only about 10 percent of Bodos are Christian), they had lasting influences on Bodo society. As elsewhere, missionaries opened schools that taught in local vernaculars, and many Bodos went to these schools (Sarmah 2014). At this time, there were several Bodo dialects, and none was a written language. The missionaries therefore selected one dialect and created a system of writing for it. And in teaching in this language and providing printed material in it, missionaries played a vital role creating both a standardized Bodo language and a Bodo literary tradition.

Given that the Bodo community is based primarily on language and that many Bodos were gravitating toward the Assamese language when missionaries arrived, the role that missionaries played in the strengthening of a Bodo communal consciousness should not be understated (Sarmah 2014, 2018). Indeed, the preservation and use of the Bodo language was a major political issue spearheaded by various communal literary organizations, including the Bodo Chatra Sanmilani and the Bodo Sahitya Sabha. Most notably, the Bodo Sahitya Sabha fought successfully for the teaching of Bodo in secondary schools but unsuccessfully for the use of a Romanized script, which was the original script used by missionaries for the Bodo language and which the Assamese government opposed as "foreign" (Sarmah 2014). In the 1970s, the issue of script mobilized many Bodos, and leaders organized protests to demand control of their language (Das 2014). The government suppressed the movement and opened fire at one protest, killing 15 people. Over the next few years, continued conflict and a growing fear of reduced cultural and political autonomy led some Bodo nationalists to begin a civil war.

Thus, similar to Karens, reserved seats helped politicize the Bodo community, missionaries helped organize them to pursue communal interests, and both made them sensitive to losing autonomy. Assamese national chauvinism, in turn, frightened many Bodos so much that they organized to protect their community. And seeing several nationalist civil wars in the region (all influenced by British colonial pluralism), Bodo leaders copied their neighbors and began a nationalist civil war.

Colonial Pluralism and Religious Nationalism in India

Religion is arguably the core component of nationalism in South Asia. The link between religion and national chauvinism is clearest in Pakistan and Bangladesh, both of which are self-declared Muslim states. In India, Hindu national chauvinism was initially more subtle given Congress's secular stance and its dominance of Indian politics during the first three decades after independence. That beings said, many influential leaders in Congress were Hindu national chauvinists, Congress commonly played the Hindu card to defeat rival parties, and Congress actively exploited Hindu religious symbolism in ways depicting the "real" Indian nation as Hindu (Kaufman 2015: 157–59; van der Veer 1994). The Indian constitution, in turn, offered few protections to religious minorities and empowered the Hindu majority (Anderson 2013; Deol 2000: 41; Singh and Shani 2021: 112). By the 1970s, overt Hindu nationalist parties gained strength at Congress's expense, and the Hindu nationalist Bharatiya Janata Party (BJP) has dominated Indian politics in recent decades. In this way, Hindu national chauvinism has been present throughout the postcolonial period but has only gained official recognition over the past quarter century.

Many recognize that British colonial pluralism strengthened—and in some ways created—religious national chauvinism in South Asia (Breuilly 1994; Kaviraj 1997; van der Veer 1994). This argument has two complementary components. The first is cultural and argues that colonialism transformed the character and contours of Indic religions. The second argument is political and recognizes that British colonialism politicized religion in ways that actively pitted different religious communities against one another. In the sections that follow, I argue that the resulting religious nationalism promoted the Sikh and Kashmiri nationalist civil wars, thereby implicating colonial pluralism in these conflicts.

COLONIALISM AND THE CONSTRUCTION OF HINDUISM

Today, Hinduism is considered a major world religion akin to Christianity, Islam, and Buddhism. Yet according to Bayly (1985), there is no evidence of a unified Hindu religious community until the 1860s. Similarly, Oberoi (1994) notes that Indic languages lack a term to refer to religious community. Bayly, Oberoi, and others note that British colonialism played a major role in the creation and politicization of a unified Hindu religious community. According to this position, these effects were unintended and resulted from the inability of Europeans to understand religions that were so different from their own. Through pluralist colonial policies, in turn, European religious understandings gained influence, both by forcing Indians to work within a new system dominated by Europeans and by threatening Indic religions.

The first Europeans arriving in India understood Islam, as Europeans had already interacted with Muslims for centuries and Islam is very similar to Christianity. Indic religions, however, were new to them and did not conform to Western understandings of religion. There was no singular God, and the focus was less on devotion to a deity than cultivating spirituality. Religious practitioners, in turn, did not base their beliefs on written religious texts and go to mass congregations at religious centers. Instead, gurus commonly gained followers and provided particular religious instructions based on their own learnings and experiences.

Another very important difference concerns the openness of Indic religions to other religions. In contrast to Christianity and Islam, Indic religions were not closed systems that competed with, shunned, and tried to eliminate other religions; they were syncretic and actively incorporated new ideas into them. The Brahmanical idea of dharma, or cosmic order, for example, suggests that the preservation of equilibrium requires the assimilation of foreign elements, thereby promoting incorporation instead of opposition. Given this syncretism, Indic religions had relatively fluid religious boundaries, something that limited both the recognition of religious "others" and unity among the community of practitioners. The presence of caste systems, in turn, divided practitioners vertically, thereby further reducing religious unity. Instead of a singular, organized religion, Hinduism was therefore more of a network of related religions, many of which were very localized and fractured along caste lines. Gurus, in turn, played an important role promoting religious diversity and synchronism.

Although unable to fully understand Indic religions, Europeans tried to make sense of them, and European biases greatly shaped these understandings. Orientalist scholars began using the term "Hinduism"—derived from the Indus River—to refer to a supposedly singular Hindu religion, with the term first appearing around 1830 (Oberoi 1994: 16). Given the centrality of the written word in Judeo-Christian religions, Orientalist scholars searched for Hindu religious texts. In so doing, they compiled a variety of documents and used these documents to highlight the supposed "core" of Hinduism. Because of the status of Brahmins and European respect for them, Orientalist scholars paid considerable attention to Brahminic religious practices and beliefs, and European understandings of Hinduism therefore focused greatly on caste. Thus, Oberoi (1994) concludes:

> Historically the term [Hinduism] is erroneous because the sects or communities that constituted it do not possess one single historical founder, nor unifying principles and rituals or shared ecclesiastical authority—elements that are usually taken to be hallmarks of an organized religious community. Even their notions of what constitutes the sacred and the profane remained extremely varied. There is little that can be seen to be common between Tantrism and Brahmanism. An extralocal religious community of Hindus is therefore a modern creation; linguistic and historical evidence indicates that it never existed in the past. (17)

After the Indian Rebellion, the British concluded that they needed to better understand Indian society to make it legible and thereby more controllable, and they focused on religion because they saw it as the core of Indian society. Instead of trying to better understand the characteristics of Indic religions, however, they lumped all into Hinduism and focused on categorizing and counting religions, with the census being a core element of this. Seeing caste as a central component of Hinduism, the British made a great effort to collect information on the presence and distribution of castes in colonial India. These religious categories gained new significance and strengthened boundaries between people because they affected one's opportunities under the British Raj (Cohn 1987; van der Veer 1994).

In an environment in which political strength and resources depended on mobilizing people around a category, British colonialism created incentives for the mobilization of Hindus behind this new and inclusive category. The earliest and most successful attempt at this was led by the Arya Samaj (Deol 2020: 68–69). As Jaffrelot (1996) notes, Indians founded this organization in 1875 in reaction to British colonialism and missionaries. Not only did British colonialism strengthen the Hindu category and politicize it, but both the British and missionaries threatened Hinduism by describing it as primitive and degenerate and trying to convert Hindus to Christianity. Thus, high-caste Hindus founded the Arya Samaj to protect, strengthen, and unify Hinduism through reform (van der Veer 1994: 65). Christianity influenced these reforms, and the Arya Samaj recognized the presence of one god, placed great emphasis on religious texts and learning, sought caste reform, and began its own missionary efforts. At the same time, the movement was revisionist, as it sought to return India to a golden age (Jaffrelot 1996: 11; van der Veer 1994: 65). And longing for this golden age and seeing the British as an impediment to it, the Arya Samaj was the first to popularize and demand swaraj, or Indian self-rule, thereby providing great impetus and rallying Hindus to the independence movement. Gandhi was part of this movement, although his more secular position—which in the Indian context refers not to the absence of religion but to respecting all religions—resulted from his embrace of the long Indic tradition of religious synchronism.

Thus, colonialism greatly influenced the character of Hinduism. Colonial officials made sense of Indic religions through their particular understandings of what religions were and thereby contributed to an idea of a singular religion called "Hinduism." In seeing religion as the basis of Indian society and reifying castes categories, people began to recognize its importance and self-identify with religion and caste. Finally, colonialism sparked efforts to protect and reform Hinduism by threatening Indic religions.

COLONIAL PLURALISM AND THE POLITICIZATION OF RELIGION IN INDIA

In addition to promoting a singular Hindu community, British colonialism also politicized religion and pitted members of different religions against one another (Breuilly 1994; Kaviraj 1997). While the strengthening of the Hindu category and community was necessary for religious politicization, pluralist colonial policies played a more direct role in this process and further strength-ened religious categories. Among others, discriminatory and empowering plu-ralist policies were especially influential.

When applied to democratic politics, pluralism suggests all communities require adequate representation. Such pluralist principles are most common in places with large majority communities, as their sheer numbers prevent minorities from securing representation when people vote along commu-nal lines. To prevent the exclusion of small communities, pluralist policies reserve seats for communities or provide separate communal electorates, both of which ensure minority representation. In colonial India, the British applied pluralist legislative representation to religion, thereby providing non-Hindu communities special representation to ensure their ability to participate in legislatures and represent their communities. Although Christians, Sikhs, and Muslims all received special representation in colonial legislatures, Muslims received the most and were the focus of this policy.

While conforming closely to pluralism and legitimized by it, communal legislative representation in India was more influenced by practical concerns: the desire to limit anticolonialism (Breuilly 1994; Tudor 2013; van der Veer 1994: 18–19). The post-Rebellion anticolonial movement was dominated by Hindus, especially Hindus educated in the colonial schools and working in white-collar jobs, and few Muslims were part of the movement. While most Muslims were uneducated peasants, Muslim elites were conservative landown-ers, and these leaders feared the anticolonial movement: They recognized that independence would lead to Hindu rule and a reversal of status and power from precolonial times, and they therefore opposed both independence and democracy. Sir Syed Ahmed Khan was an early and influential Muslim leader who was concerned about Indian democracy. Speaking before the Legislative Council in 1883, he declared: "the system of election pure and simple cannot be safely adopted. The larger community would totally override the interests of the smaller community, and the ignorant public would hold the Government responsible for introducing measures which might make the differences of race and creed more violent than ever" (Tudor 2013: 61). Elsewhere, he noted, "If we join the [anticolonial] political movement of the Bengalis our nation will reap a loss, for we do not want to become subjects of the Hindus" (Kumar 2000: 60). In line with this view, the Muslim League's first statement of goals declared "the best sense of the country recognizes the fact that the progress of India rests on the maintenance of order and internal peace, and that order and internal peace, in view of the conditions obtaining in our country at pre-sent and for a very long time to come, immeasurably long time to come, spell British occupation" (Tudor 2013: 63).

In this regard, the British and the Muslim elites had a common cause against the Hindu-dominated anticolonial movement. The British, however, were under growing pressure to implement democratic reforms. Given this situation, the British chose to empower "loyal" subjects—especially Muslim elites—by providing them with communal representation in the colonial and regional legislative assemblies (Tudor 2013: 64). For this, they first created communal electorates for local boards before establishing Muslim electorates for regional legislative councils and the Indian Legislative Council. In establishing separate electorates for Muslims, the British not only ensured Muslim representation but guaranteed Muslims a far greater share of seats that was merited by the size of their population. Because the British controlled many seats within the colonial legislatures, the British and the Muslims were able to cooperate to stymie anticolonial policies in the colonial legislatures. As Breuilly (1994) notes, "From that time on Indian politics was forced to organise along religious lines" (178). In this regard, colonial India has clear parallels with Myanmar, with Muslims and Karens given special representation because of their greater support for the British. And just like Myanmar, special Muslim representation politicized community and pitted the minority community against the majority community over the national character of the postcolonial nation-state. In fact, Breuilly (1994) suggests that it was necessary for the rise of Islamic nationalism in colonial India (182). One can argue, in turn, that it also promoted the rise of Hindu nationalism.

To pursue Muslim interests, the Muslim League was formed in 1906. From the beginning, it was dominated by elite landowners from the United Provinces, which was the former Mughal heartland, and worked with the colonial government to create a separate Muslim electorate (Tudor 2013). At this point, the main focus of the Muslim League was to protect the rights and power of Muslims. Being based in the United Provinces, it had very little influence in the regions with majority Muslim populations (Bengal and Punjab). As independence approached, however, the specter of Hindu dominance pushed Bengalis and Punjabis to turn to the Muslim League for leadership. At the same time, the British increasingly relied on the party for support against anticolonialists, making the League a political force (Tudor 2013).

During the Second World War, Congress continued its anticolonial position and refused to help the British, whereas the Muslim League encouraged Muslims to assist British war efforts. While this situation would seem to bolster British support of Muslim interests, the British promised Congress that they would grant India independence after the war in return for cooperation, and this forced the League to reorient its political goals away from stalling independence to ensuring Muslim power and autonomy after independence. As leader of the Muslim League, Jinnah now demanded the maintenance of separate Muslim electorates and the overrepresentation of Muslims (one-third of the seats despite being one-fifth of the population), regional autonomy for the Punjab and Bengal, and veto powers for Muslims. Congress refused. It was at this time that Jinnah first brought up the two-state solution, although evidence suggests he proposed this policy as a pressure tactic to get Congress to accept his previous demands (Tudor 2013: 95–97). Congress did not budge, however, thereby leading colonial India down the pathway to partition. Disagreement over colonial pluralism therefore promoted the division of India.

KASHMIR AND SIKH NATIONALIST CIVIL WARS

Thus, by strengthening religious identities, politicizing religion, and pitting religious communities against one another in the political arena, British colonialism channeled political conflict along religious lines, created powerful grievances, and contributed to competing religious nationalisms. This situation, in turn, increased the risk of nationalist civil war. With the subsequent partition of India into Muslim and Hindu segments at independence, this risk reduced considerably. It did not eliminate the risk, however, and partition and the politicization of religion contributed to multiple nationalist civil wars in postcolonial India.

As noted previously, several excluded areas had non-Hindu populations, with Nagaland and Mizoram being notable examples. Given their positions as religious minorities in postcolonial nation-states defined in large part by religion, these communities felt excluded and threatened by assimilationist policies. At the same time, Indian leaders increasingly viewed religious minorities as suspect. Thus, although conflict over political autonomy was the main cause of these wars, the politicization of religion contributed to them by hardening the positions of both sides of the conflict, with the minorities demanding cultural autonomy and the state refusing the demands of suspect minorities.

Religious nationalism played an even greater role in the Kashmir nationalist civil war, although it did so in a very different way. As noted previously, the British protected and mobilized Muslims to counter the anticolonial movement, and this led to the religious communalization of Indian politics and the ultimate division of India along religious lines. Partition, however, left pockets of religious minorities on both sides of the postcolonial border, and this was the most important determinant of the Kashmir nationalist civil war.

The Kashmir conflict began in 1988 and was ongoing in 2024. Dozens of anti-Indian groups have fought in the war, with some fighting for an independent Kashmir and others demanding union with Pakistan. Prior to the war, India and Pakistan fought multiple wars over the region, and Pakistan has actively aided anti-state combatants in the civil war (Chadha 2005). The region borders Afghanistan, and Afghan Islamists have also crossed the border to fight against India. In this way, the nationalist civil war has clear international components.

During British rule, the Kashmir region was an indirectly ruled princely state. Although its population was majority Muslim, the Maharajas were

Hindu, and Hindus held most elite positions and were the main landlords; Nehru's family were wealthy landowners from the region. At independence, the British let the rulers of princely states decide whether to join India or Pakistan. At this time, the Maharaja of Jammu Kashmir maneuvered himself to maintain his independence from both. Given the large Muslim population in the region, Pakistani officials organized a rebellion to take control of the region. After these forces defeated the Maharaja's army, the Maharaja agreed to join India in return for military assistance, and the Indian government sent troops to the region to secure it, resulting in the first war between India and Pakistan. This and subsequent wars led to an informal division of Kashmir between India and Pakistan, with India controlling the majority of the region (Bose 2003: 31–35; Chadha 2005).

Although Pakistan has played a very important role mobilizing anti-Indian sentiment and violence in Indian Kashmir, grievances have also mobilized the Muslim population (Chadha 2005). Historically, Hindu landlords dominated Muslim peasants, resulting in great religious-based inequalities and the exploitation of Muslims at the hands of Hindus (Bose 2003: 16). On top of this, Indian governments maintained tight control over the region and disregarded and distrusted Muslims, and state repression increased in the early 1980s in the face of a growing Islamist movement. While these heavy-handed tactics created strong grievances, Muslim anger and resentment strengthened even further in the late 1980s after the main Islamic party won far fewer seats than expected in an election that many believe was rigged (Bose 2003: 48–50). Shortly thereafter, mass movements against Indian rule began, which resulted in violence and eventually a nationalist civil war.

As this brief description suggests, the Kashmir nationalist civil war grew out of the partition of colonial India, which, in turn, was part of a larger process through which colonial pluralism communalized politics and politicized religion. British colonial policies politicized Hinduism while mobilizing Muslims to pursue their political interests. Both greatly strengthened the political divide between Hindus and Muslims, which, in turn, convinced the British that they had little choice but to reject Congress's position on a unified postcolonial India and accede to Jinnah's demand for separate Muslim and Hindu states. Although it is impossible to say what would have happened if the British did not politicize and mobilize the Hindu-Muslim divide in this way, it is clear that partition and the politicization of religion was an extremely important cause of the Kashmir nationalist civil war, and both are embedded within a long and complex process linking colonial pluralism to nationalist civil war (Brines 1968; Burke 1974).

Pluralist colonial policies that channeled conflict along religious lines also contributed to the Sikh nationalist civil war. Similar to Hinduism, British rule contributed to a more unified Sikh community (Fox 1985; Oberoi 1995;

Singh and Shani 2021). And by politicizing religion and providing Sikhs with resources, pluralist policies promoted a Sikh nationalist civil war.

The Sikh conflict began in 1983 and lasted a decade. It involved Sikh nationalists who wanted to secede from India and form an independent Sikh nation-state—Khalistan—in the Punjab region of India. Sikhism is a relatively new religion and was founded and formalized in Punjab in the sixteenth century. In the face of harsh Mughal prosecution, Sikhs rebelled and established, first, a Sikh Confederacy and, second, a Sikh empire, the latter of which was founded in 1799 and extended beyond Punjab. Only fifty years after its founding, however, the empire weakened, and the British conquered it during the Second Anglo-Sikh War.

According to Fox (1985), Sikhism was one of several "Hindu" religions prior to British rule, but British colonialism helped make it a separate religion. His main argument is that Sikhism was internally divided between two main sects, with one recognizing Sikhism as a separate religion—the Singh Sabah—and the other maintaining religious syncretism with Hinduism (and to a lesser extent Islam)—the Sanatan. Regardless of whether they were Singh Sabah or Sanatan, the rural Sikh peasants—who made up the vast majority of Sikhs—commonly had localized practices influenced by a variety of religions. He claims that the British ultimately favored the Singh Saba and thereby played an instrumental role in the creation of a distinct Sikh religion. The main way they did this was through the Indian military.

During the colonial period, Sikhs were greatly overrepresented in the colonial military: Although less than 2 percent of the Indian population, Sikhs made up over 20 percent of the colonial military. One important reason for this was that Sikhs fought bravely with the British during the Indian Rebellion of 1857. Influenced by this record, the British considered Sikhs a "martial race" that was both loyal and naturally inclined to warfare. The British, however, did not accept any Sikh—they recruited Sikhs from the Singh Sabah, the sect that viewed Sikhism as distinct from Hinduism. In fact, the British forced Sikh soldiers to take a religious oath that only the Singh Sabah practiced. Moreover, only the Singh Sabah wore turbans, did not cut their hair, grew long beards, and refused to smoke; and the British forced their Sikh soldiers to follow these practices. The colonial enforcement of Singh Sabah practices was due to the British interest in maintaining strong divisions between Sikhs and Hindus, which, in turn, was seen by the British as making Sikh regiments powerful fighting forces against Hindu anticolonialism. In a widely quoted section of the British Army Handbook, for example, Major A. Barstow writes, "Sikh soldiers, too, are required to adhere rigidly to Sikh customs and ceremonies, and every effort has been made to preserve them from the contagion of Hinduism. . . . Sikhs in the Indian Army have been studiously 'nationalised' or encouraged to regard themselves as a totally distinct and separate nation, their national pride has been fostered by every available means" (quoted in Nesbitt 2005: 72). And with such a large number of Sikhs serving in the colonial military and with these soldiers holding positions of power and respect in their communities after their military careers, British colonialism played an instrumental role in the rise of contemporary Sikhism.

At the same time, Sikhism's uniqueness clearly had precolonial roots, with British colonialism simply favoring one Sikh sect over another to suit colonial interests. Indeed, long before British rule, Sikh religious reforms differentiated Sikhism from other Indic religions, thereby attempting to establish Sikhism as a distinct, non-syncretic religion. In establishing their vast empire, however, Sikh rulers needed to relax these rules and tolerate religious syncretism to maintain control over their expanding territory (Oberoi 1995). In turn, Sikh leaders of princely states and landed elites were usually Sanatan, and the British supported these leaders and depended on them. In this way, the British ultimately supported both Sikh camps in different ways. As Oberoi (1995) notes, these different camps fought for control of the Sikh community in the late nineteenth and early twentieth centuries, and—given their greater mastery of political organization, education, and printing presses—the Singh Sabah gained influence over Sikh peasants and was thereby able to institutionalize its view of Sikhism. Notably, Protestant missionaries contributed to this success: Given its focus on religious purity, the Singh Sabah organized in reaction to growing missionary influence and copied the missionaries by founding printing presses and schools to spread their views and attract followers (Deol 2000).

Other pluralist policies also politicized and nationalized the Sikh community. Viewing Sikhs as "loyal" subjects, the British reserved seats for them at both the colony level and in provincial assemblies (Singh and Shani 2021: 77–78). Consequently, Sikh politicians looked out for Sikh interests at different levels of politics. Throughout most of the colonial period, the Punjab Legislative Assembly had "a modern consociational (power-sharing) arrangement, with religious proportionality in state employment, a de facto religious veto, [and] segmented autonomy," something that further politicized religious community (Singh and Shani 2021: 70). Finally, although the British never provided Sikhs with political autonomy through indirect forms of rule, they formalized a sort of communal shadow state—the Shiromani Gurdwara Prabandhak Committee—that managed Sikh holy sites, ran schools and universities, and employed thousands (Singh and Shani 2021: 64–65). Its political wing, the Akali Dal, developed into the leading nationalist organization (Oberoi 1995).

During the independence movement, Sikhs were wary of both Congress and the Muslim League, and some began to mobilize for a separate Sikh state. In the end, however, most Sikhs reacted to Jinnah's demand that the Punjab be granted to Pakistan by supporting Congress, which supported a "secular" state. With partition, Sikhs living on the Pakistan side of the border were attacked, and millions fled to Indian Punjab. As a result of this large population move-ment, Sikhs became the majority population in the Indian Punjab for the first time, and many Sikhs expected to gain political autonomy by controlling a regional state within India. One reason a Sikh state was so desired is that the Indian state stopped reserving legislative seats for Sikhs after independence, thereby increasing concern about their very survival as a community, and Sikh leaders viewed political autonomy as a means of regaining political control and protecting their community (Deol 2000: 94). At this time, the Indian state was reorganizing regional politics to create linguistically based polities, but—given Hindu national chauvinism—Congress refused to consider these reforms in several regions with large non-Hindu populations, including Punjab (Deol 2000: 93). Over the next decades, Sikh nationalists mobilized to demand a Sikh regional state, but the Indian government opposed these efforts in a great vari-ety of ways (Deol 2000: 96; Singh and Shani 2021). One way was by eliminating the Sikh majority by adding regions with large Hindu populations to Punjab. And after Sikh's regained their majority, the Indian state recognized Sikhs as Hindus and categorized Punjabi as a dialect of Hindi (Deol 2000: 95–96). While categorizing Sikhs as Hindus and Punjabi as a dialect of Hindi justified the Indian state's refusal to create a Sikh/Punjabi regional state, its refusal to recognize Sikhs as a distinct community fueled great popular resentment.

In 1966, the Indian state finally created a Punjabi state with a population that was majority Sikh. The Indian state, however, left the regional govern-ment little power by increasingly interfering in the Punjabi government and continually declaring presidential rule over the region. One element of state interference that greatly angered many Sikhs was the Indian state's hydro-electric projects in Punjab and its diversion of up to 75 percent of the water to neighboring "Hindu" states (Deol 2000: 103). In this environment, Jarail Singh Bhindranwale—a radical Sikh teacher—joined forces with Akali Dal and organized a Sikh shadow government (Deol 2000: 104–5). Bhindranwale demanded an independent Sikh country and immediate action pursuant of this goal. His followers attacked Hindus and moderate Sikhs, killing hundreds. He and many of his most radical supporters took up residence at Sikhism's most holy site—the Golden Temple of Amritsar.

To contain this growing threat, Indira Gandhi organized a military opera-tion to remove Bhindranwale and his followers from the Golden Temple in 1984, and Bhindranwale and several hundred of his followers were killed, with over 1,000 others arrested. After taking control of the temple, the military ruled Punjab and rounded up thousands of Sikh nationalists. In reaction to Indian military attacks on Sikhism's most holy site and extreme repression, two of Indira Gandhi's Sikh bodyguards murdered her, sparking deadly anti-Sikh riots that killed thousands (Deol 2000: 109). The Indian government did not attempt to stop the violence, and some officials assisted participants

(Deol 2000: 109; Singh and Shani 2021: 135–36). In reaction to the desecration of Sikhism's most holy site and the Indian government's involvement in systematic and extreme violence, many Sikhs joined the nationalist movement, including thousands of soldiers, and Sikh nationalists took up arms to fight for an independent Khalistan.

British colonialism is linked to the Sikh nationalist civil war through a long process, making it difficult to gauge the extent to which British colonial pluralism contributed to the conflict. That being said, it is clear that British colonial pluralism contributed to the war, and it is very uncertain whether a Sikh nationalist civil war would have occurred without a history of British colonial pluralism. British colonial pluralism strengthened and nationalized the Sikh community while promoting contentious religious nationalism and Hindu national chauvinism, and all were necessary parts of this conflict. And similar to Karens in Myanmar, the ending of communal legislative representation created strong grievances and redirected the political focus of Sikh politicians to communal autonomy. Finally, the militarization of Sikhs provided important resources and training that helped Sikh combatants wage a nationalist civil war.

Conclusion

Although impossible to determine whether nationalist civil wars in postcolonial India would have occurred without a history of British colonialism, this chapter shows that pluralist colonial policies clearly shaped the processes leading to all conflicts. The analysis therefore supports chapter 3's statistical findings that British colonial pluralism greatly increased the risk of nationalist civil war.

Paralleling the Shan, Karenni, and Kachin nationalist civil wars in Myanmar, British colonialism contributed to several nationalist civil wars through its effects on communal self-rule. Pluralist policies commonly provide communities with some degree of autonomy, and the British gave several Indian communities considerable political autonomy through communalized indirect rule. When postcolonial governments removed this autonomy and pursued assimilationist policies, these communities rebelled. Several Indian conflicts—including the Naga, Mizo, and Garo nationalist civil wars—occurred in excluded areas that provided extreme autonomy and isolation, thereby making the loss of autonomy particularly galling. In addition, a few princely states ruled in the name of particular communities, and their loss of autonomy contributed to nationalist civil warfare in Manipur and Tripura. While highlighting the influence of forced political inclusion into postcolonial nation-states in ways that limited the cultural and political autonomy of communities, the cases offer evidence that nationalist grievances were particularly strong when accompanied by political powerlessness, assimilationist policies, and the arrival of many migrants.

Similar to the Karens in Myanmar, colonial India also shows how communalized legislative representation can politicize communities in ways that increase the risk of nationalist civil warfare. Most notably, the British provided Muslims with special representation, and this politicized religion in ways contributing to partition and nationalist civil wars that were influenced by it. The Bodo civil war, in turn, highlights how even communal legislative representation in regional councils politicized community and promoted expectations and demands for greater communal power and self-rule. Although less central to processes leading to the Sikh nationalist civil war, communal legislative representation politicized religious community and created strong grievance when communal legislative representation was dismantled at independence.

Like Myanmar, British colonial pluralism in India also had framing effects by shaping the strength and contours of community. In colonial India, censuses were more influential in this regard relative to Myanmar, and pluralist military policies were also important, especially concerning the Sikhs. Protestant missionaries also strengthened communal frames. This effect was strongest among Nagas and Mizos, but missionaries also affected communal frames among communities with few converts. Missionary activities among Sikhs, for example, pushed them to protect their religion by enforcing clear boundaries between Sikh and non-Sikh. Among Bodos and Assamese, in turn, missionaries popularized writing in vernaculars, something that helped stop their assimilation into other communities and strengthened Bodo and Assamese communal identities. In the case of the Assamese, missionaries also limited assimilation and strengthened the Assamese identity by actively lobbying government to separate Assam from Bengal and recognize Assamese as the official language in the region.

Another way in which British colonial pluralism contributed to nationalist civil warfare was by providing communities with mobilizational resources needed to organize nationalist movements. Most notably, communalized indirect rule provided communities with their own autonomous polities. In addition, missionaries helped communities found communal associations, communal legislative representation promoted communal parties, communalized security forces provided communities with soldiers and weapons, and all empowered communities to act on their grievances over forced incorporation into postcolonial nation-states and mobilize nationalist civil warfare.

Finally, British colonial pluralism contributed to Hindu national chauvinism, which strengthened both the nationalist demands of religious minorities and state opposition to these demands. British colonialism shaped Hindu national chauvinism by promoting a unified Hindu community and organizing politics along religious lines. Hindu national chauvinism, in turn, helps explain why the Indian state has used pluralist reforms to deal with caste and linguistic issues but has generally ignored the political demands of religious minorities.

6

Additional Cases of British Colonial Pluralism

In addition to Myanmar and India, seven other former British colonies—all with histories of colonial pluralism—have experienced at least one nationalist civil war. These include Bangladesh, Iraq, Israel/Palestine, Nigeria, Pakistan, Sri Lanka, and Sudan. In this chapter, I analyze these cases to explore whether the mechanisms and processes highlighted in Myanmar and India offer insight into additional nationalist civil wars. The chapter also tests the theoretical framework in a new and more critical way—by exploring why colonial pluralism did not promote nationalist civil war in four other former British colonies: Malaysia, Sierra Leone, Ghana, and Tanzania.

Additional Cases of Nationalist Civil Warfare in the Former British Empire

PAKISTAN AND BANGLADESH

Chapter 5 describes how colonialism contributed to nationalist civil war in postcolonial India, but colonial India also included contemporary Bangladesh and Pakistan. And just as colonial pluralism promoted nationalist violence in India, it had similar effects in Bangladesh and Pakistan. In particular, it contributed to the Bangladesh Liberation War, the two Baloch nationalist civil wars, and the Chittagong Hill conflict.

The Bangladesh Liberation War

Similar to the Kashmir conflict, the partition of India was an influential cause of the Bangladesh Liberation War. Whereas partition promoted the Kashmiri conflict by creating pockets of Muslims in a Hindu nation-state, partition pro-moted the Bangladesh Liberation War by hastily creating a seemingly unwork-able nation-state made up of contemporary Pakistan and Bangladesh. Indeed, not only did the peoples of Pakistan and Bangladesh have very different cul-tures and lack a shared history, but they were over 2,000 kilometers apart.

After the creation of Pakistan in 1947, conflict flared between West Paki-stan (now Pakistan) and East Pakistan (now Bangladesh). Despite having the majority of the population, East Pakistan quickly found itself politically subor-dinate to Mohajir politicians and Punjabi soldiers. Mohajirs are Urdu-speaking Muslims who moved to West Pakistan from Indian territories after partition, and—under the leadership of Jinnah—many Mohajirs became influential political leaders in postcolonial Pakistan. At the same time, Muslim Punjabis in West Pakistan had been a powerful force within the colonial military and subsequently dominated the Pakistani military.

State policies clearly reflected the dominance of West Pakistan. Shortly after independence, politicians made Urdu the sole official language even though only a fraction of the Pakistani population spoke it; over half spoke Bengali. At the same time, government spending and services were concen-trated in the West, with East Pakistan receiving only 40 percent of the gov-ernment expenditures per capita of West Pakistan. On top of all this, Pakistan was a Muslim state, and most influential Bangladeshi political leaders—while Muslim—demanded a secular state.

Given the cultural and geographical gulf between East and West Pakistan and discriminatory policies, Bangladeshi politicians founded the Awami League in 1949 to counter West Pakistan's Muslim League and pursue the interests of East Pakistanis. The Awami League quickly gained support and became increasingly nationalistic. Given its popularity and the numerical dominance of East Pakistan, the Awami League won a majority of seats in the 1970 Pakistani elections. The government and military refused to acknowledge the results, however, creating a political deadlock and growing demands for secession. A few months later, a cyclone hit East Pakistan and killed 300,000 people. Bangladeshis blamed the devastation on government inaction, and nationalist mobilization accelerated further. The government used extreme violence to quell the movement, and nationalist politicians reacted by declar-ing independence, which began the nationalist civil war. Although the Ban-gladeshi side won in only a matter of months, it paid an extremely heavy price, with hundreds of thousands—and possibly millions—of casualties.

Ultimately, colonial pluralism shaped processes leading to the Bangladesh civil war, including partition and the communalization of politics. Yet these effects were indirect, and many other factors contributed to the conflict. In the remaining nationalist civil wars in Pakistan and Bangladesh, however, colonial pluralism played a much more direct and influential role.

The Baloch Nationalist Civil Wars

The first Baloch nationalist civil war began only a few years after the Bangla-desh Liberation War, and the processes leading to it—as well as the second Baloch war two decades later—closely parallel those of Manipur and Tripura in India: Balochistan was an indirectly ruled princely state and subsequently experienced nationalist civil wars seeking either secession from or greater autonomy within Pakistan. And like Manipur and Tripura, a form of indirect colonialism that institutionalized communal self-rule was a core determinant of this conflict.

Balochistan borders Afghanistan and Iran, and many Balochs live in Afghanistan and Iran. Its population has diverse origins and speaks a variety of languages. Overwhelmingly, however, the population is Muslim, and the most common language is Balochi, which includes several dialects. Until rela-tively recently, large segments of Balochistan's population were nomadic or semi-nomadic pastoralists living in tribes. In the mid-sixteenth century, many of the tribes joined forces in the face of expanding Safavid and Mughal Empires and formed the Khanate of Kalat. The Khanate was a non-hereditary tribal confederacy in which the Khan, or leader, was selected from among the tribal chiefs and led the confederacy's military. Beyond this military arrangement, however, the tribes retained considerable autonomy. In subsequent years, the Khanate lost its independence and paid tribute to either the Safavids, Mughals, or Afghans, although these empires left Balochs to rule themselves. During the second half of the eighteenth century, the Khanate was ruled by Mir Noori Nasir Khan. During his long rule, the Khanate's territory expanded greatly, and the Khan was able to exert greater control over the tribes. After his death, both the size and centralization of the Khanate decreased, and it was during this period that the British began interfering in Balochistan, gaining control of the region by the 1870s (Bangash 2015: 51–52).

The main interest of the British in the area was geopolitical, as they wanted a buffer between India and the expanding Russian Empire. Under the British, the Khanate of Kalat was ruled as a princely state, although the British gave the region greater autonomy than most princely states. In so doing, British colonial-ism initially restrengthened the Khan vis-à-vis the tribal chiefs, or Sardars, and made the Khanship hereditary instead of elected. A group of Sardars resented these changes and revolted (Axmann 2009: 29). In reaction to this conflict, Brit-ish official Robert Sandeman reduced the formal power of the Khan outside his own tribe and institutionalized a system of indirect rule that gave the Sardars considerable power (Axmann 2009: 30–31). At the same time, the "Sandeman system" maintained the symbolic power of the Khanate and, with the creation of security and administrative machinery through tribal levies, actively attempted to create an "identification of the people with the defence of their own coun-try and their responsibility for their welfare" (Government of India 1922: 7;

quoted in Axmann 2009: 31). Finally, the Sandeman system created an intertribal council that made decisions for all tribes. In this contradictory way, British rule empowered Sardars at the Khan's expense while strengthening a common idea of a Baloch nation that centered on the Khanate.

By the 1920s, the educated elites formed Baloch associations and began anticolonial protests (Axmann 2009; Bangash 2015: 172–74). Instead of militating for an independent India or Pakistan, this middle-class movement demanded an independent Balochistan. The Khan of Kalat actively supported the movement, seeking not only Baloch independence but to reassert his powers. The Sardars also supported the movement, although they wanted to give the Khan symbolic power while maintaining or strengthening their power and authority. At independence, the Khan declared the independence of the Khanate of Kalat and established a bicameral legislature. Believing that the Khan was attempting to usurp power, leaders in three regions decided to join Pakistan (Axmann 2009: 232–33). Although initially recognizing the independence of what remained of the Khanate, Pakistan pressured the Khan to join Pakistan less than a year later and sent in troops to suppress an uprising against the forced merger. A decade later, another uprising occurred over the government's removal of all local autonomy. Although this movement was suppressed, the Baloch nationalist movement remained active underground. And when the Pakistani government created democratic openings in the 1970s, Baloch leaders founded nationalist parties demanding secession. When the Pakistani government subsequently outlawed these parties, Baloch militants took up arms, thereby beginning the first nationalist civil war. Fighting between nationalists and the government lasted three years, and a second nationalist civil war began in 2004 after the assassination of Nawab Akbar Bugti. Several Baloch actors were involved in these wars, and the anti-state forces were decentralized and had different goals, with some demanding independence from Pakistan and others insisting on Baloch autonomy within Pakistan.

In his analysis of the origins of the Baloch nationalist civil wars, Sheikh (2018) notes that their causes are far from evident. Most notably, the Baloch population is linguistically heterogeneous, which obstructs nationalist movements. In addition, the Baloch population is overwhelmingly Muslim, and Pakistan is a self-declared Muslim nation-state. He concludes that postcolonial Pakistan's refusal to recognize ethnicity and its exclusion of Balochs from political power was the main cause of the nationalist movement. That being said, postcolonial Pakistan was led by the two communities that had the most power during the colonial period (Punjabis and Mohajirs), and all other communities were excluded from power. Of the dozens of communities, however, only the Balochs and the Bengalis fought nationalist civil wars for greater autonomy. While helping to explain nationalist warfare, the exclusion hypothesis offers little evidence into why only these two communities rebelled.

As noted previously, two factors made exclusion particularly galling for the Bengalis. First, they made up more than half the total population, and the democratic principle made their exclusion particularly bothersome. Second, the partition of colonial India resulted in a Pakistani state that was noncontiguous and separated by India, with East Pakistan over 2,000 kilometers from West Pakistan.

Instead of population size and geography, a history of communal autonomy through indirect rule is the main reason why exclusion promoted nationalist civil warfare in Balochistan. British colonialism helped build an autonomous and decentralized Baloch state based on "custom" that was symbolized by the Khanate, and the indigenous leaders of this polity did not view themselves as part of colonial India. A communalized form of indirect rule therefore made Balochs very sensitive to threats to their autonomy. As a result, the Khan of Kalat refused to join Pakistan, declared independence, and ruled Kalat as an independent country for half a year. Pakistan's forceful incorporation of Balochistan followed by the cultural, political, and economic marginalization of the region, in turn, only strengthened Baloch nationalism and inspired many to join the nationalist movement. Thus, although on the opposite edge of South Asia, a communalized form of princely rule contributed to nationalist civil warfare in ways similar to Northeast India.

The Chittagong Hill Nationalist Civil War

After its separation from India and then Pakistan, Bangladesh was a very unlikely candidate for nationalist civil warfare because of its homogeneity: 98 percent spoke Bengali, and 90 percent of the population were Muslim. Only four years later, however, a nationalist civil war began. This war pitted the Bangladeshi state against a variety of small communities known as the Chittagong Hill peoples who collectively make up less than 1 percent of the Bangladeshi population. While the war seemed improbable to many, the region's history as an excluded area helps explain its occurrence.

The Chittagong region is located in the extreme southeastern corner of Bangladesh and borders both India and Myanmar. Similar to Nagaland and Mizoram, the British designated the Chittagong Hill Tracts (CHT) an excluded area (Bala 2022: 44–47; Uddin 2010). As a result, tribes were able to maintain local autonomy, "customary" chiefs ruled, laws passed in the colonial legislatures were not implemented in the region, and nonlocals needed special passes to travel in the CHT (Adnan 2004: 20–21; van Schendel et al. 2000: 25–34). The population, in turn, was very different from the rest of southeastern India: Whereas East Bengal was overwhelmingly Bengali and Muslim, the majority of peoples living in the uplands were Buddhist or Hindu "tribals." The Chittagong range surrounds Chittagong, the second largest city in Bangladesh and a bustling port during the colonial period. The British designated the hills an excluded area to protect the region's population from the dual threat posed by Bengalis: Officials feared the demise of hill communities through assimilation into Bengali culture as well as the potential spread of Bengali anticolonialism to the CHT.

During independence negotiations, both India and Pakistan demanded the CHT, and the British belatedly awarded the region to Pakistan. Initially, the Pakistani government formally retained the region's autonomous status and chiefs (Adnan 2004: 23; van Schendel et al. 2000: 71–76). By the late 1950s, however, the government increasingly interfered in regional affairs in the name of "development," and it removed the Chittagong Hill's special autonomy in 1962 (Adnan 2004: 24–25; Uddin 2010: 287–88). As Uddin (2010) notes, "The Pakistani government saw the 1900 Act [which made the CHT an excluded area] as a legacy of British colonial administration, which helped separate the CHT from the rest of the country" (287). It therefore sought to forcibly integrate the region into Pakistan and remove communal autonomy.

After the secession of Bangladesh from Pakistan, the new government supported an even more aggressive form of national chauvinism and rejected demands from Chittagong Hill leaders to regain their special autonomy (Chakraborty 2014). On top of this, the Bangladeshi government refused to recognize the Chittagong Hill peoples in any way, made Islam the national religion and Bengali the national language, resettled Bengalis in the region, took large tracts of lands from the local population, and militarized the CHT (Adnan 2004: 26–27; Bala 2022: 57–59; Uddin 2010: 298–99). Whereas only 2 percent of the population in the CHT was Bengali in 1947, their percentage increased to 39 percent by 1981 (Adnan 2004: 15; Chakraborty 2014: 298). Faced with a loss of autonomy and becoming minorities in their own lands, several leaders began a nationalist movement demanding greater autonomy, and government violence against it quickly sparked the nationalist civil war. In this way, the Chittagong Hill conflict follows the same path as the Naga, Mizo, Karenni, Kachin, and Shan nationalist civil wars: Colonial pluralism promoted communal self-rule and extreme isolation, both were lost after independence, and nationalist movements arose to regain this cultural and political autonomy.

SRI LANKA

The nationalist civil war in Sri Lanka between the Sinhalese-dominated state and Tamil nationalists highlights several of the same dynamics as the nationalist civil wars analyzed in previous cases. British pluralist policies and missionary influence advantaged the Tamil community over the much larger Sinhalese community and created expectations for special power and representation, and both made Sinhalese national chauvinism more assertive and vindictive.

And because colonial pluralism also increased Tamil sensitivity to Sinhalese national chauvinism, Tamil nationalists began a secessionist civil war.

After taking Sri Lanka from the Dutch in 1796, the British controlled the entire island through a direct form of rule. Despite the absence of indirect rule, other pluralist colonial policies were present, as the British "chose to identify people with social categories and to control those people through their use of those categories" (Peebles 2006: 48). They used censuses to divide Sri Lankans along racial, ethnic, religious, caste, and tribal lines and treated Sri Lankans differently depending on their categories (Lieberman and Singh 2017; Peebles 2006; Wickramasinghe 2006). Moreover, direct rule in Sri Lanka depended on the Native Administration, which employed local elites to serve as administrators for the colonial government (Peebles 2006: 56–57). These indigenous authorities had considerable local power and were members of the community that they administered. The British also maintained multiple systems of civil law, with Tamils, Kandian Sinhalese, Muslims, and Mukkuvars (peoples of southern Indian origin) having their own legal codes (Cooray 1974; Nissan and Stirrat 1990: 28; Peebles 2006). Colonial education was also pluralist. With the assistance of missionaries, colonial officials created separate vernacular systems of education for Sinhalese and Tamils. In reaction to Christian education, both Sinhalese and Tamils also organized their own private schools. In addition to teaching different languages and religions, the educational systems taught opposing histories that catered to their different communities (Lange 2012; Perera 1991; Siriwardena et al. 1985; Udagama 1990). Due in part to British policies that limited missionary influence among the Sinhalese out of fear that missionary activities would provoke reactions that destabilized colonial rule, the Tamils had a substantial educational advantage that gave them greater access to elite education and white-collar employment, inequalities that fueled Sinhalese resentment against Tamils and contributed to a popular belief that Tamils were taking the state away from the Sinhalese (de Silva 1984: 127; de Silva 1986: 87; Samarasinghe 1984: 178).

A final pluralist colonial policy was a community-based system of legislative representation. Sri Lanka was the first British colony to have communalized legislative representation, and this pluralist policy began in the 1830s, a quarter century before the initial implementation of pluralist policies in neighboring India. As elsewhere, communalized representation allowed communities to pursue and protect their political interests at the colony level. In Sri Lanka, however, communal representation differed from the system in Myanmar and India because it reserved seats for nearly all communities, including the Sinhalese majority (at least until the late colonial period, when only Tamils received reserved seats) (Welhengama and Pillay 2014: 54). This representative system institutionalized and politicized communal difference, greatly overrepresented minorities while underrepresenting the Sinhalese, and was the main source of early competition and conflict between Sinhalese and Tamils. Most notably, debates about reforming communal representation became very heated in the 1920s, as Low Country Sinhalese (Sinhalese living along the coast) wanted to abolish it to increase their representation whereas other communities fought to maintain communal representation because they benefited from it (de Silva 1986: 58; Nissan and Stirrat 1990; Welhengama and Pillay 2014). Not coincidentally, the first community-based political parties were founded at this time, and Russell (1982) documents how debates over communal legislative representation effectively institutionalized a competitive and conflictual system of communal politics pitting Sinhalese against Tamil. Welhengama and Pillay (2014), in turn, note that colonial officials actively opposed Sinhalese demands to eliminate communal representation, supported the Tamils, and stoked fear of Sinhalese rule.

As in Myanmar, social divisions, group inequalities, and heightened communal competition all strengthened Sinhalese national chauvinism and made advantaged minorities—especially Tamils—favored targets (de Silva 1981). Sinhalese nationalism emerged in the late nineteenth century as part of a Sinhalese revival movement led by Angarika Dharmapala (1864–1933) and Munidasa Cumaratunga (1887–1944) (Tambiah 1992). Dharmapala focused on Buddhism as the basis of the Sinhalese nation and suggested that Sri Lanka had been unfairly taken from the Buddhists (Tambiah 1992). He therefore demanded reinstating Sinhalese-Buddhist culture before its demise and vilified British colonialism, Christian missionaries, Tamils, and Muslims as foreign invaders who were destroying a great civilization. Cumaratunga focused more on the protection and assertion of the Sinhala language. His ideas and leadership were instrumental in the rise of the Hela movement, which sought to return Sinhalese culture to its past splendor by shunning Indian, colonial, and other alien practices. Influenced by Dharmapala and Cumaratunga, a growing number of Sinhalese desired Sinhalese self-rule over all Sri Lanka and believed Sri Lanka belonged to the Sinhalese. A major focus of this Sinhalese national chauvinism was the restoration of an imagined precolonial "golden age" that the British destroyed and that other communities threatened (Jayawardena 2010: 45).

Despite the strength of Sinhalese national chauvinism, severe communal violence in India and colonial pressure combined to push Sri Lanka's first independent government to make concessions to non-Sinhalese communities and recognize the Sri Lankan nation as multicultural (de Silva 1981: 490; Little 1993: 55–57; Tambiah 1992; Wickramasinghe 2006: 169). Because Sri Lanka had a functioning democratic system for several decades before independence and did not experience Japanese rule during the Second World War, the transfer of power was much smoother than in Myanmar. Popular Sinhalese opinion, however, opposed postcolonial multiculturalism, seeing it as an illegitimate legacy of colonialism that stripped the Sinhalese of the power that they deserved (Tambiah 1986; Welhengama and Pillay 2014). As Little (1993) writes, "The majority believed their culture and religion had been violated by a long line of colonial oppressors, particularly by the British, and they were enraged that the Tamils and other minorities might dare to obstruct the fulfillment of their historic destiny" (62). In the mid-1950s, S.W.R.D. Bandaranaike, an Oxford-educated elite who was more comfortable speaking English than Sinhala and raised a Christian, tapped into this resentment and was elected prime minister (Devotta 2005). Bandaranaike demanded that Sri Lanka be a Sinhalese nation-state, something requiring that Sinhala be the only official language and Buddhism the only official religion, and his chauvinistic policies contributed to severe anti-Tamils riots. Shocked by this violence, he attempted to reign in Sinhalese national chauvinists by reversing the policies, but a Buddhist monk reacted to Bandaranaike's "treasonous" backtracking by murdering him. After his death, Bandaranaike's wife assumed power and—learning from her husband's misfortune—proved herself a staunch national chauvinist.

While British colonial pluralism contributed to Sinhalese national chauvinism by weakening the Sinhalese community and increasing the relative power of other communities, divisive British policies also made Tamils very sensitive to Sinhalese national chauvinism. Because Tamils had received special recognition, accommodation, and representation during colonialism, many expected the continuation of pluralist policies after independence and strongly opposed government policies institutionalizing Sinhalese dominance (Welhengama and Pillay 2014: 225–27). Such opposition only intensified the anger of Sinhalese nationalists, and popular opinion pushed all nonminority political parties to support Sinhalese national chauvinism. Thus, policies declaring Sinhala the official language and Buddhism the national religion sparked widespread Tamil protests and civil disobedience in 1956 and 1958, and Sinhalese nationalists reacted by killing hundreds of Tamils. This cycle of violence continued intermittently and escalated into a civil war in 1983, a bloody conflict that lasted three decades.

As in Myanmar, missionaries also contributed to nationalist conflict by antagonizing the Sinhalese while strengthening Tamil nationalism. The case is different, however, because the missionaries did not convert many Tamils and contributed to Tamil nationalism primarily by promoting reactions against missionary influence. In Sri Lanka, the American Ceylon Mission arrived in Jaffna—the region with the greatest concentration of Tamils—in 1813; the British had forbidden the Americans from working with the Sinhalese out of fear that missionary activities would worsen Sinhalese anticolonial resistance. According to Sabaratnam, a Tamil intellectual and editor of the most popular nationalist newspaper, American missionaries came to Jaffna to preach Christianity but ultimately helped create a new Tamil nation (Ilankai Tamil Sangam

2010). Missionaries strengthened Tamil communal consciousness in several ways, including by standardizing Tamil, promoting mass education, and contributing to a vibrant Tamil literature. Their greatest influence, however, was more indirect: It sparked a Tamil revival movement. Because so many Tamils attended missionary schools, Tamils worried about the standing of Hinduism. Several Protestant missions, in turn, publicly berated Hinduism, something that caused a backlash. The revivalist intelligentsia championed Tamil literature and art and popularized the Saiva doctrines of Hinduism, thereby helping to create a "heightened cultural and linguistic consciousness" among Tamils (Tambiah 1986: 108). Arumuga Navalar (1822–1879) was the key figure among the Tamil-Hindu revival movement in Sri Lanka. Navalar viewed Tamil culture as severely threatened by colonialism and missionaries and actively preached the need for a Hindu revival. In pursuit of this goal, he copied the very techniques used by Protestants to attract followers, including running a printing press and promoting the use of Tamil. His greatest concern was education, declaring that "education was the indispensable instrument of religious recovery" (de Silva 2007: 147). These schools therefore began teaching a nationalistic Tamil curriculum, and it was this very Tamil nationalism and assertiveness that so many Sinhalese reviled as a threat to their community (Lange 2012).

At the same time that missionary activities strengthened a Tamil national consciousness, their influence also strengthened Sinhalese national chauvinism by creating intercommunal inequalities. Because the missionaries were the major source of education and because missionary schools were concentrated in regions inhabited by Tamils, Tamils became much more educated than the Sinhalese majority during the colonial period. This educational advantage gave Tamils special access to white-collar employment, especially in the public sector. In 1955, 26 percent of the elite Ceylon Civil Service were Tamil despite making up only 10 percent of the population, and they were even more overrepresented among government specialists (Samarasinghe 1984: 178). This Tamil advantage also occurred in higher education, especially in the most prestigious programs like medicine, law, and engineering. Indeed, 25 percent of university admissions to the science faculties were Tamil in 1970, and their percentages were over 40 percent in engineering and medicine (de Silva 1984: 127). In a context of high unemployment and ethnic polarization, many Sinhalese scapegoated Tamils for "stealing" Sinhalese jobs and pushing Sinhalese out of higher education (Tambiah 1986: 56). This situation, in turn, conformed with and strengthened an aggressive and exclusionary Sinhalese national chauvinism, which depicted Tamils as a severe alien threat to the nation.

Thus, British colonial pluralism did not provide communities with autonomy, which was the most common pathway through which colonial pluralism promoted nationalist civil warfare in Myanmar and India. Similar to the Karen case, however, colonial pluralism politicized community and contributed to intercommunal inequalities in a variety of ways, and both caused severe political conflict between Sinhalese and Tamil communities. The Sinhalese resented the negative effects that colonialism had on their community as well as the "special" treatment that Tamils received. In contrast, Tamils sought to retain the protections and power that they gained through colonial pluralism. Thus, when Sinhalese politicians pursued aggressive and chauvinistic policies that sought to marginalize Tamils, Tamils mobilized opposition, Sinhalese national chauvinists reacted to this opposition by attacking Tamils, and Tamils countered with a nationalist civil war.

SUDAN

Similar to other British colonies in Africa, the British made a concerted effort to construct an indirect system of rule in Sudan after conquering it in 1898. This task was difficult because Mahdi rule had preceded British conquest and destroyed local political institutions, resulting in "young [British] administrators searching for lost tribes and vanished chiefs, and trying to resurrect a social system that had vanished forever" ('Abd al-Rahim 1969: 203). The British made such a concerted effort to use indirect rule because it was the dominant colonial model at the time, was cheap, and could weaken anticolonial resistance, which was strong in Sudan throughout the colonial period and caused the British to fear a fate similar to that of their Turco-Egyptian predecessors (Deng 1995). In an effort to divide anticolonial resistance, the British ruled Sudan through a large number of regional authorities, thereby destroying the more centralized state run by the precolonial Mahdi regime. On top of this, the British implemented a "Closed District Ordinance" in Darfur, the Nuba Mountains, Beja, and southern Sudan to build autonomous polities based on indigenous customs that were separate from the Arab and Islamic heartland (Idris 2013; Said 1956). Similar to the Frontier Areas in Myanmar and the excluded areas in India, this policy sought to both protect minority communities from majority communities and weaken the potential for broad-based anticolonial resistance, with the latter being of utmost importance.

Over time, the British improved relations with three Nile Valley Arab tribes in central Sudan (the Ja'aliyiin, the Shaiqiyya, and the Danagla), which had been very influential during the period of Turco-Egyptian rule and lost power under Mahdi rule. During the late colonial period and after independence, these tribes—which make up only 5 percent of the total population—controlled the majority of elite positions within the state, military, and economy (Natsios 2012: 11–12). The British eventually rescinded the Closed District Ordinance in all regions except the South, where the British felt they needed to "protect" the "primitive" Africans from the more advanced Arabs and their anticolonialism (Deng 1995; Tounsel 2018: 347). As a result, the precolonial Arab elite eventually held a privileged position in the British colonial state, although the British effectively ruled southern Sudan as a separate colony and actively restricted northern influence in the region. This "Southern Policy" sought to limit the dual processes of Arabization and Islamization through a variety of processes, including restricting Arabs from traveling to the South, preventing southerners from residing in the North, creating a system of indirect rule through "customary" chiefs, promoting the use of vernaculars and English, and restricting northern employment in the southern administration and military (Daly 1986: 396–419; Mayo 1993: 167). Summing up the divide-and-rule-style reasoning behind the Southern Policy, one influential colonial official noted: "In time we shall reap our own advantage, for a series of self-contained racial units will be developed with structure and organisation based on the solid rock of indigenous traditions and beliefs . . . and in the process a solid barrier will be created against the insidious political intrigue which must in the ordinary course of events increasingly beset our path in the north" (Daily 1986: 410).

To limit Arabic and Islam, the southern administrators turned to missionaries for support. In 1900, Governor Wingate linked financial support of missionaries to their ability to "build a strong Christian counter-weight in the South to balance Muslim strength in the North" (Mailer 2007: 206). In particular, the British depended on missionaries to provide all education in the South, something that was necessary to train southerners to work in the southern administration, and the schools employed local vernaculars and English. As elsewhere, missionaries helped forge a strong communal identity by making schools "arenas where Christianity was promulgated, ethnic pride and cross-ethnic unity encouraged, vernaculars and English taught, and new communities of belonging forged" (Tounsel 2018). Believing that they were on a mission to save the southerners from Islam, the missionaries—like the southern administrators—presented northerners as a terrible danger. Mission schools, for example, taught how northern Muslims had enslaved southerners and how the British now protected southerners from the North (Mailer 2007: 215).

Sudanese anticolonialism was present throughout the colonial period but gained strength in the 1930s and 1940s and was led by Arab elites from the Nile Valley who sought the return of an independent Islamic state ruling over an Arab nation. Similar to Myanmar and Sri Lanka, the leading anticolonialists were therefore national chauvinists. Prior to independence, the nationalists declared their intention to Arabize and Islamize the entire population (Idris 2005, 2013; Mayo 1993; Sharkey 2008). As part of this effort, they passed policies excluding non-Arabs and non-Muslims from the nation. For example, the *Nationality Act* of 1948 defined citizenship based on ethnicity and privileged Arabs, who were all Muslims (O'Brien 1998: 67).

The nationalist elites were particularly concerned about the South, which they saw as having been unfairly separated from the rest of Sudan by the Southern Policy (Daly 1991: 65–83; Mayo 1993; Sharkey 2008: 34). From their perspective, the Southern Policy "was aimed at the elimination, by administrative means, of all traces of Muslim/Arabic culture in the South and the substitution of tribal customs, Christianity and the English language with the ultimate objective of giving the southern provinces a character and outlook different from that of the country as a whole" (Mayo 1993: 168). Under pressure from northern politicians, the British reversed course and merged the North and South into a single administration in 1947, thereby abruptly replacing decades of southern isolation from "dangerous" northerners with a Sudanization policy that cemented the domination of northerners over the South (Leach 2013: 13). Once in power, the new government began aggressive policies to assimilate southerners (Deng 1995; Idris 2005, 2013; Leach 2013; Poggo 2002; Sharkey 2008). Part of this effort involved nationalizing missionary schools, kicking all missionaries out of Sudan, using Arabic as the language of instruction, and teaching Islam (Poggo 2002; Tounsel 2018: 360–61). As the head of the Sudanese Department of Religious Affairs declared in 1959, "The nationalization of the Mission schools was an important step in the direction which recognizes cultural unification," noting that the government's ultimate goal was "cultural Islamic unity" (Mailer 2007: 226).

Given half a century of separate administration that was justified as a means of protecting the southerners from the northerners and an indirect form of rule that institutionalized cultural autonomy and self-rule, the southern Sudanese population resented and feared Arab Muslim rule and strongly opposed Sudanization policies. Southern politicians reacted by demanding a federal system of government that would retain the autonomy and recognition that they had gained under British colonial rule, but the government in Khartoum rejected these demands and made support for federalism a criminal offense (Deng 1995: 137). In reaction to chauvinistic policies, southern military officers mutinied in 1955, one year before independence. A report written jointly by colonial officials and northern politicians noted that the Southern Policy contributed to the violence by creating "fear and mistrust in the mind of Southern Sudanese against his fellow countryman in the North" and "perpetuating and exacerbating southern prejudice against the north" (Mayo 1993: 165; Colony of Sudan 1956: 17). Popular southern resistance also increased as successive Sudanese governments implemented aggressive integration and assimilation policies. This was especially the case for General Abbud's military regime, which came to power in 1958 and emphasized "One religion (Islam), one culture, and one language (Arabic)—one nation (Sudan)" (Deng 1995: 12; Idris 2013; Leach 2013: 44; Mailer 2007: 226; Natsios 2012: 43). As Deng (1995) notes, "southern resistance was not so much to Islam or the Arab culture, which had already been accepted in certain parts of the South, especially in urban centers, as it was to the rigidity of the assimilationist policy and the forceful ruthlessness of its implementation" (136). The nationalist movement gained momentum and military personnel after soldiers arrested for mutinying were released from prison in the early to mid-1960s, and the first war began shortly thereafter (Rolandsen 2011: 115).

The first nationalist civil war ended in 1972 with a peace agreement that gave southern Sudan greater autonomy and ended coerced assimilation. By the early 1980s, however, Arab politicians once again popularized Arab and Islamic national chauvinism as a means of mobilizing support and imposed sharia law throughout Sudan, and renewed national chauvinism sparked a second civil war that lasted until 2005 (Deng 1995: 12–13; Idris 2005: 53; Sharkey 2008). This civil war was different from the first in two main ways. First, although southern communities led the civil war, they collaborated with non-Arab communities from other regions who also opposed the government's assimilationist policies and the marginalization of non-state communities. As a result, conflict was not limited to the South; the genocidal violence in Darfur was part of government efforts to fight this war. The second war was also different in that the leaders of the anti-state forces sought political reform instead of secession. One element of these reforms involved changing the communal character of the Sudanese nation, with anti-state combatants opposing Arabization and recognizing the Sudanese nation as diverse. In addition, they demanded a system of ethnic federalism making possible minority self-rule. [1]

In 2011, only six years after the second civil war had ended, southern Sudanese nationalists began a third war. With growing problems elsewhere, the Sudanese government feared that the South could once again join forces with anti-state combatants from other regions to topple the regime. They therefore accepted southern demands, and South Sudan became an independent country.

As this description shows, the nationalist civil wars in Sudan have close parallels with the civil wars in the excluded and Frontier Areas of India and Myanmar. Like the Garo, Kachin, Karenni, Mizo, Naga, and Shan cases, policies separated southern Sudan from the North, made possible communal self-rule, limited interactions between the North and South, and increased southerner opposition to northern dominance. Even more, colonial officials working with minorities in Myanmar, India, and Sudan all increased intercommunal antagonism by viewing the larger communities as a danger to the smaller. Finally, missionaries were active in all these cases and contributed to the conflict in important ways.

NIGERIA

Igbo leaders began a nationalist civil war—the Biafra War, or the Nigerian Civil War—to secede from Nigeria and create their own independent nation-state in 1967. The war lasted three years and was extremely deadly, with an

---

1. Because of this difference, UCDP categorizes the second Sudanese civil war as over government compatibility, not territorial compatibility, so the war is not scored as a nationalist civil war in chapter 3's statistical analysis.

estimated 100,000 military casualties and between 500,000 and two million civilian deaths. The Nigerian state won the war, and Igboland remained part of Nigeria. After the return to civilian rule and growing political openings 30 years later, a small group of actors in the oil-producing region of southeastern Nigeria tried to forcefully take control of the oil reserves and increase their autonomy, resulting in a second—albeit much briefer and less deadly—nationalist civil war led by the Ijaw community.

Previous statistical analyses find that oil production is related to nationalist civil wars, and the Nigerian case supports claims that this relationship is causal: Oil is concentrated in southeastern Nigeria, and the Igbo and—especially—the Ijaw communities mobilized nationalist movements to assert greater control over these reserves in the face of regimes that excluded them and controlled the oil revenue (Hunziker and Cederman 2017; Iwilade and Okwechime 2022: 493–96). At the same time, colonial pluralism contributed to both nationalist civil wars by communalizing politics, something that was especially important for the Biafra conflict. Paralleling Sudan, the British institutionalized regional self-rule but handed power to national chauvinists from the largest community. With limited autonomy and facing extreme ethnic violence, the Igbos reacted by seceding from Nigeria, thereby beginning the region's history of nationalist strife.

Throughout most of the colonial period, the British effectively ruled Nigeria as three different colonies—the North, Southeast, and Southwest, with the North making up the majority of the territory and having more than half the population. Although Nigeria is very diverse and has hundreds of different communities, all three regions had a communal core that made up the majority of the population: Both the northern Hausa-Fulani and southeastern Igbo made up approximately two-thirds of their region's population, and three-quarters of the population in the Southwest were Yoruba. As a result, the regional form of rule in colonial Nigeria contributed to a communalization of politics, with the dominant community of each region controlling a regional state (Young 1976). In so doing, "the colonial state institutionalized acrimonious ethnicity as a primary site of politics and set the stage for many of the narratives and counter-narratives of marginalization, dominance, and resistance" (Iwilade and Okwechime 2022: 488).

Colonial officials established indirect forms of rule in all three regions, although the forms of indirect rule varied depending on precolonial conditions. In northern Nigeria, which had a history of precolonial statehood and was ruled by the large and powerful Sokoto Caliphate, the colonizers recognized and gave special status and power to the authorities of the precolonial state. In the western Yoruba region, precolonial politics were dominated by smaller city-states, and the British established an indirect form of rule through these city-states. Finally, precolonial political institutions in the eastern Igbo region were village-based and acephalous, complicating the creation of an indirect form of rule through "customary" authorities. Similar to Sudan, the British therefore effectively created chiefs—the Warrant Chiefs—to rule the region indirectly.

The three regions were officially amalgamated in 1914, but each retained a strong and communalized regional government. After the Second World War, the British strengthened regional administrations and created legislative assemblies at both the regional and colony level. With these changes, cultural organizations turned into political parties that participated in both regional and colonial legislatures, thereby communalizing the political system, something Coleman (1958) refers to as the "regionalization of nationalism" (319). As Suberu (2022) notes, the federal system established during colonialism produced "a combustible, polarizing convergence of ethnic, regional, and political cleavages" (378).

At this time, Igbos and Yorubas spearheaded an independence movement, while "loyal" Hausa-Fulani elites demanded the maintenance of British rule. Recognizing that the Hausa-Fulani dominated the North and that the North had the majority of Nigeria's population, the southern-led anticolonial movement demanded reforms dismantling the colony's three-region structure and replacing it with a new federal state that included many new regions. The northern elites, however, vehemently opposed this and demanded either the retention of the three regions or a separate northern colony. In the end, the British protected their loyal supporters by retaining the tri-partite structure at independence. As a result, Nigeria became independent with a federal structure that allowed one community—the Hausa-Fulani—to dominate national politics, thereby violating John Stuart Mill's "Law of Stability" stating that no unit of a federation can be as strong as all other units combined (Suberu 2022: 380).

In addition to this regionalization and communalization of politics, the British contributed to regional and communal inequalities that increased competition over the control of the postcolonial state. One element of inequality is that the emirs and sultans of the North retained great authority, much more than any indigenous authority in the indirect systems of rule in the southern regions. Although the British faced strong resistance from the Sokoto Caliphate and had to conquer it militarily, Lord Lugard copied techniques he had learned in India and retained precolonial leaders as "traditional" authorities in a new indirect system of rule. As part of this, British colonialism celebrated the precolonial heritage of the leaders and allowed the rulers to continue to serve as religious authorities. This included transplanting a revamped Durbar ceremony from India that celebrated the traditional authorities of northern Nigeria in a way that separated them from the South and cemented the special status of the northern sultans, emirs, and chiefs (Apter 2008). As a result, politics in northern Nigeria remained semi-feudal and Islamic throughout the colonial period. The British also stacked the highest positions in the administration with Hausa-Fulani, and the only reserved seats in the colonial legislature were for Hausa-Fulani traditional authorities. And because the British saw southern Nigerians as a potentially disruptive force who could weaken the "Black squires" of the North, they passed laws limiting the ability of southerners to travel, live, and buy property in the North and preventing missionaries from working in the region (Chimee 2013: 112; Osaghae and Suberu 2005; Reed and Mberu 2015: 421).

Through this isolation, traditional Islamic rule in the North ultimately disadvantaged the North educationally. Relative to the other regions, southeastern Nigeria developed advanced educational systems during British colonialism (Abernethy 1969: 262–65). From early on, Protestant missionaries were influential in southeastern Nigeria, and they established schools throughout the region. Although less influential, they were also active in southwestern Nigeria, thereby promoting educational expansion in this region as well. In northern Nigeria, however, missionaries were absent, and the indigenous leaders promoted Islamic education at the expense of Western forms of education. Thus, in 1965, the enrollment in secondary schools was 110,000 in southern Nigeria but only 10,000 in northern Nigeria despite the fact that the majority of the population lived in the North (Abernethy 1969: 265). Similarly, primary enrollment was nearly universal in southern Nigeria at independence but only 10 percent in the North (Curle 1973: 89). As a result, southerners—and especially Igbos—were overrepresented in white-collar jobs.

Both before and after Nigerian independence, rates of unemployment were high among the educated (Abernethy 1969: 206; Callaway 1963). Because of particularly limited economic opportunities in the Southeast, many educated Igbos moved to other regions with lower levels of education and soon became a conspicuous minority holding desirable positions. This situation caused many Hausa-Fulani to fear and resent Igbos (Abernethy 1969: 253–77; Diamond 1983: 471–72; Paden 1971; Young 1976: 278). As a result, northerners commonly discriminated against Igbos, and fear and anger over Igbo dominance intensified as the British prepared Nigeria for independence by expanding and Africanizing the civil service, a move that provided greater opportunities to Igbos. Recognizing the relatively advantaged position of Igbos, the most influential Hausa-Fulani leader declared that ethnic competition for civil service jobs was "a matter of life and death to us" and one that warranted violence in pursuit of Hausa-Fulani interests (Abernethy 1969: 264). Given the strength of resentment against Igbo educational superiority and competition for elite jobs, Igbos living in the North became the targets of several ethnic riots killing tens of thousands (Abernethy 1969: 266–67; Paden 1971; Young 1976: 472).

After independence, northern leaders cemented their control over the state and increasingly centralized their rule (Suberu 2022: 387). In so doing, they implemented reforms favoring northerners for administrative and military positions and focused nearly all development funding on the North. To maintain their dominance, they arrested southern political leaders, systematically failed to process the candidacies of politicians running for rival parties, annulled a census that would have provided the South with more seats, and mobilized extreme violence (Doron 2022: 402; Falola and Heaton 2008: 164–71). To democratize the state and eliminate northern dominance and cronyism, Igbo officers led a military coup that took over the Nigerian state in 1966. In reaction, pogroms in northern Nigeria targeted Igbos, killing as many as 50,000, and northern officers quickly organized a countercoup that successfully reinstated northern control of the state (Doron 2022: 404; Young 1976: 294–95). Thus, faced with continual violence, excluded from state power, and fearing the loss of regional autonomy, Igbo nationalists declared independence from Nigeria, thereby beginning the Biafran civil war.

Although the Biafra civil war might have occurred without British colonial pluralism, the case clearly shows that pluralist policies increased its risk in different ways. Most importantly, it communalized politics by creating community-based administrative units and regional legislatures that reified and politicized community and strengthened expectations for communal power and self-rule. The particular form of British pluralism also promoted communal inequalities that made communalized politics all the more competitive. Finally, pluralist policies contributed to both pogroms against Igbos and strong Igbo expectations for continued self-rule, suggesting that the risk of nationalist civil war would have been much less without a history of colonial pluralism. Along these lines, Osaghae and Suberu (2005) conclude that colonialism became "the single most important factor in the crystallization of contemporary identities and identity conflicts in Nigeria" (16).

ISRAEL/PALESTINE AND IRAQ

Israel/Palestine and Iraq are two additional former British colonies that experienced nationalist civil warfare. Given histories of colonial pluralism, it seems likely that British colonial pluralism contributed to nationalist civil warfare in both cases. In fact, Iraq and Palestine were Type A Mandate Territories granted to the British by the League of Nations after the First World War, and, as part of the agreement passing these former Ottoman territories to British control, the British were required to recognize and look out for the well-being of minority communities. As the cases of Myanmar, India, and other former British colonies show, colonial policies protecting minorities against other larger and stronger communities contributed to nationalist civil warfare. An analysis of the processes leading to the wars in Israel/Palestine and Iraq, however, offers evidence that the nationalist civil wars would almost certainly have occurred without histories of colonial pluralism (although not necessarily without histories of British colonialism).

Colonialism is commonly blamed for the nationalist civil war between Palestinian anti-state combatants and the Israeli state. The argument is that British colonialism opened the colony to Jewish settlement and declared Palestine a Jewish homeland, and the influx of a population seeking their own nation-state in lands that others viewed as their natural state promoted nationalist conflict. Notably, the migration of large numbers of non-British settlers to British colonies is not unique to Palestine, with Chinese and Indian migrants settling in many Asian, African, and Caribbean colonies. In none of these other cases, however, did the settlers fight nationalist civil wars, suggesting that something was unique about colonial Palestine. One important difference is that Jewish settlement in Palestine was influenced by a Zionist movement seeking a Jewish national homeland, whereas Indian and Chinese settlers moved to British colonies overwhelmingly for economic reasons. When faced with settlers who wanted to establish a Jewish state in a region that they viewed as their own inalienable land, many Palestinians reacted by claiming that Jewish settlers had no place in Palestine, thereby pitting Palestinian and Jewish nationalist movements against one other and resulting in a violent conflict that continues to this day (Muslih 1998; Sayegh 2013).

While Jewish settlement and the pursuit of a Jewish homeland are the key elements leading to nationalist civil war, it is possible that pluralist policies contributed to this conflict in different ways. For one, British colonial pluralism might have promoted Jewish settlement, with pluralist policies encouraging the immigration of peoples to the colony. Evidence, however, does not strongly support this claim, as pluralism does not necessarily encourage settlement; it is simply compatible with the settlement of new populations. Moreover, colonial pluralism had little influence on the motivation behind the Balfour Declaration. In addition to the influence of the Zionist lobby and either sympathy for Zionism or antisemitism, the main reason why British officials supported the creation of a Jewish homeland in Palestine was to increase support from Jewish communities in North America and Russia during the First World War.

Evidence therefore suggests that the Israeli-Palestinian nationalist civil war would have occurred without a history of colonial pluralism, as the migration of hundreds of thousands of Jewish settlers seeking a national homeland was the main cause of the conflict. That being said, colonial pluralism weaves into the historical processes leading to the conflict in ways that reinforced this outcome. For example, a divisive pluralist mindset influenced the decision to make Palestine a Jewish homeland, with British officials viewing Jewish settlers as a potential ally against unruly Palestinians. While Military Governor of Jerusalem in 1917, for example, Ronald Storrs famously noted that Jewish settlement could "form for England a 'little loyal Jewish Ulster' in a sea of potentially hostile Arabism" (Specia 2023). As already mentioned, however, this was not the main motive for supporting Jewish settlement.

After taking control of Palestine, the British also implemented pluralist policies that exacerbated conflict. One notable example was the creation of a legislature based on communal representation. The first legislature was created in 1920, but Arabs boycotted the assembly because it reserved seats for the Jewish population (Friesel 1987). Protests against communal representation mobilized Palestinian nationalists in pursuit of self-rule and against a Jewish homeland and contributed to the Jaffa Riot (1921) and subsequent conflict. That being said, communal legislative representation was a lightning rod bringing preexisting opposition to a Jewish homeland into action rather than creating this opposition, and the different nationalist goals of Palestinian and Jewish settler communities would almost certainly have led to nationalist civil war without this policy.

In colonial Iraq, British pluralism had even less influence on the nationalist civil war between Kurdish nationalists and the state, as Kurdish demands for autonomy preceded British rule and the British did not actually implement pluralist policies increasing Kurdish autonomy. Iraq was a colonial creation that combined three regions of the Ottoman Empire, and the Ottomans ruled the northern region in which the Kurdish population is concentrated (the Mosul vileyat) separately from the remainder of contemporary Iraq (Izady 2004). Kurdish leaders had lobbied the Ottoman Empire for greater autonomy before British rule, and, in an effort to strengthen Kurdish support for the British during the First World War, the British promised Kurds an independent homeland (Atarodi 2003: 147–48; McDowall 2021: 151, 173). After the war, the first officer charged with negotiating an agreement with the Kurds, Major E. W. Noel, strongly supported the idea of a Kurdistan for Kurds under British protection and increased expectations for it (Atarodi 2003: 149). Other priorities, however, caused the British to reverse course: British interest in protecting Mesopotamia (southern Iraq) from the Ottomans, making Iraq a viable entity, and protecting the position of King Faisal (a foreigner who had led an Arab nationalist movement in Syria and who the British imposed as king of Iraq) ultimately trumped support of Kurdish nationalism, and the British merged the Mosul vileyat with Arab Iraq without any provision for Kurdish autonomy (Atarodi 2003; McDowall 2021: 164, 177–81). This not only contributed to Kurdish rebellions during British rule but also lies at the heart of the postcolonial nationalist civil war. The case therefore shows that Kurdish demands for autonomy preceded formal British control and that the British dealt with Iraqi Kurds in a nonpluralist way, albeit after promises of pluralism had bolstered nationalist expectations.

Colonial Pluralism and No Nationalist Warfare: Malaysia, Singapore, Sierra Leone, Ghana, and Tanzania

Although Bangladesh, Pakistan, Sri Lanka, Sudan, and Nigeria offer additional evidence that British colonial pluralism contributed to several nationalist civil wars, Israel/Palestine and Iraq show that colonial pluralism was not necessary for nationalist civil war. At the same time, some places with British colonial pluralism did not experience nationalist civil war, suggesting that British colonial pluralism was not sufficient for nationalist civil war. In this section, I analyze five former British colonies that did not experience nationalist civil warfare despite histories of British colonial pluralism—Malaysia, Singapore, Sierra Leone, Ghana, and Tanzania. The purpose of this analysis is to investigate why colonial pluralism did not always promote nationalist conflict, an issue that the next chapter also considers.

MALAYSIA

So far, this book has considered every former British colony coded in chapter 3's statistical analysis as having experienced nationalist civil warfare except one: Malaysia. A closer look suggests that the conflict in Malaysia was more of an international conflict than a civil war, and I therefore do not consider the conflict a nationalist civil war. Instead of helping my argument, this recoding complicates it because the absence of nationalist civil warfare in Malaysia is surprising for two reasons: Malaysia had a highly pluralist form of colonial rule, and the Malaysian Federation merged distinct regions that had not previously been part of the same polity and possessed distinct cultures, something that the conflict between East and West Pakistan shows can contribute to nationalist civil war. The analysis highlights two factors that help explain why pluralism did not promote war in this context: the conditions under which colonial pluralism increases sensitivity to the national chauvinism of others and how the popular acceptance of pluralism transforms the effects of pluralist policies.

Contemporary Malaysia consists of two land masses separated by hundreds of kilometers. Although smaller in terms of territory, 80 percent of the Malaysian population lives on the Malay Peninsula, and the remainder lives on the island of Borneo in the states of Sarawak and Sabah. Prior to colonialism, several states were present on the peninsula, and the vast majority of peoples in these states were ethnic Malays who practiced Islam and spoke Malay. Small numbers of indigenous non-Malays lived in isolation on the peninsula, and some Chinese resided along the coast. In contrast, Malaysian Borneo was divided into a great number of localized polities that sometimes paid allegiance to neighboring empires, and the population was very diverse and overwhelmingly non-Malay and non-Muslim.

European influence in what became British Malaya (i.e., peninsular Malaysia) began with the Portuguese conquest of Malacca in 1511, and the Dutch subsequently gained influence throughout much of the region a century later. British colonialism in the region began prior to the Napoleonic wars but expanded greatly thereafter, and the British established the Straits Settlement over Penang, Malacca, and Singapore in 1824. In the 1870s, British colonial control expanded throughout most of the Malay states, with the exception of the northern states controlled by Thailand (then Siam). Among the British Malay states, colonial officials continued to recognize the authority of the Malay sultans, although they gradually removed most of the sultans' powers and centralized control over them (Harper 1999). This was especially the case for the Federated Malay States, whereas the sultans of the Unfederated Malay States retained somewhat greater autonomy and authority. In both the Federated and Unfederated Malay States, however, the British employed Malay rulers as "customary" authorities and emphasized that they were ruling with and in the interests of these rulers. Highlighting the similarity between this form of rule and rule through the princely states in colonial India, the British regularly organized celebratory meetings with all Malay sultans and referred to these gatherings as Durbars, thereby repurposing the Indian ceremony described in the introduction.

Colonial officials opened Malaya to migration, and many workers from India and—especially—China immigrated to the colony. These population movements made Malaya much more diverse and threatened Malay demographic dominance. In general, the migrant communities worked in urban areas and the export sectors, whereas Malays remained overwhelmingly subsistence farmers. In this way, British Malaya is a prime example of a segmented colonial labor force, a character that is commonly linked to communal conflict (Bonacich 1973; Horowitz 1985).

Pluralist policies in British Malaya focused on distinguishing Malays from Chinese and Indians. Different from Myanmar, where pluralist policies hurt the largest community, the British sought to protect Malays from other communities, especially the Chinese. As Comber (1983) notes, the British acted "as an 'umpire' mainly to keep the alien Chinese at bay and to look after the special interests of the Malays" (11). In addition to preserving the political authority of the Malay sultans, the British reserved government positions for Malays, underrepresented non-Malay communities in legislative councils, and restricted the purchase of Malay lands by Chinese. The British implemented these policies because their form of rule depended on the Malays, because the Malays did not organize an anticolonial movement, and because many colonial officials viewed Chinese as pushy and disrespectful foreigners who were a potential source of instability (Comber 1983; Kheng 2002).

The political strength of Malays, in turn, increased greatly at the expense of non-Malays during the independence transition. Similar to Myanmar, the

Japanese captured Malaya during the Second World War. The Malay authorities did not fight the Japanese and sometimes collaborated with them, whereas Chinese communists from the colony led a guerrilla campaign against the Japanese. Although this situation could have promoted colonial policies favoring the Chinese, the communists turned their attention to the British after the defeat of the Japanese and led a decade-long war—the Insurgency. To combat the communists, the British centralized and strengthened the colonial state, something that required close collaboration with the sultans (Lange 2009a). Because the Chinese led the communist insurgents and because the British were working closely with the Malay communities, the reforms further marginalized the position of the Chinese. Chinese communists, in turn, commonly attacked Malays, thereby increasing intercommunal tension and forcing Chinese Malays to keep their heads low and accept Malay political dominance (Lange 2009a). To protect their economic interests, the Chinese and Indian elites formed parties that joined a coalition with the leading Malay party, and the postcolonial state was therefore multi-communal but clearly Malay-dominated. Highlighting the dominance of Malays, Islam was named the national religion, Malay became the national language, and policies limited the abilities of Chinese and Indians to gain Malay citizenship (Kheng 2002).

By the late 1960s, new Chinese parties formed to oppose Malay dominance, and these parties made important gains in the 1969 elections. After the election results were announced, many Chinese celebrated with parades and gatherings, and a number of Malays reacted by attacking Chinese, killing hundreds and injuring thousands more. Influential Malay politicians interpreted the situation as Chinese attempting to extend their economic dominance into the political arena, and subsequent government policy sought not only to reassert Malay political dominance but to privilege Malays economically. The flipside of these policies was that Chinese and Indian communities faced growing political exclusion and economic and educational discrimination. Although supposed to be temporary, these policies continue to this day.

The combination of the country's history of colonial pluralism with growing Malay national chauvinism seems an ideal environment for nationalist civil warfare, and the absence of nationalist civil warfare therefore requires consideration. Two factors help explain this exceptionalism, both of which limited the sensitivity of Chinese and Indians to Malay national chauvinism. First, British colonial pluralism was unusual in that it actively protected the state community against non-state communities. As a result, British colonialism treated non-state communities as foreigners and did not empower them, and the Chinese and Indians therefore did not have expectations for communal power and self-rule like the non-state communities in Myanmar, India, and elsewhere. Second, most members of the Chinese and Indian communities self-identified with their sending societies, and this transnationalism weakened support for a

Chinese or Indian homeland in Malaya. Kheng (2002), for example, notes that many Chinese were more concerned about losing their Chinese citizenship than gaining Malayan citizenship during the independence transition. In this regard, Chinese and Indian communities were different from many Jewish settlers in Palestine because they already had a homeland and came to Malaya for economic reasons. This helps explain why Chinese and Indian communities have generally continued to collaborate with Malays as junior parties to protect their economic interests despite discriminatory policies.

As noted previously, Sabah—located in Malaysian Borneo—experienced one minor war that my coding of UCDP and EPR data suggests was a nationalist civil war but that qualitative evidence suggests was an international war. The conflict occurred in 2013 and was led by the Sultan of Sulu and his supporters. Sulu is an island off the north coast of Sabah, and much of Sabah had been—at least nominally—part of the Sulu Sultanate prior to the founding of the British North Borneo Company in 1881. Even before the sultan conceded Sabah to European companies, however, the Spanish—who controlled the neighboring Philippines—had gained influence over the Sultanate of Sulu, and the American military subsequently forcibly incorporated Sulu into the Philippines after the Spanish-American War. When North Borneo became a formal British colony in 1946, the Philippine government declared the transfer from the British North Borneo Company to the British government illegal and demanded that the region be "returned" to the Philippines. To bolster their claims, the Philippine government reinstated a Sultan of Sulu. In 1993, the Philippine government agreed with the Malaysian government to drop its demands for Sabah, which angered the Sultan of Sulu and caused him to threaten to retake the region on his own. In 2013, after feeling betrayed for being excluded from peace talks with the Moro Islamic Liberation Front, the Sultan of Sulu (who at this time was no longer recognized by the Philippine government) sent a boat with 200 fighters to reclaim Sabah, resulting in a short military battle easily won by Malaysia. Given that these combatants were Filipino nationals, this conflict was not a civil war.

Even more than peninsular Malaysia, the absence of nationalist civil war in the Bornean states of Sabah and Sarawak requires some explanation because they have several characteristics that promote nationalist strife. For one, they possess overwhelmingly non-Malay populations, whereas the state is dominated by Malays. More importantly, Malays never controlled precolonial Sarawak and Sabah, and both regions were never part of colonial Malaya. And the Frontier Areas, excluded areas, and southern Sudan all show how the merging of different territories with distinct populations promotes nationalist civil warfare when one dominates the others. Finally, like East and West Pakistan, the Malay Peninsula and the Bornean states are hundreds of kilometers from each other, with the South China Sea separating the two.

Different factors help explain the lack of nationalist civil warfare in Malaysian Borneo, but the short answer is that both the Malaysian government and Malaysian Borneans supported postcolonial pluralism. Whereas communities in Myanmar's Frontier Areas actively opposed merger with the rest of the colony at independence, the decision to merge Sarawak and Sabah with Malaya—while encouraged by the British—was not imposed and therefore required support from populations in both colonies. Although some opposed merger and many others had serious reservations, the majority of people in both Sabah and Sarawak were supportive. One reason was that both Bornean states found themselves surrounded by hostile neighbors and saw Malaya as less threatening: Indonesia claimed both Sarawak and Sabah and began a military operation to take control of the regions, and—as already mentioned—the Philippines claimed Sabah. A second factor making union with Malaya more acceptable is that the Malayan government agreed to a long list of demands, including domestic autonomy, language rights, restriction of Malay travel to the Bornean states, reservations for Borneans, and freedom of religion (Kheng 2002). In contrast to Myanmar, India, Sri Lanka, and elsewhere, where national chauvinists dismantled colonial pluralism, a national chauvinist government agreed to implement pluralist policies that protected minorities. The main reason for this unlikely situation is that Great Britain proposed the formation of a Malaysian Federation that would join Malaya, the Straits Settlements, and Sarawak and Sabah, and Malay leaders were willing to make pluralist concessions to gain control of these new territories. In this case, the state community accepted pluralism because the merger provided them with political and economic benefits, and non-state communities accepted incorporation into a Malay-dominated state in exchange for military protection and pluralist guarantees.

Since the creation of Malaysia in 1963, the Malaysian state has encroached on Sarawak and Sabah autonomy in certain ways, and Malaysian governments have increasingly emphasized that Malays are the only true national community (Kheng 2002; Ongkili 1973: 113). As a result, resentment over union with Malaysia has increased in Malaysian Borneo, and nationalist movements are present (Lim 2015). To date, however, the movements are weak because the Bornean states retain considerable autonomy, and no major crisis—like the famine in Mizoram or mass Bengali migration in Tripura—has catalyzed nationalist movements. Should the Malaysian state decide to radically erode the autonomy of the Bornean states or should the Bornean states lack the autonomy to deal with a severe crisis, however, evidence from other former British colonies suggests that the risk of nationalist civil war in Malaysian Borneo would be very high.

Malaysia therefore shows that pluralism does not always promote nationalist civil war. In the Malay Peninsula, pluralist policies did not promote nationalist civil war because the character of colonial pluralism and the nonnative status of the other communities limited the nationalist aspirations of non-Malays, thereby making them less sensitive to Malay national chauvinism. This contrasts greatly with Myanmar, where colonial pluralism increased the sensitivity of non-state communities to Bamar national chauvinism. The comparison therefore suggests that colonial pluralism is most likely to promote nationalist civil war when it empowers communities in ways that make them very sensitive to the national chauvinism of others. In Malaysian Borneo, in turn, postcolonial pluralism did not promote nationalist conflict because all sides supported it, a situation that sets the case apart from Myanmar but that is similar to another former British colony: Singapore.

SINGAPORE

Singapore was the capital of the Straits Settlements Crown Colony and a major colonial trading hub attracting many immigrants from China, Malaya, Indonesia, India, and elsewhere. Although separate from colonial Malaya, the British applied many of the same policies to both Malaya and the Straits Settlements, including a variety of divisive pluralist policies that strengthened boundaries between and politicized the Malay, Chinese, and Indian communities (Ang and Stratton 2018; Chee et al. 2019; Chong 2020; Goh 2017). Whereas all other regions of the Straits Settlements had merged with Malaya by independence, Singapore remained autonomous and became an independent country in 1959. In 1963, Malayan and Singaporean politicians and the British government agreed to combine Singapore, Malaya, and the two British territories in Borneo to form Malaysia. Whereas three-quarters of Singapore's population was Chinese, Malay national chauvinists controlled Malaya, and this mismatch created a serious crisis for the new state. After a political deadlock between Malay and Chinese leaders and a bloody communal riot, Singapore left Malaysia in 1965, thereby becoming an independent country for the second time in only six years (Chee et al. 2019: 17). At this time, antipathy between Malay and Chinese Singaporeans was very high, and some Malays wanted to restore Malay dominance through reunification with Malaysia.

After leaving Malaysia, the ethnically Chinese leaders of postcolonial Singapore could have followed the examples of Malaysia, Myanmar, Sudan, Sri Lanka and elsewhere and tried to build a nation-state around their community. Yet such efforts almost certainly would have sparked a strong Malay nationalist movement that could have led to both a civil war and a larger regional conflict. On top of this, the Chinese community did not view Singapore as its natural homeland but instead self-identified as an immigrant community. Given their precarious geopolitical position, a desire for stability, and weak national chauvinism, postcolonial leaders sought to avoid conflict by creating an inclusive and egalitarian form of pluralism that recognized all Singaporeans as full and equal members of the nation and protected minorities from domination and discrimination (Ang and Stratton 2018; Chee et al. 2019; Chong 2020). The major goal of Singaporean pluralism was to build a viable nation-state out of a conflict-ridden "plural society" by recognizing, accommodating, and empowering all communities (Ang and Stratton 2018; Chee et al. 2019; Chong 2020; Goh 2017).

Over the next decades, postcolonial pluralism helped reduce intercommunal tensions and prevent nationalist violence in Singapore. To this day, Malay nationalists have been unable to organize a movement, and equitable pluralism obstructed Malay nationalism in two important ways. First, postcolonial pluralism prevented the strengthening of Chinese Singaporean national chauvinism, and—as highlighted in Myanmar and other cases—such chauvinism is a crucial factor strengthening popular support for nationalist movements. Second, pluralist policies recognized, accommodated, and empowered all communities, and Malays were the biggest beneficiaries of postcolonial pluralism. In this situation, most Malay Singaporeans felt included and respected and either grudgingly accepted or openly embraced Singaporean multiculturalism.

Different from Myanmar and other regions in which pluralism was the focus of nationalist conflict, Singapore—like Malaysian Borneo—shows that pluralism can contain nationalist tensions when the dominant communities accept it and use it to protect smaller communities. In so doing, the cases help pinpoint how the refusal of postcolonial states to recognize, accommodate, and empower smaller communities—especially when the smaller communities have nationalist frames, expectations, and mobilizational resources—sparks nationalist violence. That being said, postcolonial pluralism in Singapore was very different from the divisive and discriminatory colonial pluralism that preceded it, and colonial pluralism was limited in British Borneo. Postcolonial pluralism therefore was not a continuation of colonial pluralism in either case, so colonial pluralism did not limit postcolonial nationalist conflict. As described in the following sections, British colonial pluralism was more universal and less discriminatory in other cases and persisted after independence, thereby linking colonial pluralism to postcolonial peace more strongly and directly in cases like Sierra Leone, Tanzania, and Ghana.

SIERRA LEONE

Although Sierra Leone has never experienced a nationalist civil war, the country has important characteristics that create a high risk of nationalist conflict. Of greatest relevance to this work, the country experienced high levels of British colonial pluralism, with a pluralist index score of 0.9 out of 1. In addition, Sierra Leone suffered a decade-long civil war, and many of the factors that contributed to this civil war—such as state ineffectiveness—also contribute to nationalist civil warfare. Finally, Hunziker and Cederman (2017) find that nationalist civil warfare is very common in places with lootable natural resources like Sierra Leone's rich alluvial diamond deposits, and a large literature describes how a "resource curse" contributes to poverty, conflict, and instability (Ross 1999; Sachs and Warner 1995). Nationalist civil warfare was therefore a real possibility.

Colonial Sierra Leone included the small Sierra Leone Crown Colony along the coast and the much larger Sierra Leone Protectorate in the interior. The British founded the Colony in 1787 to resettle freed slaves and ruled it directly. The main inhabitants of the Colony were Creoles, who had greater cultural similarities with the colonizers than the inhabitants of the Protectorate: They spoke an English-based creole and commonly English, had relatively high levels of education, and were mostly Christian. The Protectorate was created in 1896 and ruled over the 27,000 square miles surrounding the Colony. Prior to colonialism, the inhabitants of the Protectorate were organized into a dozen decentralized polities. Through indirect rule, the British maintained chiefly authority in the Protectorate, although they broke the precolonial polities into smaller units after experiencing violent resistance, thereby turning the dozen precolonial polities into over 200 "customary" chiefdoms (Abraham 1978).

Although only making up a small segment of the Sierra Leonean population, Creoles were initially very influential because they controlled many key administrative positions. Over time, their influence diminished due to medical improvements, which made it safer for British officials to live in Sierra Leone and take positions previously held by Creoles, and the adoption of indirect rule in the Protectorate, which emphasized that African authorities should be customary (Lange 2009b: 95; Reno 1995). As a result of both, chiefs became the dominant African elites (Lange 2009b).

In Sierra Leone, colonial pluralism recognized and institutionalized communal difference through censuses, vernacular education, and customary law. The cornerstone of colonial pluralism, however, was indirect rule. Different from Myanmar, Nigeria, and elsewhere, indirect rule in Sierra Leone did not promote conflict over the communal character of the postcolonial nation-state, communalize politics, or institutionalize communal self-rule. One important reason for limited conflict over the communal character of the nation-state is that indirect rule was used universally instead of discriminatorily, so all communities—except Creoles—were ruled indirectly. As a result, all communities supported the retention of indirect rule and a multicultural postcolonial nation-state. Indirect rule, in turn, did not promote communal self-rule because each indirectly ruled polity was small and few ruled over entire communities. There were, for example, dozens of different chiefdoms ruled by Temne and Mande chiefs. And different from Nigeria, where regional administrations were communalized, a single administration ruled over the entire Sierra Leone Protectorate. And a unified administration ruling over divided communities did not communalize politics.

As part of their pluralist system of rule in Sierra Leone, the British also provided communal legislative representation, something that contributed to nationalist civil warfare in other British colonies. In Sierra Leone, however, communal legislative representation did not allow particular communities to look out for communal interests in the political arena. This is because the British reserved a total of three seats for Mande and Temne chiefs to ensure the presence of chiefs on the Legislative Council. As a result, reserved seats strengthened chiefs, not communities.

At independence, a former chief leading a coalition of chiefs became prime minister, and chiefly rule continued. Chiefs were therefore able to maintain their political power, which helped prevent conflict between the chiefdoms and the state. The risk of nationalist conflict was also limited by the fact that the two largest communities were divided into many chiefdoms and did not control their own polities. As a result, Mande and Temne communities—each of which makes up 30 percent of the total population—were not organized to pursue their communal interests in politics. Even more, Mande and Temne elites never made demands for reforms unifying Mande or Temne chiefdoms because such reforms would have removed or weakened most Mande and Temne chiefs.

Similar to the colonial state that preceded it, the postcolonial state was the center of a patronage system through which central leaders collaborated with peripheral chiefly authorities (Lange 2009b; Reno 1995). The resulting state structure was very decentralized and patrimonial, a combination that promoted extremely limited state capacity (Hayward 1989; Lange 2009b; Reno 1995). In this situation, Charles Taylor, a Libyan-backed warlord and future president of Liberia, was able to invade Sierra Leone with a small force in 1991, organize an army locally, and capture the diamond producing regions, thereby beginning a decade-long war (Fanthrope 2001; Kadeh 2002). The war transformed a weak state into a collapsed state, thereby creating an enormous opening for nationalist movements. The fact that none arose suggests that communities lacked nationalist aspirations and accepted the Sierra Leonean nation-state.

While several factors explain the lack of nationalist civil war in Sierra Leone, the case shows that pluralism need not promote nationalist civil war when used broadly and relatively equitably, as all communities have the same stake in it and therefore have similar interests in its maintenance. And in recognizing all communities, colonial pluralism promoted a multicultural postcolonial nation-state that did not privilege or exclude communities, so communities did not try to free themselves from it even after the state broke down. In this way, Sierra Leone contrasts starkly with Myanmar, where only a few communities benefited from indirect rule and where intense conflict erupted at independence over the communal character of the nation-state. Another difference is that indirect rule in Sierra Leone was based on chiefdom, not community. As such, there were many Temne and Mande chiefdoms but no single polity for the Temne or Mande, thereby limiting the extent to which colonial pluralism nationalized communities. In this regard, Sierra Leone is similar to most princely states in colonial India. Although communities in Nigeria were also commonly divided between several indirectly ruled chiefdoms, all Sierra Leonean chiefdoms were run by the same administration, whereas communal and administrative boundaries aligned in Nigeria. Overall, colonial pluralism in Sierra Leone was more unifying than divisive.

GHANA

Like Sierra Leone, indirect rule was used almost universally in Ghana and contributed to a multicultural nation-state that limited nationalist conflict. Yet the case very nearly experienced a nationalist civil war, and a communalized regional administration similar to that in Nigeria and Sudan helps explain this near outcome. Ghana differs from these cases, however, in that nationalist mobilization over reduced communal autonomy forced the Ghanaian state to maintain communal autonomy, thereby stopping nationalist movements in their tracks. The case therefore clearly shows how the maintenance of a pluralist state helped prevent nationalist civil war by safeguarding communal power and autonomy. Similar to Malaysia and Sierra Leone, the key to this outcome was that all communities supported pluralism, thereby avoiding conflict over the maintenance of pluralism like in Myanmar, Sudan, Sri Lanka, and elsewhere.

The British established the Gold Coast Colony along the coastal zone of contemporary Ghana in 1821 in lands that had previously been claimed by the Crown's Royal Trading Company. The British conquered the Asante Confederacy in 1896 and declared a separate protectorate over it in 1901. In 1902, the British conquered the territory north of the Asante Protectorate—the Northern Territories—and also made it a separate British protectorate. Finally, German Togo was divided between the British and the French after the First World War, and British Togoland was a thin vertical strip along the eastern border of the Gold Coast Colony, Asante Protectorate, and Northern Territories Protectorate. The British ruled all four territories separately until the Second World War.

Given greater European influence and the location of large urban centers along the coast, the British ruled parts of the Gold Coast Colony directly. Throughout most of the Gold Coast's territory and population, however, they institutionalized indirect rule through chiefs. The British used similar forms of indirect rule more exclusively in the other regions of colonial Ghana. In the Asante Protectorate, this form of rule changed over time. Because of the military power of the Asantes, the British exiled the Asante king after defeating the Asante Confederacy. To rule the Asante Protectorate, the British kept the Asante administrative structure intact—thereby maintaining chiefs and subchiefs—and ruled through it, with the British Resident effectively taking the spot of the king (Wilks 2000). The Asante king was repatriated in 1924 and made traditional ruler of Kumase, the Asante capital, and the kingship was formally restored in 1935. After this, the British gave the Asante king special status and privileges, including a reserved seat on the colonial legislature. Throughout most of the colonial period, the British also favored Asantes for the colonial security forces.

Ghana has over 100 different communities, although three groups make up nearly half of the population. Approximately 13 percent of the population are Asante, most of whom live in what was the Asante Protectorate. The Ewe also make up 13 percent of the total population and are concentrated in the region that was British Togoland. Finally, 16 percent of the Ghanaian population is ethnic Mole-Dabani, who are concentrated in what was the Northern Territories. Like Nigeria, the administrative units therefore overlapped with community, although the major communities in each region make up less than half the regional population.

Despite a communalized system of rule, the political elites in Ghana have followed an inclusive nationalist model since independence. In recognizing, accommodating, and empowering all communities in similar ways, colonial pluralism promoted support for pluralist policies among all communities. According to Lentz and Nugent (2000), postcolonial Ghanaian "multiculturalism operates according to which elements of 'traditional' culture from different parts of the country are plucked and then incorporated into a cannon of 'national' tradition" (16). As such, all cultures are celebrated as part of the Ghanaian nation, with presidents wearing clothing from all cultures, the national dance ensemble performing dances and songs from all major ethnic groups, and radio and television programs broadcasted in all major languages. Kwame Nkrumah, Ghana's first prime minister and president, actively promoted this model, and he developed and exploited a great number of unifying symbols to try to build the new Ghanaian nation (Fuller 2014; Hess 2001). At the same time, Nkrumah feared the communalization of politics and enforced his national model by outlawing communal parties and forbidding communal flags. After a coup removed Nkrumah from power in 1966, subsequent governments have maintained this multicultural model.

The presence of postcolonial multiculturalism instead of national chauvinism therefore helps explain why communalized politics did not promote nationalist civil war in Ghana like in Nigeria. Yet there were severe impediments to inclusive nationalism in Ghana, and a nationalist civil war was barely avoided during the independence transition. Chiefs—as protectors and politicizers of community—were strong at independence, but Nkrumah sought to weaken them to build a powerful postcolonial state. In contrast to the maintenance of chiefs in Sierra Leone, Nkrumah therefore tried to remove them. The Asante king, however, founded the Asante National Liberation Movement in opposition to these policies and mobilized against Nkrumah (Allman 1993; Rathbone 2000). The resulting conflict became violent, and British officials avoided travel in the Asante Protectorate and feared that the struggle would turn into a nationalist civil war (Allman 1993: 170). To avoid this outcome, top British officials urged Nkrumah to maintain chiefs and create regional assemblies for them, and Nkrumah grudgingly accepted this recommendation to speed up the independence process. As a result, the Asante king and other chiefs maintained a high level of self-rule and ended all demands for secession. The case therefore pinpoints the influence of communal autonomy on nationalist movements, showing how threats to remove pluralist policies promoted nationalist conflict whereas the decision to retain pluralist policies quickly ended nationalist mobilization.

TANZANIA

Despite having a relatively low pluralist index score (0.45), colonial Tanzania was clearly pluralist. Although similar to Sierra Leone and Ghana in that colonial pluralism was based on indirect rule and treated all indigenous communities the same, Tanzania is different from these cases and more similar to Myanmar and India in that postcolonial reforms ended indirect rule in an effort to strengthen the postcolonial state. In Tanzania, these reforms did not promote nationalist civil warfare because the reforms affected all indigenous communities similarly, because the chiefdoms were small and disorganized, and because the postcolonial state implemented other policies that recognized and accommodated communities.

Prior to colonialism, the Tanzanian population consisted of many small, autonomous communities that practiced local religions, and the population was very diverse. Presently, 125 recognized ethnic communities live in Tanzania and speak over 100 languages, and Papua New Guinea is the only country in the world with a higher ethnic fractionalization index score (Fearon 2003). European colonization of Tanzania began with the German conquest of the region in 1885, but the British gained control of the region during the First World War. The British colonized Tanzania until 1961 and implemented an indirect form of rule that employed local chiefs as intermediaries. Due to the absence of large and centralized precolonial polities, the British had difficulty implementing indirect rule and—as in Igboland and Sudan—resorted to "creating" many chiefs who controlled small territories and populations (Iliffe 1979). While the presence of Middle Eastern and Asian traders preceded European colonialism, the British opened the region to Indian settlement, and a small Indian population served as a middleman minority and dominated key areas of the colonial economy.

While dividing populations in a variety of ways, Aminzade (2013: 41) notes that British pluralism emphasized ethnic and racial divisions. Indirect rule institutionalized ethnic difference within the African population by ruling through chiefs, using indigenous languages, and maintaining "customary" law (Iliffe 1979: 329–41; Tripp 1999). In urban areas, Africans, Asians, and Europeans intermingled, and race was the dominant cleavage. Racial stratification was extreme, with Africans at the bottom, Asians in the middle, and Europeans on top. Racialized legal institutions, education, economies, and representative systems played important roles institutionalizing racial difference (Aminzade 2013; Bertz 2007). Notably, this racial focus helps explain the region's relatively low pluralist index score: The pluralist index focuses on policies institutionalizing divisions between indigenous communities, but many pluralist policies in colonial Tanzania focused exclusively on racial divisions between indigenous and non-indigenous communities.[2]

Like nearly all former British colonies, Tanzania transformed into a nation-state at independence. Although uninational models were hegemonic at that time, the extreme diversity of the Tanzanian population made this model unworkable. Tanzania's first prime minister and president, Julius Nyerere, presided over and directed this transition to nation-state. He was influenced by Nkrumah and pursued a very inclusive model that celebrated diversity, with the Nyerere government declaring Tanzania a multicultural nation comprised of a religiously, linguistically, and racially diverse population (Aminzade 2013; Mamdani 2012; Omari 1995; Tripp 1999). Two core elements of this were the passing of citizenship laws that did not privilege any community and using education to emphasize national unity through diversity (Aminzade 2013: 115–16; Miguel 2004; Omari 1995; Tripp 1999: 46).

At the same time, Nyerere (1966) declared that nation-building efforts in Tanzania needed "to break up tribal consciousness among the people and . . . build up a national consciousness" (39). To limit divisions and integrate the population, the Nyerere government made Kiswahili—a trading language known by many Tanzanians but that was not the vernacular of any indigenous community—the national language. The government also dismantled the system of indirect rule, replaced customary law with a unified body of law, and outlawed community-based political parties.

---

2. The case's relatively low score also results from the absence of education in multiple vernaculars, as Nyerere made Kiswahili the sole language of education at independence.

In contrast to Ghana, these policies did not provoke strong opposition. One reason for this difference is that all Tanzanian chiefdoms were very small and localized. Tanzania therefore lacked any equivalent of the Asante Protectorate—a large and powerful indirectly ruled polity that had a large stake in the maintenance of indirect rule and that was able to prevent reforms that removed local autonomy. And unlike Sierra Leone, chiefs did not organize a party to look out for their interests at the national level, thereby clearing the way for the reforms. The reforms also faced little opposition because they did not disadvantage any community and, instead, recognized and celebrated all communities as part of the Tanzanian nation, and scholars commonly link Tanzanian multiculturalism to peaceful intercommunal relations (Bjerk 2015; Koff and Von der Muhll 1967; Miguel 2004).

Like Sierra Leone and Ghana, the case therefore offers evidence that pluralist colonial policies that recognized and empowered communities equally contributed to inclusive postcolonial politics, thereby reducing the risk of nationalist civil war. The maintenance of pluralism, in turn, was possible because all communities supported it, something that was not the case in Myanmar and elsewhere. A comparison of the cases highlights one very important cause of this difference: the strength of national chauvinism. Indeed, national chauvinism was weak or absent in Sierra Leone, Tanzania, and Ghana but very strong in Myanmar, India, Sri Lanka, Sudan, Nigeria, and elsewhere. Why, then, is national chauvinism strong in some places but weak in others? This question is vital for explaining when pluralism promotes nationalist civil war and when it impedes it and is the focus of the next chapter.

Conclusion

This chapter finds that British colonial pluralism contributed to the nationalist civil wars in Nigeria, Pakistan, Sri Lanka, and Sudan, thereby supporting the findings from chapters 4 and 5 and offering additional evidence that the statistical relationship between colonial pluralism and nationalist civil warfare is causal. At the same time, the chapter provides evidence that the nationalist civil wars in Israel/Palestine and Iraq would likely have occurred without British colonial pluralism, suggesting that British colonial pluralism was not the only cause of nationalist civil wars in the former British Empire. Finally, the chapter analyzes five former colonies with histories of colonial pluralism but no nationalist civil war and explores why colonial pluralism did not promote nationalist strife in these cases. The Malaysian case highlights how unique conditions made communities more accepting of either the national chauvinism of others or postcolonial pluralism. In peninsular Malaya, pro-Malay colonial pluralism combined with Chinese and Indian transnationalism to limit sensitivity to Malay national chauvinism. In Malaysian Borneo, all sides accepted the creation of more pluralist institutions after independence because of compatible interests, and postcolonial pluralism helped contain nationalist conflict. Similarly, postcolonial leadership in Singapore created an inclusive form of pluralism that protected minorities from the majority, and this helped defuse conflict. Like postcolonial pluralism in Malaysian Borneo and Singapore, Sierra Leone, Ghana, and Tanzania offer evidence that pluralism limited nationalist conflict by promoting more pluralist postcolonial states, although the cases differ in that colonial pluralism provided the bases for postcolonial pluralism in the three African countries. Indirect rule was the cornerstone of colonial pluralism in all three regions and—in contrast to Myanmar and India—was used to rule all communities in similar ways. As a result, most communities had similar interests in its maintenance or reform, and popular postcolonial pluralism promoted inclusive politics that celebrated communities and maintained much of their autonomy. And even in Tanzania, where the postcolonial state ended indirect rule, postcolonial pluralism weakened grievances over the removal of indirect rule. The chapter therefore provides evidence that colonial pluralism had opposing effects on nationalist civil war, promoting it in some places but helping to contain it in others, something that supports chapter 3's statistical findings. Whereas chapter 3 offers evidence that the level of historical statehood mediates the effects of colonial pluralism, however, this chapter ignores historical statehood and focuses exclusively on colonial pluralism. The next chapter brings historical statehood back into the equation, thereby exploring how colonial pluralism and historical statehood interact.

7

Colonial Pluralism, Historical Statehood, and Nationalist Civil Warfare

This chapter reassesses case studies from chapters 4, 5, and 6 by bringing historical statehood into the analysis. Ultimately, it shows how the level of historical statehood affects the character of colonial pluralism and the strength, contours, and character of national chauvinism, all of which shape how colonial pluralism influences nationalist civil war. This further clarifies why colonial pluralism promoted nationalist civil war in Myanmar and India but not in Sierra Leone and Tanzania. At the same time, the analysis offers evidence that the effects of historical statehood on nationalist civil war depended considerably on colonial pluralism.

Cases with High Levels of Colonial Pluralism and High Levels of Precolonial Statehood

MYANMAR

With the highest score of precolonial statehood of all former British colonies (and the sixth highest in the world between 1001 and 1700 AD), Myanmar is an extreme case of historical statehood. And because the case also has a history of extreme colonial pluralism, it is ideal for exploring potential ways in which precolonial statehood and colonial pluralism interact to affect nationalist civil warfare. The case highlights a complicated relationship between precolonial statehood, colonial pluralism, and nationalist civil warfare, with precolonial statehood having independent effects, interaction effects with colonial pluralism, and indirect effects through colonial pluralism. Given the influence of precolonial statehood on national chauvinism and discriminatory colonial pluralism, it is unlikely that colonial pluralism would have promoted nationalist civil war without a large and long-standing precolonial state. At the same time, the risk of nationalist civil warfare would have been much lower with only high levels of historical statehood because colonial pluralism was at the center of the processes leading to war.

Myanmar has been a crossroads of people moving between South and Southeast Asia for several millennia. Settled agriculture began approximately 10,000 years ago, and the first major polities emerged around 2000 BC. These early city-states were founded by Pyu peoples who had migrated from the Yunnan region of contemporary China. They settled in the rich Irrawaddy River Valley and founded city-states on the trade route between India and China, thereby allowing both Indian and Chinese cultures to influence ancient Myanmar. Pyu peoples dominated the region until the ninth century AD, when the Nanzhao Kingdom of contemporary Yunnan repeatedly attacked the region. Shortly thereafter, Bamar began migrating into Myanmar from Yunnan and founded the Pagan city-state, which expanded to take control of the entire Irrawaddy Valley by the mid-eleventh century, thereby forming the first Bamar-led polity that controlled most of contemporary Myanmar's territory. The Pagan Kingdom ruled for 250 years and began spreading Bamar language and culture throughout the region. At the kingdom's height, the city of Pagan was one of the largest in the world, with as many as 200,000 people. After the Pagan Kingdom, two subsequent Bamar kingdoms—the Toungoo Empire and Konbaung dynasty—ruled the region and continued the process of Bamarization. These were decentralized imperial states in which communities in peripheral regions had considerable autonomy and commonly paid allegiance to multiple powers simultaneously (Ferguson 2021: 35–36; Lieberman 1987; Wolters 1997). By the onset of British colonialism, approximately two-thirds of the population was Bamar, but large pockets of non-state communities were present.

Chapter 4 provides evidence that Bamar national chauvinism played a key role in the country's many nationalist civil wars. Although the chapter focuses on how colonial pluralism affected Bamar national chauvinism, precolonial statehood also shaped it in very important ways. As described in chapter 4, Bamar national chauvinism was revivalist in that it focused on regaining control of what was "rightfully theirs." Given the centrality of powerful precolonial states—especially the Konbaung dynasty—in the Bamar myth-symbol complex, state history both pushed people to pursue Bamar national chauvinism and legitimized it. In the minds of many Bamar, the Konbaung dynasty was a glorious Bamar state, British colonialism had destroyed it, and they therefore sought to reestablish a new and reinvigorated Bamar nation-state to pick up where the Konbaung dynasty had left off. Highlighting the influence of historical statehood on Bamar national chauvinism, Laoutides and Ware (2016) found that many Kachin claimed Bamar national chauvinism was the most influential cause of the Kachin nationalist civil war, describing how Bamar officials saw "themselves as guardians of the legacy of the great Burmese conquering kings, and that their nationalistic duty is to perpetuate this historic vision of an expansionist center subduing competing kingdoms and other minority peoples" (57).

A second way in which state history contributed to Bamar national chauvinism was by shaping Myanmar's communal demography. As a result of Bamar political dominance over the past millennium, many non-Bamar assimilated into Bamar culture, thereby increasing the size of the Bamar community. Indeed, early Bamar kingdoms ruled over diverse communities that greatly outnumbered Bamar, but non-Bamar adopted the Bamar language, religion, and customs. As a result, the population of the Bamar heartland became overwhelmingly Bamar. Thus, with a proud and very long history of statehood and over two-thirds of the total population, many Bamar proclaimed the postcolonial nation-state a Bamar nation-state, and Bamar national chauvinism played an influential role in processes leading to nationalist civil war.

While recognizing that historical statehood contributed to nationalist civil warfare through its effects on national chauvinism, chapter 4 shows how British colonial pluralism reinforced these effects in important ways. One way colonial pluralism amplified the effects of historical statehood was by making Bamar national chauvinism more aggressive and vindictive, which strengthened the reactions of non-state communities to it. British colonial pluralism did this by decreasing Bamar power and status relative to non-state communities and creating a strong desire to reinstate Bamar dominance by putting non-state communities back in their marginalized precolonial positions or getting rid of them all together.

A more influential way through which colonial pluralism strengthened the impact of national chauvinism was by making non-state communities highly sensitive to Bamar national chauvinism, and it did so in three ways. First, pluralist policies increased concern over Bamar national chauvinism by creating expectations for communal recognition, accommodation, and empowerment. Due to these expectations, non-state communities were much more likely to react to Bamar national chauvinism—which sought to remove their cultural and political autonomy—by mobilizing nationalist movements. This was especially clear with the Karens, Karennis, and Kachin, who were empowered by pluralist policies, did not accept being ruled by Bamar, and began nationalist civil wars shortly after independence.

The second way through which British colonial pluralism intensified nationalist reactions to Bamar national chauvinism was by strengthening and politicizing communal frames. These nationalist frames increased the likelihood that people viewed politics in terms of their community and predisposed them to pursue and protect communal power and self-rule. Most importantly, without powerful nationalist frames, non-state communities would have focused less on communal power and autonomy and, thereby, been less likely to experience grievances over Bamar national chauvinism. Indeed, without them, many non-state communities would likely have assimilated into Bamar culture. The Karens provide one clear example: There is little evidence of a Karen communal identity prior to colonialism, colonialism helped construct a powerful and Karen national identity, and Karens ultimately paid great attention to their community and were very sensitive to Bamar national chauvinism.

Third, British colonial pluralism strengthened communal reactions to Bamar national chauvinism by providing non-state communities with important mobilizational resources. Most notably, indirect rule institutionalized communal self-rule, communal legislative representation organized communities politically, and communalized security forces provided communities with military training and resources. Without these mobilizational resources, the capacity of non-state communities to organize nationalist movements and fight civil wars would have been greatly reduced, potentially preventing nationalist civil war. For example, without a history of indirect rule that institutionalized Karenni autonomy, it seems very unlikely that Karennis, who make up 1 percent of the total population, would have been able to mount a nationalist civil war. Similarly, without missionary influence, empowerment through special legislative representation, and overrepresentation in the colonial military, the ability of Karens to mobilize a nationalist movement would have been greatly diminished.

While recognizing that colonial pluralism interacted with precolonial statehood to promote nationalist civil warfare in Myanmar in these ways, some of the effects of colonial pluralism are partially attributable to precolonial statehood because precolonial statehood contributed to discriminatory colonial pluralism. Given the Konbaung dynasty's military might, the British faced great resistance when conquering Myanmar, and the British had a very difficult time controlling the Bamar heartland throughout the colonial period, with constant dacoity and occasional rebellion. As part of their efforts to limit anticolonial resistance, the British stacked the colonial security forces with "loyal" non-state communities, and they provided select non-state communities with reserved seats in the colonial legislature, which—when combined with seats reserved for colonial officials and other Europeans—allowed the British to control the legislature and thereby stymie the nationalist agenda of Bamar politicians. Another aspect of divide and rule involved removing peripheral regions of the former Konbaung dynasty and making them autonomous zones within colonial Myanmar. In the Frontier Areas, the British claimed to "protect" non-state communities from the Bamar and, in so doing, framed the Bamar as a danger to the survival of non-state communities. While some colonial officials were concerned about protecting the cultures of non-state communities, the main reason why the British offered this type of "protection" was to prevent the Bamar from engaging the non-state communities in their anticolonial efforts, and the British isolated Frontier Areas from Bamar influence in three main ways: They established a separate administration for the Frontier Areas, barred non-residents from entering the regions without formal permission, and excluded the Frontier Areas from the colonial legislature.

In summary, Myanmar offers evidence that precolonial statehood and colonial pluralism combine in complicated ways, and bringing historical statehood into the analysis further clarifies the processes causing nationalist civil war. Yet just as it is difficult to distinguish which rope is which in a complex knot, it is hard to disentangle the effects of precolonial statehood and colonial pluralism when analyzing the processes leading to nationalist civil warfare in Myanmar. And just as a knot can disappear when you remove one rope, nationalist civil warfare would have almost certainly been much rarer—and possibly absent— without both precolonial statehood and colonial pluralism.

SUDAN AND NIGERIA

The nationalist civil wars in Sudan and Nigeria are similar to those in Myanmar in that they pitted state communities that wanted to reassert their dominance over non-state communities against the non-state communities that mobilized to retake the communal autonomy that they had gained through pluralist colonial policies. The cases also highlight how historical statehood contributed to the national chauvinism of state communities and how colonial pluralism strengthened the reactions of non-state communities to it.

The first large-scale polities of Sudan emerged in northern Sudan near the confluence of the White and Blue Nile Rivers. Nearly 5,000 years ago, Kerma— the first known major city-state in the region—was formed, and it dominated the region for 1,000 years. In 1550 BC, Egyptian forces conquered the region and ruled it for the next 500 years. After the disintegration of the Egyptian Empire during the Late Bronze Age Collapse, the Kingdom of Kush was formed and ruled northern Sudan and parts of southern Egypt from 1000 BC until the mid-fourth century AD. After this, various Christian Nubian states controlled the region for a millennium. Arabs began to influence the region in 651 AD and promoted dual processes of Arabization and Islamization, although their early efforts to conquer the Christian Nubian states failed. With the eventual decline of the Christian Nubian states, Arabized Sudanese founded the Funj Sultanate in 1504, which controlled most of northern Sudan until 1821. In that year, the Turco-Egyptian government conquered Sudan and continued the dual processes of Arabization and Islamization. After 60 years of Egyptian rule, Sudanese Arabs rebelled under the leadership of the self-proclaimed Mahdi, kicked out the Egyptians, and established an independent Islamic state over most of contemporary Sudan. Although lasting only fourteen years, Mahdi rule further entrenched Islam and Arab dominance, and approximately two-thirds of the Sudanese population practiced Islam and one-third spoke Arabic by the turn of the twentieth century. The remainder of Sudanese spoke as many as 400 different languages and practiced a great variety of localized religions. The historical processes of Islamization and Arabization were strongest in the central Nile Valley, moderate in the West, and weakest in southern Sudan.

Similar to Myanmar, the British had a difficult time conquering and controlling Sudan and separated peripheral regions from the Nile heartland explicitly to isolate resistance (Idris 2013; Said 1956). The case therefore shows the link between precolonial statehood, anticolonial resistance, and divisive colonial pluralism. After gaining control of Sudan, however, relations improved between the British and several communities in the Arab heartland, and the British subsequently reintegrated all regions except for southern Sudan, which remained under a separate administration until the independence transition.

In addition to promoting divisive colonial pluralism in the form of southern isolationism, precolonial statehood also contributed to northern national chauvinism, which focused on the nation as Muslim and Arab. The Mahdi state has a central position within the northern myth-symbol complex, and the Mahdi state inspired anticolonialism in the form of a neo-Mahdist movement (Daly 1993: 4; Ibrahim 1977; Kaufman 2006: 62). The precolonial Mahdi state was jihadist and sought to establish an independent Muslim state. The neo-Mahdists took control of the postcolonial state and created a more centralized administration under northern control. They also implemented assimilationist policies to Arabize and Islamize the population.

While British administrators in the North recognized the Arab Muslims as superior to other Sudanese and supported northern national chauvinism, southern administrators sought to protect southern Sudanese from the northerners by isolating them politically and socially. At independence, northerners dominated the Sudanese state and saw the North–South divide as illegitimate and an impediment to their dominance. During the independence transition, the northern government—with colonial support—therefore reimposed its dominance over the South by forcibly integrating the South into the postcolonial state and pursuing assimilationist policies.

Although it is impossible to assess the extent to which British colonialism shaped Arab national chauvinism, British colonial pluralism strengthened it and made it more aggressive. Of greater importance, however, British colonial pluralism bolstered southern opposition to northern national chauvinism, and the nationalist civil wars likely would not have occurred if British rule did not make southerners so sensitive to northern dominance and empower them to resist. In isolating the South and providing it with cultural and political autonomy under the guise of "protection" from the "dangerous" northerners, British rule made the southerners very fearful of northerners. Not only did British officials and missionaries vilify northerners, but they also provided expectations for autonomy and a variety of mobilizational resources in the form of communalized regional political institutions and a southern military force. In combination, northern national chauvinism and strong southern opposition promoted a vicious circle leading to nationalist war.

Precolonial statehood and colonial pluralism combined to promote nationalist civil warfare in Nigeria in ways similar to Sudan: Both had a northern state community controlling an Islamic empire and many southern non-state communities that were usually non-Muslim, colonialism institutionalized political divisions between state and non-state communities, and leaders of the state communities in both colonies were national chauvinists. That being said, precolonial statehood was more limited in Nigeria, and the state community—while still controlling the postcolonial state—was confronted with more powerful non-state communities. As a result, attempts to impose northern dominance in Nigeria were as much about maintaining power as it was about a return to past glories.

While the Benin Kingdom and Oyo Empire were precolonial states present in southwestern Nigeria, the largest historical states were present in northern Nigeria, and this region was the dominant power at the time of colonial onset. Several small Hausa states began controlling northern Nigeria around 1000 AD, but they were subsequently conquered by the Kanem, Songhai, and Sokoto Empires, all of which were expansionist Islamist states. The Sokoto Caliphate was founded in 1804 and controlled most of northern Nigeria and parts of southwestern Nigeria at the time of British colonial onset. The Empire was founded by the Fulani, who had entered the region from the West, thereby settling among the North's Hausa population and creating a Muslim Hausa-Fulani community.

Relative to the rest of Nigeria, the British had a difficult time subduing the Sokoto Caliphate. Even more so than Sudan, however, Nigeria contrasts with Myanmar in that the British employed carrots more than sticks to limit anticolonialism. For this, British officials celebrated the prestige of indigenous rulers. Similar to Sierra Leone, however, the British also limited anticolonialism by dividing the Sokoto Caliphate, which had been an imperial state combining several smaller polities, into its component parts and ruling all separately. Lord Lugard, who began his career in India, was the architect of this form of rule in northern Nigeria and reapplied the divisive but celebratory form of customary rule used in India.

Given the more limited history of precolonial statehood, the Hausa-Fulani—while the largest community—were less than 40 percent of the population. Even more, although larger than any preceding precolonial state, the Sokoto Caliphate did not control all Nigeria, with polities in the South either paying tribute to the Caliphate or being completely autonomous from it. Despite this, Hausa-Fulani national chauvinism was assertive and had a grand vision focused on reestablishing a great and expansionist Islamist state by taking control of Nigeria.

While precolonial statehood contributed to Hausa-Fulani national chauvinism, it is unlikely that Nigeria would have experienced nationalist civil warfare without a history of British colonial pluralism both because pluralist policies influenced Hausa-Fulani national chauvinism and—especially—because it made non-state communities sensitive to Hausa-Fulani dominance. As described in chapter 6, the British created three regional administrations in Nigeria, each of which had majority populations from different communities, and promoted communalized administrations and politicized communities. Similar to northern Sudan, British officials in the northern administration encouraged northern national chauvinism by giving special powers to the traditional rulers, celebrating their customary authority, and providing customary leaders with both political and religious authority. In contrast to Sudan, however, colonial influence was much greater in southern Nigeria, and British colonialism isolated northern Nigeria from the social changes going on in the South. Through the resulting educational and economic advantages of the South, British colonial pluralism promoted a more defensive Hausa-Fulani national chauvinism, and Hausa-Fulani leaders felt very threatened and insecure during the independence process and believed the control of the postcolonial state was a matter of national survival, thereby promoting violent reactions to Igbo mobility and the Igbo-led coup. Different from Sudan, Hausa-Fulani leaders therefore focused on controlling the state not only in pursuit of the return to a precolonial golden age but especially to protect themselves from southerner whippersnappers.

British colonial pluralism also contributed to Igbo reactions to Hausa-Fulani national chauvinism. There was no Igbo state prior to British rule, but the British created a separate administration for the Igbo, thereby institutionalizing a polity ruling over all of Igboland that made possible—under the heavy hand of British tutelage—Igbo national self-rule. High levels of missionary influence in the region, in turn, combined with colonial policies to create a strong Igbo communal frame and organize them politically. And all this made Igbos particularly sensitive to Hausa-Fulani dominance and violence and gave them an administrative base from which they could coordinate their war efforts.

COLONIAL INDIA

Precolonial statehood also promoted national chauvinism in South Asia, which contributed to several nationalist civil wars in India, Pakistan, and Bangladesh.

Like Myanmar, Sudan, and Nigeria, in turn, colonial pluralism strengthened and shaped the contours of national chauvinism while making communities very sensitive to the national chauvinism of others. The regions that made up colonial India are different from Myanmar, Sudan, and Nigeria, however, because they include multiple state communities that controlled large and long-standing precolonial states. And when state communities were incorporated into another state community's nation-state, they were especially sensitive to lost communal autonomy, thereby reducing—but not eliminating—the influence of colonial pluralism.

Although large polities were present in South Asia much earlier, most of the region was unified into a single polity for the first time under the Nanda Empire in 345 BC. This Empire was short-lived, but several other large imperial states followed, including the Maurya (322–184 BC), Satavahana (approximately 150 BC–250 AD), Gupta (319–542 AD), Chalukya (543–753 AD), and Cholas Empires (850–1279 AD). Throughout this period, South Asia became more culturally unified, thereby creating an Indian "civilization." In the thirteenth century, Turkic Muslims invaded northern India and founded the Delhi Sultanate, which ruled much of contemporary India, Bangladesh, and Pakistan over the next 300 years. In 1526, the Mughal Empire replaced the Delhi Sultanate and created an even larger empire.

This long and complex history of precolonial statehood over such a large area ultimately promoted multiple state communities. Ancient Indian populations practicing Indic religions, the majority of the Indian population is Hindu, and—as proclaimed by Modi and the BJP—Hindus are the dominant state community in contemporary India. For the 650 years preceding British rule, however, Muslim empires dominated India, and many Indians converted to Islam, making Muslims a second state community. Large regional state communities were also present in South Asia. Bengal, for example, was part of different Indian Empires but also had its own history of statehood, including the Gauda Kingdom (320–626 AD), the Pala Empire (750–1161 AD), the Sena Empire (1070–1230 AD), and the Bengal Sultanate (1332–1576 AD). Similarly, Assam was an independent kingdom from 1228 to 1819 AD.

Given the presence of multiple state communities, precolonial statehood promoted several national chauvinisms, and competing national chauvinisms contributed to different nationalist civil wars. Both Muslim and Hindu national chauvinism recognized their communities as rightful rulers of the postcolonial state and mobilized revivalist movements that reasserted their claims as the true national community (Reetz 1997: 289). Because of the demographic dominance of the Hindus, however, Muslim leaders eventually focused on maintaining British rule and, subsequently, partition. After partition, the Pakistani and Indian governments clearly supported national chauvinism. Hindu national chauvinism, in turn, contributed to efforts to fully integrate the Punjab, Kashmir, and Northeast India into postcolonial India both politically and culturally, thereby promoting nationalist civil wars in these regions (Franke 2009: 67–68).

Alternatively, Assamese and Bangladeshi national chauvinisms inspired nationalist movements in Assam and East Pakistan, with Assamese and Bangladeshi nationalists wanting either greater autonomy within the postcolonial state or their own nation-state. Both cases had proud histories of autonomous statehood, and this precolonial statehood contributed to movements for greater autonomy after the postcolonial states failed to protect their interests. Notably, the Baloch, Sikh, Manipuri, and Tripuri communities also had histories of precolonial statehood and sought to regain autonomy after forced integration with either India or Pakistan, thereby beginning nationalist civil wars. Colonial India therefore shows that national chauvinism promoted nationalist civil warfare in a very different way than in Myanmar: By making subordinate state communities sensitive to losing cultural and political autonomy to the postcolonial nation-state.

Assamese national chauvinism also influenced additional nationalist civil wars in Northeast India. After independence, Assam became a regional state and gained control of the excluded areas of Northeast India. While some Assamese wanted their own independent nation-state, Assamese leaders joined Congress and focused on maintaining Assamese communal autonomy within India. Viewing British rule as unrightfully breaking up the Assamese state in a divide-and-rule fashion by creating the indirectly ruled autonomous zones, Assamese governments attempted to establish or reestablish their dominance over all other communities in the regional state through political integration and cultural assimilation (Franke 2009: 68–69). As Franke (2009) notes, "the Assamese wanted what they saw as a political, cultural and administrative reunification of the hills and the plains as quickly as possible. The moment was there to build a Greater Assam, including the hill regions reaching until the international borders of China, Burma and East Pakistan" (69). Over time, these aggressive nationalizing policies aggrieved Nagas, Bodos, and Mizos in ways that motivated nationalist civil wars. In a similar way, Bangladeshi national chauvinism promoted aggressive assimilationist policies after its secession from Pakistan, something that also motivated non-state communities in the Chittagong Hill Tracts to fight a nationalist civil war (Adnan 2004: 26–27; Bala 2022: 57–59).

Although precolonial statehood contributed to multiple national chauvinisms in postcolonial India, Pakistan, and Bangladesh, colonial pluralism clearly combined with precolonial statehood to promote nationalist civil warfare in these cases. Most importantly, British pluralist policies made communities very sensitive to the national chauvinisms of others. Pluralist colonial policies strengthened communal frames, politicized communities, and provided communities with important mobilizational resources. They also institutionalized communal self-rule, thereby creating expectations for the continuation of communal self-rule after independence. In the excluded areas, pluralist policies also enforced communal isolation and heightened fear of the neighboring "plains" Indians, thereby making forced integration all the more unacceptable. Finally, British colonial pluralism shaped the contours of national chauvinism by promoting religious nationalism. As described in chapter 5, it did so both by helping create a unified Hindu community and by politicizing and nationalizing religion, and both contributed to most nationalist civil wars.

Similar to Myanmar, however, precolonial statehood influenced discriminatory colonial pluralism by creating a severe anticolonial threat, thereby making it difficult to disentangle the effects of precolonial statehood and colonial pluralism. As described in chapter 2, the great Indian anticolonial war of 1857–59 was the main event promoting colonial pluralism in India and, thereby, the British Empire, showing a clear link between anticolonialism and pluralist reactions. Colonial India also highlights how anticolonialism contributed to more discriminatory pluralist policies. With the rise of a powerful Hindu-led anticolonial movement in the late nineteenth century, British colonial pluralism began to "protect" more loyal communities. Most notably, the British implemented policies to weaken the anticolonial movement, including moving the colonial capital from Calcutta to Delhi. They also increasingly emphasized that the numerical dominance of Hindus necessitated pluralist policies empowering Muslims to protect their community. One notable aspect of this was the division of Bengal into separate administrative units, with one half being majority Hindu and the other majority Muslim. This move, in turn, sought to weaken the Bengali Hindu nationalists, who dominated Bengal politics, while allowing the more "loyal" Muslims to have greater influence in East Bengal. Another more influential policy was the reservation of legislative seats for non-Hindus, something that allowed them to work with the British to obstruct Hindu anticolonialists in the legislature. Finally, the British stacked the colonial military with Sikhs and Punjabi Muslims and used them to contain Hindu nationalists.

All in all, colonial India parallels Myanmar in that historical statehood contributed to multiple nationalist civil wars by promoting national chauvinism and creating a divisive form of colonial pluralism. The case is different from Myanmar, however, because there were multiple state communities. And because historical statehood strengthens nationalist frames and creates nationalist expectations, several communities in colonial India were very sensitive to the national chauvinism of others. The Assamese, Bengalis, Balochs, and Manipuris were all sensitive to the national chauvinism of dominant state communities because of their own histories of statehood. That being said, British colonial pluralism ratcheted up this sensitivity to higher levels by strengthening communal frames, celebrating custom, increasing expectations for self-rule, and providing a variety of mobilizational resources. It is very possible, for example, that the Assamese would have assimilated into the Bengali community without a history of British colonial pluralism despite their history of precolonial statehood. And for communities like the Nagas and Mizos that did not have precolonial states, the impact of colonial pluralism was greater.

SRI LANKA

Sri Lanka has a long history of precolonial statehood and state-sponsored religion, and both increased social homogeneity by the time the British conquered the island in 1796. Although Indian kingdoms had ruled Sri Lanka beforehand, the first indigenous polity controlling the entire island was the Anuradhapura Kingdom, which lasted in different forms for nearly a millennium and a half (437 BC–1037 AD). During this long period, Sinhalese became the dominant language, and Buddhism was made the state religion and spread throughout the island. After being conquered and integrated into the Indian Chola dynasty for two decades, the Polonnaruwa Kingdom (1056–1232 AD) established another island-wide Sinhalese state. Following its decline, Sri Lanka was ruled by a variety of smaller kingdoms, and Portugal began colonizing the island's coastal regions in 1505. A century later, the Dutch defeated the Portuguese to take control of Sri Lanka. The Portuguese and Dutch, however, only colonized a thin coastal zone surrounding the island. The interior was controlled by the Kandy Kingdom, which was founded in 1596, and the British only defeated the Kandy Kingdom in 1815.

Throughout this time, Sri Lanka was greatly influenced by India through population movements, trade, and occasional conquest. Indian cultural influence was especially strong in northern Sri Lanka, which is only 55 kilometers from India at the closest point. Many Tamil-speaking Hindus lived in the North and controlled their own kingdoms prior to Portuguese conquest. That being said, nearly all precolonial kingdoms were dominated by the Sinhalese, and roughly three-quarters of the island's population spoke Sinhalese and practiced Buddhism at the time of British colonial conquest. Of the remaining population, approximately 15 percent were Tamils, and relatively small communities of Muslims, Keralans, and individuals of mixed Sri Lankan and European descent lived along the coast.

Both Tamils and Sinhalese were part of and ruled precolonial states, so it is inaccurate to claim that Sri Lanka has only one state community. That being said, most precolonial states were dominated by the Sinhalese, and the majority of the population is Sinhalese, making the Sinhalese a clear state community and giving the Tamils characteristics similar to non-state communities.

And viewing itself as the majority community that controlled Sri Lanka from its mythic beginnings, many Sinhalese supported national chauvinism and demanded a postcolonial nation-state that was ruled by Sinhalese for the Sinhalese, something epitomized by the policies of the Bandaranaike governments and the multiple episodes of ethnic violence targeting Tamils. Because this national chauvinism and violence pushed Tamils to mobilize a nationalist movement, precolonial statehood contributed to the civil war.

Echoing the findings from previous cases, however, British colonial pluralism also contributed to Sinhalese national chauvinism in very important ways. One was by communalizing politics and increasing communal competition. For this, communal legislative representation was particularly influential, as it focused colonial politics on communal power and the needs of different communities. Even more, it provided Tamils and Sinhalese with similar numbers of seats, thereby giving them similar levels of political influence. With democratic reforms in the early twentieth century, Sinhalese politicians demanded the end of communal legislative representation, whereas Tamil leaders mobilized to maintain them. In general, the communalization of politics interacted with historical statehood to push the Sinhalese to try to take greater control of the state and reassert their historical dominance.

An increasingly organized and powerful Tamil community also strengthened Sinhalese national chauvinism, and colonial pluralism contributed to this. Communal legislative representation was one way, but vernacular education also increased the relative status of Tamils. Due to their greater education, Tamils were overrepresented in government services, elite professions, and higher education. And because they were much more influenced by missionaries, Christianity threatened Tamil culture more and promoted a Hindu revival movement led by Navalar and others. Many Sinhalese saw the growing mobility and assertiveness of Tamils as a threat to their community's standing, which promoted an aggressive and vindictive Sinhalese national chauvinism. Of potentially greater importance, an organized Tamil community mobilized against Sinhalese national chauvinism, something that Sinhalese national chauvinists reacted to with violence.

At the same time, Tamils also have a history of statehood in Sri Lanka and are linked to an even longer history of statehood with Tamil kingdoms in India. This history was part of the Tamil myth-symbol complex, and Tamils saw themselves as a founding community of Sri Lanka, thereby making Sinhalese national chauvinism all the more unacceptable. Similar to colonial India, the presence of multiple state communities therefore contributed to Tamil sensitivity to Sinhalese national chauvinism, suggesting that British colonialism—while very influential—was not the only determinant of Tamil nationalist reactions.

Colonial Pluralism and Limited Statehood:
Sierra Leone, Tanzania, Ghana, and Singapore

Similar to the cases analyzed in the last section, Sierra Leone, Tanzania, Ghana, and Singapore have histories of British colonial pluralism. These cases differ, however, in that they either did not have precolonial states or had more limited and sporadic histories of precolonial statehood. Sierra Leone, Tanzania, Ghana, and Singapore therefore provide insight into the combined effects of colonial pluralism and more limited precolonial statehood. Overall, Sierra Leone, Tanzania, and Ghana offer evidence that colonial pluralism was applied to all communities in similar ways and did not radically transform communal hierarchies, limited state history promoted little or no national chauvinism, and nondiscriminatory colonial pluralism in a colony with little national chauvinism decreased the risk of nationalist civil warfare by promoting inclusive postcolonial politics. In contrast, colonial pluralism in Singapore was greatly influenced by colonial Malaya and was highly divisive and discriminatory. This form of rule communalized politics to a much greater extent and contributed to communal violence. The combination of moderate historical statehood with high levels of divisive colonial pluralism therefore created an elevated risk of nationalist civil war, but this was avoided by postcolonial pluralist reforms that protected minorities, something that postcolonial leaders in Myanmar, India, Sri Lanka, Sudan, and elsewhere failed to do and that led to nationalist civil war in these cases.

SIERRA LEONE AND TANZANIA

Among former British colonies, both Sierra Leone and Tanzania have among the lowest levels of precolonial statehood. In Sierra Leone, chiefdoms formed during the period of the Atlantic slave trade to protect populations, but these chiefdoms were relatively small and decentralized. In Tanzania, the islands of Zanzibar and Pemba were trading centers with states prior to colonialism, but the vast Tanzanian mainland included many very small polities comprised of villages or collections of villages. With limited precolonial statehood, political pressures and opportunities did not promote assimilation into one community, and the populations of Sierra Leone and Tanzania are therefore diverse.

Without a large and long-standing precolonial state, important determinants of national chauvinism were lacking in both Sierra Leone and Tanzania. Given localized and multicommunal precolonial polities, no community had a glorious history of conquest and rule. Furthermore, the absence of historical statehood promoted diverse populations. And without myth-symbol complexes focused on glorious precolonial states or the demographic dominance of one community, no community saw Sierra Leone or Tanzania as exclusively or especially "theirs." Very limited precolonial statehood therefore created a low risk of nationalist civil war by deterring national chauvinism.

Colonial pluralism reinforced this effect. As described in the previous chapter, the British employed pluralist policies relatively universally and nondiscriminatorily because all communities posed similar and limited risks to British colonial rule. And because no community saw itself as the true national community or lost more power and autonomy during colonialism, all had similar interests in maintaining or reforming pluralist policies after independence. Popular postcolonial pluralism, in turn, portrayed all Sierra Leonean and Tanzanian communities as full members of the national community. While postcolonial pluralism limited nationalist movements by maintaining extreme communal power and autonomy in Sierra Leone, postcolonial pluralism also limited nationalist pressures in Tanzania despite the removal of chiefs because indirect rule was not as communalized as elsewhere and because other pluralist policies made this reduction in local autonomy more palatable.

Thus, limited historical statehood created a low risk of nationalist civil war in Sierra Leone and Tanzania, and colonial pluralism further reduced this risk. Whereas colonial pluralism was divisive and discriminatory in Myanmar and India, the British applied it much more universally in Sierra Leone and Tanzania. As a result, colonial pluralism neither benefited certain communities at the expense of others nor transformed communal hierarchies. And given weak national chauvinisms, pluralist policies were broadly accepted, posed little threat to postcolonial states, and were maintained or adjusted after independence. And popular postcolonial pluralism deterred nationalist civil war by promoting inclusive politics.

GHANA

In all likelihood, nationalist civil war would not have occurred in Sierra Leone or Tanzania with or without a history of colonial pluralism due to the presence of many small communities that did not view themselves as the true national community. In contrast, Ghana's more moderate levels of historical statehood create a greater risk of nationalist civil war. And because of this possibility and the clear ways in which colonial pluralism helped contain violence, Ghana offers the strongest evidence of how colonial pluralism can reduce the risk of nationalist civil war in places with more limited historical statehood.

Prior to the onset of British colonial rule, the Asante Confederacy—which consisted of the Asante state and several smaller polities that collaborated with and paid tribute to the Asante king—controlled much of contemporary Ghana. The history of Asante statehood is at the center of the Asante myth-symbol complex and is the basis of customary authority, with the Asante king and Queen Mother remaining influential authorities. That being said, historical statehood did not promote strong Asante national chauvinism proclaiming Ghana an Asante nation-state. Instead, Asante leaders have accepted their incorporation into a multicultural Ghana while maintaining considerable autonomy and emphasizing their central position in a multicultural Ghanaian nation-state. In this way, Ghana contrasts with Sudan and Nigeria in that the state community did not demand control of the postcolonial nation-state but accepted communal power within it.

One reason for weaker Asante national chauvinism is the relatively small size of the Asante community: The Asantes make up only 13 percent of the total population and are not even Ghana's largest community, and the democratic principle therefore suggests that the Ghanaian nation-state is not Asante. In contrast, the Arab and Hausa-Fulani were the largest communities, made up nearly half of the Sudanese and Nigerian populations, and therefore had stronger expectations to rule the postcolonial state. Moreover, whereas the Hausa-Fulani felt they needed to control the postcolonial Nigerian state to prevent domination by more "modern" southerners, Asantes were not disadvantaged and could hold their own against other communities. Ghana therefore shows how moderate precolonial statehood limited Asante national chauvinism.

With communalized regional governments, the real risk of nationalist civil war in Ghana involved regional communities trying to gain autonomy from the rest of Ghana. As noted in chapter 6, Ghana was poised to begin a trajectory similar to that of the Shan, Naga, and South Sudanese cases whereby the removal of communal autonomy after independence provoked secessionist struggles. Due to their size and history of statehood, however, Asantes posed a much greater threat than any of these communities, and forceful Asante opposition forced Nkrumah to backtrack and maintain pluralist policies that provided communities with autonomy. On top of this, Nkrumah was neither a national chauvinist nor backed by national chauvinists, so Asante demands were not as provocative as those of Karens or Tamils. Consequently, Nkrumah made concessions that defused Asante opposition, and a multicultural nation-state deterred further nationalist conflict.

Ultimately, Ghana shows how the particular combination of precolonial statehood and colonial pluralism contained nationalist conflict. Moderate levels of precolonial statehood limited country-wide national chauvinism and focused attention on more regional self-rule. Non-state communities therefore did not feel overly threatened by Asantes (although some were worried about the possibility of Asante dominance). Moreover, a universal application of colonial pluralism and the maintenance of pluralist policies after independence satisfied Asantes—and all other communities—because it recognized and empowered communities.

With limited national chauvinism and postcolonial pluralism, people from all communities recognized the Ghanaian nation as mixed and viewed themselves as part of it. Data from the Afrobarometer survey support this finding: Of the 28 countries in the survey, Ghana is tied for having the *fewest* respondents—3.9 percent—who self-identify more with ethnicity than country-based nation (Afrobarometer 2015). Notably, Tanzania is the country tied with Ghana, and Sierra Leone is a close third with only 4.1 percent, showing how the combination of colonial pluralism and low to moderate levels of historical statehood strengthened self-identification with the country-based nation in these cases. In contrast, 27.5 percent of Nigerian respondents self-identified most strongly with ethnicity, a total that is much higher than any other country in the survey (Sudan is not included in the Afrobarometer survey). As noted previously, Nigeria differs from Ghana, Sierra Leone, and Tanzania in that its precolonial state and British colonial pluralism strengthened northern national chauvinism, and the combination of national chauvinism with colonial pluralism promoted contestation over the continuation of pluralism and the communal character of the postcolonial nation-state, both of which limited self-identification with the Nigerian nation.

SINGAPORE

Conforming with the statistical analysis, Singapore has limited historical statehood and no nationalist civil war. That being said, the region was part of some precolonial empires, both the Malay and Chinese communities have attributes of state communities, and this situation had the potential to promote nationalist civil war by strengthening rival national chauvinisms. On top of this, Singapore is different from Sierra Leone, Tanzania, and Ghana in that colonial pluralism was much more divisive and discriminatory, thereby increasing intercommunal conflict and antipathy and creating an elevated risk of nationalist civil war at independence. The case therefore requires explanation for why the combination of moderate historical statehood and high levels of discriminatory colonial pluralism did not promote nationalist civil war.

Because of its strategic location at the opening of a strait linking the Indian and Pacific Oceans, Singapore was part of different empires since at least 1000 AD. When the British took over the island in 1819, however, no empire had ruled the island for 200 years, and only a few small and autonomous villages of Malays and Orang Laut (sea people who are indigenous to the Malay Peninsula) were present on the island. Singapore therefore has a rather particular history of statehood: It was claimed by and controlled by different empires for long periods, but it was usually peripheral to these empires and was abandoned by all long before British rule.

Given this history of moderate but limited historical statehood, no community is a clear state community, and national chauvinism has therefore been relatively weak in Singapore. As Ang and Stratton (2018) note, an overwhelmingly immigrant population in a polity that was a complete colonial construct prevented the rise of myth-symbol complexes depicting Singapore as a natural, glorious, and ancient homeland of any community. That being said, both Malay and Chinese communities have attributes that promote national chauvinism. Malays, for example, are indigenous to the region and view Singapore as part of a "great" Malay civilization that dominated the region for centuries before British rule. In contrast, Chinese Singaporeans lack any claim of indigeneity, as all arrived in Singapore after British colonial onset. Yet demographic dominance is an important determinant of national chauvinism, and three-quarters of Singaporeans self-identify as ethnically Chinese. With such a large majority, Chinese Singaporeans could easily claim Singapore as their own. And during the independence transition, both Chinese and Malay communities mobilized to pursue their opposing interests, thereby promoting heightened competition and conflict, and nationalist civil war was a real possibility.

As noted in chapter 6, one very important reason why nationalist civil war did not occur was that postcolonial leaders implemented pluralist reforms that recognized all communities as equal members of the Singaporean nation. These inclusive policies recognized, accommodated, and empowered all communities and contributed to a more multicultural view of the Singaporean nation-state. Because the numerical dominance of Chinese Singaporeans allowed them to control the postcolonial state and economy, pluralism was especially important for weakening Malay nationalism and national chauvinism. Indeed, pluralist policies do not formally favor the Chinese in any way and benefit Malays more than any other community. And because Malays are not excluded, are actively assisted by pluralist policies, and feel part of a prosperous postcolonial nation-state, there is little or no nationalist mobilization to merge Singapore into Malaysia. In this way, an inclusive and egalitarian form of postcolonial pluralism helped ease nationalist tensions and weaken national chauvinism, thereby transforming the trajectory resulting from the combination of moderate precolonial statehood and divisive colonial pluralism.

Conclusion

This chapter uses comparative-historical methods to explore how precolonial statehood affects nationalist civil warfare. In Myanmar, India, Pakistan, Bangladesh, Sri Lanka, Sudan, and Nigeria, precolonial statehood contributed to national chauvinism among state communities, and national chauvinism shaped the processes leading to nationalist warfare by promoting arrogant and assertive efforts to build a nation-state around the state community. At the same time, colonial pluralism commonly made national chauvinism more assertive and exclusive by increasing the relative power and status of non-state communities, especially when colonial pluralism was overtly discriminatory and disadvantaged state communities in a divide-and-rule style. Even more, colonial pluralism created expectations for communal power and autonomy among non-state communities and provided them with mobilizational resources, both of which helped transform grievances over the national chauvinism of state communities into nationalist civil wars. Yet precolonial statehood sometimes contributed to discriminatory colonial pluralism, making it difficult to differentiate the effects of precolonial statehood and colonial pluralism. Ultimately, the analysis suggests that large and long-standing precolonial states increased the risk of nationalist civil war; that this risk was especially high in places like India with multiple state communities; but that colonial pluralism magnified the effects of precolonial statehood by promoting more aggressive national chauvinism, making communities more sensitive to the national chauvinism of others, and providing them with resources to organize nationalist movements. Nationalist civil war was therefore most likely in places with both historical statehood and colonial pluralism.

In contrast, Sierra Leone, Tanzania, and Ghana offer evidence that nationalist civil war is rare in places with low to moderate levels of precolonial statehood because limited precolonial statehood weakened national chauvinism. At the same time, colonial pluralism was more universal and less discriminatory in this context. As a result, all communities supported pluralism, and inclusive postcolonial politics further diminished the risk of nationalist conflict. In Singapore, however, moderate historical statehood was combined with highly divisive colonial pluralism, and this combination created a high risk of nationalist civil war at independence. Inclusive pluralist reforms after independence, however, weakened the national chauvinism of Chinese and Malay communities and helped repair intercommunal relations, thereby alleviating nationalist tensions.

These comparative-historical findings coincide with and help interpret the statistical results from chapter 3 showing that historical statehood and colonial pluralism interact to affect nationalist civil war in different ways. Yet the statistical analysis also provides evidence that historical statehood can affect nationalist civil warfare independent of colonial pluralism, but this chapter's comparative-historical analysis has difficulty isolating the impact of precolonial statehood from colonial pluralism because all cases experienced colonial pluralism. More analysis is therefore needed to understand the independent effects of historical statehood.

8

Historical Statehood without Colonial Pluralism

VIETNAM, CAMBODIA, THAILAND, ETHIOPIA, BOTSWANA, AND EGYPT

To isolate the impact of historical statehood on nationalist civil warfare, this chapter analyzes six cases with moderate to high levels of precolonial statehood and low levels of colonial pluralism (see table 8.1). Among the non-British colonies, I analyze three cases from Southeast Asia: Vietnam, Cambodia, and Thailand. I selected these cases because their histories of statehood and communal demographies are very similar to those of Myanmar and Northeast India, and these similarities increase insight that can be gained through qualitative comparison. As noted in the introduction, I also selected the cases because nationalist civil wars are highly concentrated in Southeast Asia, suggesting that regional characteristics unrelated to British colonial pluralism might explain the large number of nationalist civil wars in Northeast India and Myanmar. I therefore analyze countries in the region that were never colonized by the British and compare them with Myanmar, Northeast India, and Bangladesh to better isolate the impact of British colonialism on nationalist civil warfare in the region.

Ethiopia is the final non-British colony. Similar to Myanmar, many communities have fought nationalist civil wars in the country, but Ethiopia differs in that it experienced only limited colonial pluralism, as the Italians implemented pluralist policies over a very short period. The case therefore helps highlight mechanisms through which historical statehood affects nationalist civil war in places with limited colonial pluralism.

TABLE 8.1. Cases with Historical Statehood but Limited Colonial Pluralism

Country	State History Index	Level of Colonial Pluralism	Number of Nationalist Civil Wars
Vietnam	39.9	Low	0
Ethiopia	49.2	Low	7
Cambodia	48.0	Very Low	0
Thailand	37.3	Absent	1
Egypt	42.1	Low	0
Botswana	21.4	Low	0

In addition to these cases, the chapter analyzes two former British colonies: Botswana and Egypt. Although the level of colonial pluralism is positively related to the level of historical statehood in the British Empire, Botswana and Egypt are outliers with moderate or high levels of historical statehood but very low levels of colonial pluralism. The cases therefore offer insight into how precolonial statehood affected nationalist conflict when colonial pluralism was limited.

Vietnam

Historical statehood contributed to national chauvinism in South Vietnam and—to a lesser extent—communist Vietnam. Yet without colonial pluralism, non-state communities did not react to national chauvinism with nationalist warfare. Overall, the case therefore provides evidence that the impact of historical statehood on nationalist civil war is much weaker without colonial pluralism. There is a partial and telling exception to this general pattern, however: The French employed pluralist policies to empower Montagnards, the community that organized the most violent nationalist movement in postcolonial Vietnam.

The first states in the region that became Vietnam formed along the Red River in the country's north before the Christian era. In 111 BC, China conquered these states, thereby beginning a historical cycle of Chinese conquest followed by Vietnamese independence that lasted until the early fifteenth century. During the periods of self-rule, the states in northern Vietnam strengthened and gradually extended their rule to the south. The leaders of these states were ethnic Vietnamese, or Kinh. In the late fifteenth century, a Vietnamese state unified northern and southern Vietnam for the first time. This period of unification lasted a century, after which the country divided into several Vietnamese states. In 1802, a Vietnamese kingdom unified all Vietnam once again, and this polity lasted until the onset of French colonialism in 1858. By this time, Kinh culture had spread widely throughout the Vietnamese lowlands.

French colonial rule began in reaction to Vietnamese attacks on French Catholic missionaries and resulted in the French colonization of southern Vietnam, known as Cochinchina. Formally, the French ruled Cochinchina directly, although they included elements of indirect rule at the local level (Goscha 2016: 81). Thirty years later, the French conquered the remainder of contemporary Vietnam. Different from colonial rule in Cochinchina, the French tried to limit anticolonial violence by retaining the Vietnamese emperor and transferring his authority to the colonial state. Faced with very strong resistance, the French also employed a second technique to limit anti-colonialism: They divided northern and central Vietnam, and the emperor was the "puppet" ruler of the central Annam region, with the northern Tonkin region being a protectorate administered by the French.

As described in chapter 2, the dominant French colonial model of political community—at least on paper—was more assimilationist and associational than pluralist. In colonial Vietnam, one sees posturing and policies that supported this colonial ideal, although colonialism was usually something very different on the ground. For one, Vietnam attracted thousands of French settlers, who subsequently gained considerable economic and political clout and commonly opposed Republicanism in favor of an opposing colonial ideology—white supremacy (Boittin et al. 2011; Vann 2003). In addition, French officials focused on exploiting the colony's economic resources, and assimilationist and associational policies generally hindered this goal. Instead of being dictated by Republicanism, *réal politique* was therefore the dominant influence, and the French employed a variety of techniques and policies in their efforts to extract resources and control foreign lands and peoples, thereby resulting in considerable variation in the character of colonial rule over both time and place. Due to this variation, French colonial rule had a bit of everything, including pluralism.

Japan controlled Vietnam during the Second World War. Instead of fighting the Japanese, the French colonial administration collaborated with them, whereas the Viet Minh, a communist and anticolonial force, fought against both Japanese and French rule. After the war, the French tried to reestablish colonial rule, but the Viet Minh continued their operations and took control of northern Vietnam in 1954 after defeating the French. The independence agreement separated northern and southern Vietnam but stated that a future election would select a government for the entire country, thereby reunifying Vietnam. Before any election could occur, leaders from the South—with the backing of the French and American governments—declared themselves the leaders of the Republic of Vietnam, thereby beginning the Second Vietnam War. This war ended in 1975 after the American withdrawal from South Vietnam.

Although experiencing a bloody anticolonial conflict that morphed into a war that was both civil and international, Vietnam has not experienced a nationalist civil war. Nationalist civil wars are relatively rare, but Vietnam has two characteristics that make this absence somewhat unexpected. First, Vietnam has high levels of historical statehood, which is positively related to nationalist civil warfare. Second, Vietnam has upland non-state communities that historically had considerable autonomy and that are surrounded by a proud state community.

One reason why nationalist civil warfare has not occurred in postcolonial Vietnam is that Vietnam is very homogeneous, with approximately 85 percent of the population categorized as Kinh. Although assimilation was common during the precolonial period, it continued under French colonial rule through policies that recognized the Kinh as the national community and only rarely recognized, accommodated, and empowered non-state communities (Aldrich 1996: 76–81: Boittin et al. 2011; Goscha 2016; Raffin 2013). While this suggests that limited colonial pluralism reduces the risk of nationalist civil war by promoting more homogeneous populations, the Chittagong Hill nationalist civil war in hyper-homogeneous Bangladesh shows that nationalist civil war remains possible in places with very limited diversity.

A second yet related reason for the absence of postcolonial nationalist civil warfare is that French rule maintained the precolonial communal hierarchy while simply placing the French on top. Through a weak form of association-alism, the French worked through Vietnamese elites—including the maintenance of the emperor as a national symbol—and did not advantage indigenous minorities. Moreover, French colonial education taught almost exclusively in French and Vietnamese and was concentrated in regions with large Kinh populations (Hien 2020; Kelly 1977: 100). Relatedly, the French rarely encouraged the use of minority languages and helped spread the Vietnamese language during the colonial period. Finally, with colonial encouragement, Kinh migrated to peripheral regions during the colonial period, thereby creating a greater Kinh presence throughout the territory and diluting potential homelands of non-state communities. And due to these factors, non-state communities did not threaten ethnic Vietnamese, and non-state communities were not sensitive to Kinh dominance.

At the same time that French rule minimized communal divisions, maintained preexisting hierarchies, and facilitated assimilation into the Kinh community, it also created extremely strong divisions between colonizer and colonized through a variety of policies and practices, thereby directing the attention of the colonized away from intercommunal divisions and toward the division between citizen and subject (Kelly 1982). One very important element of this was the construction of a dual legal system based on citizenship status, with French law for citizens and the *régime de l'indigénat* for all colonial subjects. Through the *indigénat*, subjects from all communities were forced to provide corvée labor, paid much higher taxes than citizens, and received few rights (Aldrich 1996: 213; Goscha 2016: 86; Mann 2009). Informally, in turn, French citizens were allowed to interpret and enforce the *indigénat*, thereby allowing a sort of vigilante justice in which many settlers harassed and exploited the colonized. At the same time, the colonial state, French settlers, and Catholic Church gained control of vast territories, so much so that three-quarters of the colonized population became landless (Khổng Diễn 2002: 75–76; Quincy 1995: 114). The extensive use of corvée labor to build infrastructure and clear lands further impeded the ability of these landless peasants to provide for their families, especially because they did not receive any food or housing when working.

To analyze a negative case of nationalist civil warfare, it is helpful to compare it to a positive case, and this comparison is more insightful when the cases share key traits. Several factors make Myanmar appropriate for comparison with Vietnam. Both Myanmar and Vietnam had large precolonial states, large state communities living in lowland areas, and subordinate non-state communities residing in the mountainous and forested periphery. Even more, both cases experienced a period of Japanese rule during the Second World War that resulted in co-nationals fighting one another on different sides of the conflict. The cases differ, however, in terms of the extent of colonial pluralism.

Although British officials in Myanmar also created very stark divisions between the colonized and the colonizers and actively exploited the colonized, Myanmar contrasts with Vietnam in that the colonizers institutionalized clear and powerful communal divisions among the colonized and transformed communal hierarchies. As a result, divisions between different colonized communities were as meaningful as divisions between colonizer and colonized. In this situation, assimilation into the Bamar community slowed or halted, and many communities opposed the Bamar-led anticolonial movement. As described in chapter 4, British policies recognized the division between diverse communities and formally institutionalized the power and autonomy of several non-state communities through communal legislative representation and indirect rule, going so far as to prevent Bamar from traveling in some minority regions. In contrast, the French paid much less attention to non-state communities, empowered them only in exceptional cases, and opened up all regions to Kinh settlement. Moreover, the British encouraged the use of minority languages and rarely used Burmese to communicate with non-state peoples, whereas French colonial officials used French or Vietnamese almost exclusively. An important symbolic difference, in turn, is that the British destroyed the Konbaung dynasty and exiled the ruling family, whereas the French tried to maintain the Vietnamese emperor as a symbol to legitimize French rule. In this way, British colonialism marginalized Bamar, but French colonialism maintained

Kinh symbolic dominance over non-state communities. Finally, discriminatory pluralist policies strengthened non-state communities at the expense of the Bamar, which also contributed to stronger intercommunal divisions and antipathy in Myanmar than in Vietnam and provided non-state communities with resources to fight for self-rule.

All of these factors, in turn, made the anticolonial movement in Myanmar a Bamar affair, and many minorities opposed independence because they feared Bamar national chauvinism and helped the British fight anticolonial militants who joined forces during the Second World War. The French also tried to gain support from non-state communities in their efforts to defeat anticolonial forces after the Second World War, but these brief policies were far less successful because colonialism had not strengthened intercommunal divisions prior to these efforts and because the Viet Minh did not resent the non-state communities as colonial stooges and were already actively courting them for support (McElwee 2004: 191; Safman 2007: 50). According to Nguyen Khac Vien (1968), "whereas the colonialists, the feudalists and the nationalist parties treated the minority peoples as 'savages,' the Communists were the first to believe in their revolutionary potential and to advocate joint action by all the nationalities with a view to national liberation and social emancipation" (11). The main reason for the more communally inclusive form of Vietnamese anticolonialism is that the lack of discriminatory and empowering colonial pluralism limited communal divisions and antipathy, which made a weak version of national chauvinism more acceptable to ethnic Kinh while making Kinh dominance more tolerable to non-state communities.

After reunifying Vietnam, the communist government continued to recognize non-state communities but became increasingly chauvinistic (McElwee 2004; Vasavakul 2003). Kinh dominated the state and economy, and non-state communities faced heavy repression whenever they asserted their identities through unofficial channels. Linguistically, the government actively promoted the use of Vietnamese while at the same time taking largely symbolic steps to protect other languages. Vietnamese national chauvinism was therefore present but less formal and more muted than Bamar national chauvinism, and it did not provoke nationalist civil war.

Comparison with Myanmar therefore highlights how limited colonial pluralism impeded nationalist civil warfare in Vietnam by restraining Kinh national chauvinism and weakening reactions to it. As noted previously, however, the French did employ some pluralist policies in colonial Vietnam. Supporting previous findings, the Montagnards were the community most affected by colonial pluralism, and they organized Vietnam's most violent nationalist movement.

Also called "Dega," Montagnards received considerable autonomy during much of the colonial period. In fact, they were a rare example of a community in the French Empire that controlled its own "customary" tribunals and administrations, suggesting a form of indirect rule that was more British in character than French (Lange 2009b; Salemink 2003: 80–82). Even more, the French organized Montagnards into a short-lived autonomous polity—the Montagnard Country of South Indochina—that formally separated the Montagnard region from colonial Annam as a means of gaining Montagnard support against anticolonial forces (Safman 2007: 49; Salemink 1995).

Similar to other non-state communities in the Southeast Asian highlands, Montagnards include diverse peoples speaking many languages, and colonial policies promoted the rise of a Montagnard communal consciousness (Hickey 1982; Salemink 1995). As the term "Montagnard" suggests, these peoples live in the mountains of south-central Vietnam, a region that has relatively low population density and that was located at the periphery of the precolonial states and experienced relatively limited Kinh influence. During the early colonial period, the French had very little presence among Montagnard peoples. When French influence in the region expanded, a handful of French officials devised an indirect form of rule that codified "traditional" law and recognized and maintained Montagnard chiefs. Léopold Sebatier spearheaded these efforts (Salemink 2003). He recognized the Kinh and Chinese as more advanced and sought to protect Montagnards from them by safeguarding their autonomy and limiting the influence of Kinh, Chinese, and French settlers (Salemink 2003: 81–82). While Catholic missionaries were present in the region by the mid-nineteenth century, Protestant missionaries—a rarity in French Vietnam—arrived in the early twentieth century and taught in a local vernacular, something that the Catholics subsequently copied. And through education and communal organizations, all missionaries "played an important part in the rise of ethnonationalism among the highland people" (Hickey 1982: 210).

The French did not employ these pluralist policies universally among Montagnards, however, and competing forces pushed the French to waver between direct and indirect rule. Recognizing the disruptive effect of French settlers and Kinh migrants, Sebatier tried to prevent them from moving to the region in the 1920s. This move opposed an important colonial directive to further integrate the central highlands into Indochina, so Sebatier's superiors removed him from power in 1926, ended indirect rule, and controlled the region through a more direct form of rule. By the mid-1930s, however, growing opposition to French rule and Kinh settlement pushed the French to reapply Sebatier's model of customary law (Salemink 1995: 270). After the Second World War, French officials greatly increased Montagnard autonomy by creating a separate Montagnard administration as part of their effort to limit anticolonial influence in the region. Despite some partial backtracking during the final years of French rule, Montagnards retained autonomy, and the Sabatier system of indirect rule continued to function (Christie 1996: 93–92; Salemink 1995:

285–86). According to Salemink (1995), this eight-year period of Montagnard self-rule successfully popularized an idea of a Montagnard homeland, thereby creating expectations for Montagnard autonomy (264).

At independence in 1954, the Montagnard region merged with South Vietnam, and relations between Montagnards and the South Vietnamese government were very contentious due to the latter's strong national chauvinism. After coming to power in 1954, the southern Vietnamese government formally ended the indirect rule of Montagnard communities, implemented aggressive assimilationist policies, and resettled refugees from North Vietnam in the central highlands (Dharma 2006; Hickey 1982: 5–12, 16). Like upland communities in Myanmar, Montagnard leaders mobilized against discriminatory treatment and lost autonomy (Christie 1996; Dharma 2006; Hickey 1982). UCDP data, however, suggests that the Montagnard conflict never escalated into a nationalist civil war. The main factor that limited the expansion of this conflict is that the violence was part of a larger international war, with the Americans, Cambodians, and Viet Minh fracturing the movement by organizing their own Montagnard supporters (Christie 1996; Dharma 2006: 69; Salemink 1995).

Because of their strategic location, Montagnard peoples found themselves at the epicenter of the Vietnam War: No side was in control, all sides insisted that the Montagnard support them, and Montagnard communities were under constant attack. The Viet Minh made considerable inroads into the central highlands and successfully engaged many Montagnards in their efforts (Salemink 1995). Thousands of other Montagnards joined the Front Unifié de Lutte des Races Opprimées (FURLO), an organization created and run by the Cambodian government to destabilize Vietnam in the hopes of regaining control of regions that Cambodia had lost to Vietnam prior to French rule (Dharma 2006; Salemink 1995). Finally, the American military followed the example set by the French during the First Vietnam War and trained many Montagnards to fight the Viet Minh.

Although international warfare and interference fractured the Montagnard nationalist movement, the actual scale of nationalist violence was likely greater than commonly recognized. Montagnard forces in FURLO and the South Vietnamese government fought against one another despite efforts by American forces to reconcile their differences, and many soldiers and civilians died in these clashes. Because the Cambodian government organized FURLO, this violence is usually considered part of an international war instead of as a conflict over Montagnard autonomy. Most FURLO combatants, however, were Montagnards who fought for their communal rights and autonomy, not for an enlarged Cambodian state (Christie 1996; Hickey 1982: 117). In fact, FURLO gained great support from Montagnard communities by absorbing BAJARAKA, a Montagnard nationalist movement started in 1956 in reaction to the removal of Montagnard cultural and political autonomy by the South

Vietnamese government (Dharma 2006; Hickey 1982). The Montagnard nationalist conflict therefore parallels the nationalist civil wars in Myanmar, Northeast India, Sudan, and elsewhere in showing how pluralist colonial policies that formally provided non-state communities with autonomy and self-rule contributed to nationalist conflict after postcolonial governments pursued chauvinistic policies that undermined the cultural and political autonomy of these communities.

Cambodia

French Indochina was a colonial federation that included the three Vietnamese territories (Cochinchina, Annam, and Tonkin) as well as Cambodia and Laos. Of Vietnam, Cambodia, and Laos, data on historical statehood suggest that Cambodia had the highest level of precolonial statehood. In fact, with a score of 48 out of 50 for the period between 1001 and 1700 AD, Cambodia has the highest precolonial state index of all former British and French colonies and one of the highest in the world. At the same time, Cambodia experienced a form of colonialism that was more Republican than in Vietnam and that lacked pluralist exceptions like the Montagnards. Ultimately, the case offers evidence that precolonial statehood and French rule strengthened Khmer national chauvinism but did not promote nationalist civil war due to the absence of non-state communities with both expectations for nationalist self-rule and mobilizational resources to pursue this goal.

Beginning in the third century BC, states formed and coalesced into larger polities in what is presently Cambodia. Between the eighth and fifteenth centuries, the Khmer Empire dominated contemporary Cambodia and much of the surrounding regions, and it was during this time that Angkor Wat flourished. By the end of the fifteenth century, military defeat resulted in the collapse of the Empire, and the subsequent states that ruled Cambodia were commonly vassal states of either the Siamese or Vietnamese empires.

The French usually ruled colonies and protectorates in very similar ways given a common focus on geopolitical control and economic gain. As a result, French officials made all important political decisions in colony and protectorate alike. In Cambodia, however, protectorate status shaped the form of French rule in important ways. Similar to central Vietnam, the French recognized the authority of the Cambodian King in an effort to transfer his legitimacy to the colonial state. Moreover, the French worked through the precolonial state during the first decades of colonial rule because they lacked personnel and resources and only gradually reformed legal-administrative institutions to bolster French control. In maintaining the Cambodian monarchy and administrative structure, the king continued to symbolize the political community and helped unify the colonized population. Moreover, the French did not recognize, accommodate, or empower non-state communities in any way and implemented policies that strengthened ideas of a unified Cambodian nation. In particular, the French were obsessed with Angkor Wat and popularized ideas that Cambodians were the descendants of a glorious Khmer civilization, thereby using Angkor Wat as the symbol of this ancient nation and constructing a myth-symbol complex around it (Edwards 2008).

Through these policies, assimilation into Khmer culture, which had long preceded French rule, continued. Presently, Cambodia has a very homogeneous population, with approximately 85 percent of the population being ethnic Khmer, nearly all of whom are Buddhist. The remaining population is made up of several relatively small communities, many of which live in isolated upland regions.

Although precolonial statehood contributed to Khmer national chauvinism through its effects on communal demography and myth-symbol complexes, French colonialism also strengthened it, and Khmer national chauvinism has been present throughout the postcolonial period (Edwards 2008; Ovesen and Trankell 2004: 241–45). Yet this national chauvinism was not as aggressive and exclusive as in Myanmar and commonly incorporated indigenous non-state communities into the Khmer nation as junior partners (Ovesen and Trankell 2004: 245; Safman 2007: 43–44). Governments recognized the Cham as the "middle" Khmer due to their concentration along the central Mekong River. The communities in the mountainous region, in turn, were recognized as the earliest inhabitants of the region and referred to as the "original Khmer." In contrast, the Chinese and Vietnamese were recognized as non-indigenous and excluded from the Khmer nation (Ovesen and Trankell 2004: 248; Safman 2007: 44).

With the rise to power of the Khmer Rouge in 1975, Khmer national chauvinism gained a new and extreme form focused on rejuvenating the ancient Khmer Empire. The Khmer Rouge mixed Marxism with national chauvinism, thereby describing "real" Khmers as peasants and seeking both economic and nationalist reforms. Seeing the Vietnamese and Chinese as foreign bourgeois elements who destroyed traditional livelihoods, the Khmer Rouge targeted both. Like the Khmer, all non-state communities suffered greatly under the Khmer Rouge, but—with the possible exception of the Cham—the Khmer Rouge did not target them because of their communal difference and accepted them as members of the Khmer nation on the condition that they lived according to the Khmer Rouge's version of "tradition" (Kiernan 2008).

In enforcing a Khmer "tradition" through the use of extreme violence, the Khmer Rouge forced non-state communities to assimilate, and many died. The previous chapters offer evidence that forced assimilation and violence greatly increase the risk of nationalist civil warfare, suggesting that its absence in Cambodia requires explanation. Communal homogeneity likely deterred nationalist civil warfare to some extent, but—as already noted—very small communities fought large state communities in the former British Empire. Another possible explanation is that Pol Pot's extreme violence prevented nationalist civil warfare. Yet previous chapters also provide evidence that non-state reactions to integration and assimilation are strong when states coerce and repress them. Instead of communal demography or violence, comparison with Myanmar and other former British colonies highlights the absence of colonial pluralism as the crucial difference that explains the absence of nationalist warfare. In contrast to neighboring Myanmar and India, French colonialism in Cambodia did not politicize community or pit state and non-state communities against each other. As a result, non-state communities did not have nationalist frames, expectations, and mobilizational resources and did not react to the Khmer Rouge's national chauvinism with nationalist movements.

Thailand

Thailand is one of only a handful of countries in the Global South that was never a European overseas colony. As a result, the region did not experience colonial pluralism in any form, and the contemporary state is the continuation of a long line of Thai states that have ruled the region for nearly a millennium. The country's history of nationalist civil warfare is mixed, with one conflict in southern Thailand but the absence of nationalist warfare in all other regions. Ultimately, the case shows that historical statehood promoted Thai national chauvinism during the transition from imperial state to nation-state but that national chauvinism only sparked nationalist civil warfare when non-Thai communities had distinct cultures and possessed their own historical state.

Known as Siam until 1939, the term "Thailand" declares the country the land of the Thais. Thais trace their origins to Thai-speaking peoples who immigrated from China over 1,000 years ago. By that time, many people lived in the region, and Indian culture had influenced social relations, including the introduction of Hinduism and Buddhism. The first major Thai polity was the Sukhothai Kingdom, which lasted from 1228 to 1438 and controlled most of contemporary Thailand. In 1335, the rival Ayutthaya Kingdom was founded, and it overthrew the Sukhothai Kingdom to dominate the region. At its height, the city of Ayutthaya was a bustling economic and political port and possibly the largest city in the world. The Ayutthaya Kingdom lasted over 400 years, finally collapsing in 1767 as a result of Bamar attacks. After the destruction of the Ayutthaya Kingdom, the region divided into several competing kingdoms, but the Chakri dynasty was founded in 1782, which continues to rule Thailand to this day. Like other major polities in the region, the early Chakri state was imperial and ruled over diverse peoples, with power being greatest in Bangkok and weakening as the distance from the center increased. At the extreme, the most peripheral regions simply paid tribute to the king and, in return, were left to rule themselves.

With the British to the west and south and the French to the east, Chakri kings did an adept job playing both colonial powers off one another to maintain Thai independence. Despite this, they lost considerable territory, and colonial pressures greatly influenced Thai politics by promoting wide-ranging political reforms that sought to transform Thailand from an empire to a nation-state (Keyes 2003: 187). For this, the leaders sought to eliminate local intermediaries and replaced them with administrators who reported directly to Bangkok. They also centralized state control over Buddhism. Finally, Thai kings sought to create a homogeneous nation through aggressive assimilationist policies. As part of this, they formalized the Central Thai dialect, made this dialect the national language, created a compulsory system of education, and taught a curriculum that focused on strengthening Thai nationalism by emphasizing the three pillars of nation, religion, and monarchy (Buadaeng and Leepreecha 2018; Keyes 2003). These assimilationist policies were very successful: In the late nineteenth century, Thais made up approximately 15 percent of the population, but over three-quarters of the population presently self-identify as ethnic Thai (Keyes 2003: 181).

Karens live on both sides of the Myanmar-Thai border, and Thai Karens provide an example of assimilation. The case also informs the counterfactual from chapter 4 about whether Myanmar Karens would have fought a nationalist civil war without a history of British colonial pluralism. Thai Karens are the largest recognized minority in northern Thailand. Similar to their precolonial Myanmar counterparts, they were not organized politically over the past few hundred years, did not have strong communal identities, were marginalized, and faced considerable discrimination (Buadaeng 2007). Thailand, however, was never colonized by a European power, and Thai officials did not attempt to implement any sort of pluralist policy that recognized communal difference between Thais and Karens, let alone any policy that privileged Karens over Thais. Instead, the Thai state attempted to integrate Karens into the Thai nation while increasing its control over them. For example, the Thai government created government schools for minorities that taught in Thai, used a Thai nationalist curriculum, and thereby facilitated the inclusion of minorities into the Thai nation. Because Buddhism was the official religion and was a source of state legitimacy, Thai officials also limited the influence of Christian missionaries among minorities and countered missionary efforts by sponsoring their own Buddhist missions. Given government pressure, Protestant missionaries who worked with Thai Karens simply helped Karens attend government schools instead of running their own schools. Thus, whereas "Christian missionaries helped create a separate Karen consciousness [in Myanmar]," they "aided the Karen to better integrate into Thai society" (Buadaeng 2007: 84).

Due in large part to these differences, Thai Karens never became an assertive political community, and most Karens have developed hybrid political identities that are both Thai and Karen (Buadaeng 2007). Although one cannot assume that the outcome would have been exactly the same in Myanmar without a history of British rule, a similar outcome seems likely because there is no apparent reason why a Bamar-led state would have privileged Karens, recognized them as a distinct community, and opened the door to missionary conversion. Indeed, the most likely scenario is that the Bamar would have treated Karens in ways like the Thais and that Myanmar Karens would have reacted to this treatment in ways similar to Thai Karens.

The comparison of Thai and Myanmar Karens pinpoints colonial pluralism as the key factor explaining their different histories of nationalist civil warfare, but an alternative explanation is population size—there are ten times more Karens in Myanmar than Thailand. The Isan, on the other hand, make up one-third of the entire Thai population, so they would be especially likely to fight nationalist civil wars if population size matters. Even more, the Isan are concentrated in a peripheral region and face economic, political, and cultural marginalization. Similar to the Thai Karen, however, the Isan never mobilized a nationalist movement.

Formerly known as Lao, the Isan are concentrated in the Khorat Plateau, a region in northeastern Thailand that borders Laos and Cambodia. Like ethnic Thais, the Isan are from the Thai-linguistic family, but the Isan language is closer to Laotian than Thai. Historically, the Khorat Plateau was part of the Khmer Empire, and Isan began moving into the region from present-day Laos half a millennium ago. Due to this population movement, Isan became the dominant community in the Khorat Plateau, although Isan culture—including its language—was influenced by the Khmer. Similar to the Shan in Myanmar, the Isan formed several polities on the hinterlands of different imperial states, so they were never completely independent but generally retained considerable autonomy. With the growing strength of the Thai state in the late eighteenth century, the region transferred from Laotian to Thai influence. At first, the Thais ruled the region as vassal states. With Thai state-building in the late nineteenth century, however, the Thai government built a new administrative system in the region that reported directly to the central state and greatly reduced local autonomy. As with Thai Karens, these reforms were combined with nation-building efforts focused on linguistic assimilation and Buddhism.

The Thai government was particularly concerned about nation building among the Isan because of the ever-present threat of colonialism. With French control of neighboring Laos and Cambodia, Thai leaders feared French intrusions into the Khorat Plateau. Even more, the French saw the Isan as Laotian and encouraged them to join French Laos. At this time, a religiously motivated rebellion occurred in the Khorat Plateau, thereby heightening Thai fears of losing the region. In 1904, the Thai state therefore decided to make the Isan Thais. The first concrete step they took toward this goal was to stop employing the term "Lao" in favor of the term "Isan," which referred to the region (Liu and Ricks 2022: 27). And although the Thai state had previously considered the Isan non-Thais, it now noted new "scientific" evidence proving that the Isan were Thais (Streckfuss 2012: 308). With this reclassification, the Isan community was erased from the Thai map, and Thai Karens—who number far less than the Isan—became the largest recognized non-state community in northern Thailand.

Despite continued inequalities and condescending treatment from "real" Thais, nation-building efforts among the Isan have been successful, especially relative to non-state communities in Myanmar. Although Isan has emerged as a regional identity, the Isan community is not politicized. As a result, there is neither an Isan political party protecting communal interests nor an Isan nationalist movement (Ricks 2019). Even more, surveys consistently show that Isan self-identify with and value the Thai nation even more than Central Thais (Ricks 2020).

The case of the Isan therefore shows that Thai national chauvinism was present and linked to the transition from empire-state to nation-state. Unlike communities in Myanmar, India, and other former British colonies, however, this national chauvinism did not push the Isan to demand greater autonomy despite aggressive state integration and assimilation. Unlike the British colonies, the Thai model of political community was anything but pluralist, as it neither recognized, empowered, nor accommodated minorities and, instead, strove to assimilate all communities into the Thai national community. Although Isan polities had considerable autonomy when incorporated into the Thai state, this autonomy was not granted based on communal status, and polities were very localized. A history of autonomy therefore had limited effect on expectations for Isan self-rule, and subsequent assimilationist policies did not provide communal mobilizational resources. The Isan contrast greatly with Karens, Shan, Karennis, and other communities in Myanmar, which mobilized nationalist movements against forced integration and assimilationism because they had frames and expectations for continued autonomy and the capability to mobilize support for it, all resulting from a history of British colonial pluralism.

While the Thai Karens, Isan, and other non-state communities have largely—if at times grudgingly—accepted Thai national chauvinism, one community in Thailand has fought a nationalist civil war over it: the Southern Insurgency led by Malay nationalists in the Patani region. This secessionist conflict began in the early twentieth century, and violence resurfaced the 1940s and 1960s. In 2004, a nationalist civil war began and caused thousands of deaths, most resulting from government force. The case is similar to the Isan in that the Patani region was on the periphery of the Chakri dynasty and retained great autonomy until the implementation of nation-state-building reforms. The cases are also similar in that the Thai government pursued particularly harsh assimilationist policies among the Malay over fear of colonial interference, as the British controlled neighboring Malaya. Yet, two factors put the Patani region on a different path: culture and historical statehood.

Whereas most Isan speak a language that is similar to Thai and are Buddhist, the population of southern Thailand speaks a language that is not related to Thai—Malay—and is primarily Muslim. As a result, the region's population was more sensitive to Thai assimilationist policies and resisted them, especially in terms of religion (Barter 2014; Chalermsripinyorat 2021). That being said, the Southern Insurgency has been active in only four of the five southern provinces: The conflict has been concentrated in Pattani, Yala, Narthiwat, and Eastern Songkhla but has been absent from Satun, which also has a majority Malay population (Barter 2014: 127). One important characteristic that separates Satun from the other provinces is that it is the only one that was not part of the Sultanate of Patani.

The Sultanate of Patani was formed in the late fourteenth century and included much of northern Malaysia (Christie 1996). As its name suggests, it was a Muslim state, with the ruler having both political and religious authority. The Sultanate grew and prospered as an important center of regional trade, something that placed it in direct competition with the Thai imperial state. After being defeated in the late sixteenth century, the Sultanate became a vassal state of the expanding Ayutthaya Kingdom, but it retained great autonomy and began its "golden age" at this time. Half a century later, Patani gained complete autonomy from the Thais, but Thai troops forcibly reestablished it as a tributary state in 1786, which it remained until the Sultan was removed in 1902. In 1909, the Thai state took direct control of the region.

Different from Isan, this history of statehood provided a powerful myth-symbol complex that created strong expectations for self-rule. In addition, statehood promoted cultural homogeneity, with the Patani state ruling in the name of Islam and employing the Malay language. Because Thai nationalism imposed both the Thai language and Buddhism and removed the Patani Sultan and his administrators from power, forced integration and assimilationism promoted strong grievances in Patani, provoked an uprising almost immediately, and motivated subsequent conflicts (Brown 1988; Melvin 2007; Safman 2007: 34). In contrast, these policies also greatly limited cultural autonomy in neighboring Satun, but the population in this region had a much weaker national consciousness because it was regularly moving from one polity to another. Overall, the Patani conflict therefore highlights that the absence of colonial pluralism did not prevent nationalist civil warfare in southern Thailand because a separate history of statehood in Patani—but not Satun—had similar effects as British colonial pluralism.

Botswana and Egypt

So far, this chapter has analyzed non-British colonies, thereby exploring how precolonial statehood affected nationalist civil war in regions with limited or no history of colonial pluralism. Another way to consider this issue is to analyze the two former British colonies with precolonial states that experienced low levels of colonial pluralism: Botswana and Egypt. Similar to Cambodia, British rule maintained the dominance of the state community in both regions, and the absence of pluralist policies limited non-state sensitivity to the national chauvinism of the state communities. As a result, neither country has experienced nationalist civil war.

Influential analyses arguing that historical statehood limits ethnic warfare use Botswana to support their claims (Englebert 2000; Wimmer 2018). In contrast, this book focuses on nationalist civil warfare, argues that historical statehood promotes this type of conflict, and points to limited colonial pluralism as a more likely explanation for relatively peaceful intercommunal relations in Botswana. And similar to Vietnam, Cambodia, and northern Thailand, limited pluralism in colonial Botswana—known as the Bechuanaland Protectorate—did not promote nationalist warfare because non-state communities lacked nationalist frames, expectations for self-rule, and mobilizational resources to pursue autonomy. Thus, although some non-state communities were aggrieved by postcolonial policies that maintained Tswana dominance, no nationalist civil war occurred.

Botswana's moderate state history index score (21.5 out of 50) suggests that historical statehood should have more limited effects on nationalist civil warfare than in Myanmar, Sri Lanka, or even Nigeria. Yet, Botswana possesses two traits commonly associated with historical statehood that contributed to nationalist civil warfare in these cases: a communal demography characterized by one large state community and several small non-state communities and national chauvinism. Due to the latter, the postcolonial state recognizes the Tswana as the core national community; the term "Botswana" means the Tswana.

Prior to colonialism, Botswana was controlled by five large kingdoms, usually referred to as chiefdoms, all of which were governed by Tswana rulers (Schapera 1943). The Tswana peoples first entered the region around 600 AD, and the first powerful Tswana chiefdom—the Kwena—was founded around 1500 AD. Over the next three centuries, populations broke off from the Kwena Chiefdom (and subsequent chiefdoms) to form new Tswana chiefdoms, with the last—the Tawana Chiefdom—founded in the 1790s. These states enforced communal hierarchies, with ethnic Tswana having the highest status, non-Tswana having lower statuses, and some non-Tswana being little more than slaves. The boundaries between Tswana and non-Tswana were usually fluid, however, and communities that assimilated into Tswana society became Tswana. In the earliest analysis of the communal composition of the population, Schapera (1952) finds that Tswana were easily the largest community but that the majority of the African population—53 percent—was non-Tswana.

Unlike nearly all former British colonies of occupation, the British did not implement overtly pluralist policies in Botswana and, instead, left the Tswana chiefs to rule their subjects without recognizing, empowering, or accommodating non-state communities in any way. The main reason for the absence of common pluralist policies is the way in which Botswana became a British possession: Boer intrusions into Tswana territories pushed Tswana chiefs to travel to England and request British protection, so the British did not conquer and impose their rule on recalcitrant subjects. In this situation, the British had no need for divide-and-rule-style policies, and pluralism would have simply turned the Tswana chiefs against the British. Colonial officials therefore only recognized, accommodated, and empowered Tswana.

Protestant missionaries in Botswana were also unique in that they strengthened Tswana dominance instead of promoting pluralism. For practical reasons, Tswana chiefs were open to missionary influence prior to the establishment of the British protectorate. Because Tswana elite wanted to monopolize the benefits of missionaries (education, health care, and political influence), they demanded that the missionaries only work closely with them. As a result, the missionaries worked with Tswana chiefs and their royal families but did not work among non-Tswana (Mgadla 2003). For their part, the missionaries accepted this situation because their ability to proselytize depended on chiefly accommodation and because the missionaries believed—correctly— that Christianity would diffuse from the Tswana elite to the rest of the population. One outcome of collaborative relations between missionaries and Tswana chiefs is that the missionaries only used the Tswana language (Setswana), thereby failing—with one partial exception—to develop writing for the non-state communities and teaching exclusively in Tswana and English (Mgadla 2003: 52). Missionaries monopolized education in colonial Botswana until the 1930s, and subsequent government schools also used Setswana as the sole vernacular. And unlike elsewhere, Protestant missionaries did not mobilize to protect non-state communities from the state community.

Given the dominance of Tswana, a form of Tswana national chauvinism is present, and it suggests that Tswana are the core community of the Botswana nation-state and disregards diversity for the sake of national unity (Werbner 2000: 4). In this way, assimilationist pressures are present, the national ideology emphasizes that the nation is Tswana, and the state neither recognizes, accommodates, nor empowers non-Tswana. While less aggressive and exclusionary than national chauvinism in Myanmar, Sudan, and elsewhere, Tswana national chauvinism has helped Tswana maintain their dominant positions at the expense of non-state communities and therefore had the potential to provoke minority opposition. Instead of reacting violently, however, non-state communities have grudgingly accepted Tswana dominance, and assimilation is common. Thus, whereas the majority of the population was non-Tswana in the 1950s, 80 percent of the contemporary population self-identify as Tswana.

Two main factors explain why Tswana national chauvinism did not promote nationalist civil war. First, and of greatest relevance to this book, colonial rule was nonpluralist and limited the strength of communal divisions, the politicization of communities, and the mobilizational resources of non-state communities. Indeed, by failing to acknowledge, accommodate, and empower non-Tswana, non-state communities accepted continued Tswana dominance and continued to assimilate into the Tswana community. According to Bennett (2002), "In some parts of Africa, colonial governments used tactics of 'divide and rule' in relation to ethnic groups. But in the Bechuanaland Protectorate [colonial Botswana], it was quite the reverse. The administration had no interest in the sort of rule which dividing would permit; rather they wished to maintain the power of the chiefs as the most convenient form of government. Attempts by minorities to resist Tswana power were swatted down, with the colonial government backing the chief" (8). Importantly, limited communal mobilization against Tswana dominance promoted a virtuous circle that weakened nationalist mobilization among non-state communities even further: Tswana did not feel threatened by minorities and therefore did not support aggressive policies targeting non-state communities, and a milder Tswana national chauvinism limited the grievances of non-state communities. Given this situation, Botswana provides a glimpse of what could have happened to communities like the Karens in Myanmar—who were a subordinate community living among the state community—if colonial actors did not strengthen a Karen national consciousness, privilege Karens, and communalize politics.

The second reason for limited mobilization by non-state communities against Tswana national chauvinism concerns the country's particular transition to independence. As elsewhere in the British Empire, indirect rule strengthened chiefs relative to their subjects, and some chiefs ruled their non-Tswana subjects very harshly, thereby provoking resistance to Tswana overrule (Bennett 2002: 7; Lange 2009a; Maundeni 1998: 119; Wylie 1990). Most notably, Chief Tshekedi Khama of the Ngwato, the largest and most powerful Tswana chiefdom during the British colonial period and one with a large non-Tswana majority, centralized his rule and demanded more and more tribute and labor from non-Tswana communities (Parsons 1987; Wylie 1990). Yet Tshekedi was a regent chief ruling in the place of his nephew, Seretse Khama, during the latter's childhood and education in London. While getting his law degree in the UK in the 1950s, Seretse married a white woman, which sparked outrage among South African officials because of a long-standing agreement that South Africa would eventually take control of Botswana (Lange 2009a). Due to South African influence, the British refused to allow Seretse to become chief. The population in the Ngwato Chiefdom and in the other chiefdoms strongly backed Seretse, and this support was especially strong among non-Tswana, who wanted to depose Tshekedi because of the hardships they experienced under his rule (Lange 2009a; Parsons 1987). After renouncing his chieftaincy several years later, Seretse returned to Botswana. His fame, education, and chiefly heritage allowed him to gain great popular support, and he became Botswana's first prime minister. After independence, Prime Minister Khama removed chiefs from power and replaced them with local councils, an act that endeared many non-Tswana to him because it removed Tswana chiefs who had commonly ruled non-Tswana harshly.

All in all, the Botswana case shows that the absence of colonial pluralism helps explain the country's lack of nationalist civil warfare despite its history of precolonial statehood. Like other places with precolonial states, Botswana has a state community supporting national chauvinism. Tswana national chauvinism is relatively mild when compared to that in Myanmar, Sudan, and elsewhere, a difference resulting in large part from the absence of pluralist policies that threatened Tswana. That being said, Tswana national chauvinism still discriminates against non-state communities and could provoke nationalist conflict. The main reason why non-state communities have not reacted to Tswana national chauvinism is their relatively weak nationalist frames, motives, and mobilizational resources, outcomes that colonial pluralism promoted in other British colonies but that were absent in Botswana because of an exceptionally nonpluralist form of British colonial rule.

Among former British colonies, Egypt is second only to Myanmar in terms of its state history index score between 1001 and 1700 AD, suggesting a very long history of precolonial statehood. At the same time, it has very low levels of colonial pluralism. Like Botswana, the British ruled Egypt "lightly" through precolonial institutions, thereby maintaining indigenous authorities while not recognizing, accommodating, or empowering non-state communities. The country is also similar to Botswana in that it has not experienced a nationalist civil war.

The lack of nationalist civil warfare might not seem surprising given Egypt's high levels of ethnic homogeneity. The country's ethnic fractionalization index score is only 0.16, and approximately 90 percent of the population speak Arabic and are Sunni Muslim. There are, however, many minorities. Roughly 10 percent of the population are Coptic Christians and commonly experience violence and exclusion. Linguistically, there are small numbers of Amazigh (Berber) speakers in the western desert and Nubian and Beja speakers in the South, and roughly one-quarter of Egyptians speak Sa'idi Arabic, which—depending on the dialect—is commonly incomprehensible to speakers of Egyptian Arabic. Finally, many Egyptians—especially those living away from the Nile Valley who presently or recently led nomadic or semi-nomadic life-styles and speak Sa'idi Arabic—are organized into tribes. Several non-state communities, in turn, historically had considerable political autonomy from the precolonial state centered in the lower Nile. Given this situation, nationalist movements were a real possibility.

Similar to Botswana, however, the British did not implement pluralist poli-cies but ruled through precolonial authorities in ways that maintained the state community's political and cultural dominance. The case is also similar to Cam-bodia in that the ancient heritage of Egypt and the presence of magnificent ruins and monuments underlay a colonial understanding of Egypt as a grand civilization with a unified national population. Reinforcing this situation, Brit-ish rule of Egypt was informal except for an eight-year period and was there-fore supposed to simply guide Egyptian authorities, causing British officials to maintain the precolonial political institutions and authorities much more than in other colonial possessions. As Tignor (1966) notes, "The British ruled Egypt through, or more precisely, behind, the Egyptian governmental apparatus" (184). In this situation, pluralist policies would have weakened the authority of the colonized Egyptian state, so the British did not implement them.

It is impossible to say whether Egypt would have suffered nationalist civil warfare if the British implemented pluralist policies like in neighboring Sudan, where the southern periphery was ruled separately from the rest of the colony. Such a policy seems a realistic possibility in colonial Egypt; given the British record throughout the empire, the absence of colonial pluralism in Egypt is more surprising. And if the British divided state and non-state communities and favored the later, the risk of nationalist civil warfare would have been very high.

Ethiopia

So far, the cases analyzed in this chapter provide evidence that historical state-hood rarely promotes nationalist civil warfare in the absence of colonial plural-ism, a finding that contrasts with the statistical findings of chapter 3 showing a positive relationship between precolonial statehood and nationalist civil war onset. The cases, however, had either no or limited nationalist civil warfare, and the sample is therefore poorly suited for highlighting mechanisms through which historical statehood promotes nationalist civil warfare in the absence of colonial pluralism. In this section, I analyze a much more appropriate case: Ethiopia, a country with an ancient state, limited colonial pluralism, and seven nationalist civil wars. The five communities that have fought nationalist civil wars include the Afars, Amharas, Eritreans, Oromo, and Somalis.

Although only covering a small portion of contemporary Ethiopia, the earli-est Ethiopian kingdoms formed thousands of years ago. The first large imperial state for which information is available was the Aksumite Empire (150 BC–960 AD). It was centered in northern Ethiopia, expanded to include much of the Arabian Peninsula, and dominated trade in the Red Sea. Syrian monks introduced Christianity in the fourth century, and Christianity quickly became the Empire's dominant religion. Once losing control of regional trade, the Aksumite Empire declined. The Zagwe Empire replaced it (960 AD–1270 AD), and the Solomonic dynasty, which lasted over 700 years until the deposition of Haile Selassie in 1974, followed the Zagwe Empire. The rulers of the Solomonic dynasty supported Coptic Orthodox Christianity and based their authority on mythic claims of descendance from King Solomon's son, Menelik I, whose mother, the Queen of Sheba, was supposedly Ethiopian and returned to the region with her son. The Solomonic dynasty was feudalistic and very decentralized, with highly autonomous polities within the empire, and imperial power regularly shifted among leaders from the three main regions—Tigray, Amhara, and Shoa.

Weakened by internal conflict and foreign invasions on multiple fronts, the Solomonic dynasty experienced a period of crisis in the seventeenth and eighteenth centuries. Although Ethiopian forces eventually repelled invasions by the Ottomans and other Muslims, the Oromo—who had increasingly migrated into Ethiopian lands from the south over the previous two centuries—gained greater influence due to their military prowess and participation in Ethiopia politics (Dilebo 1974: 37). In the nineteenth century, however, Amhara and Tigrayan leaders curbed Oromo influence and began modernizing the imperial state, with Tewados II and Yohannes IV reducing local autonomy and promoting greater centralization. Menelik II was an Amhara prince from Shoa who was adopted by the Tigrayan Tewados II after Tewados defeated Shoa and reduced its autonomy, and Menelik maneuvered himself to become emperor after the death of Yohannes IV. Menelik introduced modernizing military reforms that allowed him to expand the empire to the south, east, and west (Dilebo 1974). This expansion was aided by access to European military equipment (Dilebo 1974: 49–52, 60). At the same time that European technologies assisted Ethiopian expansion, European powers had their eyes on Ethiopia as a potential colony. In the Battle of Adowa, Menelik's forces defeated an Italian colonial invasion. Four decades later, Italy attacked Ethiopia again and was more successful. Although Italy never conquered all Ethiopia, it exiled Emperor Haile Selassie and occupied most of the country from 1936 to 1941, when Ethiopian and Allied forces expelled the Italians.

Similar to India, Ethiopia has multiple and different types of state communities. Prior to the eighteenth century, Amhara and Tigrayan communities were the dominant imperial communities, and many people assimilated into them (Levine 1974). The decentralized form of Ethiopian empires combined with mountainous barriers to maintain the autonomy and distinctiveness of both state communities—as well as others—throughout Ethiopia's long history of statehood. With the weakening of the Empire during the seventeenth and eighteenth centuries, Oromo leaders became more influential, and Tigrayan, Amhara, and Oromo communities jockeyed for power within the Empire. When the rule of Emperor Yohannes IV, a Tigrayan, was followed by Menelik II, an Amhara, Amhara leaders—especially those from the Shoa region—began cementing their community's political dominance. After increasingly subjugating the Oromo, Menelik II viewed the Tigrayans as his main imperial rival, and he agreed to allow Italy to colonize Eritrea—in part—because nearly half of the Tigrayan population lived there (Jacquin-Berdal 2002: 92).

In addition to centralizing his control over the historical core of the Solomonic dynasty, Menelik II led military expeditions that incorporated vast territories with millions of people into Ethiopia. Many of these conquered peoples did not have precolonial states, although some—like the Somalis and Afars—did. As a result, Ethiopia has both the ancient state communities of the Amharas and the Tigrayans, the more recent Oromo state community, as well as recently conquered state communities outside of the imperial homeland. Today, the four largest communities are the Oromo (35 percent), Amharas (27 percent), Somalis (6 percent), and Tigrayans (6 percent).

Emperor Haile Selassie, an Amhara from the Shoa region, ruled Ethiopia from 1930 to 1974 and continued Menelik II's state- and nation-building efforts. Noting the constant threat of colonial conquest, he focused on making Ethiopia a "modern" state by creating a more direct and centralized form of rule and building an Amhara nation-state. In this way, Selassie embraced an aggressive and exclusionary Amhara national chauvinism even though three-quarters of the Ethiopian population were non-Amhara. Amhara national chauvinism contributed to a variety of discriminatory policies: "Their language became the national language, their army was made the national army, and the Coptic Orthodox Church . . . became the national church and the emerging bureaucracy filled with the Amhara elite" (Abbay 1998: 12). As Gellner (1983) notes, "The Amhara empire was a prison-house of nations if ever there was one" (85).

Given that the Amharas were one of the two dominant state communities in Ethiopia over the past millennium, historical statehood contributed to a myth-symbol complex that strengthened Amhara national chauvinism. That being said, other aspects of Ethiopia's history of statehood created obstacles to the pursuit of Amhara national chauvinism. The decentralized character of Ethiopian imperial states and a mountainous terrain limited assimilation into a single community, and the historical state was multicultural and under the control of several communities. In fact, the ancient Aksumite Empire, which was the predecessor of the Solomonic dynasty, was centered in Tigray, something the popular Tigrayan myth-symbol complexes emphasize. Despite great communal diversity, international pressure and the dominant uninational model of the nation-state promoted very aggressive national chauvinism: Amhara leaders pursued national chauvinism to build a powerful state based on the European model of a nation-state that was capable of fending off colonial intrusions and cementing Amhara power within a competitive imperial polity. While more hidden in Thailand because the historical state was dominated by ethnic Thais over a long period, the Thai monarchy also pursued national chauvinist agendas to fend off colonizers and create a viable state. These cases therefore suggest that the determinants of national chauvinism in land-based empires transitioning to nation-states are different from those in overseas colonies transitioning to nation-states, with the leaders of land-based empires struggling to create a viable polity in the face of foreign aggression and internal adversaries whereas the postcolonial leaders of former colonies tried to reclaim and nationalize a state that colonizers had taken away.

Like the Patani Malays in Thailand, several Ethiopian communities reacted to Amhara national chauvinism with nationalist movements and violence. The Tigrayans, Afars, Oromo, and Somalis all recognized histories of past self-rule and autonomy and greatly resented Amhara efforts to impose their dominance. Tigrayan nationalists, for example, recognized the Aksumite Empire as their own and saw Amhara national chauvinism as deviant and illegitimate, noting that the Tigrayan Emperor Yohannes IV respected the autonomy of other regions and demanding that Amhara emperors do the same (Abbay 1998: 38; Clapham 1991). After Haile Selassie regained control of Ethiopia in 1941, he began extensive state-building efforts in the Tigray region and elsewhere. These reforms removed local officials, replaced customary law with Ethiopian law, and installed Amhara administrators and officials. In reaction, many Tigrayans participated in a violent rebellion in 1943—the Weyane—over the retention of autonomy within Ethiopia, and the violence only ended after British aerial bombings (Abbay 1998: 51). In the 1970s, the Second Weyane began and was led by the Tigray People's Liberation Front (TPLF). Although also proclaiming the need to protect Tigrayan culture and increase Tigrayan autonomy, the TPLF has focused primarily on taking over the Ethiopian state, something it did successfully after defeating the Derg in 1991. In this way, the Second Weyane was a center-seeking ethnic civil war, not a nationalist civil war. One reason why it did not pursue national autonomy is that the Tigrayans were a core state community in the Ethiopian region for several millennia, and their myth-symbol complexes therefore consider Ethiopia the Tigrayan homeland (Clapham 1991).

Instead of a center-seeking civil war, Afars have fought a nationalist civil war over secession. Afars have a long history of sultanates along the Red Sea that were either autonomous or retained autonomy within larger empires. Most recently, Afars ruled the Aussa Sultanate from 1734 until the early twentieth century. Although Ethiopian rulers claimed the region as part of their empire, Afars did not recognize Ethiopian authority until the late nineteenth century, and the Sultanate retained considerable autonomy even after Ethiopian state- and nation-building efforts. In 1974, however, a military coup led by Marxist Amharas removed Haile Selassie from power, and the new Derg government—which was "imbued with centralising Jacobism" and attacked any regionalism as a counterrevolutionary threat—removed all Afar autonomy (Clapham 1991: 250). In reaction, the Afar Liberation Front began a nationalist civil war.

Despite its limited duration, Italian colonialism also contributed to the Afar nationalist civil war. Because the Italian colonial forces faced great resistance and only controlled part of Ethiopia, Italian officials implemented divide-and-rule-style policies that favored non-Amharas to divide resistance and gain local support. With some irony, the Italians proclaimed themselves the protectors of Muslims against Christian domination and actively privileged Muslims to gain their support (Sbacchi 1985: 161–65). Afars are Muslim, and they supported Italian colonial efforts, thereby increasing conflict between Afars and Amharas.

Along with Afars, the Italians actively courted Somalis for support, and these policies—in combination with Somali historical statehood—also contributed to Somali nationalist civil wars. Somalis are overwhelmingly Muslim and live in the Ogaden region bordering Somalia. Italians successfully gained support from the Somalis for a variety of reasons. For one, Ethiopia only conquered the region in the late nineteenth century. In addition, Somalis resented Amhara rule because they lost much of their best land to Amhara settlers and had a history of statehood under a variety of different polities, including the Ifat Sultanate (1285–1403 AD), the Adal Sultanate (1415–1577 AD), and the Emirate of Harar (1647–1887 AD). The Italians, in turn, merged Ogaden with Italian Somaliland, thereby creating a larger Somali polity and encouraging support for a Somali homeland. After the Second World War, the Ethiopian government successfully lobbied for the return of Ogaden over the strong opposition of its population, and Ethiopian Somalis reacted to growing Amhara national chauvinism by beginning a nationalist civil war in 1964.

The Italians also sought to gain support among the largely Muslim Oromo peoples, although the latter were much more reticent despite Italian efforts to "free" the Oromo from Amhara domination (Sbacchi 1985: 160–61). Similar to other communities, however, many Oromo resented Amhara national chauvinism and their community's growing marginalization in Ethiopia. For example, the Ethiopian government banned Afan Oromo—the main language of the Oromo—from administrative use, schools, and even public places after retaking Ethiopia in 1941. Historically, in turn, the Oromo were autonomous from Ethiopia, and the Oromo heartland was only forcibly incorporated by Menelik II in the late nineteenth century. In this way, the combination of recent forced incorporation, Italian efforts to separate the Oromo from Amharas, a proud history of conquest and expansion, and the exclusion and marginalization of the Oromo all promoted a nationalist civil war.

The unique history of Italian colonialism and British rule in Eritrea made colonialism an especially influential cause of the Eritrean nationalist civil war. Unlike the rest of Ethiopia, Eritrea was colonized by the Italians for 51 years and was controlled by the British military between 1941 and 1952, thereby formally separating the region from the Ethiopian imperial state. During the 11 years of British control, military leaders implemented policies strengthening an Eritrean national frame to prepare it for incorporation into British Sudan (Jacquin-Berdal 2002: 98–99). Under pressure from the United States and the United Nations, these efforts failed, and Great Britain returned Eritrea to Ethiopia in 1952 on the condition that the region retain considerable autonomy within the Ethiopian state, including its own flag and legislature (Jacquin-Berdal 2002: 109). Over time, the Selassie government removed this autonomy, with the closing of Eritrean Legislature, the removal of the Eritrean flag, the replacement of local leaders with Amharas, and the declaration of Amharic as the official language of Eritrea (Abbay 1998; Jacquin-Berdal 2002: 109). In reaction, Eritrean nationalists began a nationalist civil war in 1964.

Finally, an Amhara general began a brief civil war in 2019 to increase the autonomy of Amharas, and the Ethiopian military quickly defeated his forces with only limited casualties. Since the fall of the Derg in 1991, non-Amharas have dominated the Ethiopian state and repressed Amhara political opposition. Many Amharas resented their marginalization, viewing themselves as the true national community. General Asaminew Tsige was a leading Amhara national chauvinist and organized forces in a failed attempt to increase the autonomy of the Amhara regional state.

All in all, Ethiopia provides another example of how the transition from empire to nation-state commonly promotes nationalist civil warfare. Instead of being an overseas colony, however, Ethiopia was a land-based empire with a brief and partial history of Italian conquest, and emperors focused their nation-state-building reforms on making Ethiopia a viable state that was recognized and respected by world powers. The purpose of analyzing Ethiopia in this chapter, however, was to analyze the independent effects of historical statehood on nationalist civil warfare, and the case shows that the transition from land-based empire to nation-state was very violent because forced integration under the guise of Amhara national chauvinism promoted strong reactions. Similar to Thailand, international pressure made Amhara national chauvinism extremely aggressive and promoted efforts to build a cohesive nation around the state community. And, like the Patani region, the presence of multiple state communities promoted strong opposition to forced integration, as histories of political and cultural autonomy made these communities very sensitive to Amhara national chauvinism. Like the Patani nationalist civil war in Thailand, the case therefore shows how transitions from land-based empires to nation-states promoted aggressive national chauvinism, which communities reacted to with nationalist movements when they had their own histories of statehood and autonomy. Colonial pluralism was not completely absent from the case, however, and influenced multiple nationalist civil wars, with Italian (and British) colonialism being an especially influential cause of the Eritrean conflict.

Conclusion

Although varying in strength and aggressiveness, the cases analyzed in this chapter all had state communities pursuing national chauvinism and offer evidence that historical statehood contributed to national chauvinism. In Thailand and Ethiopia, extremely aggressive national chauvinism was an important determinant of nationalist civil warfare, thereby suggesting that historical statehood can promote nationalist civil warfare independent of colonial pluralism (although divisive colonial pluralism also influenced most conflicts in Ethiopia). Yet national chauvinism did not promote nationalist civil warfare in Vietnam, Cambodia, Botswana, and Egypt because it was usually more moderate and—especially—because non-state communities were less sensitive to it. Comparison with other cases suggests that the absence of colonial pluralism helps explain limited reactions to national chauvinism, as non-state communities lacked histories of autonomy and empowerment and had limited nationalist frames, all of which made the national chauvinism of state communities less repulsive and antagonistic.

That being said, some communities in Thailand and Ethiopia reacted to the national chauvinisms of others with nationalist movements, showing that colonial pluralism was not necessary for nationalist civil war. These cases highlight the presence of multiple state communities as key to explaining variation in nationalist civil warfare among cases with limited or no colonial pluralism: With their own histories of statehood, subordinate state communities had nationalist frames and expectations for continued autonomy, both of which created strong grievances when faced with forced integration into the nation-states of others. In this way, historical statehood has powerful independent effects on nationalist civil wars in countries with multiple communities that have their own historical states. Notably, the Arakanese and Mon nationalist civil wars in Myanmar, the Baloch and Bangladesh nationalist civil wars in Pakistan, the Tamil nationalist civil war in Sri Lanka, and the Assamese, Manipuri, Sikh, and Tripuri nationalist civil wars in India also involved communities with their own histories of precolonial statehood revolting against postcolonial states for greater autonomy and self-rule. These findings therefore suggest that the presence of multiple state communities promotes nationalist civil war through many of the same mechanisms as colonial pluralism and is the main reason for the positive relationship between state history and nationalist civil war onset.

These findings begin to outline a more general model of nationalist civil warfare. During transitions from empire to nation-state, leaders from state communities try to build a nation-state around their community by forcibly imposing their culture and rule on others. While this forced integration commonly aggrieves communities, they rarely react with nationalist movements because national chauvinism is commonly mild and because they lack the nationalist frames, expectations, and mobilizational resources that make possible nationalist reactions. Colonial pluralism is one very influential factor making the national chauvinism of state communities aggressive and vindictive, increasing the sensitivity of communities to national chauvinism, and providing them with resources to organize nationalist movements, thereby explaining why nationalist civil warfare is so common in former British colonies with precolonial states. At the same time, the Patani Malays in Thailand shows that a history of statehood makes communities very sensitive to the national chauvinism of others in similar ways. And in cases like the Arakanese and Manipuri conflicts, both colonial pluralism and the presence of multiple state communities combined to fuel strong reactions to the national chauvinism of others.

9
Conclusions, Contributions, and Comparisons

In the British Empire, pluralism and divide and rule were often two sides of the same coin. Pluralism recognized, accommodated, and empowered communities, although it commonly benefited some communities at the expense of others. For the communities benefiting from these policies, colonial pluralism prevented large communities from dominating them. For the communities that lost relative power and status, colonial pluralism was dangerous and needed dismantling.

The main finding of this book is that the two-sidedness of colonial pluralism commonly sparked nationalist civil warfare over communal autonomy through multiple mechanisms. One way in which it did so was by motivating conflict. During and after the independence process, leaders of state communities sought to eliminate pluralist policies as part of the decolonization process, whereas members of non-state communities saw these efforts as an affront to their community and a return to communal subjugation. Instead of promoting compromise, this conflict strengthened the resolve of each side, with state communities seeing demands for pluralism as illegitimate and destructive and non-state communities declaring anti-pluralist reforms as proof that state communities sought to remove all their powers and forcibly assimilate or eliminate them.

A second way that colonial pluralism promoted nationalist civil war was by promoting nationalist frames, something that increased the tendency of people to perceive community and heightened concerns about communal power and self-rule. Colonial pluralism strengthened and politicized communal frames through a variety of policies. At the most basic, colonial censuses counted communities in ways that made them tangible, legible, and comparable. Other pluralist policies like indirect rule, communal legislative representation, and community-based military regiments nationalized communal frames by focusing attention on communal power and self-rule. Policies providing non-state communities with power and self-rule also created expectations for their continuation, and the combination of nationalist frames and expectations promoted strong opposition to reforms that reduced communal power and autonomy.

Finally, colonial pluralism provided communities with a variety of resources that could put nationalist grievances into action. Indirect rule endowed communities with their own political institutions, which are arguably the most important mobilizational resources for nationalist civil war. Communalized military recruitment, in turn, gave communities military training, weaponry, and leadership, all of which facilitated the organization of fighting forces. And communal legislative representation promoted communal associations and political parties that could mobilize support for the nationalist cause, whereas vernacular schools provided ready-made organizations and easy access to nationalist supporters.

While British colonial states were the main source of colonial pluralism, other actors also contributed to it. Several colonized communities that benefited from colonial pluralism supported the system and encouraged its maintenance and expansion. In addition, this book provides strong evidence that Protestant missionaries were often influential supporting actors in the colonial enterprise and bolstered British colonial pluralism in ways that increased the risk of nationalist civil war. By teaching in vernaculars, printing a variety of material in local languages, and striving to build religious communities, they helped create imagined national communities, something that is necessary for nationalist civil warfare. Missionaries also created powerful communal grievances through their effects on communal inequalities. Most notably, education was an important source of mobility in the British Empire, and Protestant missionaries provided some communities with much more of it than others. Missionaries also lobbied colonial administrations in favor of the communities with whom they worked, and many colonial officials believed Christians were more loyal than non-Christians and therefore hired Christians for sensitive colonial positions and reserved seats for them in the colonial legislature. Finally, missionaries contributed to nationalist civil warfare by provoking fear and resentment among communities resisting missionary influence. Many communities opposed missionaries because they sought to protect their religions and viewed those communities that converted as both degenerate and dangerous.

Colonial pluralism, however, did not always promote nationalist civil war, and this book offers evidence that these destructive effects depended greatly on the presence of large and long-standing precolonial states. Regions with high levels of precolonial statehood usually had a state community that strongly resisted colonial rule and several non-state communities that posed a much weaker anticolonial threat, and this situation created ideal conditions for divide-and-rule-style policies. To legitimize these policies, the British framed the measures as needed to protect small communities from the domination of powerful communities. Both state and non-state communities were therefore very concerned about pluralism but for very different reasons, with state communities seeking its elimination but non-state communities demanding its retention. Missionaries, in turn, reinforced this process. Because state communities mobilized greater opposition to missionary incursions, Protestant missionaries usually influenced non-state communities much more than state communities, thereby increasing nationalist conflict between state and non-state communities.

Precolonial statehood also promoted national chauvinism among state communities, which intensified conflict over colonial pluralism. Large and long-standing states commonly homogenized populations in ways making state communities demographically dominant, and numbers legitimized national chauvinism. At the same time, communities that controlled large and powerful precolonial states had myth-symbol complexes that focused on these states and depicted the state community as the natural community. Because colonialism recognized, accommodated, and empowered non-state communities, non-state communities were very sensitive to the national chauvinism of state communities and were able to mobilize resistance to it. And because of their national chauvinism, state communities were enraged by pluralist policies that empowered non-state communities, sought to eliminate colonial pluralism as a means of decolonization, and saw resistance to their nation-state-building efforts as illegitimate and a danger to the true nation.

In the absence of precolonial states, colonial pluralism had very different effects. Communal hierarchies were usually limited in places without precolonial states, and national chauvinism was weak or absent because all communities were small and lacked proud histories of statehood. At the same time, all communities posed similar anticolonial threats and were equally open to missionary influence. As a result, colonial officials employed pluralist policies more universally and less discriminatorily, and missionaries had similar effects on all communities. And when colonial pluralism was employed equitably in regions without national chauvinism, all communities had similar stakes in pluralism, no community was threatened by it, and pluralist policies continued after independence. Popular postcolonial pluralism, in turn, promoted more plurinational understandings of the nation and more inclusive politics, thereby reducing the risk of nationalist civil war.

While the impact of colonial pluralism depended on the presence of large and long-standing precolonial states, colonial pluralism also mediated the effects of historical statehood. This is because colonial pluralism affects the character, contours, and strength of national chauvinism, the sensitivity of communities to national chauvinism, and the mobilizational resources of non-state communities; and historical statehood is less likely to promote nationalist civil war in the absence of these conditions. This helps explain why nationalist civil war has been absent in northern Thailand, Cambodia, Botswana, Egypt, and Vietnam.

Through these findings, this book makes several important contributions to different literatures, including the literatures on ethnic civil warfare, pluralism, and colonial legacies. Considering the first, "ethnic civil war" is a broad term including different subtypes, and recent statistical analyses find that the two most common subtypes—nationalist and center-seeking ethnic civil wars—have different correlates, suggesting that they might have different causal dynamics (Cederman et al. 2009; Hunziker and Cederman 2017; Lange and Jeong 2024). Despite this finding, the literature continues to focus on ethnic civil warfare more broadly, and this book is one of the first to rigorously explore the causes of nationalist civil war.

Although focusing primarily on the former British Empire, the book provides a lens through which one can clearly see the causes of nationalist civil war and offers general insight that can be applied to a variety of cases. In contrast to past findings that political exclusion promotes ethnic civil war, this analysis finds that the most common core process leading to nationalist civil war is the loss of political and cultural autonomy to chauvinistic states. And because historical statehood strengthens national chauvinism, places with large and long-standing states have an elevated risk of nationalist civil war. Most communities, however, do not react to national chauvinism and lost autonomy with nationalist movements but, instead, accept them without a fight. I find that the aggressiveness and vindictiveness of national chauvinism, the strength of nationalist frames, expectations for communal autonomy, and the control of mobilizational resources are the main factors making communities very sensitive to the removal of their autonomy and empowering them to mobilize a nationalist movement in opposition. And because British colonial pluralism commonly provided these conditions, nationalist civil wars are very concentrated in the former British Empire.

Land-based empires that avoided European overseas colonialism highlight the broader applicability of this book's findings. Chapter 8 analyzes Thailand and Ethiopia and shows how historical statehood promoted national chauvinism in both cases during transitions from land-based empire to nation-state, with the threat of colonial conquest making the national chauvinism particularly aggressive. And although these cases had little or no history of colonial pluralism, they highlight how the presence of two or more state communities promoted reactions to national chauvinism in ways very similar to

British colonial pluralism. Most notably, a history of statehood created strong nationalist frames, made the national chauvinism of others more galling, and created expectations for communal power and self-rule, all of which sparked strong nationalist reactions.

The book also makes important contributions to past works on states and collective action. This literature focuses on social movements and notes that states shape their character and success by influencing the frames, mobilizational resources, motives, and openings of movement participants. While applying this general framework to nationalist civil war, the present analysis differs by considering the influence of historical states instead of contemporary ones. Taking a more historical institutionalist approach, I argue and offer evidence that precolonial and colonial states have lingering effects by promoting enduring structures and institutions and influencing frames and schema that people use to make sense of community and politics. Precolonial states shape communal demographies and are core elements of myth-symbol complexes that underpin ideas of nation, and both promote national chauvinism among state communities. Similarly, colonial pluralism had long-term effects on nationalist frames, grievances, and mobilizational resources.

In making these claims, *Legacies of British Rule* also enters a long-standing debate over how colonialism affects the prevalence of ethnic conflict but reorients it by focusing on how one form of colonialism—colonial pluralism— shapes one type of conflict—nationalist civil war. And whereas past analyses generally use the identity of the colonizer as a proxy for the form of rule, I focus on colonial pluralism, recognize diverse forms of rule within empires, and explore how a variety of pluralist policies affected the risk of nationalist civil war. The book therefore narrows previous claims that colonialism promotes violence by noting how certain types of colonialism promote a particular type of conflict and focusing on particular policies instead of the identity of the colonizer. The book also redirects past findings in another way: Previous works usually focus on colonialism as an omnipotent force determining long-term legacies, but this analysis shows that its influence depended on precolonial conditions. Finally, past works pay little attention to missionaries, but this book recognizes that missionaries were part of the colonial system and provides evidence that they influenced colonial legacies.

The book also contributes to the literature on pluralism. Although some scholars draw on social identity theory and claim that pluralism strengthens communal frames and grievances in ways that promote conflict, most analyses of nationalist conflict argue that pluralism weakens grievances by increasing political inclusiveness. This book provides evidence that both positions offer important insight. It finds that pluralism is commonly an important source of conflict, with some communities demanding it but others strongly opposing it, and the evidence from the previous chapters shows that this conflict commonly promotes nationalist civil war. At the same time, pluralism can limit nationalist violence by creating more inclusive nation-states to accommodate plurinational populations. The book provides strong evidence that conflict over pluralism is most common in places with historical states, whereas pluralism is most likely to promote inclusive politics in places with limited historical statehood.

Pluralism Elsewhere

While making these contributions, the book fails to resolve other issues. Most importantly, I focus on the former British Empire, and it is uncertain whether these findings hold for other empires or in non-imperial settings. Moreover, this work focuses on nationalist civil war and does not consider whether pluralism affects other types of conflict. In this final section, I briefly consider these issues and, in so doing, end the book by pointing to new areas of research.

PLURALISM IN NATION-STATES

Colonialism is unique from other social settings in a variety of ways, and it is uncertain whether pluralism has similar effects in noncolonial contexts. Most notably, colonialism commonly combines pluralism with divide and rule, and this mix has toxic effects on intercommunal relations. Yet colonialism amplifies certain elements that are also present in independent polities, so this book highlights processes that can also occur in noncolonial settings.

Pluralism recognizes all communities and protects smaller communities from larger and stronger ones, and its varying effects promote contrasting views: Members of smaller communities see pluralism as fair and protective, members of larger communities that oppose pluralism see it as discriminatory, and members of larger communities that accept pluralism see it as either a necessary evil or proof of their beneficence. In a colonial setting, foreign powers impose pluralism, and these policies often discriminate against larger communities. In this situation, members of larger communities almost always view colonial pluralism as discriminatory instead of helpful, necessary, or beneficent and seek to remove it as part of the decolonization process. Because the smaller communities see pluralism as just and protective, they mobilize to retain colonial pluralism, thereby promoting conflict.

In a noncolonial setting, dominant communities have greater control over pluralist policies. As a result, pluralism is rarely possible when large and powerful communities oppose it. And when powerful communities accept pluralism, they generally control its implementation and make sure that pluralism does not threaten their interests and, in fact, protects them. In Canada, for example, the state implemented multicultural policies in the face of Quebecois nationalism, Indigenous sovereignty movements, and immigration; but these pluralist reforms did not threaten the well-being of white Anglophone Canadians. As a result, smaller communities received accommodation, and most members of the dominant community felt safe and magnanimous.

At the same time, members of dominant communities might disagree with their leaders' decisions to implement pluralist policies that benefit smaller communities. Affirmative action provides one notable example of how members of communities whose interests conflict with pluralist policies can revolt against it. Nondominant communities can also oppose pluralism. In Quebec, for example, many oppose Canadian multiculturalism because they see it as downplaying the special place of the Quebecois in the Canadian nation-state, benefiting other communities at their expense, failing to protect the French language, and hiding a reality of Anglophone dominance.

Even in noncolonial settings, therefore, a fine line can exist between viewing pluralism as protective or discriminatory, and pluralism can be a source of nationalist conflict. That being said, pluralism seems much less likely to promote nationalist civil war in noncolonial settings because noncolonial states are unlikely to implement pluralist policies when powerful communities oppose them. Although smaller communities can mobilize to demand pluralism, movements for the creation of pluralist institutions are usually weaker than movements for the retention of pluralism given the impact of preexisting pluralist institutions on mobilizational resources, grievances, frames, and expectations. At the very least, this book shows that pluralism can promote nationalist violence and contestation when communities disagree strongly over it, a finding that can occur in colonial and noncolonial settings alike.

PLURALISM AND ETHNIC CIVIL WARFARE IN OTHER EMPIRES

Another unresolved issue is whether this book's findings help explain patterns of conflict in other overseas colonies. In this final section, I briefly analyze the French and Spanish Empires. Instead of focusing exclusively on nationalist civil war, I expand the scope to consider whether different types of colonialism promoted different types of conflict.

This book compares British and French colonialism and finds that British colonialism was usually much more pluralist than French colonialism. Another difference is that nationalist civil wars per former colony are nearly three times more prevalent in former British colonies. The case studies of Vietnam and Cambodia in chapter 7 offer evidence that a more limited use of pluralist policies contributed to the relative rarity of nationalist civil warfare in the French Empire. French rule of the Montagnards in Vietnam, however, was quite unique in that it institutionalized communal autonomy, and this helps explain the rise of a Montagnard nationalist movement.

A few other French colonies have also experienced nationalist strife. France's longest nationalist civil war occurred in Senegal, and—like the Montagnard nationalist movement and numerous nationalist civil wars in former British colonies—a form of colonialism that promoted regional autonomy and isolation contributed to this civil war: French colonialism in Senegal effectively isolated the Casamance region both politically and culturally, and a nationalist civil war began in the region in the early 1980s in reaction to forced integration into the postcolonial nation-state.

Casamance is only attached to the rest of Senegal through a thin strip of land, with Gambia separating most of the region from the rest of Senegal. At the same time, the region's population is distinct in terms of culture; unlike most Senegalese, relatively few Casamançais are Muslim or speak Wolof as their first language. Because the physical separation of Casamance created problems with communication and because the local social structure was poorly suited for the form of rule used in northern Senegal, the French ruled Casamance as a distinct region with its own administration from the late nineteenth century until 1939 (Dalberto 2020: 75; Trzciński 2005). Even after the region formally merged with the rest of Senegal, French administrators continually emphasized the distinctiveness of Casamance and supported regional autonomy whenever it helped them deal with anticolonialists (Dalberto 2020: 75).

Missionaries also emphasized the difference between the Casamançais and Senegalese. Given the region's predominantly non-Muslim population, missionaries in Senegal concentrated their efforts in Casamance, and many Casamançais—especially Diolla in Lower Casamance—converted. Missionary influence helped make Lower Casamance the most educated in all of Senegal. And because they saw the Casamançais as different and wanted to isolate them from Muslim influence, missionaries cultivated a distinct identity (Labrune-Badiane 2010).

Shortly after the merger of Lower Casamance with Senegal, Diallo educated elites formed the Mouvement des Forces Démocratiques de Casamance (MFDC) to demand the retention of regional autonomy within Senegal. Senegal's first president, Léopold Sédar Senghor, gained the support of the MFDC by backing their demands for regionalism; he was also a Christian from a "brother" community of the Diolla. Over time, however, he implemented assimilationist policies seeking to build a nation around the Wolof, who controlled relatively large and long-standing precolonial states and made up half the population. Although most were not from the region and were unacquainted with it, Wolof dominated the postcolonial administration of Casamance despite a large number of qualified Casamançais, thereby creating what many Casamançais saw as internal colonialism (Boone 2003: 94–96;

Englebert 2004: 28). After Diouf replaced Senghor as the president in 1981 and overtly supported Wolof national chauvinism, the MFDC—which had previously disbanded—reemerged and began a nationalist movement. Faced with state repression and open disdain and discrimination, the movement organized guerrilla units to begin the fight for secession.

This book's findings also offer important insight into the nationalist civil war in Cameroon. This region was first colonized by the Germans, but the French and British replaced them as colonial rulers after the First World War. The French took control of the vast majority of German Cameroon, and the British informally incorporated their much smaller territory into Nigeria and implemented pluralist policies similar to those in Nigeria. At independence, both French and British Cameroons were reunified, and the French region dominated politics due to its much greater size. Following a pattern present in several cases analyzed in this book, a history of pluralism and self-rule combined with subsequent discrimination and reductions in cultural and political autonomy to promote a nationalist civil war.

Syria has also experienced a nationalist civil war, and, like the Montagnards in Vietnam, French rule clearly employed pluralist policies to deal with anti-colonialism, with the architect of colonialism in the region openly declaring a policy of "divide and rule" when faced with open revolt (Khoury 2004: 172). The French referred to these policies as "*la politique des races*," which involved separating different colonized communities from one another and increasing competition between them (Smith 2023: 118). French colonialism in Syria was based on several divisive pluralist techniques that disadvantaged the demographically dominant Sunni community in favor of Alawi, Druze, Christian, and Kurdish communities, and these policies contributed to the Kurdish nationalist civil war (Bou-Nacklie 1993; Fildis 2011; Khoury 1987; White 2011). At the same time, the Syrian civil war between the state and various Sunni groups was over the control of the state, not secession, so it was a center-seeking civil war instead of a nationalist civil war. The main reason why this conflict was not a nationalist civil war is that the Sunni make up 80 percent of the Syria population, whereas the Alawi—who controlled the state until 2024—are a small minority. In this context, the Sunni saw the country as rightfully theirs, thereby promoting conflict over the control of the state instead of secession.

Like Syria, two other former French colonies also had unusually high levels of colonial pluralism: Morocco and Lebanon. Although Morocco has experienced a nationalist civil war, French colonial pluralism did not contribute to it: Western Sahara was colonized by the Spanish, and Morocco unilaterally took possession of it in 1975, which sparked a secessionist war supported by Algeria. While not involving colonial pluralism, this war follows the similar sequence of many former British colonies: Autonomy during the colonial period created sensitivity to forced incorporation and lost autonomy after independence.

In colonial Morocco, pluralism focused on recognizing, accommodating, and empowering Berber, or Amazigh, communities (Bidwell 1973: 48–56; Burke 1973). Since independence, Amazigh have not mobilized a nationalist civil war. One important reason for this is that French pluralism maintained the Moroccan sultan as the formal leader of the entire protectorate. And although French administrators made all important political decisions, the sultan remained the symbol of the government, and Amazigh had pledged allegiance to him for centuries before French rule (Ben Kaddour 1973; Bidwell 1973: 65–67; Brown 1973: 205). Of equal importance, the sultan was the supreme religious leader of all Muslims in Morocco prior to French rule, and the French allowed the sultan to retain his religious authority. Nearly all Amazigh, in turn, are Muslim and continued to view the sultan as their religious leader. Finally, Amazigh autonomy had precolonial origins and was dependent on the sultan's authority, so Amazigh were the sultan's strongest supporters at independence and helped defeat modernizing opponents who sought to dismantle the monarchy (Ben Kaddour 1973; Coram 1973). In recognition of this support, the sultan—renamed king after independence—continued to recognize and empower Amazigh communities. Thus, even with colonial pluralism, the colonial state created centripetal forces that kept non-state communities part of the greater Moroccan nation, and the retention of pluralist policies that recognized and accommodated Amazigh communities maintained these centripetal pressures (Aslan 2015).

In colonial Lebanon, the French also implemented pluralist policies that recognized, accommodated, and empowered the colony's main religious communities. Instead of nationalist civil wars over communal self-rule, however, the country has suffered two center-seeking civil wars whereby different communities fought to increase their control of the state. While seemingly opposed to this book's findings, the case is similar to Morocco in that French colonialism promoted centripetal forces. Most notably, French colonialism in Lebanon did not promote indirect rule whereby communities controlled their own polities. Instead, the French institutionalized a centralized consociational state in which each community was guaranteed some political power within a centralized state (Cobban 1986; El-Solh 2004: 4; Longrigg 1958; White 2011: 52–53). French consociationalism favored Christians, Shia and Sunni viewed this as unfair, and both communities mobilized to increase their control of the postcolonial state, thereby promoting center-seeking conflicts (Cobban 1986).

This example shows that—even in a place with a history of colonial pluralism—French rule promoted centripetal forces pushing communities to focus on controlling the postcolonial state instead of communal self-rule. Instead of colonial pluralism, however, the dominant colonial model of the French Empire was more Republican and provided communities with very little recognition, accommodation, power, and resources. Because the state

TABLE 9.1. Nationalist and Center-Seeking Civil Wars per Country by Colonizer

Colonizer	Nationalist Civil Wars per Colony	Center-Seeking Civil Wars per Colony	Ethnic Civil Wars per Colony
British	0.97	0.28	1.25
French	0.38	0.63	1.01
Other	0.32	0.35	0.67

was the main source of political resources, the most logical means to increase communal power was to expand communal control of the state, not secession. Instead of nationalist civil war, French colonialism therefore appears to have increased the risk of center-seeking ethnic civil wars.

Table 9.1 presents the average number of nationalist and center-seeking ethnic civil wars per country by colonizer, and the composition of ethnic civil wars varies greatly. British cases of ethnic civil war are overwhelmingly nationalist civil wars, whereas French cases are mostly center-seeking civil wars. The table also combines nationalist and center-seeking civil wars and shows that former British colonies have experienced 25 percent more ethnic civil wars per country than the French and twice the number of conflicts of all other overseas empires.

In the former French Empire, center-seeking ethnic civil wars are most common in places with limited precolonial statehood. Most of these conflicts occurred in sub-Saharan Africa, including wars in Cameroon, Central African Republic, Chad, the Republic of Congo, Cote d'Ivoire, Niger, and Togo. In these cases, weak Republican states, limited national chauvinism, and high levels of communal diversity combined to limit centrifugal forces while focusing intercommunal conflict on the control of the state. In places with historical statehood, however, French colonialism deterred center-seeking ethnic civil wars. This is because state communities were large enough to dominate postcolonial states, and non-state communities were too weak to take over the state. Syria is an exception in this regard, as discriminatory colonial pluralism strengthened non-state communities enough to control the state.

Center-seeking civil wars are much rarer in British Africa: Only Nigeria, Sudan, and Uganda experienced center-seeking civil wars involving indigenous communities fighting over the control of the state.[1] Of these three, Nigeria and Sudan had large and long-standing precolonial states, and both countries also

1. South Africa and Zimbabwe also experienced center-seeking civil wars, but these were unique in that they pitted Africans against white settlers over the control of the postcolonial state.

experienced nationalist civil wars. In fact, both types of ethnic civil war were related in these cases and pitted state and non-state communities against one another, with the goals of the anti-state forces changing over time.[2] In contrast with former French colonies, center-seeking civil wars are therefore relatively rare in former British colonies with limited state history. As described in previous chapters, the British employed colonial pluralism more universally in this social context, and more multicultural understandings of the postcolonial nation-state promoted more inclusive states. In addition to deterring nationalist civil war, a comparison with former French colonies suggests that the combination of colonial pluralism and limited historical statehood also reduced the risk of center-seeking civil war.

This discussion suggests that pluralist and Republican colonial states promoted different types of ethnic civil warfare in different social environments. Whereas pluralist colonial states affect frames, motivation, and mobilizational resources in ways that channel conflict toward nationalist civil warfare in places with historical states, more centralized colonial states pay less attention to communal diversity and direct conflict toward the control of the state in places with limited historical statehood. In this way, British pluralism created centrifugal forces that pushed conflict toward secession and self-rule, and relatively centralized French rule promoted more centripetal forces that pushed conflict toward taking over the state. And because historical statehood affects both types of ethnic civil war differently, ethnic civil wars in the former British Empire are concentrated in places with large precolonial states whereas ethnic civil war in the former French Empire is concentrated in places with more limited historical statehood (Lange and Jeong 2024).

In addition to the British and French Empires, table 9.1 presents the prevalence of ethnic civil warfare in other European overseas empires and shows that former colonies from other empires had relatively low levels of both nationalist and center-seeking ethnic civil war. A closer look at these cases shows that Spanish colonies drive this pattern: Between 1946 and 2020, only Guatemala, Mexico, and Nicaragua experienced center-seeking ethnic civil wars over greater control of the state, and Philippines is the only former Spanish colony to experience a nationalist civil war.[3] On a per-country basis, this represents 0.06 nationalist civil wars per former Spanish colony, well below the

2. The Nigerian center-seeking civil war of 1966 involved northerners removing southerners from power, and this war sparked the Igbo nationalist civil war. In Sudan, southern nationalists joined forces with other communities to try to take over the state to implement pluralist reforms after their first attempts to secede from Sudan failed.

3. In chapters 2 and 3, I categorize the colonizer based on the last foreign colonial power that controlled the country for at least ten consecutive years. Based on this definition, Philippines is a former American colony—not a former Spanish colony. One can therefore argue that former Spanish colonies have not experienced a single nationalist civil war.

British average of 0.97. Even though former British colonies have experienced relatively few center-seeking ethnic civil wars, the per-country rate of this type of ethnic civil war is considerably lower among former Spanish colonies: There were 0.18 center-seeking ethnic civil wars per Spanish colony versus 0.28 per British colony. The relative rarity of both types of conflict is quite surprising, as Latin America has many characteristics that are strongly related to ethnic civil war (Cleary 2000; Ross 2010; vom Hau 2023).

One factor that limited ethnic civil warfare in former Spanish colonies is the time of independence. As Wimmer (2013) finds, ethnic civil wars are concentrated during and shortly after the independence process, and nearly all former Spanish colonies gained their independence in the early or late nineteenth century. The timing of independence is also important in another way: Nationalism and the nation-state model were both new and far from hegemonic when most Spanish colonies gained independence. While not necessarily limiting the national chauvinism of Spanish settlers, this political context likely weakened the nationalist reactions of non-Europeans to settler national chauvinism.

As described in chapter 2, Spanish colonialism was nonpluralist, and the form of colonialism is a second factor affecting postcolonial civil warfare in the former Spanish Empire. With few exceptions, the Spanish created mixed colonies with European settlers and Indigenous peoples; several also had large populations of African slaves and their descendants. Given the large numbers of European settlers in nearly all colonies (the Philippines and Equatorial Guinea being exceptions), Spanish colonialism was similar to British settler and forced settlement colonialism in that white settlers controlled all institutions, European culture dominated, and there was little effort to recognize, accommodate, and empower non-European communities. Paralleling the British settler and forced settlement colonies, the Spanish Empire shows that the limited cultural and political autonomy of non-Europeans severely impeded their abilities to mobilize nationalist movements despite great inequalities and hardships (Lange 2017).

Latin America is different from British settler and forced settlement colonies, however, in that postcolonial governments eventually recognized the non-European population as integral parts of the nation through *mestizaje* ideologies declaring the nation racially mixed. While hiding racial inequalities instead of addressing them, *mestizaje*—in combination with nonpluralist colonialism—helped limit centripetal forces promoting nationalist civil warfare by recognizing communities in ways that did not provide cultural or political autonomy, blurred systematic communal comparisons, and simply bound communities to institutions and cultural systems that the white population dominated. In this situation, there was a long-term trend in which Indigenous peoples became mestizos and mestizos became white, and the focus was therefore on assimilation instead of communal difference (Wimmer 2002). As a result, nationalist civil war was rarely a viable option. Instead of channeling conflict toward center-seeking civil war, the state and other social institutions marginalized and controlled non-Europeans to such an extent that they were too weak to fight the state for greater power, thereby making center-seeking ethnic civil warfare very rare in the former Spanish Empire as well.

An important part of the process limiting Indigenous identification and the politicization of Indigenous communities during most of the twentieth century was the form of state corporatism common throughout much of Latin America (Yashar 1998: 33). States recognized peasants and only offered most Indigenous peoples access to the state as peasants, and this minimized the mobilization of Indigenous communities and organized politics along class lines. As these institutions weakened with liberal reforms beginning in the 1980s, however, identification and organization along communal lines increased (Yashar 1998).

Although of more minor importance, missionaries also contributed to the relative rarity of nationalist and center-seeking ethnic civil wars in the former Spanish Empire. Catholic missionaries were present at the beginning of Spanish colonial rule in the Americas, but the first Protestant mission in Latin America was founded, on average, 350 years after the first Catholic mission. Unlike Protestant missionaries, Catholic missionaries did not employ vernaculars, provided much less education, and did not organize non-European communities. Even more, the institutional setting of mixed settler colonies greatly influenced missionary relations with non-European communities. Similar to the British settler and forced settlement colonies, governments and settlers exerted great influence over missionaries and attempted to incorporate non-European peoples into settler society in a subordinate position. While the influence of settlers suggests that the denomination of the missionaries was not important, Trejo (2009) analyzes Indigenous movements in Mexico and finds that—whereas the history of Catholic missionaries deterred such movements—the arrival of Protestant missions in the 1970s was an enormous boon to Indigenous movements. Similar to the Karens in Myanmar and elsewhere, they strengthened Indigenous identities and helped organize Indigenous peoples. Of greatest importance, however, their popularity pushed Catholics to copy their more pluralist techniques.

Despite having only 1 nationalist civil war and 3 center-seeking ethnic civil wars, former Spanish colonies have experienced 18 non-ethnic civil wars since 1946 (Lange 2024). Of these, 14 involved leftist anti-state actors—including Marxists, Leninists, Maoists, and Trotskyites—fighting in pursuit of class-based revolution (Lange 2024). Whereas former Spanish colonies have experienced 0.83 class-based civil wars per country since 1946, the corresponding figures are only 0.33 and 0.17 for former British and French colonies, respectively (Lange 2024). In this way, ethnic civil war is very rare in the former Spanish Empire, but class-based civil war is relatively common.

Although the early timing of Spanish decolonization makes it more diffi-cult to link these postcolonial patterns to colonialism, the history of civil war in the former Spanish Empire suggests that settler colonial states channeled conflict along class lines instead of communal divisions. Spanish settler colo-nialism institutionalized highly unequal societies, with landed, mercantile, and religious elites controlling land, resources, workers, and souls (Assadourian 1992; Bonner 1977; Lockhart 1969; Ramirez 1986). At the same time, this form of colonialism did not recognize, accommodate, or empower communities. In this situation, the main cleavage was class, not community, and conflict focused on economic and social reforms to uplift disadvantaged classes at the expense of the elites. Class-based civil wars in the former Spanish Empire, in turn, are most highly concentrated in the places in which the colonial elites were the strongest and remained strong after independence. Mahoney (2010), for example, notes that Argentina, Chile, Costa Rica, Paraguay, and Uruguay did not have powerful landed and mercantile classes during the colonial period and experienced broad liberal reforms that weakened colonial elites, and these five countries experienced only two class-based civil wars, or 0.4 per country. In contrast, the Spanish colonies in Latin America that either had the strongest elite classes or did not experience major liberal reforms weakening these elites fought 12 class-based civil wars, or 1.1 per country.

A comparison of the British, French, and Spanish Empires therefore high-lights three ideal types of colonial state, each concentrated imperfectly in a dif-ferent empire. Whereas British colonial pluralism increased the risk of nation-alist civil war, more Republican French rule promoted communal conflict over the control of the postcolonial state, and Spanish rule was settler-based and contributed to civil wars organized primarily along class lines. Although showing that the dominant dynamics of the British Empire cannot be trans-ferred to other major overseas empires, the comparison provides evidence that historical states shape long-term patterns of civil warfare in other former empires as well, with different types of colonial states increasing the risk of different types of conflict. Yet these findings are more impressionistic than conclusive given the cursory analyses of the French and Spanish Empires. The book's findings on British colonialism are on much more solid ground, however, and provide strong evidence that British pluralism interacted with precolonial statehood to shape postcolonial patterns of nationalist civil warfare in influential and enduring ways.

BIBLIOGRAPHY

Abbay, Alemseged. 1998. *Identity Jilted or Re-Imagining Identity? The Divergent Paths of the Eritrean and Tigrayan Nationalist Struggles.* Lawrenceville, NJ: Red Sea Press.

'Abd Al-Rahim, Muddathir. 1969. *Imperialism and Nationalism in the Sudan: A Study in Constitutional and Political Developments, 1899–1956.* Oxford: Clarendon Press.

Abernethy, David. 1969. *The Political Dilemma of Popular Education: An African Case.* Stanford, CA: Stanford University Press.

Abernethy, David. 2000. *The Dynamics of Global Dominance: European Overseas Empires 1415–1980.* New Haven, CT: Yale University Press.

Abraham, Arthur. 1978. *Mende Politics and Government under Colonial Rule.* New York: Oxford University Press.

Adnan, Shepan. 2004. *Migration, Land Alienation and Ethnic Conflict: Causes of Poverty in the Chittagong Hill Tracts of Bangladesh.* Dhaka: Research and Advisory Services.

Afrobarometer. 2015. "Afrobarometer Round 5." Retrieved August 4, 2015. http://www.afrobarometer.org/.

Albaugh, Ericka. 2014. *State-Building and Multilingual Education in Africa.* New York: Cambridge University Press.

Aldrich, Robert. 1996. *Greater France: A History of French Overseas Expansion.* New York: St. Martin's Press.

Aldrich, Robert. 2021. "Kingdoms, Empires and the French Republic: Colonisers and Indigenous Monarchs in the Asia-Pacific." *History Australia* 18 (2): 370–89.

Alesina, Alberto, Arnaud Devleeschauwer, William Easterly, Sergio Kurlat, and Romain Wacziarg. 2003. "Fractionalization." *Journal of Economic Growth* 8 (2): 155–94.

Allman, Jean Marie. 1993. *The Quills of the Porcupine: Asante Nationalism in an Emergent Ghana.* Madison: University of Wisconsin Press.

Amasyali, Emre. 2016. "Boundaries of Intrusion: A Mixed Methods Analysis of Colonialism and State Building." Civil War Seminar, McGill University, Montreal, Canada.

Amasyali, Emre. 2017. "Securing the Nation: Patterns of Crisis and Reform from Empire to Nation-State." Social Science History Association Annual Conference, Toronto, Canada.

Amenta, Edwin, and Michael Young. 1999. "Democratic States and Social Movements: Theoretical Arguments and Hypotheses." *Social Problems* 46 (2): 153–68.

American Baptist Foreign Mission Society. 1931. "The Karen Mission in Burma." Collection 4424, Folder 701-2-7. Division of Rare and Manuscript Collections, Cornell University Library.

American Baptist Historical Society. 2015. "Karen Language and Loyalty." Accessed September 15, 2015. http://judson200.org/index.php/burma-language-exhibit/57-morning-star-articles/195-karen-language-and-loyalty.

Aminzade, Ronald. 2013. *Race, Nation, and Citizenship in Post-Colonial Africa: The Case of Tanzania.* New York: Cambridge University Press.

Anderson, Benedict. 1983. *Imagined Communities: Reflections on the Origin and Spread of Nationalism.* London: Verso.

Anderson, Perry. 2013. *The Indian Ideology*. New York: Verso.

Ang, Ien, and Jon Stratton. 2018. "The Singapore Way of Multiculturalism: Western Concepts/ Asian Cultures." *Sojourn: Journal of Social Issues in Southeast Asia* 33 (S): 61–86.

Apter, Andrew. 2008. *The Pan-African Nation: Oil and the Spectacle of Culture in Nigeria*. Chicago: University of Chicago Press.

Aslan, Senem. 2015. *Nation-Building in Turkey and Morocco: Governing Kurdish and Berber Dissent*. New York: Cambridge University Press.

Assadourian, Carlos Sempat. 1992. "The Colonial Economy: The Transfer of the European System of Production to New Spain and Peru." *Journal of Latin American Studies* 24: 55–68.

Atarodi, Habibollah. 2003. *Great Powers, Oil and the Kurds in Mosul (Southern Kurdistan/Northern Iraq), 1910–1925*. Toronto: University Press of America.

Axmann, Martin. 2009. *Back to the Future: The Khanate of Kalat and the Genesis of Baloch Nationalism 1915–1955*. New York: Oxford University Press.

Bala, Sajib. 2022. *Politics of Peace Agreement Implementation: A Case Study of the Chittagong Hills Tracts (CHT) in Bangladesh*. Singapore: Palgrave Macmillan.

Ballhatchet, Kenneth. 1980. *Race, Sex, and Class under the Raj: Imperial Attitudes and Policies and their Critics, 1793–1905*. London: Weidenfeld & Nicolson.

Bangash, Yaqoob Khan. 2015. *A Princely Affair: The Accession and Integration of the Princely States of Pakistan, 1947–1955*. Karachi: Oxford University Press.

Barter, Shane J. 2014. *Civilian Strategy in Civil War: Insights from Indonesia, Thailand, and the Philippines*. New York: Palgrave Macmillan.

Baruah, Sanjib. 2005. *Durable Disorder: Understanding the Politics of Northeast India*. New Delhi: Oxford University Press.

Baruah, Sanjib. 2020. *In the Name of the Nation: India and Its Northeast*. Stanford, CA: Stanford University Press.

Bayly, Christopher A. 1985. "The Pre-History of 'Communalism'? Religious Conflict in India, 1700–1860." *Modern Asian Studies* 19 (2): 177–203.

Belmekki, Belkacem. 2008. "A Wind of Change: The New British Colonial Policy in Post-Revolt India." *Atlantis* 30 (2): 111–24.

Bendford, Robert D., and David A Snow. 2000. "Framing Processes and Social Movements: An Overview and Assessment." *Annual Review of Sociology* 26: 611–39.

Ben Kaddour, Abdaslam. 1973. "The Neo-Makhzan and the Berbers." In *Arabs and Berbers: From Tribe to Nation in North Africa*, edited by Ernest Gellner and Charles Micaud, 259–67. London: Duckworth.

Bennett, Bruce S. 2002. "Some Historical Background on Minorities in Botswana." In *Minorities in the Millennium: Perspectives from Botswana*, edited by Isaac N. Mazonde, 5–15. Gaborone: Lightbooks.

Bertz, Ned. 2007. "Educating the Nation: Race and Nationalism in Tanzanian Schools." In *Making Nations, Creating Strangers: States and Citizenship in Africa*, edited by Sara Dorman, Daniel Hammett, and Paul Nugent, 181–94. Boston: Brill.

Bettini, Francesco. 1788. "Superbe Jardin Anglais." Accessed May 1, 2023. https://gallica.bnf.fr /ark:/12148/btv1b10024391z#

Betts, Raymond. 1961. *Assimilation and Association in French Colonial Theory, 1890–1914*. New York: Columbia University Press.

Bhattacharjee, J. B. 1973. "Pattern of British Administration in Garoland." *Journal of Indian History* 153: 509–20.

Bidwell, Robin. 1973. *Morocco under Colonial Rule: French Administration of Tribal Areas 1912–1956*. London: Frank Cass.

Bjerk, Paul. 2015. *Building a Peaceful Nation: Julius Nyerere and the Establishment of Sovereignty in Tanzania, 1960–1964*. Rochester, NY: University of Rochester Press.

Blanton, Robert, David Mason, and Brian Athow. 2001. "Colonial Style and Post-Colonial Ethnic Conflict in Africa." *Journal of Peace Research* 38: 473–91.

Boittin, Jennifer, Christina Firpo, and Emily Musil Church. 2011. "Hierarchies of Race and Gender in the French Colonial Empire, 1914–1946." *Historical Reflections* 37 (1): 60–90.

Bonacich, Edna. 1973. "A Theory of Middleman Minorities." *American Sociological Review* 38 (5): 583–94.

Bonner, Fred. 1977. "Peruvian Encomendoros in 1630: Elite Circulation and Consolidation." *Hispanic American Historical Review* 57 (3): 633–59.

Boone, Catherine. 2003. *Political Topographies of the African State: Territorial Authority and Institutional Choice*. Cambridge: Cambridge University Press.

Borcan, Oana, Olsson, Ola, and Louis Putterman. 2018. "State History and Economic Development: Evidence from Six Millennia." *Journal of Economic Growth* 23: 1–40.

Bose, Sumantra. 2003. *Kashmir: Roots of Conflict, Paths to Peace*. Cambridge, MA: Harvard University Press.

Bou-Nacklie, N. E. 1993. "Les Troupes Spéciales: Religious and Ethnic Recruitment, 1916–46." *International Journal of Middle East Studies* 25 (4): 645–60.

Bowerman, J. F. 1946. "The Frontier Areas of Burma." *Journal of the Royal Society of Arts* 95 (4732): 44–55.

Bowser, Matthew J. 2021. "Partners in Empire? Co-Colonialism and the Rise of Anti-Indian Nationalism in Burma, 1930–1938." *The Journal of Imperial and Commonwealth History* 49 (1): 118–47.

Brara, Vijaylakshmi. 2022. "Manipur: The Sociocultural Continuum." In *Northeast India Through the Ages: A Transdisciplinary Perspective on Prehistory, History, and Oral History*, edited by Rituparna Bhattacharyya, 281–305. London: Routledge India.

Brass, Paul R. 1997. *Theft of an Idol: Text and Context in the Representation of Collective Violence*. Princeton, NJ: Princeton University Press.

Breuilly, John. 1994. *Nationalism and the State*. Chicago: University of Chicago Press.

Brines, Russell. 1968. *The Indo-Pakistani Conflict*. New York: Pall Mall Press.

Brown, David. 1988. "From Peripheral Communities to Ethnic Nations: Separatism in Southeast Asia." *Pacific Affairs* 61 (1): 51–77.

Brown, Kenneth. 1973. "The Impact of the Dahir Berbere in Sale." In *Arabs and Berbers: From Tribe to nation in North Africa*, edited by Ernest Gellner and Charles Micaud, 201–15. London: Duckworth.

Brubaker, Rogers. 2004. *Ethnicity Without Groups*. Cambridge, MA: Harvard University Press.

Brunnschweiler, Christa, and Erwin Bulte. 2009. "Natural Resources and Violent Conflict: Resource Abundance, Dependence, and the Onset of Civil Wars." *Oxford Economic Papers* 61 (4): 651–74.

Buadaeng, Kwanchewan. 2007. "Ethnic Identities of the Karen Peoples in Burma and Thailand." In *Identity Matters: Ethnic and Sectarian Conflict*, edited by James Peacock, Patricia Thorton, and Patrick Inman, 73–97. New York: Berghahn Books.

Buadaeng, Kwachewan, and Prasit Leepreecha. 2018. "Modern Education Systems and Impact on Ethnic Minorities." In *Education, Economy, and Identity: Ten Years of Educational Reform in Thailand*, edited by Supat Chupradit and Audrey Baron-Gutty, 37–55. Bangkok: Institut de Rescherche sur l'Asie du Sud-Est Contemporaine.

Bunce, Valerie. 1999. "Peaceful Versus Violent State Dismemberment: A Comparison of the Soviet Union, Yugoslavia, and Czechoslovakia." *Politics and Society* 27 (2): 217–37.

Bunker, Alonzo. 1902. *Soo Thah: A Tale of the Making of the Karen Nation*. London: Oliphant, Anderson, & Ferrier.

Burke, Edmund III. 1973. "The Image of the Moroccan State in French Ethnological Literature: A New Look at the Origin of Lyautey's Berber Policy." In *Arabs and Berbers: From Tribe to nation in North Africa*, edited by Ernest Gellner and Charles Micaud, 175–99. London: Duckworth.

Burke, R. M. 1974. *Mainsprings of Indian and Pakistani Foreign Policies*. Minneapolis: University of Minnesota Press.

Burma Legislative Council. 1928. "Proceedings of the Burma Legislative Council, Volumes 12 and 13." British Library, IOR/V/9/4065.

Burma Legislative Council. 1929. "Proceedings of the Burma Legislative Council, Volume 14." British Library, IOR/V/9/4066.

Burma Legislative Council. 1930. "Proceedings of the Burma Legislative Council, Volume 17." British Library, IOR/V/9/4069.

Burma Legislative Council. 1932. "Proceedings of the Burma Legislative Council, Volume 21." British Library, IOR/V/9/4073.

Burma Legislative Council. 1933a. "Proceedings of the Burma Legislative Council, Volume 24." British Library, IOR/V/9/4076.

Burma Legislative Council. 1933b. "Proceedings on Motions Concerning Separation Issue; Conclusions of Government of Burma." British Library, IOR/M/1/46.

Burma Legislative Council. 1935. "Proceedings of the Burma Legislative Council, Volume 30." British Library, IOR/V/9/4082.

Burma Legislative Council. 1936. "Proceedings of the Burma Legislative Council, Volume 32." British Library, IOR/V/9/4084.

Burma Legislative Council. 1938. "Proceedings of the First Senate, Volume IV." British Library, IOR/V/9/4104.

Burma Legislative Council. 1946. "Proceedings of the Burma Legislative Council, Volume 1, Number 8." British Library, IOR/V/9/4127.

Burma Reforms Committee, 1921. "Proceedings of the Burma Reforms Committee. Record of Evidence, Volume I." British Library, IOR/L/PARL/2/391.

Bush, Kenneth D., and Diana Saltarelli. 2000. *The Two Faces of Education in Ethnic Conflict*. Florence: UNICEF Innocenti Research Centre.

Cady, John F. 1958. *A History of Modern Burma*. Ithaca, NY: Cornell University Press.

Callahan, Mary P. 2003. *Making Enemies: War and State Building in Burma*. Ithaca, NY: Cornell University Press.

Callaway, Archibald. 1963. "Unemployment among African School Leavers." *Journal of Modern African Studies* 1 (3): 351–71.

Carter, David, and Curtis Signorino. 2010. "Back to the Future: Modeling Time Dependence in Binary Data." *Political Analysis* 18: 271–92.

Cederman, Lars-Erik, Halvard Buhaug, and Jan Ketil Rød. 2009. "Ethno-Nationalist Dyads and Civil War: A GIS-Based Analysis." *Journal of Conflict Resolution* 53: 496–525.

Cederman, Lars-Erik, Kristian Skrede Gleditsch, and Halvard Buhaug. 2013. *Inequality, Grievances, and Civil War*. New York: Cambridge University Press.

Cederman, Lars-Erik, Kristian Skrede Gleditsch, and Julian Wucherpfennig. 2017. "Predicting the Decline of Ethnic Civil War: Was Gurr Right and for the Right Reasons?" *Journal of Peace Research* 54 (2): 262–74.

Cederman, Lars-Erik, Simon Hug, Andreas Schädel, and Julian Wucherpfennig. 2015. "Territorial Autonomy in the Shadow of Conflict: Too Little, Too Late?" *American Political Science Review* 109 (2): 354–70.

Cederman, Lars-Erik, Andreas Wimmer, and Brian Min. 2010. "Why do Ethnic Groups Rebel? New Data and Analyis." *World Politics* 62 (1): 87–119.

Chadha, Vivek. 2005. *Low Intensity Conflicts in India: An Analysis*. New Delhi: Sage Publications.

Chakraborty, Papri. 2014. "Ethnic Conflict in the Chittagong Hill Tracts (CHT) of Bangladesh: Politics of Homogenization." *Indian Journal of Political Science* 75 (2): 297–304.

Chalermsripinyorat, Rugnrawee. 2021. "Islam and the BRN's Armed Separatist Movement in Southern Thailand." *Small Wars and Insurgencies* 32 (6): 945–76.

Chatterjee, Suhas. 1994. *Making of Mizoram*. New Delhi: MD Publications.

Chee, Chan Heng, Sharon Siddique, Irna Nurlina Masron, and Dominic Cooray. 2019. *Singapore's Multiculturalism: Evolving Diversity*. London: Routledge.

Chimee, Ihediwa Nkemjika. 2013. "The Nigerian-Biafran War, Armed Conflicts and the Rules of Engagement." In *Warfare, Ethnicity and National Identity in Nigeria*, edited by Toyin Falola, Roy Doron, and Okpeh O. Okpeh, 111–37. Trenton, NJ: Africa World Press.

Chong, Terence. 2020. "Introduction." In *Navigating Differences: Integration in Singapore*, edited by Terence Chong, 1–16. ISEAS: Singapore.

Christie, Clive J. 1996. *A Modern History of Southeast Asia: Decolonization, Nationalism, and Separatism*. New York: Tauris Academic Studies.

Clapham, Christopher. 1991. "The Structure of Regional Conflict in northern Ethiopia." *Disasters* 15 (3): 244–53.

Cleary, Matthew. 2000. "Democracy and Indigenous Rebellion in Latin America." *Comparative Political Studies* 33: 1123–53.

Clemens, Elizabeth S., and James M. Cook. 1999. "Politics and Institutionalism: Explaining Durability and Change." *Annual Review of Sociology* 25: 441–66.

Cobban, Helena. 1986. *The Making of Modern Lebanon*. New York: Routledge.

Cogneau, Denis, and Alexander Moradi. 2014. "Borders that Divide: Education and Religion in Ghana and Togo since Colonial Times." *Journal of Economic History* 74 (3): 694–729.

Cohn, Bernard. 1983. "Representing Authority in Victorian India." In *The Invention of Tradition*, edited by Eric Hobsbawm and Terrance Ranger, 165–209. New York: Cambridge University Press.

Cohn, Bernard. 1987. *An Anthropologist Among the Historians*. Delhi: Oxford University Press.

Coleman, James. 1958. *Nigeria: Background to Nationalism*. Berkeley: University of California Press.

Collier, David. 2011. "Understanding Process Tracing." *PS: Political Science and Politics* 4: 823–30.

Collier, Paul, and Anke Hoeffler. 2002. "On the Incidence of Civil War in Africa." *Journal of Conflict Resolution* 46 (1): 13–28.

Collier, Paul, Anke Hoeffler, and Dominic Rohner. 2009. "Beyond Greed and Grievance: Feasibility and Civil War." *Oxford Economic Papers* 61 (1): 1–27.

Collier, Ruth Berins. 1982. *Regimes in Tropical Africa: Changing Forms of Supremacy, 1945–1975*. Los Angeles: University of California Press.

Colony of Sudan. 1956. *Report of the Commission of Inquiry into the Disturbances in the Southern Sudan During August, 1955*. Sudan: McCorquedale & Co.

Comber, Leon. 1983. *13 May 1969: A Historical Survey of Sino-Malay Relations*. Singapore: Graham Brash.

Conklin, Alice L. 1997. *A Mission to Civilize: The Republican Idea of Empire in France and West Africa, 1895–1930*. Stanford, CA: Stanford University Press.

Cooper, Frederick. 2014. *Citizenship Between Empire and Nation*. Princeton, NJ: Princeton University Press.

Cooray, L.J.M. 1974. "The Reception of Roman-Dutch Law in Sri Lanka. *Comparative and International Law Journal of Southern Africa* 7 (3): 295–320.

Coram, Andre. 1973. "Note on the Role of the Berbers in the Early Days of Moroccan Independence." In *Arabs and Berbers: From Tribe to Nation in North Africa*, edited by Ernest Gellner and Charles Micaud, 269–76. London: Duckworth.

Crowder, Michael. 1964. "Indirect Rule: French and British Style." *Africa* 34 (3): 197–205.

Crowder, Michael. 1968. *West Africa Under Colonial Rule*. Evanston: Northwestern University Press.

Curle, Adam. 1973. *Educational Problems of Developing Societies: With Case Studies of Ghana, Pakistan, and Nigeria*. New York: Praeger Publishers.

Dalberto, Séverine Awenengo. 2020. "Hidden Debates over the Status of the Casamance during the Decolonizerion Process in Senegal: Regionalism, Territorialism, and Federalism at the Crossroads, 1946–62." *Journal of African History* 61 (1): 67–88.

Dalrymple, William. 2002. *White Mughals: Love and Betrayal in Eighteenth-Century India*. London: HarperCollins.

Daly, M. W. 1986. *Empire on the Nile: The Anglo-Egyptian Sudan, 1898–1934*. New York: Cambridge University Press.

Daly, M. W. 1991. *Imperial Sudan: The Anglo-Egyptian Condominium, 1934–1956*. New York: Cambridge University Press.

Daly, M. W. 1993. "Broken Bridge and Empty Basket: The Political and Economic Background of the Sudanese Civil War." In *Civil War in the Sudan*, edited by M.W. Daly and Ahmad Alawad Sikainga, 1–26. New York: St. Martin's Press.

Das, Bitasta. 2014. "The Bodo Movement and Situating Identity Assertions in Assam." *Pragmata: Journal of Human Sciences* 2 (2): 173–84.

Das, Debojyoti. 2022. "Colonial and Post-Colonial Anthropology among the Nagas." In *The Cultural Heritage of Nagaland*, edited by G. Kanato Chophy and Sarit K. Chaudhuri, 67–90. London: Routledge.

Davies, Lynn. 2004. *Education and Conflict: Complexity and Chaos*. New York: Routledge Falmer.

De, Ranjit Kumar. 1998. *Socio-Political Movements in India: A Historical Study of Tripura*. New Delhi: Mittal Publications.

Debbarma, Mohan. 2015. "Identity, Conflict and Development: A Study of the Borok Community in Tripura." In *Identity, Contestation and Development in Northeast India*, edited by Komol Singha and M. Amarjeet Singh, 151–72. London: Taylor and Francis.

de Maaker, Erik. 2022. "Rethinking Ethnographies on Garo Hills." In *Routledge Handbook of Highland Asia*, edited by Jelle J.P. Wouters and Michael T. Heneise, 298–311. London: Routledge.

Deng, Francis M. 1995. *War of Visions: Conflict of Identities in the Sudan*. Washington, DC: Brookings Institution.

Deol, Harnik. 2000. *Religion and Nationalism in India: The Case of Punjab*. London: Routledge.

de Silva, Chandra Richard. 1984. "Sinhala-Tamil Relations and Education in Sri Lanka: The University Admissions Issue—The First Phase, 1971–7." In *From Independence to Statehood: Managing Ethnic Conflict in Five African and Asian States*, edited by Robert B. Goldmann and A. Jeyaratnam Wilson, 125–46. London: Frances Pinter Publishers.

de Silva, K. M. 1981. *A History of Sri Lanka*. Berkeley: University of California Press.

de Silva, K. M. 1986. *Managing Ethnic Tensions in Multi-Ethnic Societies: Sri Lanka, 1880–1985*. Lanham, MD: University Press of America.

de Silva, K. M. 2007. *Sri Lanka's Troubled Inheritance*. Kandy: International Centre for Ethnic Studies.

Devotta, Neil. 2005. "From Ethnic Outbidding to Ethnic Conflict: The Institutional Bases for Sri Lanka's Separatist War." *Nations and Nationalism* 11 (1): 141–59.

Dharma, Po. 2006. *Du FLM au FULRO: Une Lutte des Minorités du Sud Indochinois, 1955–1975*. Paris: Les Indes Savantes.

Diamond, Jared, and James Robinson, eds. 2010. *Natural Experiments of History*. Cambridge, MA: Belknap Press.

Diamond, Larry. 1983. "Class, Ethnicity, and the Democratic State: Nigeria, 1950–1966." *Comparative Studies in Society and History* 25: 457–489.

Dilebo, Getahun. 1974. "Emperor Menelik's Ethiopia, 1865–1916: National Unification or Amhara Communal Domination." PhD diss., Howard University.

Dirks, Nicholas. 2001. *Castes of Mind: Colonialism and the Making of Modern India*. Princeton, NJ: Princeton University Press.

Doron, Roy. 2022. "The Nigerian Civil War and Its Legacies." In *The Oxford Handbook of Nigerian History*, edited by Toyin Falola and Matthew M. Heaton, 399–420. New York: Oxford University Press.

Dutta, Uddipan. 2005. *Language Management and Transition of Assamese Identity, 1826–2005*. Guwahati: Omeo Kumar Das Institute of Social Change and Development.

Edwards, Penny. 2008. *Cambodge: The Cultivation of a Nation, 1860–1945*. Honolulu: University of Hawai'i Press.

Elliot, John H. 1992. "A Europe of Composite Monarchies." *Past and Present* 137: 48–71.

El-Solh, Raghid. 2004. *Lebanon and Arabism: National Identity and State Formation*. New York: I.B. Tauris Publishers.

Englebert, Pierre. 2000. *State Legitimacy and Development in Africa*. Boulder, CO: Lynne Rienner Press.

Englebert, Pierre. 2004. "Should I Stay or Should I Go? Compliance and Deviance to National Integration in Barotseland and Casamance." Unpublished manuscript. Accessed July 21, 2023. http://www.politics.pomona.edu/penglebert/ Compliance%20and%20Defiance-afrika%20spectrum.pdf

Evans, Peter B., Dietrich Rueschemeyer, and Theda Skocpol, eds. 1985. *Bringing the State Back In*. New York: Cambridge University Press.

Falola, Toyin, and Matthew M. Heaton. 2008. *A History of Nigeria*. New York: Cambridge University Press.

Fanthrope, Richard. 2001. "Neither Citizen nor Subject? Lumpen Agency and the Legacy of Native Administration in Sierra Leone." *African Affairs* 100: 363–86.

Fatih, Zakaria. 2013. "Colonial 'Gimmicks' of French Cultural Education." *French Cultural Studies* 24 (4): 332–45.

Fearon, James. 2003. "Ethnic and Cultural Diversity by Country." *Journal of Economic Growth* 8 (2): 195–222.

Fearon, James, and David Laitin. 2003. "Ethnicity, Insurgency and Civil War." *American Political Science Review* 97 (1): 75–90.

Feenstra, Robert C., Robert Inklaar, and Marcel P. Timmer. 2015. "The Next Generation of the Penn World Table." *American Economic Review* 105 (10): 3150–82.

Ferguson, Jane M. 2021. *Repossessing Shanland: Myanmar, Thailand, and a Nation-State Deferred*. Madison: University of Wisconsin Press.

Fildis, Ayse Tekdal. 2011. "The Troubles in Syria: Spawned by French Divide and Rule." *Middle East Policy* 18 (4): 129–39.

Fink, Christina. 2001. "Introduction." In *Burma and the Karens* by Po San C. White Lotus: Bangkok, ix–xliii.

Firmin-Sellers, Kathryn. 2000. "Institutions, Context, and Outcomes: Explaining French and British Rule in West Africa." *Comparative Politics* 32 (3): 253–72.

Fisher, Michael. 1991. *Indirect Rule in India: Residents and the Residency System, 1764–1858*. Delhi: Oxford University Press.

Fox, Richard G. 1985. *Lions of the Punjab: Culture in the Making*. Berkeley: University of California Press.

Franke, Marcus. 2009. *War and Nationalism in South Asia: The Indian State and the Nagas*. New York: Routledge.

Friesel, Evyatar. 1987. "British Officials on the Situation in Palestine, 1923." *Middle Eastern Studies* 23 (2): 194–210.

Frydenlund, Iselin, and Michael K. Jerryson. 2020. *Buddhist-Muslim Relations in a Theravada World*. Singapore: Palgrave Macmillan.

Fuller, Harcourt. 2014. *Building the Ghanaian Nation-State: Kwame Nkrumah's Symbolic Nationalism*. New York: Palgrave Macmillan.

Furnivall, John S. 1948. *Colonial Policy and Practice*. London: Cambridge University Press.

Gallego, Francisco, and Robert Woodberry. 2010. "Christian Missionaries and Education in Former African Colonies: How Competition Mattered." *Journal of African Economies* 19 (3): 294–329.

Gan-Chaudhuri, Jagadish. 1980. "Tripuri Political Consciousness." In *Tripura: The Land and its People*, edited by Jagadis Gan-Chaudhuri, 153–58. Delhi: Leeladevi Publications.

Gellner, Ernest, 1983. *Nations and Nationalism*. London: Basil Blackwell.

George, Alexander, and Andrew Bennett. 2005. *Case Studies and Theory Development in the Social Sciences*. Cambridge, MA: MIT Press.

Gifford, Prosser, and Timothy C. Weiskel. 1971. "African Education in a Colonial Context: French and British Styles." In *France and Britain in Africa: Imperial Rivalry and Colonial Rule*, edited by Prosser Gifford and William Roger Louis, 663–711. New Haven, CT: Yale University Press.

Goertz, Gary. 2016. "Multimethod Research." *Security Studies* 25 (1): 3–24.

Goertz, Gary, and James Mahoney. 2013. *A Tale of Two Cultures: Qualitative and Quantitative Research in the Social Sciences*. Princeton, NJ: Princeton University Press.

Goh, Daniel P. S. 2017. "Diversity and Nation-Building in Singapore." Global Centre for Pluralism, https://www.pluralism.ca/wp-content/uploads/2017/10/Singapore_EN.pdf.

Goodwin, Jeff. 2001. *No Other Way Out: States and Revolutionary Movements, 1945–1991*. New York: Cambridge University Press.

Goscha, Christopher. 2016. *The Penguin History of Modern Vietnam*. New York: Penguin.

Goswami, Namrata. 2009. "The Indian Experience of Conflict Resolution in Mizoram." *Strategic Analysis* 33 (4): 579–89.

Government of India. 1922. *Administration Report of the Baluchistan Agency for the Year 1920–21*. Quetta: Qasim Printers.

Gravers, Mikael. 1999. *Nationalism as Political Paranoia in Burma: An Essay on the Historical Practice of Power*. Richmond: Curzon Press.

Gravers, Mikael, 2002. "Conversion and Identity: Religion and the Formation of the Karen Ethnic Identity in Burma." In *Exploring Ethnic Diversity in Burma*, edited by Mikael Gravers, 227–58. Copenhagen: NIAS Press.

Greenfeld, Liah. 2019. *Nationalism: A Short History*. Washington, DC: Brookings Institute Press.

Gurr, Ted R. 1993. *Minorities at Risk: A Global View of Ethnopolitical Conflict*. Washington, DC: United States Institute of Peace Press.

Hall, John A. 2015. "Varieties of State Experience." In *Oxford Handbook of the Transformations of the State*, edited by Stephan Liebfried, Evelyne Huber, Matthew Lange, Jonah Levy, Frank Nullmeier, and John Stephens, 61–73. New York: Oxford University Press.

Hall, John A. 2024. *Nations, States and Empires*. Cambridge: Polity Press.

Hall, John, and Siniša Malešević. 2013. "Introduction: Wars and Nationalisms." In *Nationalism and War*, edited by John Hall and Siniša Malešević, 1–28. New York: Cambridge University Press.

Hanjabam, Shukhdeba Sharma. 2008. "The Meitei Upsurge in Manipur." *Asia Europe Journal* 6 (1): 157–69.

Harper, T. A. 1999. *The End of Empire and the Making of Malaya*. Cambridge: Cambridge University Press.

Harriden, Jessica. 2002. "'Making a Name for Themselves': Karen Identity and the Politicization of Ethnicity in Burma." *Journal of Burma Studies* 7: 84–144.

Hayward, Fred. 1989. "Sierra Leone: State Consolidation, Fragmentation, and Decay." In *Contemporary West African States*, edited by Donal Cruise O'Brien, John Dunn, and Richard Rathbone, 165–80. New York: Cambridge University Press.

Hechter, Michael. 2000. *Containing Nationalism*. New York: Oxford University Press.

Henderson, Errol A. 2000. "When States Implode: The Correlates of Africa's Civil Wars, 1950–92." *Studies in Comparative International Development* 35 (2): 28–47.

Hess, Janet. 2001. "Exhibiting Ghana: Display, Documentary, and 'National' Art in the Nrumah Era." *African Studies Review* 44 (1): 59–77.

Hickey, Gerald C. 1982. *Free in the Forest: Ethnohistory of the Vietnamese Central Highlands 1954–1976*. New Haven, CT: Yale University Press.

Hien, Luong Quang. 2020. "French Educational Reforms in Indochina Peninsula and the Appearance of the Western Intellectual Hierarchy in Vietnam in the Early Twentieth Century." *American Journal of Educational Research* 8 (4): 208–13.

Holt, Benjamin. 2022. "Building the State and Conceiving the Nation: The Origins of Separatist insurgency in the Mizo Hills, 1945–61." *Contemporary South Asia* 30 (3): 313–30.

Holt, John C. 2019. *Myanmar's Buddhist-Muslim Crisis: Rohingya, Arakanese, and Burmese Narratives of Siege and Fear*. Honolulu: University of Hawai'i Press.

Horowitz, Donald. 1985. *Ethnic Groups in Conflict*. Berkeley: University of California Press.

Hunziker, Philipp, and Lars-Erik Cederman. 2017. "No Extraction Without Representation: The Ethno-Regional Oil Curse and Secessionist Conflict." *Journal of Peace Research* 54: 365–81.

Hutchinson, John. 2005. *Nations as Zones of Conflict*. London: Sage.

Ibrahim, Azeem. 2016. *The Rohingyas: Inside Myanmar's Hidden Genocide*. London: Hurst & Company.

Ibrahim, Hassan Ahmed. 1977. "The Development of Economic and Political Neo-Mahdism in the Sudan 1926–1935." *Sudan Notes and Records* 58: 44–64.

Idris, Amir. 2005. *Conflict and Politics of Identity in Sudan*. New York: Palgrave Macmillan.

Idris, Amir. 2013. *Identity, Citizenship, and Violence in Two Sudans: Reimagining a Common Future*. New York: Palgrave Macmillan.

Ilankai Tamil Sangam. 2010. "American Ceylon Mission." Accessed June 7, 2023. https://sangam.org/2010/04/ACMission.php?uid=3922

Iliffe, John. 1979. *A Modern History of Tanganyika*. Cambridge: Cambridge University Press.

Iliffe, John. 1995. *Africans: The History of a Continent*. Cambridge: Cambridge University Press.

Indian Statutory Commission. 1929. "Seventh Meeting of the Commission, Deputations from the British Burman Association, the Karen Elders and the Karen National Association, the Burma Muslim Society, the Muslim League, Burma, and the Provincial Tanzim." Rangoon, February 5, 1929. British Library, IOR/Q/13/1/33, item 7.

Iwilade, Akin, and Iwebunor Okwechime. 2022. "Ethnic Nationalism and Minority Politics in Nigeria." In *The Oxford Handbook of Nigerian History*, edited by Toyin Falola and Matthew M. Heaton, 483–500. New York: Oxford University Press.

Izady, M. R. 2004. "Kurds and the Formation of the State of Iraq." In *The Creation of Iraq, 1914–1921*, edited by Reeva Spector Simon, Eleanor Tejirian, and Gary Sick, 95–109. New York: Columbia University Press.

Jacquin-Berdal, Dominique. 2002. *Nationalism and Ethnicity in the Horn of Africa: A Critique of the Ethnic Interpretation*. Lewiston, NY: Edwin Mellen Press.

Jaffrelot, Christophe. 1996. *The Hindu Nationalist Movement in India*. New York: Columbia University Press.

Jaquet, Carine. 2018. *The Kachin Conflict: Testing the Limits of the Political Transition in Myanmar*. Bangkok: Institut de Recherche sur l'Asie du Sud-Est Contemporaine.

Jayawardena, Kumari. 2010. *Perpetual Ferment, Popular Revolts in Sri Lanka in the 18th and 19th Centuries*. Colombo: Social Scientists' Association.

Jenkins, J. Craig. 1983. "Resource Mobilization Theory and the Study of Social Movements." *Annual Review of Sociology* 9 (1): 527–53.

Jenkins, Richard. 2008. *Rethinking Ethnicity: Arguments and Explorations.* London: Sage Publications.

Jenne, Erin K., Stephen M. Saideman, and Will Lowe. 2007. "Separatism as a Bargaining Posture: The Role of Leverage in Minority Radicalization." *Journal of Peace Research* 44 (5): 539–58.

Jeong, Tay. 2023. "Community-Based Legislative Representation and Postcolonial Ethnic Civil Warfare in Former British and French Colonies." *Nations and Nationalism* 29 (1): 311–30.

Johnston, Hank. 2011. *States and Social Movements.* Malden, MA: Polity Press.

Jones, Thomas-Jesse. 1925. *Education in Africa: A Study of West, South, and Equatorial Africa by the African Education Commission, under the Auspices of the Phelps-Stokes Fund and the Foreign Mission Societies of North America and Europe.* New York: Phelps-Stokes Fund.

Jørgensen, Anders Baltzer, 1997. "Forward," in H. I. Marshall, *The Karen People of Burma: A Study of Anthropology and Ethnology*, v–xi. Bangkok: White Lotus.

Judicial Advisers' Conference. 1957. *Native Courts and Native Customary Law in Africa.* London: H.M. Stationery Office.

Julien, C. A. 1950. "From the French Empire to the French Union." *International Affairs* 26 (4): 487–502.

Kandeh, Jimmy. 2002. "Subaltern Terror in Sierra Leone." In *Africa in Crisis: New Challenges and Possibilities*, edited by Tunde Zack Williams, Diane Frost, and Alex Thomson, 179–95. Sterling, VA: Pluto Press.

Kasfir, Nelson. 1972. "Cultural Sub-Nationalism in Uganda." In *The Politics of Cultural Sub-Nationalism in Africa*, edited by Victor A. Olorunsola, 49–148. Garden City, NY: Anchor Books.

Kaufman, Stuart. 2006. "Symbolic Politics or Rational Choice? Testing Theories of Extreme Ethnic Violence." *International Security* 30 (4): 45–86.

Kaufman, Stuart. 2015. *Nationalist Passions.* Ithaca, NY: Cornell University Press.

Kaviraj, Sudipta. 1997. "Religion and Identity in India." *Ethnic and Racial Studies* 20 (2): 325–44.

Keenan, Paul. 2017. "Karen National Identity in the Early 20th Century—the Daw K'lu: The Karen National Association." Retrieved January 16, 2019, https://paullkeenan.net/2017/04/18/karen-national-identity-in-the-early-20th-century-the-daw-klu-the-karen-national-association/.

Keese, Alexander. 2007. *Living with Ambiguity: Integrating an African Elite in French and Portuguese Africa, 1930–61.* München: Martin-Behaim-Preis.

Kelly, Gail P. 1977. "Colonial Schools in Vietnam, 1918 to 1938." *Proceedings of the Meeting of the French Colonial Historical Society* 2: 96–106.

Kelly, Gail P. 1982. "Schooling and National Integration: The Case of Interwar Vietnam." *Comparative Education* 18 (2): 175–95.

Kemper, Theodore D. 1978. *A Social Interactional Theory of Emotions.* New York: Wiley.

Keyes, Charles F. 1977. *The Golden Peninsula: Culture and Adaptation in Mainland Southeast Asia.* New York: MacMillan Publishing.

Keyes, Charles F. 2003. "The Politics of Language in Thailand and Laos." In *Fighting Words: Language Policy and Ethnic Relations in Asia*, edited by Michel E. Brown and Sumit Ganguly, 177–210. Cambridge, MA: MIT Press.

Khama, Seretse. 1970. *Botswana: A Developing Democracy in Southern Africa.* Uppsala: Scandinavian Institute of African Studies.

Khan, Saqib. 2023. *The Tribe-Class Linkages: The History and Politics of the Agrarian Movement in Tripura.* London: Routledge India.

Kheng, Cheah Boon. 2002. *Malaysia: The Making of a Nation.* Singapore: Institute of Southeast Asian Studies.

Khổng Diễn. 2002. *Population and Ethno-Demography in Vietnam.* Chiang Mai: Silkworm Books.

Khoury, Gérard D. 2004. "Robert de Caix et Louis Massignon: Deux Visions de la Politique Française au Levant en 1920." In *The British and French Mandates in Comparative Perspective*, edited by Nadine Méouchy and Peter Sluglett, 165–83. Boston: Brill.

Khoury, Philip. 1987. *Syria and the French Mandate: The Politics of Arab Nationalism, 1920–1945*. Princeton, NJ: Princeton University Press.

Kiernan, Ben. 2008. *The Pol Pot Regime: Race, Power, and Genocide in Cambodia under the Khmer Rouge, 1975–79*. New Haven, CT: Yale University Press.

King, Elisabeth. 2014. *From Classrooms to Conflict in Rwanda*. New York: Cambridge University Press.

Kirk-Greene, Anthony. 1980. "'Damnosa Hereditas': Ethnic Ranking and the Martial Races Imperative in Africa." *Ethnic and Racial Studies* 3 (4): 393–414.

Kirk-Greene, Anthony. 1995. "'Le Roi est Mort! Vive le Roi!': The Comparative Legacy of Chiefs after the Transfer of Power in British and French West Africa." In *State and Society in Francophone Africa since Independence*, edited by Anthony Kirk-Greene and Daniel Bach, 16–33. London: Macmillan Press.

Kitschelt, Herbert P. 1986. "Political Opportunity Structures and Political Protest: Anti-Nuclear Movements in Four Democracies." *British Journal of Political Science* 16 (1): 57–85.

Kocher, Matthew A., and Nuno P. Monteiro. 2016. "Lines of Demarcation: Causation, Design-Based Inference, and Historical Research." *Perspectives on Politics* 14 (4): 952–75.

Koff, David, and George Von der Muhll. 1967. "Political Socialization in Kenya and Tanzania: A Comparative Analysis." *Journal of Modern African Studies* 5 (1): 13–51.

Kumar, Krishna. 2003. *The Making of English National Identity*. Cambridge: Cambridge University Press.

Kumar, Krishna. 2017. *Visions of Empire: How Five Imperial Regimes Shaped the World*. Princeton, NJ: Princeton University Press.

Kumar, Kuldeep. 2016. *Police and Counterinsurgency: The Untold Story of Tripura's COIN Campaign*. New Delhi: Sage Publications.

Kumar, Satinder. 2000. *Educational Philosophy in Modern India*. New Delhi: Anmol Publications.

Kymlicka, Will. 1995. *Multicultural Citizenship: A Liberal Theory of Minority Rights*. New York: Oxford University Press.

Labrune-Badiane, Céline. 2010. "Peut-On Parler d'un 'Désir d'école' en Casamance? (1860–1930)." *Histoire de l'Éducation* 128: 29–52.

Laitin, David D. 1986. *Hegemony and Culture: Politics and Religious Change among the Yoruba*. Chicago: University of Chicago Press.

Lalchungnunga. 1994. *Mizoram: Politics of Regionalism and National Integration*. New Delhi: Reliance Publishing House.

Lange, Matthew. 2009a. "Developmental Crises: A Comparative-Historical Analysis of State Building in Colonial Botswana and Malaysia." *Commonwealth & Comparative Politics* 47: 1–27.

Lange, Matthew. 2009b. *Lineages of Despotism and Development: British Colonialism and State Power*. Chicago: University of Chicago Press.

Lange, Matthew. 2012. *Educations in Ethnic Violence: Identity, Educational Bubbles, and Resource Mobilization*. New York: Cambridge University Press.

Lange, Matthew. 2013. *Comparative-Historical Methods*. London: SAGE.

Lange, Matthew. 2015. "State Formation and Transformation in Africa and Asia: The Third Phase of State Expansion." In *Oxford Handbook of the Transformations of the State*, edited by Stephan Liebfried, Evelyne Huber, Matthew Lange, Jonah Levy, Frank Nullmeier, and John Stephens, 116–30. New York: Oxford University Press.

Lange, Matthew. 2017. *Killing Others: A Natural History of Ethnic Violence*. Ithaca, NY: Cornell University Press.

Lange, Matthew. 2020. "A Path-Dependent Approach to Communal Transformation: Recognizing Cognitive and Structural Views of Collective Community." *Canadian Journal of Sociology* 45 (4): 313–35.

Lange, Matthew. 2024. "Colonial Patterns of Civil War: British, French, and Spanish Empires in Comparative Perspective." Social Science History Association Annual Conference, Toronto, Canada.

Lange, Matthew, and Hrag Balian. 2008. "Containing Conflict or Instigating Unrest? A Test of the Effects of State Infrastructural Power on Civil Violence." *Studies in Comparative International Development* 43: 314–33.

Lange, Matthew, and Andrew Dawson. 2009. "Dividing and Ruling the World? A Statistical Test of the Effects of Colonialism on Postcolonial Civil Violence." *Social Forces* 88: 785–818.

Lange, Matthew, and Tay Jeong. 2024. "Fighting over Nation or State: States, Communal Demography, and the Type of Ethnic Civil War." *Nations and Nationalism*, 1–18.

Lange, Matthew, Tay Jeong, and Emre Amasyali. 2021. "The Colonial Origins of Ethnic Warfare: Re-Examining the Impact of Communalizing Colonial Policies in the British and French Empires." *International Journal of Comparative Sociology* 62 (2): 141–65.

Lange, Matthew, Tay Jeong, and Charlotte Gaudreau. 2022. "A Tale of Two Empires: Models of Political Community in British and French Colonies." *Nations and Nationalism* 28 (3): 872–989.

Lankina, Tomila, and Lullit Getachew. 2012. "Mission or Empire, Word or Sword: The Human Capital Legacy in Postcolonial Democratic Development." *American Journal of Political Science* 56 (2): 465–83.

Lankina, Tomila, and Lullit Getachew. 2013. "Competitive Religious Entrepreneurs: Christian Missionaries and Female Education in Colonial and Postcolonial India." *British Journal of Political Science* 43 (1): 103–31.

Laoutides, Costas, and Anthony Ware. 2016. "Reexamining the Centrality of Ethnic Identity to the Kachin Conflict." In *Conflict in Myanmar: War, Politics, Religion*, edited by Nick Cheesman and Nicholas Farrelly, 47–65. Singapore: ASEAS-Yusof Ishak Institute.

Lattimore, Owen. 1962. *Studies in Frontier History: Collected Papers, 1928–1958*. New York: Oxford University Press.

Lawrence, Adria. 2013. *Imperial Rule and the Politics of Nationalism: Colonial Protest in the French Empire*. New York: Cambridge University Press.

Leach, Justin D. 2013. *War and Politics in Sudan: Cultural Identities and the Challenges of the Peach Process*. New York: I.B. Tauris.

Lee, Alexander. 2020. *From Hierarchy to Ethnicity: The Politics of Caste in Twentieth-Century India*. Cambridge: Cambridge University Press.

Lentz, Carola, and Paul Nugent. 2000. "Ethnicity in Ghana: A Comparative Perspective." In *Ethnicity in Ghana: The Limits of Invention*, edited by Carolina Lentz and Paul Nugent, 1–28. London: Macmillan Press.

Levine, Donald N. 1974. *Greater Ethiopia: The Evolution of a Multiethnic Society*. Chicago: University of Chicago Press.

Lewis, James Lee. 1924. "The Burmanization of the Karen People: A Study in Racial Adaptability." Master's thesis, University of Chicago.

Lewis, Martin D. 1962. "One Hundred Million Frenchmen: The 'Assimilation' Theory in French Colonial Policy." *Comparative Studies in Society and History* 4 (2): 129–53.

Lieberman, Evan, and Prerna Singh. 2017. "Census Enumeration and Group Conflict: A Global Analysis of the Consequences of Counting." *World Politics* 69 (1): 1–53.

Lieberman, Victor B. 1987. "Reinterpreting Burmese History." *Comparative Studies in Society and History* 29 (1): 162–94.

Lijphart, Arend. 1977. *Democracy in Plural Societies: A Comparative Exploration*. New Haven, CT: Yale University Press.

Lim, Regina. 2015. *Federal-State Relations in Sabah, Malaysia*. Singapore: ISEAS-Yusof Ishak Institute.

Little, David. 1993. *Sri Lanka: The Invention of Enmity*. Washington, DC: United States Institute of Peace Press.

Liu, Amy H., and Jacob I. Ricks. 2022. *Ethnicity and Politics in Southeast Asia*. New York: Cambridge University Press.

Lockhart, James. 1969. "Encomienda and Hacienda: The Evolution of the Great Estate in the Spanish Indies." *Hispanic American Historical Review* 49 (3): 411–29.

Longrigg, Stephen H. 1958. *Syria and Lebanon under French Mandate*. London: Oxford University Press.

Loveman, Mara. 2014. *National Colors: Racial Classification and the State in Latin America*. New York: Oxford University Press.

Lugard, Frederick. 1922. *The Dual Mandate in British Tropical Africa*. Edinburgh: William Blackwood and Sons.

Mahoney, James. 2000a. "Path Dependence in Historical Sociology." *Theory and Society* 29 (4): 507–48.

Mahoney, James. 2000b. "Strategies of Causal Inference in Small-N Analysis." *Sociological Methods and Research* 28 (4): 387–424.

Mahoney, James. 2010. *Colonialism and Postcolonial Development: Spanish America in Comparative Perspective*. New York: Cambridge University Press.

Mailer, Gideon. 2007. "Anglo-American and European Missionary Encounters in Southern Sudan, 1898-Present." In *Missions, States, and European Expansion in Africa*, edited by Chima J. Korieh and Raphael Chijioke Njoku, 203–33. New York: Routledge.

Malešević, Siniša. 2019. *Grounded Nationalisms: A Sociological Analysis*. Cambridge: Cambridge University Press.

Mamdani, Mahmood. 1996. *Citizen and Subject*. Princeton, NJ: Princeton University Press.

Mamdani, Mahmood. 2001. *When Victims Become Killers: Colonialism, Nativism, and Genocide in Rwanda*. Princeton, NJ: Princeton University Press.

Mamdani, Mahmood. 2012. *Define and Rule: Native as Political Identity*. Cambridge, MA: Harvard University Press.

Mangrai, Sao Saimong. 1965. *The Shan States and the British Annexation*. Ithaca, NY: Cornell University Press.

Mann, Gregory. 2009. "What Was the Indigénat? The 'Empire of Law' in French West Africa." *Journal of African History* 50: 331–53.

Mann, Michael. 1986. *The Sources of Social Power, Volume 1: A History of Power from the Beginning to AD 1760*. New York: Cambridge University Press.

Mann, Michael. 1988. *States, War and Capitalism: Studies in Political Sociology*. Oxford: Blackwell.

Mann, Michael. 1993. *The Sources of Social Power, Volume II: The Rise of Classes and Nation-States*. New York: Cambridge University Press.

Mann, Michael. 2005. *The Dark Side of Democracy: Explaining Ethnic Cleansing*. New York: Cambridge University Press.

Mantena, Karuna. 2010. *Alibis of Empire: Henry Maine and the Ends of Liberal Imperialism*. Princeton, NJ: Princeton University Press.

Marshall, Monty G., and Ted Gurr. 2020. *Polity5: Political Regime Characteristics and Transitions, 1800–2018. Dataset Users' Manual*. Center for Systemic Peace, http://www.systemicpeace.org/inscr/p5manualv2018.pdf.

Marx, Anthony. 1998. *Making Race and Nation: A Comparison of the United States, South Africa, and Brazil*. New York: Cambridge University Press.

Mason, Ellen Huntly Bullard. 1862. *Civilizing Mountain Men or Sketches of Mission Work among the Karens*. London: James Nisbet & Co.

Mason, Francis. 1860. *Burmah, Its People and Natural Productions*. London: Trubner and Company.

Mason, Francis. 1870. *The Story of a Working Man's Life: With Sketches of Travel in Europe, Asia, Africa, and America, as Related by Himself*. New York: Oakley, Mason, and Co.

Maundeni, Zibani. 1998. "The Struggle for Political Freedom and Independence." In *Botswana: Politics and Society*, edited by W. A. Edge and M. H. Lekorwe, 118–33. Pretoria: J.L. van Shaik Publishers.

Maung, U Maung. 1990. *Burmese Nationalist Movements, 1940–1948*. Honolulu: University of Hawai'i Press.

Maxwell, Neville. 1973. *India and the Nagas*. London: Minority Rights Group.

Mayo, David Nailo. 1993. "The British Southern Policy in Sudan: An Inquiry into the Closed District Ordinances (1914–1946)." *Northeast African Studies* 1 (2/3): 165–85.

Mazrui, Ali. 1983. "Francophone Nations and English-Speaking States: Imperial Ethnicity and African Political Formations." In *State Versus Ethnic Claims: African Policy Dilemmas*, edited by Donald Rothchild and Victor Olorunsola, 25–43. New York: Routledge.

McAdam, Doug. 1982. *Political Process and the Development of Black Insurgency, 1930–1970*. Chicago: University of Chicago Press.

McCarthy, John D., and Mayer N. Zald. 1977. "Resource Mobilization and Social Movements: A Partial Theory." *American Journal of Sociology* 82 (6): 1212–41.

McDowall, David. 2021. *A Modern History of the Kurds*. 4th ed. New York: I.B. Tauris.

McElwee, Pamela. 2004. "Becoming Socialist or Becoming Kinh? Government Policies for Ethnic Minorities in the Socialist Republic of Viet Nam." In *Civilizing the Margins: Southeast Asian Government Policies for the Development of Minorities*, edited by Christopher R. Duncan, 182–213. Ithaca, NY: Cornell University Press.

McEvoy, Joanne, and Brendan O'Leary, eds. 2013. *Power Sharing in Deeply Divided Places*. Philadelphia: University of Pennsylvania Press.

McMahon, A. R. 1876. *The Karens of the Golden Chersonese*. London: Harrison and Sons Printers.

Meetei, Naorem Malemsanba. 2015. "Consilidation of British 'Indirect Rule' in Manipur." In *Colonialism and Resistance: Society and State in Manipur*, edited by Arambam Noni and Kangujam Sanatomba, 147–58. London: Routledge India.

Melvin, Neil J. 2007. "Conflict in Southern Thailand: Islamism, Violence and the State in the Patani Insurgency. SIRPI Policy Paper No. 20." Accessed June 20, 2023. https://www.sipri.org/sites/default/files/files/PP/SIPRIPP20.pdf

Merry, Sally Engle. 1991. "Law and Colonialism." *Law and Society Review* 25 (4): 889–922.

Metcalf, Thomas. 1960. "The Impact of the Mutiny on British Attitudes to India." *Proceedings on the Indian History Congress* 23: 24–31.

Metcalf, Thomas. 2016. *Aftermath of Revolt: India 1857–1970*. Princeton, NJ: Princeton University Press.

Metcalf, Barbara D., and Thomas R. Metcalf. 2006. *A Concise History of Modern India*. New York: Cambridge University Press.

Meyer, Jean, Jean Tarrade, Annie Rey-Goldzeiguer, and Jacques Thobie. 1991. *Histoire de La France Colonial: Dès origins à 1914*. Paris: Armand Colin.

Meyer, John W., John Boli, George M. Thomas, and Francisco O. Ramirez. 1997. "World Society and the Nation-State." *American Journal of Sociology* 101 (1): 144–81.

Mgadla, Part Themba. 2003. *A History of Education in the Bechuanaland Protectorate to 1965*. New York: University Press of America.

Michaud, Jean. 2010. "The Southeast Asian Massif." Accessed May 2, 2023. https://commons .wikimedia.org/wiki/File:GENERAL-Massif_2May2010.jpg

Michelman, Frederic. 1995. "French and British Colonial Language Policies: A Comparative View of Their Impact on African Literature." *Research in African Literatures* 26 (4): 216–25.

Miguel, Edward. 2004. "Tribe or Nation? Nation Building and Public Goods in Kenya Versus Tanzania." *World Politics* 56: 327–62.

Miles, William F. 1994. *Hausaland Divided: Colonialism and Independence in Niger and Nigeria.* Ithaca, NY: Cornell University Press.

Mill, John Stewart. 1843/2012. *A System of Logic, Ratiocinative and Inductive: Being a Connected View of the Principles of Evidence, and the Methods of Scientific Investigation.* New York: Cambridge University Press.

Misra, Sanghamitra. 2021. "The Customs of Conquest: Legal Primitivism and British Paramountcy in Northeast India." *Studies in History* 37 (2): 168–90.

Misra, Tilottoma. 1987. *Literature and Society in Assam: A Study of the Assamese Renaissance, 1826–1926.* New Delhi: Omsons Publications.

Mohanta, Bijan. 2004. *Tripura: In the Light of Socio-Political Movements since 1945.* Kolkata: Progressive Publishers.

Mukherjee, Shivaji. 2021. *Colonial Institutions and Civil War: Indirect Rule and Maoist Insurgency in India.* New York: Cambridge University Press.

Müller-Crepon, Carl. 2020. "Continuity or Change? (In)direct Rule in British and French Colonial Africa." *International Organization* 74 (4): 707–41.

Muslih, Huhammad. 1988. *The Origins of Palestinian Nationalism.* New York: Columbia University Press.

Natsios, Andrew S. 2012. *Sudan, South Sudan, and Darfur: What Everyone Needs to Know.* New York: Oxford University Press.

Nayak, Purusottam, and Komol Singha. 2015. "Identity, Deprivation and Demand for Bigurcation of Meghalaya." In *Identity, Contestation and Development in Northeast India,* edited by Komol Singha and M. Amarjeet Singh, 121–30. London: Taylor and Francis.

Nemoto, Kei. 2000. "The Concepts of Dobama ('Our Burma') and Thudo-Bama ('Their Burma') in Burmese Nationalism, 1930–1948." *Journal of Burma Studies* 5: 1–16.

Nesbitt, Eleanor. 2005. *Sikhism: A Very Short Introduction.* Oxford: Oxford University Press.

Newbury, Catharine. 1983. "Colonialism, Ethnicity, and Rural Ethnic Protest: Rwanda and Zanzibar in Comparative Perspective." *Comparative Politics* 15 (3): 253–80.

Nguyen Khac Vien. 1968. "A Mosaic of Nationalities." *Vietnamese Studies* 15: 4–23.

Nissan, Elisabeth, and R. L. Stirrat. 1990. "The Generation of Communal Identities." In *Sri Lanka: History and the Roots of Conflict,* edited by Jonathan Spencer, 19–44. London: Routledge.

Nunn, Nathan. 2014. "Gender and Missionary Influence in Colonial Africa." In *Africa's Development in Historical Perspective,* edited by Emmanuel Akyeapong, Robert Bates, Nathan Nunn, and James Robinson, 489–514. New York: Cambridge University Press.

Nyerere, Julius. 1966. *Freedom and Unity: A Selection from Writings and Speeches 1952–1965.* Oxford: Oxford University Press.

Oberoi, Harjot. 1994. *The Construction of Religious Boundaries: Culture, Identity, and Diversity in the Sikh Tradition.* Chicago: University of Chicago Press.

O'Brien, Jay. 1998. "Power and the Discourse of Ethnicity in Sudan." In *Ethnicity and the State in Eastern Africa,* edited by M. A. Mohamed Salih and John Markakis, 62–71. Uppsala: Nordiska Africainstitutet.

Okoye, Dozie, and Roland Pongou. 2014. "Historical Missionary Activity, Schooling, and the Reversal of Fortunes: Evidence from Nigeria." MPRA Paper. Accessed May 10, 2023. https://papers.ssrn.com/sol3/papers.cfm?abstract_id=2484020

Omari, C. K. 1995. "The Management of Tribal and Religious Diversity." In *Mwalimu: The Influence of Nyerere*, edited by Colin Legum and Geoffrey Mmari, 23–31. Trenton, NJ: Africa World Press.

Ongkili, James P. 1975. "The 'Dacing' in Sabah and Sarawak." *Southeast Asian Affairs*: 109–14.

Osaghae, Eghosa E., and T. Rotimi Suberu. 2005. *A History of Identities, Violence, and Stability in Nigeria*. Oxford: Centre for Research on Inequality, Human Security and Ethnicity.

Our World in Data. 2024. "Oil Production." Accessed August 30, 2024. https://ourworldindata .org/grapher/oil-production-by-country

Ovesen, Jan, and Ing-Briitt Trankell. 2004. "Foreigners and Honorary Khmers: Ethnic Minorities in Cambodia." In *Civilizing the Margins: Southeast Asian Government Policies for the Development of Minorities*, edited by Christopher R. Duncan, 241–69. Ithaca, NY: Cornell University Press.

Owolabi, Olukunle. 2023. *Ruling Emancipated Slaves and Indigenous Subjects: The Divergent Legacies of Forced Settlement and Colonial Occupation in the Global South*. New York: Oxford University Press.

Pachuau, Joy L. K. 2014. *Being Mizo: Identity and Belonging in Northeast India*. Delhi: Oxford Academic.

Pachuau, Joy L. K., and Willem van Schendel. 2015. *The Camera as Witness: A Social History of Mizoram, Northeast India*. Delhi: Cambridge University Press.

Paden, John. 1971. "Communal Competition, Conflict ad Violence in Kano." In *Nigeria: Modernization and the Politics of Communalism*, edited by Robert Melson and Howard Wolpe, 113–44. East Lasing: Michigan State University Press.

Paine, Jack. 2019. "Ethnic Violence in Africa: Destructive Legacies of Pre-Colonial States." *International Organizations* 73: 645–83.

Panwar, Namrata. 2017. "Explaining Cohesion in an Insurgent Organization: The Case of the Mizo National Front." *Small Wars and Insurgencies* 28 (6): 973–95.

Parsons, Neil. 1987. "The Central District: The BaNgwato Crisis, 1948–1956." In *The Birth of Botswana: A History of the Bechuanaland Protectorate from 1910 to 1966*, edited by Morton, F. and J. Ramsay, 123–33. Gaborone: Longman Botswana.

Pathak, Suryasikha. 2010. "Tribal Politics in the Assam: 1933–1947." *Economic and Political Weekly* 45 (10): 61–69.

Peebles, Patrick. 2006. *The History of Sri Lanka*. Westport, CT: Greenwood Press.

Pelletier, Alexandre. 2021. "Identity Formation, Christian Networks, and the Peripheries of Kachin Ethnonational Identity." *Asian Politics & Policy* 13: 72–89.

Pérelle, Adam. 1680. "View of Versailles, Garden Facade, 1680s." Accessed May 1, 2023. https:// commons.wikimedia.org/wiki/File:Adam_Perelle,_View_of_Versailles,_garden_facade, _1680s.jpg

Perera, Sasanka. 1991. "Teaching and Learning Hatred: The Role of Education and Socialization in Sri Lankan Ethnic Conflict." PhD diss. University of California, Santa Barbara.

Pettersson, Therese, and Magnus Öberg. 2020. "Organized Violence, 1989–2019." *Journal of Peace Research* 57 (4): 597–613.

Poggo, Scopas S. 2002. "General Ibrahim Abboud's Military Administration in the Sudan, 1958–1964: Implementation of the Programs of Islamization and Arabization in the Southern Sudan." *Northeast African Studies* 9 (1): 67–101.

Pollis, Adamantia. 1973. "Intergroup Conflict and British Colonial Policy: The Case of Cyrus." *Comparative Politics* 5 (4): 575–99.

Posen, Barry. 1993. "Nationalism, the Mass Army, and Military Power." *International Security* 18 (2): 80–124.

Price, Gareth. 1997. "The Assam Movement and the Construction of Assamese Identity." PhD diss., Bristol University.

Putnam, Robert. 2000. *Bowling Alone: The Collapse and Revival of American Community*. New York: Simon and Schuster.

Quincy, Keith. 1995. *Hmong, History of a People*. Cheney, WA: Eastern Washington University.

Raffin, Anne. 2013. "Native Policy and Colonial State Formation in Pondicherry (India) and Vietnam: Recasting Ethnic Relations, 1870s–1920s." In *Sociology and Empire: The Imperial Entanglements of a Discipline*, edited by George Steinmetz, 415–35. Durham, NC: Duke University Press.

Rajah, Ananda. 2002. "A 'Nation of Intent' in Burma: Karen Ethno-Nationalism, Nationalism and Narrations of Nation." *Pacific Review* 15: 517–37.

Rameriz, Susan Elizabeth. 1986. *Provincial Patriarchs: Land Tenure and the Economics of Power in Colonial Peru*. Albuquerque: University of New Mexico Press.

Rathbone, Richard. 2000. *Nkrumah and the Chiefs: The Politics of Chieftaincy in Ghana 1951–60*. Athens: Ohio University Press.

Ray, Animesh. 1982. *Mizoram: Dynamics of Change*. Calcutta: Pearl Publishers.

Ray, Subhasish. 2012. "The Nonmartial Origins of the 'Martial Races': Ethnicity and Military Service in Ex-British Colonies." *Armed Forces & Society* 39 (3): 560–75.

Ray, Subhasish. 2018. "Beyond Divide and Rule: Explaining the Link Between British Colonialism and Ethnic Violence." *Nationalism and Ethnic Politics* 24 (4): 367–88.

Ray, Subhasish. 2019. "History and Ethnic Conflict: Does Precolonial Centralization Matter?" *International Studies Quarterly* 63: 417–31.

Reed, Holly E. and Blessing U. Mberu. 2015. "Ethnicity, Religion, and Demographic Behavior in Nigeria." In *The International Handbook of the Demography of Race and Ethnicity, Volume 4*, edited by Rogelio Sáenz, David Embrick, and Néstor Rodríguez, 419–54. Dordrecht: Springer.

Reetz, Dietrich. 1997. "In Search of the Collective Self: How Ethnic Group Concepts Were Cast through Conflict in Colonial India." *Modern Asian Studies* 31 (2): 285–315.

Reno, William. 1995. *Corruption and State Politics in Sierra Leone*. New York: Cambridge University Press.

Rey, Charles. 1988. *Monarch of All I Survey: Bechuanaland Diaries 1929–37*, edited by Neil Parsons and Michael Crowder. Gaborone: Botswana Society.

Ricks, Jacob. 2019. "Proud to be Thai: The Puzzling Absence of Ethnicity-Based Political Cleavages in Northeastern Thailand." *Pacific Affairs* 92 (2): 257–85.

Ricks, Jacob. 2020. "Integration despite Inclusion: Thai National Identity among Isan People." *Kyoto Review of Southeast Asia*, 27. Accessed August 9, 2023. https://kyotoreview.org/issue-27/integration-despite-exclusion-thai-national-identity-among-isan-people/

Rohlfing, Ingo. 2008. "What You See and What You Get: Pitfalls and Principles of Nested Analysis in Comparative Research." *Comparative Political Studies* 41 (11): 1492–1514.

Rolandsen, Øystein H. 2011. "A False Start: Between War and Peace in the Southern Sudan, 1956–62." *Journal of African History* 52: 105–23.

Ross, Michael. 1999. "The Political Economy of the Resource Curse." *World Politics* 51 (2): 297–322.

Ross, Michael. 2010. "Latin America's Missing Oil Wars." Accessed June 9, 2023. https://www.sscnet.ucla.edu/polisci/faculty/ross/papers/working/Latin%20America's%20Missing%20Oil%20Wars.pdf

Ruane, Joseph, and Jennifer Todd. 2004. "The Roots of Intense Ethnic Conflict May not in Fact be Ethnic: Categories, Communities, and Path. Dependence." *European Journal of Sociology* 45 (2): 209–32.

Russell, Jane. 1982. *Communal Politics under the Donoughmore Constitution, 1931–1947*. Dehiwala: Tisara Prakasakayo.

Sachs, Jeffrey, and Andrew Warner. 1995. "Natural Resource Abundance and Economic Growth." NBER Working Paper (5398).

Sadan, Mandy. 2013. *Being and Becoming Kachin: Histories Beyond the State in the Borderworlds of Burma*. Oxford: Oxford University Press.

Safman, Rachel M. 2007. "Minorities and State-Building in Mainland Southeast Asia." In *Myanmar: State, Society, and Ethnicity*, edited by N. Ganesan and Kyaw Yin Hlaing, 30–69. Singapore: Institute of Southeast Asian Studies.

Saha, K. C. 2002. "Learning from the Ethnic Conflict and the Internal Displacement in Tripura in Northeast India." *Human Rights Review* 3 (3): 50–64.

Said, Beshir Mohammed. 1956. *The Sudan Crossroads of Africa*. London: Bodley Head.

Salemink, Oscar. 1995. "Primitive Partisans: French Strategy and the Construction of a Montagnard Ethnic Identity in Indochina." In *Imperial Policy and Southeast Asian Nationalism, 1930–1957*, edited by Hans Antlöv and Stein Tønnesson, 261–93. Richmond: Curzon Press.

Salemink, Oscar. 2003. *The Ethnography of Vietnam's Central Highlanders: A Historical Contextualization, 1850–1990*. Florence: Routledge.

Samarasinghe, S.W.R. de A. 1984. "Ethnic Representation in Central Government Employment and Sinhala-Tamil Relations in Sri Lanka, 1948–1981." In *From Independence to Statehood: Managing Ethnic Conflict in Five African and Asian States*, edited by Robert B. Goldmann and A. Jeyaratnam Wilson, 173–84. London: Frances Pinter.

Sambanis, Nicholas. 2002. "A Review of Recent Advances and Future Directions in the Quantitative Literature on Civil War." *Defence and Peace Economics* 13 (3): 215–43.

Sanatomba, Kangujam. 2015. "Polemics of the Manipur Merger Agreement, 1949." In *Colonialism and Resistance: Society and State in Manipur*, edited by Arambam Noni and Kangujam Sanatomba, 206–17. London: Routledge India.

Sarbahi, Anoop. 2021. "The Structure of Religion, Ethnicity, and Insurgent Mobilization: Evidence from India." *World Politics* 73 (1): 82–127.

Sarmah, Satyendra Kumar. 2014. "Script Movement Among the Bodo of Assam." *Proceedings of the Indian History Congress* 75: 1335–40.

Sarmah, Satyendra Kumar. 2018. "The Role of Language in Identity Formation among the Bodos of Assam: A Historical Review." *International Journal of Interdisciplinary Research in Science, Society and Culture* 4 (2): 8–19.

Sayegh, Fayez. 2013. "Zionist Colonialism in Palestine." *Settler Colonial Studies* 2 (1): 206–25.

Sbacchi, Alberto. 1985. *Ethiopia Under Mussolini: Fascism and the Colonial Experience*. London: Zed Books.

Schapera, Isaac. 1943. *Native Land Tenure in the Bechuanaland Protectorate*. London: Lovedale Press.

Schapera, Isaac. 1952. *The Ethnic Composition of Tswana Tribes*. London: Lund Humphries.

Scott, James C. 2009. *The Art of Not Being Governed: An Anarchist History of Upland Southeast Asia*. New Haven, CT: Yale University Press.

Seawright, Jason. 2016. "Better Multimethod Design: The Promise of Integrative Multimethod Research." *Security Studies* 25 (1): 42–49.

Shannon, G. B. 1953. "Dispatch No. 12." Foreign Office 371 file 106853.

Sharkey, Heather. 2008. "Arab Identity and Ideology in Sudan: The Politics of Language, Ethnicity, and Race." *African Affairs* 107 (426): 21–43.

Sharma, Jayeeta. 2002. "The Making of 'Modern' Assam, 1826–1935." PhD diss., Cambridge University.

Sharma, S. C. 2000. *Insurgency or Ethnic Conflict: With Reference to Manipur*. New Delhi: Magnum Business Associates.

Sheikh, Salman Rafi. 2018. *Genesis of Baloch Nationalism: Politics and Ethnicity in Pakistan, 1947–1977*. New Delhi: Routledge India.

Silverstein, Josef. 1980. *Burmese Politics: The Dilemma of National Unity*. New Brunswick, NJ: Rutgers University Press.

Singh, Gurharpal, and Georgio Shani. 2021. *Sikh Nationalism: From a Dominant Minority to an Ethno-Religious Diaspora.* Cambridge: Cambridge University Press.

Singh, M. Amarjet. 2013. "Revisiting the Naga Conflict: What Can India Do to Resolve this Conflict?" *Small Wars and Insurgencies* 24 (5): 794–811.

Singh, Naorem Joykumar. 2002. *Colonialism to Democracy: A History of Manipur, 1819–1972.* Guwahati: Spectrum Publications.

Singh, N. William. 2017. "Mizo Identity: The Role of the Young Mizo Association (YMA) in Mizoram." In *Geographies of Difference: Explorations in Northeast Indian Studies,* edited by Mélanie Vandenhelsken, Meenaxi Barkataki-Ruscheweyh, and Bengt G. Karlsson, 233–52. London: Routledge India.

Singh, Oinam Jitendra. 2011. "Armed Violence in Manipur and Human Rights." *Indian Journal of Political Science* 72 (4): 887–1006.

Singh, S. N. 1994. *Mizoram: Historical, Geographical, Social, Political, and Administrative.* New Delhi: Mittal Publications.

Singha, Komol, and Purusottam Nayak. 2015. "Reconsidering Ethnic-Based-Autonomy Movements in Maghalaya: An Analysis." *MPRA.* https://mpra.ub.uni-muenchen.de/64745/1/MPRA_paper_64745.pdf. Accessed April 17, 2023.

Siriwardena, Reggie, K. Indrapala, Suil Basian, and Sepali Kottegoda. 1985. *School Text Books and Communal Relations in Sri Lanka.* Colombo: Council for Communal Harmony through the Media.

Skocpol, Theda. 1979. *States and Social Revolutions: A Comparative Analysis of France, Russia, and China.* Cambridge: Cambridge University Press.

Skocpol, Theda. 1992. *Protecting Soldiers and Mothers: The Political Origins of Social Policy in the United States.* Cambridge, MA: Harvard University Press.

Smeaton, Donald MacKenzie. 1920. *The Loyal Karens of Burma.* London, Kegan Paul: Trench, Trubner & Co.

Smith, Anthony D. 1986. *The Ethnic Origin of Nations.* Oxford: Basil Blackwell.

Smith, Leonard V. 2023. *French Colonialism: From the Ancien Régime to the Present.* New York: Cambridge University Press.

Smith, Martin J., 1991. *Burma: Insurgency and the Politics of Ethnicity.* London: Zed Books.

Snow, David A., and Robert D. Benford. 1992. "Master Frames and Cycles of Protest." In *Frontiers in Social Movement Theory,* edited by Aldon D. Morris and Carol M. Mueller, 135–55. New Haven, CT: Yale University Press.

Societé des Missions Étrangères. 1890. *Comte Rendu des Travaux de 1889.* Paris: Seminarie des Missions Étrangères.

South, Ashley. 2003. *Mon Nationalism and Civil War in Burma: The Golden Sheldrake.* New York: Routledge Curzon.

Specia, Megan. 2023, December 2. "Tracing the Deep Roots of Ireland's Support for Palestinians." *New York Times.* Accessed December 13, 2023. https://www.nytimes.com/2023/12/02/world/europe/ireland-palestinians-support.html

Steinmetz, George. 2003. "'The Devil's Handwriting': Precolonial Discourse, Ethnographic Acuity, and Cross-Identification in German Colonialism." *Comparative Studies in Society and History* 45 (1): 41–95.

Steinmo, Sven, Kathleen Thelen, and Frank Longstreth, eds. 1992. *Structuring Politics: Historical Institutionalism in Comparative Analysis.* New York: Cambridge University Press.

Stepan, Alfred, Juan Linz, and Yogendra Yadav. 2011. *Crafting State-Nations: India and Other Multinational Democracies.* Baltimore: Johns Hopkins University Press.

Stern, Theodore, 1968. "*Ariya* and the Golden Book: A Millenarian Buddhist Sect Among the Karen." *Journal of Asian Studies* 27: 297–328.

Streckfuss, David. 2012. "An 'Ethnic' Reading of 'Thai' History in the Twilight of the Century-Old Official 'Thai' National Model." *South East Asia Research* 20 (3): 305–27.

Suberu, Rotimi T. 2022. "Federalism and the First Republic of Nigeria, 1960–1966." In *The Oxford Handbook of Nigerian History*, edited by Toyin Falola and Matthew M. Heaton, 377–98. New York: Oxford University Press.

Suny, Ronald Grigor. 1994. *The Revenge of the Past*. Stanford, CA: Stanford University Press.

Suykens, Bert. 2015. "Comparing Rebel Rule Through Revolution and Naturalization: Ideologies of Governance in Naxalite and Naga India." In *Rebel Governance and Civil War*, edited by Ana Arjona, Nelson Kasfir, and Zachariah Mampilly, 138–57. New York: Cambridge University Press.

Swettenham, Frank. 1907. *British Malaya: An Account of the Origin and Progress of British Influence in Malaya*. London: Lane Publishers.

Tajfel, Henri. 1970. "Experiments in Intergroup Discrimination." *Scientific America* 223: 96–102.

Tajfel, Henri. 1974. "Social Identity and Intergroup Behavior." *Social Science Information* 13: 65–93.

Tambiah, Stanley. 1986. *Sri Lanka: Ethnic Fratricide and the Dismantling of Democracy*. Chicago: University of Chicago Press.

Tambiah, Stanley. 1992. *Buddhism Betrayed: Religion, Politics, and Violence in Sri Lanka*. Chicago: University of Chicago Press.

Tarapot, Phanjoubam. 2003. *Bleeding Manipur*. New Delhi: Har-Anand Publications.

Tarrow, Sydney. 1998. *Power in Movement*. New York: Cambridge University Press.

Taylor, Robert H. 2009. *The State in Myanmar*. London: Hurst & Company.

Thangjam, Homen. 2015. "Colonial Administration, Knowledge and Intervention: Colonial Project of Ethnicisation in Manipur." In *Colonialism and Resistance: Society and State in Manipur*, edited by Arambam Noni and Kangujam Sanatomba, 28–41. London: Routledge India.

Thawnghmung, Ardeth Maung. 2012. *The "Other" Karen in Myanmar: Ethnic Minorities and the Struggle without Arms*. Lanham, MD: Lexington Books.

Thomas, John. 2015. *Evangelising the Nation: Religion and the Formation of the Naga Political Identity*. London: Routledge India.

Tignor, Robert L. 1966. *Modernization ad British Colonial Rule in Egypt, 1882–1914*. Princeton, NJ: Princeton University Press.

Tilly, Charles. 1978. *From Mobilization to Revolution*. Reading, MA: Addison Wesley.

Tilly, Charles. 1992. *Coercion, Capital, and European States, AD 990–1992*. Cambridge, MA: Blackwell.

Tilly, Charles. 2004. *Social Movements, 1768–2004*. Boulder, CO: Paradigm Publishers.

Tounsel, Christopher. 2018. "'Render to Caesar': Missionary Thought and the Sudanese State, 1946–1964." *Social Sciences and Missions* 31: 341–74.

Trejo, Guillermo. 2009. "Religious Competition and Ethnic Mobilization in Latin America: Why the Catholic Church Promotes Indigenous Movements in Mexico." *American Political Science Review* 103: 329–42.

Tripp, Aili M. 1999. "The Political Mediation of Ethnic and Religious Diversity in Tanzania." In *The Accommodation of Cultural Diversity: Case Studies*, edited by Crawford Young, 37–71. London: Palgrave Macmillan.

Trzciński, Krzysztof. 2005. "Origins of Armed Separatism in Southern Senegal." *Africana Bulletin* 53: 169–208.

Tudor, Maya. 2013. *The Promise of Power: The Origins of Democracy in India and Autocracy in Pakistan*. New York: Cambridge University Press.

Turner, Jonathan, and Jan E. Stets. 2006. "Moral Emotions." In *Handbook of the Sociology of Emotions*, edited by Jonathan Turner and Jan E. Stets, 544–66. Boston, MA: Springer.

Udagama, P. 1990. "Education and National Integration in Sri Lanka." *Sri Lanka Journal of Social Sciences* 13: 9–17.

Uddin, Nasir. 2010. "Politics of Cultural Difference: Identity and Marginality in the Chittagong Hill Tracts of Bangladesh." *South Asian Survey* 17 (2): 183–94.

Upper Burma Muslims. 1929. "Memorandum from the Upper Burma Muslims." British Library, IOR/Q/13/2/28, E-Bur-993.

Uppsala Conflict Data Program. 2024. "Countries in Conflict View." Accessed August 28, 2024. https://ucdp.uu.se/encyclopedia

van der Veer, Peter. 1994. *Religious Nationalism: Hindus and Muslims in India.* Berkeley: University of California Press.

Vann, Michael G. 2003. "The Good, the Bad, and the Ugly: Variation and Difference in French Racism in Colonial Indochine." In *The Color of Liberty: Histories of Race in France*, edited by Sue Peabody and Tyler Stovall, 187–205. Durham, NC: Duke University Press.

van Schendel, Willem, Wolfgang Mey, and Aditya Kumar Dewan. 2000. *The Chittagong Hill Tracts: Living in a Borderland.* Bangkok: White Lotus.

Varshney, Ashutosh. 1997. "Postmodernism, Civic Engagement, and Ethnic Conflict: A Passage to India." *Comparative Politics* 30 (1): 1–20.

Vasavakul, Thaveeporn. 2003. "Language Policy and Ethnic Relations in Vietnam." In *Fighting Words: Language Policy and Ethnic Relations in Asia*, edited by Michael E. Brown and Sumit Ganguly, 212–38. Cambridge, MA: MIT Press.

Verghese, Ajay. 2016. *The Colonial Origins of Ethnic Violence in India.* Palo Alto, CA: Stanford University Press.

Verghese, B. G. 1996. *India's Northeast Resurgent.* Delhi: Konark Publishers.

Vogt, Manuel, Nils-Christian Bormann, Seraina Rüegger, Lars-Erik Cederman, Philipp Hunziker, and Luc Girardin. 2015. "Integrating Data on Ethnicity, Geography, and Conflict: The Ethnic Power Relations Data Set Family." *Journal of Conflict Resolution* 59 (7): 1327–42.

vom Hau, Matthias. 2023. "Social Movements and Nationalism in Latin America." In *The Oxford Handbook of Latina American Social Movements*, edited by Federico M. Rossi, 162–79. New York: Oxford University Press.

Ware, Anthony, and Costas Laoutides. 2019. *Myanmar's 'Rohingya' Conflict.* New York: Oxford University Press.

Weber, Eugen. 1976. *Peasants into Frenchmen: The Modernization of Rural France, 1870–1914.* Stanford, CA: Stanford University Press.

Weber, Jacques. 2010. "L'assimilation par les institutions." In *Les Élections Législatives et Sénatoriales Outre-Mer*, edited by Laurent Jalabert, Bertrand Joly, and Jacques Weber, 15–27. Paris: Les Indes Savantes.

Weber, Max. 2019. *Economy and Society: A New Translation.* Translated by Keith Tribe. Cambridge, MA: Harvard University Press.

Welhengama, Gnanapala, and Nirmala Pillay. 2014. *The Rise of Tamil Separatism in Sri Lanka: From Communalism to Secession.* New York: Routledge.

Werbner, Richard. 2000. "The Minorities Debate and Cosmopolitan Ethnicity in Botswana." Challenging Minorities' Difference and Tribal Citizenship Conference. University of Botswana, Gaborone.

Wheeler, James Talboys. 1877. *The History of the Imperial Assemblage at Delhi, Held on the 1st January 1877, to Celebrate the Assumption of the Title of Empress of India by Her Majesty the Queen, Including Historical Sketches of India and Her Princes, Past and Present.* London: Longmans, Green, Reader, and Dyer.

White, Benjamin T. 2011. *The Emergence of Minorities in the Middle East: The Politics of Community in French Mandate Syria.* Edinburgh: Edinburgh University Press.

Wickramasinghe, Nira. 2006. *Sri Lanka in the Modern Age: A History of Contested Identities.* London: Hurst and Company.

Wight, Matin. 1950. *The Development of the Legislative Council, 1606–1945*. London: Faber & Faber Limited.

Wilder, Gary. 2005. *The French Imperial Nation-State: Negritude and Colonial Humanism between the Two World Wars*. Chicago: University of Chicago Press.

Wilkinson, Steven. 2004. *Votes and Violence: Electoral Competition and Ethnic Riots in India*. New York: Cambridge University Press.

Wilkinson, Steven. 2015. *Army and Nation: The Military and Indian Democracy since Independence*. Cambridge, MA: Harvard University Press.

Wilks, Ivor. 2000. "Asante Nationhood and Colonial Administrators, 1896–1935." In *Ethnicity in Ghana: The Limits of Invention*, edited by Carolina Lentz and Paul Nugent, 68–96. London: Macmillan Press.

Wimmer, Andreas. 2002. *Nationalist Exclusion and Ethnic Conflict: Shadows of Modernity*. New York: Cambridge University Press.

Wimmer, Andreas. 2008. "The Making and Unmaking of Ethnic Boundaries: A Multilevel Process Theory." *American Journal of Sociology* 113 (4): 970–1022.

Wimmer, Andreas. 2013. *Waves of War: Nationalism, State Formation, and Ethnic Exclusion in the Modern World*. New York: Cambridge University Press.

Wimmer, Andreas. 2018. *Nation Building: Why Some Countries Come Together While Others Fall Apart*. Princeton, NJ: Princeton University Press.

Wimmer, Andreas, Lars-Erik Cederman, and Brian Min. 2009. "Ethnic Politics and Armed Conflict: A Configurational Analysis." *American Sociological Review* 74: 316–37.

Win, Kanbawza. 1994. *A Burmese Appeal to the UN and U.S.* Bangkok: CPDSK Publications.

Wolters, O. W. 1997. *History, Culture, and Region in Southeast Asian Perspectives*. Singapore: ASEAS Publishing.

Woodberry, Robert. 2004. "The Shadow of Empire: Christian Missions, Colonial Policy, and Democracy in Post-Colonial Societies." PhD diss., University of North Carolina-Chapel Hill.

Woodberry, Robert. 2012. "The Missionary Roots of Liberal Democracy." *American Political Science Review* 106 (2): 244–74.

Wouters, Jelle J. P. 2019. *In the Shadows of Naga Insurgency: Tribes, State, and Violence in India's Northeast*. New Delhi: Oxford University Press.

Wucherpfennig, Julian, Philipp Hunziker, and Lars-Erik Cederman. 2016. "Who Inherits the State? Colonial Rule and Postcolonial Conflict." *American Journal of Political Science* 60 (4): 882–98.

Wylie, Diana. 1990. *A Little God: The Twilight of Patriarchy in a Southern African Chiefdom*. London: Wesleyan University Press.

Wyrtzen, Jonathan. 2015. *Making Morocco: Colonial Intervention and the Politics of Identity*. Ithaca, NY: Cornell University Press.

Yashar, Deborah. 1998. "Contesting Citizenship: Indigenous Movements and Democracy in Latin America." *Comparative Politics* 31 (1): 23–42.

Yawnghwe, Tzang. 2010. *The Shan of Burma: Memoirs of a Shan Exile*. Singapore: Institute of Southeast Asian Studies.

Yi, Khin. 2018. *The Dobama Movement in Burma (1930–1938)*. Ithaca, NY: Cornell University Press.

Young, Crawford. 1976. *The Politics of Cultural Pluralism*. Madison: University of Wisconsin Press.

Zeileis, Achim, Thomas Lumley, Nathaniel Graham, and Susanne Köll. 2021. "Package 'sandwich' v3.0-2." Accessed July 27, 2023. https://cran.r-project.org/web/packages/sandwich/sandwich.pdf

GPSR Authorized Representative: Easy Access System Europe - Mustamäe tee
50, 10621 Tallinn, Estonia, gpsr.requests@easproject.com

www.ingramcontent.com/pod-product-compliance
Lightning Source LLC
Chambersburg PA
CBHW031412270326
41929CB00010BA/1422